TIME IN TELEVISION NARRATIVE

TIME
IN TELEVISION NARRATIVE

Exploring Temporality in Twenty-First-Century Programming

Edited by Melissa Ames

UNIVERSITY PRESS OF MISSISSIPPI • JACKSON

www.upress.state.ms.us

The University Press of Mississippi is a member of the Association of American University Presses.

Copyright © 2012 by University Press of Mississippi
All rights reserved
Manufactured in the United States of America

First printing 2012

∞

Library of Congress Cataloging-in-Publication Data

Time in television narrative : exploring temporality in twenty-first-century programming / edited by Melissa Ames.
 p. cm.
Includes bibliographical references and index.
ISBN 978-1-61703-293-6 (cloth : alk. paper) — ISBN 978-1-61703-294-3 (ebook) 1. Time on television. 2. Television programs—United States. I. Ames, Melissa, 1978–
PN1992.8.T56T56 2012
791.450973—dc23   2011045389

British Library Cataloging-in-Publication Data available

For all who feel that "time" is never wasted on a good television show

CONTENTS

Acknowledgments   *xi*

Introduction
Television Studies in the Twenty-First Century   3

I. PROMOTING THE FUTURE OF EXPERIMENTAL TV
The Industry Changes and Technological Advancements That Paved the Way to "New" Television Ventures

1. Television's Paradigm (Time)shift
Production and Consumption Practices in the Post-Network Era   27
TODD M. SODANO

2. "A Stretch of Time"
Extended Distribution and Narrative Accumulation in Prison Break   43
J. P. KELLY

3. "It's Not Unknown"
The Loose- and Dead-End Afterlives of Battlestar Galactica and Lost   56
JORDAN LAVENDER-SMITH

4. Zero-Degree Seriality
Television Narrative in the Post-Network Era   69
NORMAN M. GENDELMAN

5. "Play It Again, Sam ... and Dean"
Temporality and Meta-Textuality in Supernatural   82
MICHAEL FUCHS

II. HISTORICIZING THE MOMENT
How the Cultural Climate Impacts Temporal Manipulation on the Small Screen

6. Temporality and Trauma in American Sci-Fi Television *97*
ARIS MOUSOUTZANIS

7. The Fear of the Future and the Pain of the Past
The Quest to Cheat Time in Heroes, FlashForward, *and* Fringe *110*
MELISSA AMES

8. *Lost* **in Our Middle Hour**
Faith, Fate, and Redemption Post-9/11 *125*
SARAH HIMSEL BURCON

9. "New Beginnings Only Lead to Painful Ends"
"Undeading" and Fear of Consequences in Pushing Daisies *139*
KASEY BUTCHER

III. THE FUNCTIONS OF TIME
Analyzing the Effects of Nonnormative Narrative Structure(s)

10. "Did You Get Pears?"
Temporality and Temps Mortality in The Wire, Mad Men, *and* Arrested Development *153*
GRY C. RUSTAD AND TIMOTHEUS VERMEULEN

11. Temporalities on Collision Course
Time, Knowledge, and Temporal Critique in Damages *165*
TONI PAPE

12. Freaks of Time
Reevaluating Memory and Identity through Daniel Knauf's Carnivàle *178*
FRIDA BECKMAN

13. The Discourse of *Medium*
Time as a Narrative Device *190*
KRISTI MCDUFFIE

IV. MOVING BEYOND THE TELEVISUAL RESTRAINTS OF THE PAST
Reimagining Genres and Formats

14. Making Sense of the Future
Narrative Destabilization in Joss Whedon's Dollhouse   205
CASEY J. MCCORMICK

15. Why 30 Rock Rocks and The Office Needs Some Work
The Role of Time/Space in Contemporary TV Sitcoms   218
COLIN IRVINE

16. Change the Structure, Change the Story
How I Met Your Mother and the Reformulation of the Television Romance   232
MOLLY BROST

17. Like Sands through the Half-Hourglass
Nurse Jackie and Temporal Disruption   245
JANANI SUBRAMANIAN

18. The Television Musical
Glee's New Directions   257
JACK HARRISON

V. PLAYING OUTSIDE OF THE BOX
The Role Time Plays in Fan Fiction, Online Communities, and Audience Studies

19. "Nothing Happens Unless First a Dream"
TV Fandom, Narrative Structure, and the Alternate Universes of Bones   273
MELANIE CATTRELL

20. Two Days before the Day after Tomorrow
Time, Temporality, and Fandom in South Park   285
JASON W. BUEL

21. Lost in Time?
Lost Fan Engagement with Temporal Play   297
LUCY BENNETT

About the Contributors   310

Index   315

ACKNOWLEDGMENTS

As with any undertaking of this magnitude, there are a myriad of people to thank. First, I want to thank the authors who contributed to this volume. Their enthusiasm for the project and diligence in producing this work is greatly appreciated. I would also like to thank my editor, Leila Salisbury, who believed in this collection from the onset, and whose encouragement early in this process was invaluable. I should also recognize the support of my colleagues and chair, Dana Ringuette, at Eastern Illinois University who value my academic pursuits and allow this television scholar to hide out in their midst in the English department. The list of friends and family members who have shared my interest in the televisual tactics traced in these essays—or have humored me while I have expounded on them in great detail—would be too long to list here, but to them I say: thank you for listening to me and helping me continue this conversation outside the walls of academe. And lastly, I thank the writers, producers, and fans of the programs analyzed within this volume; I speak for many when I urge you to continue creating and watching television shows of this caliber. May there be many more years of temporal play on the small screen.

TIME IN TELEVISION NARRATIVE

INTRODUCTION
Television Studies in the Twenty-First Century

The trends of contemporary popular television programming have received a great deal of attention both within and outside scholarly circles throughout the past few decades, even more so as the medium continues to evolve into the twenty-first century. The increasing complexity and experimental nature of television narratives have been well studied by both academics[1] and laypersons through various fan forums.[2] This collection adds to this discussion by limiting its analysis of such televisual texts to those solely in the first decade of the new millennium. This collection offers an analysis of twenty-first-century televisual texts exclusively—something that has not existed heretofore—thus expanding on this discussion and bringing into sharper focus the added complexity of this medium at present.[3]

THE POST-NETWORK ERA

Much of the recent scholarship on this influential medium has tracked the changes currently affecting the television industry. These studies include Lynn Spigel and Jan Olsson's *Television after TV: Essays on a Medium in Transition*, Amanda Lotz's *The Television Will Be Revolutionized*, and Janet McCabe and Kim Akass's *Quality TV: Contemporary American Television and Beyond*. In the latter text, the periodization of television history provided by Jimmie Reeves, Mark Rodgers, and Michael Epstein maps out the shifts leading up to the current post-network or digital era of television: TV I (1948–1975), associated with the network era or broadcast era, TV II (1975–1995), the cable era, and TV III (1991–Present), the digital era. Lotz, studying the latter era, describes three characteristics of this post-network era—convenience, mobility, and theatricality—claiming that these traits have "redefined the medium from its network-era form" (50). Similarly, Jason Mittell has demonstrated the ways in which the emergence of new media, along with changes in the industry, has resulted in the production of increasingly complex television narratives and alternative viewing practices.[4] Although these studies have been groundbreaking in reconceptualizing the current televisual landscape, continued attention is needed to explore the narrative content and stylistics of the programs resulting from recent production trends.

POST-9/11 TELEVISION

The scholarship of the past decade that has focused primarily on narrative content has often studied programming through a post-9/11 lens.[5] Although much was going on in the fictional television programs during this time period, for the most part media scholarship focused on representations of 9/11 and the early stages of the "war on terror" by studying print and television news coverage (Spigel 238). Lynn Spigel points out that the majority of the work from the academy during this time attended to "the narrative and mythic 'framing' of the events[,] the nationalistic jingoism," and the "competing global news outlets," such as Al Jazeera (238). But, as Spigel states, despite these important achievements of the academy, "the scholarly focus on news underestimates (indeed, it barely considers) the way the 'reality' of 9/11 was communicated across the flow of television's genres, including its so-called entertainment genres" (238).[6] The goal of this collection, in part, is to address this void by focusing exclusively on fictional texts and considering how these narratives work through the reality of this historic decade.

TELEVISION AND GENRE STUDY

Other recent studies have focused largely on specific televisual trends in terms of bourgeoning genres, such as those of reality television and infotainment, which many read as a response to 9/11.[7] The attention to the former is not surprising, given that by January 2003, one-seventh of all programming on major networks was reality based, a trend that continues today (Douglas 632). The rapid growth in this genre has contributed increased scholarship theorizing its popularity from both an audience and production standpoint.[8] While the numbers of reality programming caught scholars' attention during this time, the visibility and impact of the other growing genre, infotainment, has also begun to spark academic discussion.[9] An online poll conducted by *TIME* magazine in June 2009 reported that Jon Stewart, the host of Comedy Central's *The Daily Show* (1996–Present), was named the most trusted televised newscaster since Walter Cronkite.[10] The following year, *People* reported that he had been voted the "most influential man of 2010" (Silverman).[11] This suggests that such programming, originally designed for comedic/entertainment purposes, is beginning to supplant traditional news media in interesting ways. Although both of these television genres were very influential during the first decade of the twenty-first century, and while their editing practices might be important to study in terms of temporal play, these genres have been omitted from this collection as they do not fall into the neglected category of fictional programming.

THE STUDY OF (NARRATIVE) TIME ACROSS MEDIA

While all of the studies listed above have been quite instrumental in understanding the evolving state of television, few of these studies have focused on narrative content across genre or on the televisual aesthetics that have resulted from these network and genre shifts. This leaves room in television scholarship for studies that narrow their focus to specific televisual characteristics of this new era of programming, such as this anthology's focus on the phenomenon of experimental time—a subject which has yet to be given attention in terms of twenty-first-century programming.

ACADEMIA AND TIME

In its focus, this collection deals with a particular concept that has fascinated scholars for centuries: time. These essays will, in a sense, continue the work of philosophers (from Aristotle and Augustine to Edmund Husserl and Martin Heidegger to Friedrich Nietzsche and Henri Bergson)[12] and scientists (such as Isaac Newton, Albert Einstein, and Stephen Hawking),[13] applying their theories of time to the contemporary new media moment in novel ways. Many of the recent studies concerning time have moved away from looking at time as a philosophical concern and scientific inquiry and have instead studied its impact on societal development. For example, the standardization of time (from the invention of clocks and calendars to the impact of railroad schedules and daylight savings) has brought about interesting inquiries into humans' need to regulate time.[14] This impact on society is often seen in the various ways that time is depicted in cultural narratives.

NARRATIVE THEORY AND TIME

Most relevant to this project is the scholarly work of the late twentieth century in regard to the link between narrative structure and time. As Ursula Heise notes, "theorists of narrative generally agree that time is one of the most fundamental parameters through which narrative as a genre is organized and understood" (47). Therefore, it is not surprising that scholarly work abounds in this area dating back to foundational texts such as Frank Kermode's *The Sense of an Ending* (1966) and Walter Benjamin's "Storyteller" (1968) to more recent studies like Heise's own *Chronoschisms* (1997), which analyzes the experimental narratives found in postmodern literature.[15] Scholars have also attempted to theorize how time plays a role in the actual experience of reading literature. One such example is Paul Ricouer's theory concerning "the fictive experience of time," which he explains as "the temporal aspect of (the) virtual experience of being-in-the-world proposed by the text" (100). The essays in this collection draw upon many of these narrative theories, reworking and applying them to televisual narratives in new ways.

POSTMODERN LITERATURE AND TIME

Because this "age is one of unprecedented flourishing for alternative ways of understanding and inhabiting time," it is not surprising that the cultural narratives of the last half century have been obsessed with time itself (Wood ix). Nonlinearity, or temporal distortion, is one of the most common features of modern and postmodern fiction. Postmodern novels, in particular, are centrally concerned with the possibility of experiencing time in an age when temporal horizons have been drastically foreshortened. The coexistence of these competing experiences of time allows new conceptions of history and posthistory to emerge, and opens up comparisons with recent scientific approaches to temporality. Heise reads "the temporal structure of the postmodern novel" as "a way of dealing aesthetically with an altered culture of time in which access to the past and especially to the future appears more limited than before in cultural self-awareness" (67).[16]

Although a complete list of postmodern literary works that rely on experimental temporality would be too lengthy to include here, it does seem useful to include a few key examples that might have served as predecessor texts for the cinematic and televisual time experiments that followed. However, it would be misleading to include only postmodern works that could have served as inspirations for these later media creations since experimental time, at least in the form of the time-travel motif, has existed in fiction for centuries. Such motifs have surfaced in both canonical and popular texts throughout the years with increasing regularity in the most recent decades. Examples include Samuel Madden's *Memories of the Twentieth Century* (1733), Charles Dickens's *A Christmas Carol* (1843), H. G. Wells's *The Time Machine* (1895), Alison Uttley's *A Traveller in Time* (1939), Isaac Asimov's *The End of Eternity* (1955), Kurt Vonnegut's *Slaughterhouse-Five* (1969), Philip Jose Farmer's *Time's Last Gift* (1972), Octavia Butler's *Kindred* (1980), Michael Crichton's *Timeline* (1999), Audrey Niffenegger's *The Time Traveler's Wife* (2003), and Jacob LaCivita's *Timely Persuasion* (2008).

FILM AND TIME

Of course, this focus on experimental time quite obviously did not remain entrapped on the printed page. In *Time Lapse: The Politics of Time-Travel Cinema*, Charles Tryon argues that new media technologies often become associated with disruptions in our experience of chronological time. This collection claims they also explore and allegorize such disruptions. Tryon's project analyzes constructions of time, history, and memory as they are articulated cinematically in various time-travel films. While similar projects are beginning to surface in the study of film,[17] the implication of experimental temporality has often been ignored in television scholarship. Despite the uneven academic coverage between these two fields, it is clear that the films of the late twentieth century and early twenty-first century helped establish the precedent for what is occurring on the small screen today.

For example, various films focused on the narrative trope of the "do-over" where characters were able to travel back in time to revise their lives. These include action films such as Robert Zemeckis's *Back to the Future* trilogy (1985, 1989, 1990), comedies such as Burr Steer's *17 Again* (2009), dramas like James Orr's *Mr. Destiny* (1990), and adaptations along the lines of Brett Ratner's revision of *It's a Wonderful Life* (1946), *The Family Man* (2000), or Richard Donner's *Scrooged* (1988) and Penny Marshall's *Ghosts of Girlfriends Past* (2009), both updated versions of Charles Dickens's *A Christmas Carol*. Other films dealt with filmic time in more experimental ways. For example, Quentin Tarantino's *Pulp Fiction* (1994) influenced a wave of nonlinear films that followed it, including Terry Gilliam's *Twelve Monkeys* (1995), David Lynch's *Mulholland Dr.* (2001), Christopher Nolan's *Memento* (2001), Eric Bess's *The Butterfly Effect* (2004), and Tony Scott's *Deja Vu* (2006).

TELEVISION'S RELATIONSHIP WITH TIME

The majority of scholarship concerning television and time is restricted to the analysis of nonfiction, live television,[18] with the occasional study devoted to the way that time plays a part in a specific genre of television, such as the soap opera[19] or the science fiction drama.[20] Varying from these approaches, this text analyzes the role of time across a variety of television genres (including the sitcom, drama, musical, and cartoon).

Although this collection focuses on the novelty of the televisual time experiments played out during the twenty-first century, it would be amiss not to mention that such programming has existed in decades prior (although in much lesser frequency) and that some scholarship has been directed toward it.[21] Some noteworthy programs include *Doctor Who* (BBC, 1963–1989; 2005–Present), *Timeslip* (ITV, 1970–1971), *Voyagers!* (NBC, 1982–1983), *Quantum Leap* (NBC, 1989–1993), *Time Trax* (PTEN, 1993–1994), *Goodnight Sweetheart* (BBC, 1993–1999), *Crime Traveller* (BBC, 1997), and *Seven Days* (UPN, 1998–2001).[22]

THE "TIMELINESS" OF THIS INQUIRY INTO CONTEMPORARY TELEVISION'S EXPLORATION OF TEMPORALITY

Studying more recent series, this project aims to fill a void in the current scholarship concerning the temporal and narrative experimentations taking place in twenty-first-century American programming. As such, this collection analyzes television programs through various theoretical and methodological approaches. Although the television shows of the past decade are as diverse and plentiful as that of any previous time period, there appear some commonalities between the programs currently creating the most engaged fan communities, the ones that have become quick cult draws or instant hits. These types of shows often fit the complexity that Steven Johnson lists in his discussion of television's role in the smartening of culture: multiple plot threads (often stopping and starting up again) spanning large durations of time, a thickening of characterization and a multiplication of cast members, and a heavy reliance on audience intellect (and loyalty) in order to keep up with the narrative leaps and bounds. These are all characteristics that can be attributed, in part, to existing in the current media moment. However, this anthology argues that a new characteristic is sneaking into the mix: the temporal tease.

The most popular television shows of the new millennium have at their center a narrative progression unlike many of those that came before them.

These shows play with time, slowing it down to unfold the narrative at rarely before seen rates (time retardation and compression) and disrupting the chronological flow itself (through the extensive use of flashbacks and the insistence that viewers be able to situate themselves in both the present and past narrative threads simultaneously). Although temporal play has existed on the small screen prior to the twenty-first century—soap operas are well known for their use of time retardation and NBC's Emmy-award-winning sitcom, *Seinfeld* (1989–1998), had various televisual time experiments (including its 1991 episode "The Chinese Restaurant," which occurred in real time, and its 1997 episode "The Betrayal," which presented all scenes in reverse chronological order)—never before has narrative time played such an important role in mainstream television. The frequency of this practice at present seems worthy of epochal note and this collection offers explanations for not only its presence in contemporary programming, but the implications of this presence.

Drawing upon the fields of cultural studies, television scholarship, and literary studies, among others, as well as overarching theories concerning postmodernity and narratology, this collection suggests that the influx of television programs concerned with time may stem from any and all of the following: recent scientific approaches to temporality, new conceptions of (post)history, and trends in late-capitalistic production and consumption. These programs could also be viewed as being products of the new culture of instantaneity (forever focused on the fleeting present, often termed "nanosecond culture" or "throw-away culture")[23] or of the recent trauma culture amplified in the wake of the September 11 attacks. In short, these televisual time experiments may very well be an aesthetic response to the cultural climate from which they derive. However, this explanation oversimplifies the complicated, reciprocal way that societal trends affect textual production, and textual production and consumption affect society. This collection examines both ends of this continuum while also attending to another crucial variable: the television viewer/fan.

ORGANIZING (DISCUSSIONS OF) TIME
Understanding the Structure of This Text

This text is organized into five sections representing different approaches to the study of television and temporality that have yet to be brought into conversation with one another. Section 1 is titled "Promoting the Future of Experimental TV: The Industry Changes and Technological Advancements That Paved the Way to 'New' Television Ventures." In this section authors explore the ways in which production and consumption practices in the post-network era have encouraged complex television programming that disrupts previous televisual norms (especially in regard to linear storytelling). Section 2, titled "Historicizing the Moment: How the Cultural Climate Impacts Temporal Manipulation on the Small Screen," focuses on how the political and cultural climate during the first decade of the twenty-first century (one fueled by, for example, post-9/11 anxieties) contributes to narratives that depend, in part, on temporal play to achieve their goals. The chapters in Section 3, "The Functions of Time: Analyzing the Effects of Nonnormative Narrative Structure(s)," determine what these temporal practices actually *do* for the television programs they play a part in. Section 4, "Moving beyond the Televisual Restraints of the Past: Reimagining Genres and Formats," continues on this thread and discusses the ways in which these fictional depictions of time actually work to alter existing television genres in the neo-postmodern era. And, lastly, Section 5, "Playing outside of the Box: The Role Time Plays in Fan Fiction, Online Communities, and Audience Studies," shifts its focus from the television programs themselves to the viewers who consume them.

Section I. Promoting the Future of Experimental TV: The Industry Changes and Technological Advancements That Paved the Way to "New" Television Ventures

The work in this section draws upon and extends the work of influential scholars who have traced the ways in which the television industry has been altered due the technological advancements of the late twentieth and early twenty-first centuries. The essays in this section argue, in part, that the fragmented plots and experimental narrative structures of the programs analyzed are, to some extent, conditioned by the accelerated temporal rhythms of what Fredric Jameson would consider late-capitalism's technologies of production and consumption.[24] In chapter 1, "Television's Paradigm (Time)shift: Production and Consumption Practices in the Post-Network Era," Todd M. Sodano explores temporal differences between yesterday's linear television viewing and today's post-network consumption practices. As modes of content distribution have evolved, so have serial narratives and viewer discourses. Sodano argues that this paradigmatic shift from the broadcast networks' carefully orchestrated flow to individualized viewer control has complicated how viewers draw meanings and pleasures from programs. Today's viewer can time-shift and/or binge on favorite series through DVD, DVR, on-demand, and online viewing. Consequently, the standard gap (traditionally the week between new episodes) that used to predominate TV discourses now has shrunk, increased, or been eliminated altogether. Meanwhile, paratexts, which include "previously on" segments, previews, commercials, spoilers, and water-cooler discussions that surround the main text, have become critical pieces in TV conversations, due to the proliferation of online communities and social media. Sodano's end claim is that as digital platforms continue to grow in number, viewing audiences are sure to fragment into smaller pieces, thus further complicating these conversations.

The second chapter, "'A Stretch of Time': Extended Distribution and Narrative Accumulation in *Prison Break*," continues the argument that the new distributive regimes of the contemporary television industry have given rise to new narrative temporalities. In particular, a number of series, such as *24*, bear many hallmarks of what has been called "network time," namely acceleration and real-time. Although scholars maintain that "network time" is the dominant temporality of the twenty-first century, in this chapter J. P. Kelly argues that the flexibility of distribution in contemporary television has resulted in multiple narrative temporalities. To illustrate this point he uses *Prison Break* as a way to complicate and challenge many of the assumptions made by "network time" scholarship. By taking an industrial-textual approach his essay highlights the interdependent relationship between narrative and distribution, while also revealing key differences between the seriality of shows such as *Prison Break* (which uses "serialized seasons") versus series such as *24* (which uses "episodic seasons").

The next essay extends the arguments set in motion by the opening two chapters by considering the ways in which two specific programs'—*Battlestar Galactica* and *Lost*—formal and generic structures both emphasize and undermine the ostensible statements the shows offer about leadership, time, memory, and continuity, while also spotlighting the ways in which the narratives might be read as allegories for their position in the constellation of contemporary serialized TV. In "'It's Not Unknown': The Loose- and Dead-End Afterlives of *Battlestar Galactica* and *Lost*," Jordan Lavender-Smith attends to the way the shows' writers are always in the process of returning to previous material, changing the relative valences of the past because of their present situation, a situation which itself will be rewritten by and according to the future. Additionally, his chapter suggests that the very same advanced technologies that allow contemporary writers and producers the opportunity to create shows with such novelistic ambitions also compromise the narrative coherence of these elaborate, plot-heavy epics.

Chapter 4 considers Jameson's argument that by the mid-twentieth century electronic media would comprise a discretely defined "third phase" of corporate capitalism. "Zero-Degree Seriality: Television Narrative in the Post-Network Era" argues that two recent television shows preoccupied with time (*24* and *Lost*) emblematize a "fourth" moment in corporate capitalism. Norman

M. Gendelman's essay extends Jameson's claim that global capital exists as a confluence between embodied subjectivity and ethereal corporate electromagnetism and argues that as incorporated electronic serials, the shows construct narrative codes that structure a "ground" from which to confront the electronic present while likewise mapping its displacements. By stylistically and structurally foregrounding ("plotting") their own emergent contexts as obsessive speed and digressive multiplicity, these shows are semiotic/experiential modes—electronic "signatures" of our era. This chapter entertains what it means to experience and think through time-based media in the twenty-first century.

The final essay in this section, Michael Fuchs's "'Play It Again, Sam . . . and Dean': Temporality and Meta-Textuality in *Supernatural*," narrows down this discussion of contemporary television to analyze one specific drama. Like so many other contemporary television series, *Supernatural*, basically a series about two brothers hunting supernatural beings, breaks traditional linear narration in numerous episodes. This chapter argues that by departing from a chronological structure and also deconstructing seemingly fixed temporal markers such as death, *Supernatural* self-reflexively draws attention to the constructed nature of (television) narratives while also highlighting the cultural construction that is the concept of linear time. This program is thus indicative of a larger trend in our contemporary society in which the differentiation between objective and subjective time has evolved into conceiving of temporality as discontinuous and fragmented.

As the work in this section indicates, developments in technology, science, and media—along with changes in production and consumption practices—help to explain the formal experiments that contemporary televisual narratives have taken on. However, these television programs also help shape the cultural lenses through which viewers perceive and interpret those technological and social developments.[25] Therefore, the relationship between the cultural-industrial climate and the texts it produces is reciprocal in nature rather than simply being one that could be reduced to a mere cause-effect relationship. The essays in the next two sections further showcase this reciprocity.

Section II. Historicizing the Moment: How the Cultural Climate Impacts Temporal Manipulation on the Small Screen

Moving away from the first section's focus on the scientific and technological advancements of the twenty-first century, the essays in this portion of the text expand their focus to analyze how the historical time period more generally might have influenced the wave of experimental time narratives on the small screen. In chapter 6, "Temporality and Trauma in American Sci-Fi Television," Aris Mousoutzanis approaches the experimentation of temporality in recent American Sci-Fi TV shows, such as *Lost*, *FlashForward*, *Fringe*, and *The Event*, in terms of their preoccupation with the topic of psychological trauma. As a psychopathology that constantly returns patients to the traumatic incident, which they compulsively reexperience in nightmares and hallucinations, trauma is characterized by an experience of temporality that is nonlinear and repetitive; fictions of trauma often attempt to convey that aspect of the disease by employing a nonlinear, repetitive, and cyclical narrative. Mousoutzanis's discussion, however, does not read the widening interest in trauma in popular narratives only as a response to contemporary historical tragedies and crises. Instead, it combines this historicist approach with one that sees these television shows as self-reflective texts on the history and function of the medium of television itself.

While chapter 6 purposely avoids reading the televisual creations of the twenty-first century as post-9/11 products (alone), chapter 7 analyzes three programs with this very argument in mind. In "The Fear of the Future and the Pain of the Past: The Quest to Cheat Time in *Heroes*, *FlashForward*, and *Fringe*," Melissa Ames analyzes three contemporary fictional narratives that remediate the tragedy of 9/11. These programs include experimental temporality and center their plots on anxieties concerning time: the longing to correct mistakes of the past, the panic of living in a hypersensitive present, and the fear of the premediated future.[26] These shows suggest that the fear we feel as a nation post-attack unconsciously resurfaces itself and seeks resolution in narrative spaces through repetition and that the consumption of these narratives is a means by which viewers "work through" the lingering emotional trauma caused by the attacks. This essay suggests that the temporal play present within these programs is crucial to this working through and, in fact, embodies the affect of fear that prompts it.

In chapter 8, "*Lost* in Our Middle Hour: Faith, Fate, and Redemption Post 9/11," Sarah Himsel Burcon argues that both the narrative structure (flashbacks, flashforwards, and flashsideways) as well as the thematic content of *Lost* worked together to immerse viewers in the longstanding philosophical and theological debates surrounding free will/destiny and faith/reason. In her examination she draws a parallel between *Lost* and Milton's *Paradise Lost* to demonstrate that, after 9/11, Americans refocused on religious ideals given their shattered sense of freedom, righteousness, and sense of security. Ultimately, Himsel Burcon draws upon the rhetoric of political speeches contemporary to *Lost* to suggest that the program emphasized how Americans were (and perhaps still are) in their "middle hour" of grief. That is, they wished to "do over" the past at the same time that they were living in an unstable present and looking to some "Other" to help them move into the future.

Also focusing on this popular motif of the do-over, Kasey Butcher's essay analyzes the ways in which *Pushing Daisies*, the story of a man who can bring the dead back to life with the touch of his fingertip, mirrored the political discourses surrounding the 2008 presidential election and interacted with the 2007–2008 Writers' Guild of America strike. "'New Beginnings Only Lead to Painful Ends': 'Undeading' and Fear of Consequences in *Pushing Daisies*" claims that, on the surface, the show is a candy-colored fairytale romance mixed with a fast-talking crime-drama, but the major tension of the series is a push-pull between the optimism of Charlotte Charles and the pessimism of the Pie Maker, Ned—the program's two main characters. By taking ideologies about transmedia, intertextuality, and genre convention into account, this chapter argues that the larger-than-life world of *Daisies* can be understood as reflecting similar anxieties in the culture of its viewing audience, who were faced with a contentious election and a looming economic crisis.

Section III. The Functions of Time: Analyzing the Effects of Nonnormative Narrative Structure(s)

This section, housing perhaps the most eclectic gathering of essays within this text, studies the various results of such narrative experiments with time. In the wake of debates on flexi-narratives, narrative complexity, and narrative compression, Gry C. Rustad and Timotheus Vermeulen's "'Did You Get Pears?': Temporality and Temps Mortality in *The Wire*, *Mad Men*, and *Arrested Development*" discusses these three programs in terms of narrative disintegration. While scholars such as Robin Nelson and Jason Mittell emphasize the extent to which these programs complicate plot lines, Rustad and Vermeulen draw attention to the moments these lines dissipate into the details of the image and disperse into the arbitrariness of the world. In spite of their significant generic differences, *The Wire*, *Mad Men*, and *Arrested Development* all frequently begin, interrupt, or end scenes with moments in which "nothing happens." Chapter 10 researches the temporal inferences of these particular moments, arguing that these moments hint at a temporality that oscillates between *kainos* and *chromos*; between a structured, linear narrative and a rhizomatic, inexplicable there-ness of the world; and between the promise of closure and a radical, inconclusive openness.

Chapter 11, "Temporalities on Collision Course: Time, Knowledge, and Temporal Critique in *Damages*" proposes an analysis of narrative temporalities in the legal drama *Damages*. Toni Pape focuses on the show's second season, which constructs two opposing temporal trajectories: while the main narrative starts at the beginning and is told forward, the second narrative trajectory starts in the future and regresses into the past. In this way, the show creates an intricate network of temporal relations. Drawing on philosophical critiques of "modern time consciousness," this essay argues that *Damages*'s temporal structures rely on an emphatic conception of modern time. Thus, the show reveals the complicity of these temporalities with a modern knowledge economy and power structures. Secondly, this chapter argues that *Damages* ultimately discards its "modern time consciousness" in favor of a notion of time as "intelligible becoming." This shift in narrative temporalities simultaneously brings about a shift in the knowledge economy and power relations represented in the *Damages*.

Chapter 12 shifts the focus to time's impact on the formation of identity rather than knowledge. "Freaks of Time: Reevaluating Memory and Identity through Daniel Knauf's *Carnivàle*" looks into the complex temporal structures of *Carnivàle* and argues that this television series offers layers of time through which it becomes possible for characters to retrace temporality, relive events, and share pasts and/or futures. Identifying these layers as actual and virtual dimensions of time, Frida Beckman proposes that this portrayal of time and space challenges not only the notion of a continuous, causal temporality, but also the idea of individual continuity since memories and experiences are not tied to one single mind or body. Rather, there is a repetition of events traveling across generations. As such complexities need to be untied by viewers over the integral interruptions of serial television, *Carnivàle* demands active viewing. It also invites philosophical inquiries into the nature of time and selfhood.

In chapter 13, "The Discourse of *Medium*: Time as a Narrative Device," Kristi McDuffie analyzes the character Allison Dubois, a psychic who dreams about past, present, and future crimes and uses those dreams to help the district attorney's office solve crimes. Although *Medium* is primarily an episodic crime drama, its paranormal elements allow it to challenge genre limits. McDuffie evokes Sarah Kozloff's idea of discourse—how a story is told—to discuss the ways episodic crime dramas privilege the process of solving the crime over the crime itself. The paranormal elements in *Medium* allow it to utilize different temporal structures, such as flashbacks, visions of the future, and alternate realities, to further plot and discourse possibilities. This essay demonstrates how *Medium* is unique and innovative in its utilization of these time devices throughout the series.

Section IV. Moving beyond the Televisual Restraints of the Past: Reimagining Genres and Formats

This section resumes the discussion of how nonlinear narratives might reshape existing television genres. Continuing the conversation begun in chapter 13, "Making Sense of the Future: Narrative Destabilization in Joss Whedon's *Dollhouse*" attends to the practice of temporal play in another science fiction program. Casey J. McCormick uses Joss Whedon's *Dollhouse* as a case study for examining recent trends in science fiction televisual narratives, particularly the prevalence of present-tense settings. Through an examination of the narratological implications of the series' "Epitaph" episodes from the perspective of the show's creators, as well as the experience of the viewer, this chapter explores how multiple diegetic layers emerge as a result of *Dollhouse*'s complicated temporal structure. Using theories of narrative derived from Gerard Genette and Mieke Bal, in conjunction with Bruce Clarke's concept of posthuman narratology, McCormick explores how temporal complexities relate to the ontological and epistemological concerns of a hyper-narrativized culture.

Colin Irvine's work further expands this section's hypothesis that experimental temporality plays a large role in the evolution of television genres at present. "Why *30 Rock* Rocks and *The Office* Needs Some Work: The Role of Time/Space in Contemporary TV Sitcoms" draws on a combination of frame theory, embedding Mikhail Bakhtin's concept of chronotopism to assert that paying attention to the uses of humor in sitcoms enables viewers to understand how—with respect to their uses of time/space—these shows function and why, as importantly, some succeed and some fail. Chapter 15 focuses first on *Arrested Development* and the manner with which it presents complex and yet coherent scenes, episodes, and seasons that allow for manipulation of time/space. It then turns to *The Office*, noting the similar reasons and ways the show worked during its first few seasons and discussing why it eventually began to fail. Irvine's essay concludes with an analysis of *30 Rock*, a sitcom that effectively establishes an imagined and yet plausible space that allows for multiple kinds of time as well as various political and social commentary.

Molly Brost's "Change the Structure, Change the Story: *How I Met Your Mother* and the Reformulation of the Television Romance" attends to how romantic storylines are affected by strategic alterations in temporal flow. *How I Met Your Mother* began with a unique premise: in a flashback from the year 2030, a middle-aged man tells his teenage children the story of how he met their mother. From the very beginning of the series, viewers were told who the mother was *not*: Robin Scherbatsky, the journalist who would be protagonist Ted Mosby's love interest for the show's first two seasons, and intermittently thereafter. Though some critics believed that this allowed the show to sidestep the "will-they-or-won't-they" relationship drama that plagues many sitcoms, others dismissed it as merely a gimmick. Chapter 16 argues that the show's unique narrative structure allows the series to reimagine the traditional romantic comedy formula; within this reimagining, the audience's expectations for both televisual romantic relationships and traditional gender roles are challenged and subverted.

Chapter 17 also analyzes how nontraditional narrative time works to draw attention to gender issues. Janani Subramanian's "Like Sands through the Half-Hourglass: *Nurse Jackie* and Temporal Disruption" once again moves this collection's focus on time from that of traditional network television to that which can be found on the competing cable stations. Showtime has emerged in the last few years as a serious contender in the premium television league. While HBO built its reputation around narrative complexity, Showtime has incorporated the female-centric, single-camera, half-hour "dramedy" genre into its quality brand identity. In this chapter, Subramanian argues, using *Nurse Jackie* as her primary example, that the segmentation of these thirty-minute shows presents a reformulation of television time in a quality television context; along with continuing to develop Showtime's brand identity, the combination of situation comedy and melodrama in that 30-minute time frame also turn conventional rituals of heterosexual coupling and domesticity on their head, creating a space in the television landscape for female characters' renegotiation of the traditional work/home binary.

Chapter 18 closes this section by giving attention to one of the newest television genres of the twenty-first century: the musical. In "The Television Musical: *Glee*'s New Directions," Jack Harrison looks at the temporal narrative experiment taking place in Fox's *Glee*, the first successful contemporary musical television program. His essay addresses the temporalities of *Glee* in three parts. The first section explores how musical conventions are changed by seriality, arguing that the climactic narrative synthesis of the musical film is still relevant to the show, but that the indefinite temporal expansion of television creates opportunities for multiple romantic unions. In the second section, closer attention is paid to the cause of the diegetic ruptures—the musical numbers themselves—reading their lyric time against the history of televisual realism to highlight the break from tradition they represent. Finally, in order to begin to address the question of why *Glee* was the show to bring the musical to television where other series have failed, the third section reads the show's musical numbers through the lens of Amit Rai's interval, showing how their circulation, independent of the greater text, has tapped into novel flows of sensation and revenue, particularly through digital downloads.

Section V. Playing outside of the Box: The Role Time Plays in Fan Fiction, Online Communities, and Audience Studies

The final section in this anthology turns away from the programs themselves and instead studies the various viewing audiences of these programs dedicated to exploring experimental time. Melanie Cattrell's "'Nothing Happens Unless First a Dream': TV Fandom, Narrative Structure, and the Alternate Universes of *Bones*" looks at how contemporary television writers draw upon the work in fan communities to inform and inspire the directions of their shows. This essay examines the way in which *Bones* challenges traditional storytelling patterns in two episodes that play with and disrupt narrative time by breaking from its typical format to place the lead characters in different realities. Within these realities, the lead characters are placed in a romantic relationship. Thus, these episodes allow viewers to see the characters together without disrupting the larger narrative of the program. Cattrell argues that the techniques used in these episodes are similar to techniques used by fan fiction writers, as they frequently place characters in different situations and in new realities.

In chapter 20, "Two Days before the Day after Tomorrow: Time, Temporality, and Fandom in *South Park*," Jason W. Buel examines atypical narrative time and narrative experimentation in the television series *South Park*. Though narrative time is not in the foreground of *South Park* as it is in many of the other programs analyzed in this collection, temporal play is nonetheless an important and common part of the show. This chapter examines such experimentation and attends to how fans have responded to the show's subversion of their expectations. Although the series has received a great deal of attention in popular media for the way its characters subvert the conventions of society, the way its form subverts conventions of narrative time is rarely discussed. *South Park* regularly delays narrative resolutions, continues narrative arcs from episodes long past, misremembers its own history through flashbacks, and refuses to pay off cliffhangers. Through such temporal play, Buel argues the series not only delights its fans but also carries different meanings for dedicated fans compared to casual viewers.

With Lucy Bennett's "Lost in Time?: *Lost* Fan Engagement with Temporal Play," this collection closes with an essay that analyzes the show most credited with jumpstarting the narrative trend of experimental temporality—a show that, because of its importance, has appeared (at least in passing) in almost every section of this anthology. As is well known, the television program *Lost* uses experiments with time as an important part of its structure, employing flashforwards, flashbacks, flashsideways, time travel, and multiple plot threads to create quite a novel narrative development. This chapter, by focusing on a specific example of the flashforward employed in season three, seeks to examine how online fans of the show engage with, and respond to, the use of these devices surrounding narrative time and the rationale that underlies their participation in the program as a puzzle to be solved. To achieve this, Bennett considers how these fans "read" and try to make sense of the show's use of temporal play in terms of their placement as viewers following characters in past, present, and alternate timelines, often simultaneously. Exploring discussions by members of the largest online community for *Lost* fans, www.lost-forum.com, she illuminates the responses of fans initiated by the startling temporal narrative device and explains how some struggled with its inclusion.

CONCLUSION
Why Time Matters

Humans have been preoccupied by time for centuries so it is not surprising that academic works and popular culture products continue to play to this fascination. In *About Time: Einstein's Unfinished Revolution*, Paul Davies explains that "the greatest outstanding riddle" concerning time is linked to "the glaring mismatch between physical time and subjective, or psychological, time," or how the brain struggles to relate the two in a way that connects "to our sense of free will" (283). The sociologist Émile Durkheim first noted that an "individual's temporal experience is conditioned by the collective rhythms of" his or her society (Flaherty 2). That is, time itself "is shaped from the very outset by society because self-consciousness is generated through socialization" (Flaherty 2). As television is perhaps one of the most influential media products helping to shape the "collective rhythms" of the society it stems from, and is one of the most apt means of socialization, it only makes sense that the medium of television, and televisual narratives in particular, would play a role in shaping individuals' understanding of the abstract concept we call time.

Although time moves along steadily whether we fully comprehend it or not, this study suggests that temporal explorations are the result of societal trends (sometimes even to the extent that they become allegories for them), they are a way of working through contemporary cultural concerns, and that they can be influential in transforming the very narratives that we tell (and the way we tell them) generation after generation. Moreover, these programs, in surprising ways, continue the work of scientists, philosophers, and media scholars, offering up fascinating critiques of current "times" while chasing the age-old dream of understanding "time" in general.

NOTES

1. One important study is Steven Johnson's *Everything Bad Is Good for You*, which argues that entertainment media of the last three decades have been increasing in complexity and have resulted in the smartening, rather than the "dumbing down," of American consumers. Two other noteworthy studies, focused more specifically on televisual trends, would include Robert J. Thompson's *Television's Second Golden Age* and M. Keith Booker's *Strange TV.*

2. For academic studies on the role of the active fan as television scholar/critic, see Henry Jenkin's *Textual Poachers*, Camille Bacon-Smith's *Enterprising Women*, or Nancy K. Baym's *Tune In, Log On.*

3. Although no such book for this decade exists, there is a precedent for the success of academic books focusing on one decade of television alone. See Jane Feuer's *Seeing Through the Eighties: Television and Reaganism* and Aniko Bodroghkozy's *Groove Tube: Sixties Television and the Youth Rebellion* as examples of ancestor texts that study a specific televisual decade.

4. These ideas can be further explored in Mittell's "Narrative Complexity in Contemporary American Television," "Serial Boxes," and "Previously On: Prime Time Serials and the Mechanics of Memory."

5. For such examples, see Barbie Zelizer and Stuart Allan's *Journalism after September 11th*, Daya Kishan Thussu and Des Freedman's *War and the Media*, Stephen Hess and Marvin Kalb's *The Media and the War on Terrorism*, Dennis Broe's "Fox and Its Friends: Global Commodification and the New Cold War," Susan J. Douglas's "The Turn Within: The Irony of Technology in a Globalized World," and Marc Redfield's "Virtual Trauma: The Idiom of 9/11."

6. To be clear, there have been some studies on individual television shows that read their fictional contents through a post-9/11 lens. Examples include Cinnamon Stillwell's "'24': Television for a Post-9/11 World," Lynnette Porter, David Lavery, and Hillary Robson's *Saving the World: A Guide to* Heroes, and J. Wood's *Living Lost: Why We're All Stuck on the Island*. However, most of these studies analyze one single program through a post-9/11 lens rather than studying programming thematics more broadly.

7. See Douglas (2006) and Spigel (2004).

8. A full list of such studies would be impossible to include here, but some select examples include Mark Andrejevic's *Reality TV: The Work of Being Watched*, Su Holmes and Deborah Jermyn's *Understanding Reality Television*, Michael Essany's *Reality Check: The Business and Art of Producing Reality TV*, Laurie Ouellette and Susan Murray's *Reality TV: Remaking Television Culture*, Anna David's *Reality Matters: 19 Writers Come Clean About the Shows We Can't Stop Watching*, and Jennifer L. Pozner's *Reality Bites Back: The Troubling Truth About Guilty Pleasure TV.*

9. Two noteworthy studies are Bonnie Anderson's *Newsflash: Journalism, Infotainment, and the Bottom-Line Business of Broadcast News* and Daya Thussu's *News as Entertainment: The Rise of Global Infotainment.*

10. Stewart beat out other reputable newscasters, such as Katie Couric, Charles Gibson, and Brian Williams. This poll can be viewed at http://www.timepolls.com/hppolls/archive/poll_results_417.html (accessed March 11, 2011).

11. This title was given to him just days before his political event, The Rally to Restore Sanity, which drew over a quarter million people to the National Mall in Washington, D.C., on October 30, 2010.

12. See Aristotle in the fourth book of *Physics*, Augustine in book six of *Confessions*, Husserl in *The Phenomenology of Internal Time-Consciousness*, Heidegger in *Being and Time*, Nietzche in *Thus Spoke Zarathustra*, and Bergson in *Duration and Simultaneity*.

13. Perhaps the best text that traces the development of scientific debates and theories of time is Hawking's *A Brief History of Time*.

14. Two such studies are David Landes's *Revolution in Time* and Jo Ellen Barnett's *Time's Pendulum*.

15. Other noteworthy studies include Mikhail Bakhtin's "Forms of Time and the Chronotrope in the Novel," E. M. Forester's *Aspects of the Novel*, and Peter Brooks's *Reading for the Plot*.

16. For other studies on postmodernism and time, consult E. D. Ermarth's *Sequel to History*, Brian Richardson's *Beyond Story and Discourse*, and David Dickens and Andrea Fontana's "Time and Postmodernism."

17. See also Doane (2002), Tyree (2009), and Uhlin (2010).

18. See Stephanie Marriott's *Live Television: Time, Space, and the Broadcast Event*.

19. See Tania Modeleski's *Loving With a Vengeance: Mass-Produced Fantasies for Women*.

20. It is not surprising that many of the shows analyzed in this collection could loosely fall into the category of science fiction as the genre as a whole aims to accomplish what each of these time-travel narratives do on a smaller scale: work through cultural anxieties. For two highly informational studies that track this science fiction goal historically, see Nagl and Clayton (1983) and Hollinger (1999).

21. For example, Steve Anderson's "History TV and Popular Memory" studies how television crafts cultural memories and how fictional programming often remediates historical events in interesting ways.

22. It is worth noting that the majority of the television shows devoted to experimental time, or time travel, prior to the twenty-first century were British. As this collection focuses on American television series alone it is interesting to observe how American television post-2000 hijacked this focus that it had previously only occasionally dabbled in.

23. This cultural trend was noted as early as 1970, when Alvin Toffler pointed out the close relation of instant availability and disposability in what he termed the "throw-away society" (47–67).

24. See Jameson's *Postmodernism, Or, the Cultural Logic of Late Capitalism*.

25. Heise makes a very similar argument concerning postmodern literature in *Chronoschisms*.

26. For more on the concept of premediation, see Richard Grusin's *Predmediation: Affect and Mediality after 9/11*.

WORKS CITED

Anderson, Bonnie. *Newsflash: Journalism, Infotainment, and the Bottom-Line Business of Broadcast News*. San Francisco: Jossey-Bass, 2004. Print.

Anderson, Steven. "History TV and Popular Memory." *Television Histories: Shaping Collective Memory in the Media Age*. Ed. Gary R. Edgerton and Peter C. Rollins. Lexington: University Press of Kentucky, 2001. 19–36. Print.

Andrejevic, Mark. *Reality TV: The Work of Being Watched*. New York: Rowman & Littlefield, 2004. Print.

Aristotle. *Physics.* Ed. David Bostock. Trans. Robin Waterfield. Oxford: Oxford University Press, 2000. Print.

Augustine. *The Confessions of St. Augustine.* Trans. Edward Pusey. New York: Collier, 1961. Print.

Bacon-Smith, Camille. *Enterprising Women: Television Fandom and the Creation of Popular Myth.* Philadelphia: University Press of Pennsylvania, 1994. Print.

Bakhtin, Mikhail. "Forms of Time and the Chronotope in the Novel." *The Dialogic Imagination: Four Essays.* Trans. Caryl Emerson and Michael Holquist. Ed. Michael Holquist. Austin: University of Texas Press, 1981. 84–258. Print.

Barnett, Jo Ellen. *Time's Pendulum: From Sundials to Atomic Clocks, the Fascinating History of Timekeeping and How Our Discoveries Changed the World.* New York: Harvest Books, 1998. Print.

Baym, Nancy K. *Tune In, Log On: Soaps, Fandom, and Online Community.* London: Sage, 2000. Print.

Benjamin, Walter. "The Storyteller." *Illuminations: Essays and Reflections.* Trans. Harry Zohn. New York: Schocken Books, 1968. 83–110. Print.

Bergson, Henri. *Duration and Simultaneity.* 1922. Indianapolis, IN: Bobbs-Merrill, 1965. Print.

Bodroghkozy, Aniko. *Groove Tube: Sixties Television and the Youth Rebellion.* Durham, NC: Duke University Press, 2001. Print.

Booker, M. Keith. *Strange TV: Innovative Television Series from* The Twilight Zone *to* The X-Files. Westport, CT: Greenwood Press, 2002. Print.

Broe, Dennis. "Fox and Its Friends: Global Commodification and the New Cold War." *Cinema Journal* 43.4 (Summer 2004): 97–102. Print.

Brooks, Peter. *Reading for the Plot: Design and Intention in Narrative.* New York: Random House, 1985. Print.

David, Anna, ed. *Reality Matters: 19 Writers Come Clean About the Shows We Can't Stop Watching.* New York: HarperCollins, 2010. Print.

Davies, Paul. *About Time: Einstein's Unfinished Revolution.* New York: Simon & Schuster, 1995. Print.

Dickens, David R., and Andrea Fontana. "Time and Postmodernism." *Symbolic Interaction* 25.3 (2002): 389–96. Print.

Doane, Mary Ann. *The Emergence of Cinematic Time: Modernity, Contingency, The Archive.* Cambridge, MA: Harvard University Press, 2002. Print.

Douglas, Susan J. "The Turn Within: The Irony of Technology in a Globalized World." *American Quarterly* 58.3 (September 2006): 619–38. Print.

Edgerton, Gary R., and Peter C. Rollins, eds. *Television Histories: Shaping Collective Memory in the Media Age.* Lexington: University Press of Kentucky, 2001. Print.

Ermarth, Elizabeth Deeds. *Sequel to History: Postmodernism and the Crisis of Representational Time.* Princeton, NJ: Princeton University Press, 1992. Print.

Essany, Michael. *Reality Check: The Business and Art of Producing Reality TV.* Boston: Focal Press, 2008. Print.

Feuer, Jane. *Seeing Through the Eighties: Television and Reaganism.* Durham, NC: Duke University Press, 1995. Print.

Flaherty, M. G. *A Watched Pot: How We Experience Time.* New York: New York University Press, 2000. Print.

Forester, E. M. *Aspects of the Novel.* San Diego: Harcourt Brace Jovanovich, 1985. Print.

Grosz, Elizabeth. *The Nick of Time: Politics, Evolution, and the Untimely.* Durham, NC: Duke University Press, 2004. Print.
Grusin, Richard. *Premediation: Affect and Mediality after 9/11.* New York: Palgrave Macmillan, 2010. Print.
Hawking, Stephen. *A Brief History of Time.* New York: Bantam Books, 1988. Print.
Heidegger, Martin. *Being and Time.* 1927. Trans. J. Macquarrie and E. Robinson. London: SCM Press, 1962.
Heise, Ursula K. *Chronoschisms: Time, Narrative, and Postmodernism.* Cambridge: Cambridge University Press, 1997. Print.
Hess, Stephen, and Marvin Kalb, eds. *The Media and the War on Terrorism.* Washington, D.C.: Brookings, 2003. Print.
Hollinger, Veronica. "Contemporary Trends in Science Fiction Criticism, 1980–1999." *Science Fiction Studies* 26.2 (1999): 232–62. Print.
Holmes, Su, and Deborah Jermyn. *Understanding Reality Television.* New York: Routledge, 2004. Print.
Husserl, Edmund. *The Phenomenology of Internal Time-Consciousness.* 1928. Ed. Martin Heidegger. Trans. J. S. Churchill. Bloomington: Indiana University Press, 1964. Print.
Jameson, Fredric. *Postmodernism, Or, the Cultural Logic of Late Capitalism.* Durham, NC: Duke University Press, 1991. Print.
Jenkins, Henry. *Textual Poachers: Television Fans & Participatory Culture.* New York: Routledge, 1992. Print.
Johnson, Steven. *Everything Bad Is Good for You: How Today's Popular Culture Is Actually Making Us Smarter.* New York: Riverhead, 2005. Print.
Kermode, Frank. *The Sense of an Ending.* Oxford: Oxford University Press, 1966. Print.
Landes, David S. *Revolution in Time: Clocks and the Making of the Modern World.* Cambridge: Belknap, 1983. Print.
Lotz, Amanda. *The Television Will Be Revolutionized.* New York: New York University Press, 2007. Print.
Marriott, Stephanie. *Live Television: Time, Space, and the Broadcast Event.* London: Sage Publications, 2007. Print.
McCabe, Janet, and Kim Akass, eds. *Quality TV: Contemporary American Television and Beyond.* London: I. B. Tauris, 2007. Print.
Mittell, Jason. "Narrative Complexity in Contemporary American Television." *The Velvet Light Trap* 58 (2006): 29–40. Print.
———. "Previously On: Prime Time Serials and the Mechanics of Memory." *Just TV.* July 3, 2009. Web. November 6, 2010.
———. "Serial Boxes." *MediaCommons.* January 20, 2010. Web. January 22, 2010.
Modleski, Tania. *Loving With a Vengeance: Mass-Produced Fantasies for Women.* Hamden, CT: Archon Books, 1982. Print.
Nagl, Manfred, and David Clayton. "The Science-Fiction Film in Historical Perspective." *Science Fiction Studies* 10.3 (1983): 262–77. Print.
Nietzsche, Friedrich. *Thus Spoke Zarathustra.* Harmondsworth: Penguin, 1979. Print.
Ouellette, Laurie, and Susan Murray. *Reality TV: Remaking Television Culture.* New York: New York University Press, 2009. Print.
Porter, Lynnette, David Lavery, and Hillary Robson. *Saving the World: A Guide to* Heroes. Toronto: ECW Press, 2007. Print.
Pozner, Jennifer L. *Reality Bites Back: The Troubling Truth About Guilty Pleasure TV.* New York: Seal Press, 2010. Print.

Redfield, Marc. "Virtual Trauma: The Idiom of 9/11." *diacritics* 37.1 (Spring 2007): 55–80. Print.

Reeves, Jimmie L., Mark C. Rogers, and Michael M. Epstein. "Quality Control: *The Daily Show*, the Peabody and Brand Discipline." *Quality Television: Contemporary American Television and Beyond*. Ed. Janet McCabe and Kim Akass. New York: Palgrave Macmillan, 2007. 79–97. Print.

Richardson, Brian. *Beyond Story and Discourse: Narrative Time in Postmodern and Nonmimetic Fiction*. Columbus: Ohio State University Press, 2002. Print.

Ricouer, Paul. *Time and Narrative*. Vol. 1–3. Trans. Kathleen McLaughlin and David Pellauer. Chicago: University of Chicago Press, 1984. Print.

Silverman, Stephen M. "Jon Stewart Named Most Influential Man of 2010." *People*. October 27, 2010. Web. January 5, 2011.

Spigel, Lynn. "Entertainment Wars: Television Culture after 9/11." *American Quarterly* 56.2 (June 2004): 235–67. Print.

Spigel, Lynn, and Jan Olsson, eds. *Television after TV: Essays on a Medium in Transition*. Durham, NC: Duke University Press, 2004. Print.

Stillwell, Cinnamon. "'24': Television for a Post-9/11 World." *SFGate*. Web. January 31, 2007. April 10, 2008.

Thompson, Robert J. *Television's Second Golden Age: From* Hill Street Blues *to* ER. Syracuse, NY: Syracuse University Press, 1996. Print.

Thussu, Daya Kishan. *News as Entertainment: The Rise of Global Infotainment*. New York: Sage, 2007. Print.

Thussu, Daya Kishan, and Des Freedman. *War and the Media: Reporting Conflicts 24/7*. London: Sage, 2003. Print.

Toffler, Alvin. *Future Shock*. New York: Bantam Books, 1970. Print.

Tyree, J. M. "Against the Clock: *Slumdog Millionaire* and *The Curious Case of Benjamin Button.*" *Film Quarterly* 62.4 (2009): 34–38. Print.

Uhlin, Graig. "TV, Time, and the Films of Andy Warhol." *Cinema Journal* 49.3 (2010): 1–23. Print.

Wood, J. *Living Lost: Why We're All Stuck on the Island*. New Orleans, LA: Garrett County Press, 2007. Print.

Zelizer, Barbie, and Stuart Allan. *Journalism after September 11th (Communication and Society)*. New York: Routledge, 2002. Print.

PART I

PROMOTING THE FUTURE OF EXPERIMENTAL TV
The Industry Changes and Technological Advancements That Paved the Way to "New" Television Ventures

1

TELEVISION'S PARADIGM (TIME)SHIFT
Production and Consumption Practices in the Post-Network Era

TODD M. SODANO

> It seems safe to say that no decade has seen more transformations in television as an industry, a textual form, and a technology since the 1950s.
> —JASON MITTELL ("SERIAL")

In a twenty-four-hour period between Sunday, May 23 and Monday, May 24, 2010, viewers said farewell to three of the most influential dramatic series in television history: *Lost*, *24*, and *Law & Order*. Though *24* (FOX, 2001–2010) and *Law & Order* (NBC, 1990–2010) strongly influenced scripted programming, *Lost* (ABC, 2004–2010) undoubtedly captured the zeitgeist of the prime-time serial in the first decade of the twenty-first century, which American TV institution *The Simpsons* recognized.

The Simpsons (FOX, 1989–Present), whose impressive longevity has outstripped these other series', made its own meaningful contribution to conversations from those two nights: Bart Simpson, the perpetually troublemaking fourth grader who begins most episodes by suffering the punishment of scrawling a repeating chalkboard message, opened the program's twenty-first season finale with the following gag: "End of *Lost*. It was all the dog's dream. Watch us" ("Judge"). *The Simpsons* paid its respects through one of its famous popular culture references. However, for viewers who watched either show outside of the networks' scheduling context, this gesture might appear less significant.

As new media distribution platforms continue to develop, the television audience continues to splinter further. The traditional linear broadcast flow that marked the network era has been challenged and subverted by time-shifters, cable channels, online venues, emerging media, and a newer "publishing flow" (namely, DVDs).[1] Consequently, as Amanda Lotz suggests, "We need to think of the medium not as 'Television' but as televisions" because "we can no longer conceive of the technology with such singularity" (78, 80).

Television consumption continues to increase alongside the increased fracturing of the viewing audience. The average American watches more than thirty-five hours of television per week, and almost one-third of American TV households own four or more sets ("Snapshot"). The fragmentation of the viewing population continues to affect the broadcast networks. In the thirty years between the 1979–80 and 2009–10 TV seasons, ratings for the most-watched shows decreased by almost 50 percent. Overall, from 1994 to 2009, viewership for the four major networks (CBS, NBC, ABC, and FOX) decreased 42 percent (Steinberg).

"Convenience technologies" that include the VCR, the DVR, and DVDs have disrupted traditional modes of production and distribution, which have significantly changed consumption practices and discourses (Lotz 61). This chapter examines practices that have changed broadcast flow in the post-network era. This essay also looks at the gaps within (and between) episodes and across seasons, which represent a new dimension in television production, consumption, and scholarship. As the 2010 season finales of *Lost* and *The Simpsons* exemplify, the main text may remain the same, but other texts and contexts disappear in the conversations surrounding today's serials. The phenomenon of binge viewing is explored here, as viewers can bypass full seasons on linearly scheduled television in favor of watching them at once at their convenience. Finally, this chapter examines how paratexts such as watercooler conversations and spoilers have become integral pieces of post-network TV dialogues.

FLOW

Raymond Williams called "flow" the uninterrupted nature of television within, between, and across programs. However, in its incipient years, television shared more with film and literature in that viewers or readers consumed media as "discrete events" (Williams 88). They went to a movie theater, saw a film, and returned home; they pulled a book from a shelf, read it, and returned it. Television was similar, as viewers watched a program with no interruptions.

As Williams described, though, television changed once advertising entered the picture, so to speak, and changed the "intervals" between programming units. Ads glued together seamlessly the programs that used to be discrete, marking a shift "from the concept of sequence as *programming* to the concept of sequence as *flow*" (89, emphasis in original). Television never ends. One program leads into a commercial, which leads into the next program or a promo, and so on. Programs fill the gaps between ads and promos, not the reverse. Muriel Cantor plainly reminds us, "The only purpose of all programming is to sell products and therefore advertising time" (62).

A TV network's flow, or the "*seemingly* unrelated ribbon of fragments—commercials, programs, and promotional material," is anything but unrelated (Budd and Steinman 17, emphasis added). As Williams wrote, the flow is deliberate or "planned." Networks and advertisers try to "get viewers in at the beginning of a flow" (Williams 93). NBC wants us to watch not only *Community* (2009–Present) and *30 Rock* (2006–Present) on Thursday nights but also the promos for other NBC programs, commercial advertisements, and anything in between. In an ideal network flow, viewers' television sets should remain turned on well before and long after they watch their desired program(s).

Sarah Kozloff adds a third level to narrative theory, schedule—to join story and discourse—which determines how the latter two "are affected by the text's placement within the larger discourse of the station's schedule" (69). This level is carefully orchestrated around the programs, advertisements, and promos. To maintain this flow, series often implement conventions such as "staged climactic moments before each commercial break" (Gregory 25). Adrenaline-filled series like *24* use a formula in which, just before each break and at the end of every episode, something shocking, explosive, or tense happens in order to keep viewers watching.

Accordingly, context can dictate content. *The Wire* (HBO, 2002–2008), *The Sopranos* (HBO, 1999–2007), and *Dexter* (Showtime, 2006–Present), all premium cable series, need not include such exhilarating moments every eight minutes because their networks offer no commercial breaks. Kyle Killen, creator of the short-lived drama *Lone Star* (FOX, 2010), encapsulates the differences between working on broadcast and working on cable through an analogy of holding someone's dog hostage: "If I'm bored for two minutes [on network TV], I'll kill your dog. If I'm bored at the end of 43 minutes [on cable], I'll kill your dog" (2010). Killen's series was terminated after two low-rated but acclaimed episodes.

Flow has changed how television is programmed and consumed. Consequently, storytelling has grown more sophisticated narratively and aesthetically. Series' narratives can remain open. The viewer knows he can return the following week to see the same characters. This "most striking narrative feature" has enabled daily soap operas to stay on the air for as long as they have (Allen 107). When television programming developed in the late 1940s, the popular live anthology dramas and variety shows did not offer open narratives. However, as flow evolved, so did the television narrative.

Post-network era television has challenged its viewers like never before. As Jason Mittell notes, "The past decade or so of American television has seen the emergence of a widespread trend of narrative complexity" ("Serial").[2] Convenience technologies have facilitated more advanced narrative techniques, as storytellers no longer must accede to the limitations of traditional linear broadcast flow to present their stories. Steven Johnson has argued that complex television has made us smarter. Our brains work especially hard to follow the many characters and multiple storylines, while simultaneously filling in the gaps within these threads. Therefore, in what he calls the Sleeper Curve, "the most debased forms of mass diversion—video games and violent television dramas and juvenile sitcoms—turn out to be nutritional after all" (Johnson 9).

"CONVENIENCE TECHNOLOGIES"

Convenience technologies have subverted broadcast scheduling. Viewers today can ignore a network's planned flow and time-shift their favorite programs to a more convenient time. Moreover, they can miss an entire season outright and buy/rent/download/stream episodes, further complicating the relationships among viewers, networks, sponsors, and storytellers.

Lotz's three characteristics of post-network technologies—convenience, mobility, and theatricality—have "redefined the medium from its network-era form" by giving viewers more control. In fact, control has literally switched hands, as viewers can select with remote control devices and media players which programs to watch or to record. This represents a paradigmatic shift in the ways networks distribute their programs and viewers consume them. Furthermore, more viewers are watching television alone, due to "narrowly targeted programming and more sets in homes" (Levin). The idyllic image of the family gathered around one TV set has given way to either an empty living room or the family sitting together but individually juggling content across multiple platforms.

David Carr observes, "We don't watch TV anymore as much as it seems to watch us, recommending, recording, and dishing up all manner of worthy product." As a result, he adds, "our ability to produce media has outstripped our ability to consume it." Time-shifting has become a regular viewing practice. Hampton Stevens calls *24* the most influential drama series ever and points to the fact that no other drama has used the real-time format to tell its story. Perhaps, though, that says less about *24*'s influence and more about viewers who no longer consume television in real time.

The DVR's penetration into U.S. households epitomizes convenience technologies' influences in the television industry. Many believed the DVR, like its predecessor, the VCR, would destroy the broadcast networks. However, over time, the networks' reluctance, resistance, and hostility have cooled. Alan Wurtzel, president of research for NBC Universal, has begun to call the DVR their "frenemy," that is, both friend and enemy (Carter, "Later"). While the DVR allows viewers to fast-forward through commercials, there is no definitive evidence to suggest that all viewers would invariably do so. Furthermore, Bill Carter has characterized this sticky relationship between networks and DVR technology as a "media business version of the Stockholm Syndrome, [in which] television network executives have fallen in love with a former tormentor" ("DVR"). At the beginning of the 2010–11 season, more than 37 percent of TV households had a DVR, a number sure to increase ("Snapshot").

Because time-shifting has become more common, Nielsen Media Research has incorporated it into its ratings methodologies. The group now calculates live ratings as well as live-plus-three and live-plus-seven to account for viewers who take anywhere from a few days up to a week to watch a recorded program. Some content, like sporting events and talk shows, is purportedly "DVR-proof" because it most likely will be watched live (or when the networks air them). However, because of this time-sensitive nature of such programs, the live-plus-three and live-plus-seven ratings could be negligible, which could lower advertising rates (Carter, "DVR"; Leonard).

Derek Kompare has examined another type of flow that has emerged in the post-network era, one that represents the evolution of Williams's concept and how DVDs have changed the relationship between television and viewers. Kompare begins from the perspective addressed above; namely, how home video devices have enabled viewers to watch what, when, and where they want. He invokes two of Bernard Miége's three models of cultural production, publishing, and flow, and makes a careful distinction between them. While publishing "connects producers and consumers more or less directly, the flow model is premised on a different exchange: between producers, broadcasters, and advertisers" (Kompare 339).

The TV-on-DVD box set has enabled viewers to purchase series for consumption as well as collection. Kompare calls it "the video object that successfully converted broadcast flow to published text and finally made television tangible" (343). Michael Z. Newman adds, "The new technologies that give viewers the agency to program their own media mark a shift from ephemeral to collectible content." In addition to consumption, television scholars have introduced another prandial metaphor to describe how viewers watch programming—the binge.

BINGE/MARATHON VIEWING

Thanks to the plethora of series released on DVD at the turn of the century, viewers have embraced the opportunity to catch up on shows they missed when they first aired. One common practice is binge viewing, in which viewers watch numerous episodes (and sometimes complete seasons) over a concentrated period. This brings us closer to the characters, writes Newman, but removes us from the broadcast scheduling context that informs conversations surrounding a series.

For example, viewers who binge on *Modern Family* (ABC, 2009–Present) miss the commercials and promos that ABC aired during those episodes, which reveal the network's sponsors and other programming. Moreover, binge viewers might not have understood the controversy surrounding "The Kiss" episode, in which the same-sex couple Cameron (Eric Stonestreet) and Mitchell (Jesse Tyler Ferguson) finally smooch on-screen early in the second season. Some fans wondered why the heterosexual couples on the show often kissed but the gay couple merely hugged. Did the show's creators prohibit such displays of affection? Did the network or conservative advertisers discourage them? Fans created a Facebook page, "Let Cam & Mitchell Kiss on *Modern Family*," in support of this elusive plot element. Binging removes viewers from these paratextual conversations that take place across episodes and in the gaps between them.

Television binging has influenced interpersonal relationships, too. Grady Hendrix calls the box set a form of "ritualistic abuse [that] we inflict on one another." In addition to sharing our pleasures by demanding that those close to us watch a particular DVD, he continues, we are also saying, "If you don't, you are an idiot. I will still acknowledge you in public, but in my heart I will know that you are an anti-intellectual vulgarian." In his humorous diatribe against binge viewing, Hendrix declares that DVDs have "transformed television from light entertainment into homework."

Conversely, according to Mittell, DVDs allow us to examine television series aesthetically. He writes, "[V]iewing a DVD edition helps highlight the values of unity, complexity, and clear beginnings and endings, qualities that are hard to discern through the incremental releases of seriality" (Mittell, "Serial"). David Simon, creator of *The Wire*, *Generation Kill* (HBO, 2008), and *Treme* (HBO, 2010–Present), would prefer viewers to examine his whole story rather than the weekly episodic installments. In response to criticisms he received about the stories in *Treme*'s first season, Simon said,

> If you go back and watch the first episode of any season of *The Wire*, or the first episode of *Treme* or *Generation Kill*, knowing the ending, the choices

will be entirely reasonable as a first chapter of something that is novelistic. (qtd. in Sepinwall)

Many early reviews of *The Wire* in 2002, based on the few screener episodes that HBO distributed, were middling. However, toward the end of the first season, reviews grew more favorable, which Simon attributes to critics appreciating the accumulation of plot, character, and novelistic storytelling. Thus, binging can "make one more conscious of the season as a narrative unit" (Newman).

The same technologies that offer opportunities to "alter the narrative possibilities available to creators" (Mittell, "Serial") also allow viewers, including Simon's, to abandon series and the linear broadcasting flow if they do not like the rhythm, pacing, or stories. Consequently, the influences of gaps have grown more complex, and the consumers' viewing experiences have grown increasingly diverse.

GAPS

Simon and his writing team on *The Wire* embraced a "novelistic" approach in crafting what became one of television's most acclaimed series ever. TV critics lauded the series for its "Dickensian" qualities, an adjective that grew so tiresome that the writers self-referentially joked about it in the final season, which examined the mass media in Baltimore. In one episode, the clueless executive editor of the fictional *Baltimore Sun* tells his staff, "The word I'm thinking about is Dickensian. We want to depict the Dickensian lives of city children" ("Unconfirmed").

The comparisons between Charles Dickens's novels and Simon's television series did not start and end with their raw, detailed depictions of urban life; both authors embrace(d) seriality within their respective medium. Simon continues to tell his stories through the episodic mode of television production, despite any shortcomings or inevitable criticisms it may bring. According to Sean O'Sullivan, "One key component of [Dickens's serial fiction] mechanics is the gap, the space between publication of installments that differentiates serial fiction from every other art form" (116).[3] In twenty-first-century television, this gap, marked by serialized programming, convenience technologies, and time-shifting, has grown uniquely complicated.

Texts and interpretations have changed considerably. O'Sullivan continues, "[I]t is in that between-state that we as readers or viewers do most of our interpreting—speculating about plot developments or resolutions, wondering about characters and their choices, luxuriating in the details of the story's construction" (123). The traditional broadcast flow, in which episodes generally are introduced weekly (or daily) at the same time on the same channel, allows for viewers "to imagine in that gap what happens next" (Dove-Viebahn). However, today's viewer can watch new episodes of *Modern Family* an hour later on the DVR, stream them on Hulu the following morning, purchase them from iTunes to watch on an iPod, or binge through them later on DVD.

As a result, the "swaying between the ignorance of the new and the knowledge of the old" gets murkier as viewers use different technologies for consumption across seasons (O'Sullivan 123). According to O'Sullivan, "[B]etween-ness takes on an even more complicated role in a narrative that unfolds not patiently over twenty months but intensively, in three-month clusters separated by nine or more fallow months" (121). Or, in the case of *The Sopranos*, nearly two years, as twenty-one months elapsed between the fifth and sixth seasons. An impatient HBO subscriber who endured that seemingly interminable period was privy to the conversations (in person, in print, or online) about what lay ahead in the final season. A Netflix subscriber missed those discussions but could instantly bridge the gap in the time it took her to instantly stream the next season's episodes through her Nintendo Wii.

Though neither method is "better" than the other, viewing episodes in their natural broadcast flow can reveal more insight into the industrial and narrative contexts. According to Mittell, the broadcast schedule "creat[es] the structure for collective synchronous consumption and provid[es] the time to reflect upon the unfolding narrative world." He adds, "One of the chief pleasures of *Lost* is the ludic sense of play that fills the gaps between episodes and seasons, with fans congregating in online forums and wikis to theorize, investigate, evaluate, and debate" ("Serial"). Even though *Lost* has concluded its run, this "play" can still take place, just not in the synchronous structure created by the networks.

In describing the spaces within and across seasons, O'Sullivan writes, "We are always close to the beginning or end of something in a serial narrative, and so the space between has its own special import" (121), a notion evident in the first season of *Glee* (FOX, 2009–Present). In the 2009–10 TV season, the musical juggernaut instantly became one of the most popular new series. FOX premiered the pilot episode in May 2009 to more than 10 million viewers (Tanklefsky), took advantage of the summer buzz it created, and waited until the fall to broadcast the full season. The first thirteen episodes aired through December, and the back nine premiered the following April with a season finale in June.

Considering all gaps, *Glee* had five distinct campaigns in its first season. Twentieth Century Fox Home Entertainment capitalized on this by releasing the *Glee* DVDs as two separate volumes and as one complete volume. An examination of these campaigns—discretely and collectively—reveals interesting insights into post-network television, FOX's broadcast structure, and conversations surrounding a hit series.

PARATEXTS

One of the major elements that both fills and represents the gaps is the paratext, which is "anything surrounding the text that isn't considered the text itself, and it is most often used to give us better understanding of the primary text" (Ford). Examples include network promos, previouslies (recap segments that introduce episodes of serials), previews, spoilers, and DVD extras.

The TV scholar Jonathan Gray does not recognize them as a "wholly industrial entity" or something that is "peripheral." Instead, in applying this literary term to media, Gray says, "'Para' suggests a more complicated relationship to the film or show, outside of, alongside, and intrinsically part of all at the same time" (qtd. in Jenkins). Viewers who practice consumption outside of the broadcast scheduling context may never see these paratexts, thus exposing gaps in their knowledge.

On the night of the *Lost* finale, viewers in the Rochester, New York, market who tuned in to their local ABC affiliate (WHAM-TV) saw at least three parodic commercials that used the show's idioms, music, sound effects, and symbols. In one 30-second spot, the first image viewers saw was the iconic extreme close-up of someone's eye opening. A man, revealed to be wearing a dark suit à la *Lost*'s main character Dr. Jack Shephard (Matthew Fox), runs through a forest to escape the villainous smoke monster. He emerges on a mound of dirt, peers out into the distance, and sees . . . the local Dick Ide Honda dealership.

Another 10-second commercial for the car dealer lists the show's six major characters and their mythological numbers (4, 8, 15, 16, 23, 42), followed by a seventh number that reveals . . . the lease price ($249/month) for a new Accord.

Rich Ide, the marketing director who created and starred in these spots, said his company was trying to "get around the DVR problem." Because viewers fast-forward through commercials, he said, "why not make an ad that looks like the show? I [received] some emails from people saying that I faked them out, and they thought it was the show, and then they came and bought a car."

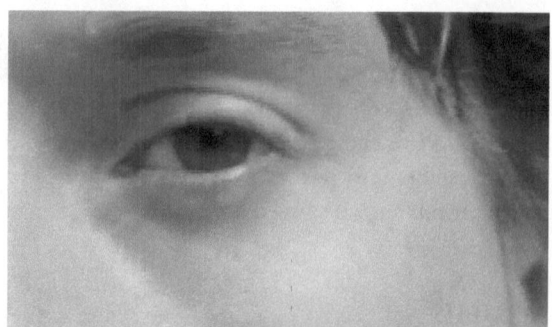

Fig. 1.1 Local *Lost* Parody Commercial: Dick Ide Honda Dealership

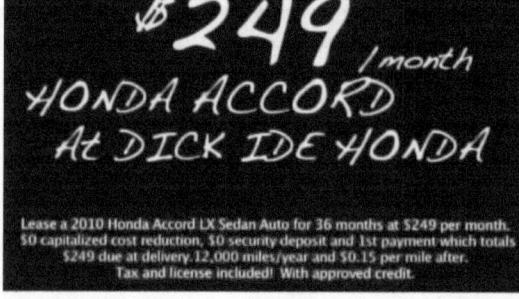

Fig. 1.2 Second Local *Lost* Parody Commercial: Honda Accord Lease

Fig. 1.3 Target's National *Lost* Parody Commercial: Smoke Detector Advertisement

Retail giant Target aired a spot that showed the smoke monster (and its concomitant sound effects) invading the beach where the original plane crashed, followed by a full-screen graphic for a $10.99 First Alert smoke detector.

In short, viewers who watched ABC on that Sunday in May 2010 witnessed these paratexts that provided a fuller understanding of the primary *Lost* text in relation to the broadcasting context. Viewers who missed the broadcast but watch(ed) it on DVD or online would see the same episode but without the elements that might have enhanced their appreciation for a concluding popular series. Mittell notes, "The ability to watch DVDs on your own time and pace, without commercials or interruptions, helps emphasize the medium's artistic merits over commercial imperatives" ("Serial"). However, such imperatives reveal considerable insight into the broadcast contexts.

Lost is not gone for good, as it will live on in syndication, on DVD, and through online consumption. Gone, though, are the synchronous conversations in between (and created by) the gaps and the "forensic fandom . . . dependent on simultaneous viewership, with everyone at the same point of the story, enabling a collaborative group process of decoding and engagement" (Mittell, "Serial"). These conversations might not be resurrected until and unless uninitiated viewers undertake the series.

WATER COOLERS AND SPOILERS

As cable television fragmented the viewing audience in the early 1980s and broke up the Big Three networks' oligopoly, sources of "water-cooler conversation" began to change. Lotz attributes network-era chatter to the "synchronicity of linear viewing," which provided "shared content for discussion" (32). However, convenience technologies have given viewers more control in selecting what, when, and where to watch, thus altering morning-after conversations. The assumption that "everyone" watched last night's episode of a hit TV show no longer holds water, as it were, because the odds have grown slimmer that everyone watched the same show at *any* time.

Water-cooler interlocutors now contend with countless consumption options. As digital and social media platforms serve as popular locations for these conversations, the water-cooler trope has given way to the water bottle, since viewers can participate privately and alone with their computers, smartphones, and portable media players.

One result of fewer in-person water-cooler dialogues is the valuable buzz these conversations can create that often persuades more viewers to watch a program. With an ever-increasing slate of series, channels, and platforms from which viewers may choose, programs with low ratings can subsist but will need help from other venues to avoid cancellation. Lotz suggests, "The conditions of the waning years of the multi-channel transition and the opening years of the post-network era have required networks to utilize pop-culture opinion leaders to lead viewers back to their sets" (112). However, TV critics who once filled these roles have begun to disappear as print and online journalism continue to struggle.

One paratext that has altered post-network era conversation is the water cooler's close relative, the spoiler. According to Gray and Mittell, "The definition of 'spoiler' varies somewhat in the eyes of the beholder, as any revelation of yet-to-unfold narrative developments could be viewed as a spoiler by some, ranging from a leaked script of an unfilmed episode to a network preview of next week's program." Nevertheless, online communities abound with Web sites and discussions devoted to spoilers from popular programs.

Productions have grown especially secretive to avoid divulging any meaningful plot points. In the summer of 2010, *Mad Men* (AMC, 2007–Present) creator Matthew Weiner expressed his dismay after a *New York Times* TV critic revealed an important piece of information about the relationship status of the main character and his wife. "I was shocked—really shocked," said Weiner. "I would love to have it known that this was done totally without my approval" (qtd. in Dawn). This runs counter to AMC sending out screener episodes to journalists in advance of the fourth season but asking them not to reveal any spoilers.

Though many viewers wish to avoid them in print or on screen, spoilers "are texts to be enjoyed, studied, interpreted, and consumed like any other text" (Gray and Mittell). Previouslies and previews, the bookends of many prime-time serials, are "network-sanctioned spoilers," which often are controlled by the networks—not necessarily the showrunners or writers—and thus are "separate texts" from the main program (Gilbert). Whereas watercooler discussions about television from the night before used to ostracize people who missed popular programs and wanted to avoid spoilers, today's marginalized viewers include the few who watch them when they first air.

CONCLUSION

The traditional television flow once prescribed by the broadcast networks has been irrevocably altered through "convenience technologies [that] encourage active selection" (Lotz 59), a shift in viewer control that has affected not only post-network era production practices but also the medium's textual and paratextual discourses. As digital platforms have grown in number and in scale, the linear programming flow has become a distant memory. New modes of distribution have enabled viewers to watch television when *they* want to watch, a development that has further splintered the already fractured audience.

Consequently, these new production and consumption practices have grown more diverse and have complicated the uniform gaps that underpinned network-era television. How viewers watch and discuss television has influenced—now more than ever before—today's conversations about the medium, a change that undoubtedly will continue to affect not only post-network discourses but also serial narratives, distribution practices, and programming strategies.

SUGGESTED EPISODES FOR ADDITIONAL STUDY

Lone Star
1:1. "Pilot." Writ. Kyle Killen. Dir. Marc Webb. September 20, 2010.

Lost
6:17–18. "The End." Writ. Damon Lindelof and Carlton Cuse. Dir. Jack Bender. May 23, 2010.

Modern Family
2:2. "The Kiss." Writ. Abraham Higginbotham. Dir. Scott Ellis. September 29, 2010.

The Sopranos
3:6. "University." Writ. Terence Winter and Salvatore J. Stabile. Dir. Allen Coulter. April 1, 2001.

24
6:1. "Day 6: 6:00 A.M.—7:00 A.M." Writ. Howard Gordon. Dir. Jon Cassar. January 14, 2007.

The Wire
1:1. "The Target." Writ. David Simon. Dir. Clark Johnson. June 2, 2002.
1:10. "The Cost." Writ. David Simon. Dir. Brad Anderson. August 11, 2002.

NOTES

1. See Kompare.
2. See Mittell ("Narrative") for more on narrative complexity.
3. Special thanks to Mittell ("Serial"), who discusses O'Sullivan's article about *Deadwood* and seriality.

WORKS CITED

Allen, Robert C. "Audience-oriented Criticism and Television." *Channels of Discourse, Reassembled: Television and Contemporary Criticism.* 2nd ed. Ed. Robert C. Allen. Chapel Hill: University of North Carolina Press, 1992. 77–103. Print.
Budd, Mike, and Clay Steinman. "Television, Cultural Studies, and the 'Blind Spot' Debate in Critical Communications Research." *Television Studies: Textual Analysis.* Ed. Gary Burns and Robert J. Thompson. New York: Praeger, 1989. 9–20. Print.
Cantor, Muriel. *The Hollywood TV Producer: His Work and His Audience.* New York: Basic Books, 1971. Print.
Carr, David. "The Glut of Shows Unwatched." *New York Times.* September 5, 2010. Web. September 6, 2010.
Carter, Bill. "Later Viewings of Shows on DVRs Brighten Ratings." *New York Times.* October 13, 2009. Web. October 13, 2009.
———. "DVR, Once a Mortal Foe, Is a Friend After All." *New York Times.* November 2, 2009. Web. November 2, 2009.
Dawn, Randee. "*Mad Men* Creator 'Shocked' by Spoilers." *Hollywood Reporter.* July 23, 2010. Web. August 24, 2010.

Dove-Viebahn, Aviva. "Serial Narratives and Viewing Demands I." *Flow Conference 2010*. University of Texas at Austin. AT&T Conference Center, Austin, TX. October 1, 2010. Roundtable Discussion.

Ford, Sam. "SCMS: Jason Mittell, Jonathan Gray, and Paratexts." *Convergence Culture Consortium*. March 26, 2008. Web. September 17, 2010.

Gilbert, Anne. "Serial Narratives and Viewing Demands I." *Flow Conference 2010*. University of Texas at Austin. AT&T Conference Center, Austin, TX. October 1, 2010. Roundtable Discussion.

Gray, Jonathan, and Jason Mittell. "Speculation on Spoilers: *Lost* Fandom, Narrative Consumption and Rethinking Textuality." *Particip@tions* 4.1 (2007). Web. September 28, 2010.

Gregory, Chris. *Be Seeing You . . . Decoding* The Prisoner. Bedfordshire, UK: University of Luton Press, 1997. Print.

Hendrix, Grady. "Boxed In." *Slate*. December 1, 2009. Web.

Ide, Rich. Re: Dick Ide TV Commercials on *Lost*. Message to the author. October 22, 2010. E-mail.

Jenkins, Henry. "On Anti-Fans and Paratexts: An Interview with Jonathan Gray (Part Two)." *Confessions of an Aca/Fan*. March 8, 2010. Web. October 8, 2010.

Johnson, Steven. *Everything Bad Is Good for You: How Today's Popular Culture Is Actually Making Us Smarter*. New York: Riverhead Books, 2005. Print.

"Judge Me Tender." *The Simpsons*. FOX. WUHF, Rochester, NY. May 23, 2010. Television.

Killen, Kyle. "*Lone Star*." *Flow Conference 2010*. University of Texas at Austin. AT&T Conference Center, Austin, TX. October 1, 2010. Screening and Q&A Session.

Kompare, Derek. "Publishing Flow: DVD Box Sets and the Reconception of Television." *Television and New Media* 7.4 (2006): 335–60. Print.

Kozloff, Sarah. "Narrative Theory and Television." *Channels of Discourse, Reassembled: Television and Contemporary Criticism*, 2nd ed. Ed. Robert C. Allen. Chapel Hill: University of North Carolina Press, 1992. 77–103. Print.

Leonard, Andrew. "Jay Leno: Too Awful to Watch, Now or Later." *Salon*. January 7, 2010. Web. October 17, 2010.

Levin, Gary. "More Sets, DVRs Have Changed the TV Picture." *USA Today*. June 10, 2010. Web. June 10, 2010.

Lotz, Amanda. *The Television Will Be Revolutionized*. New York: New York University Press, 2007. Print.

Mittell, Jason. "Narrative Complexity in Contemporary American Television." *The Velvet Light Trap* 58 (2006): 29–40. Print.

———. "Serial Boxes." *MediaCommons*. January 20, 2010. Web. January 22, 2010.

Newman, Michael Z. "TV Binge." *FlowTV.org*. January 23, 2009. Web. October 1, 2010.

O'Sullivan, Sean. "Old, New, Borrowed, Blue: *Deadwood* and Serial Fiction." *Reading Deadwood: A Western to Swear By*. Ed. David Lavery. London: I. B. Tauris & Company, 2006. Print.

Sepinwall, Alan. "Interview: *Treme* Co-creator David Simon Post-mortems Season One." *HitFix.com*. June 20, 2010. Web. June 21, 2010.

Simon, David. Personal interview. October 20, 2005.

"Snapshot of Television Use in the U.S." *Nielsen.com*. September 23, 2010. Web. September 23, 2010.

Steinberg, Brian. "The Future of TV." *Advertising Age*. November 30, 2009. Web. November 30, 2009.

Stevens, Hampton. "The Enduring Legacy of 24." *The Atlantic*. May 24, 2010. Web. May 24, 2010.

Tanklefsky, David. "Primetime Ratings: *Glee* Pilot Replay Sings into Second." *Broadcasting & Cable*. September 3, 2009. Web. October 10, 2010.

"Unconfirmed Reports." *The Wire*. HBO. January 13, 2008. Television.

Williams, Raymond. *Television: Technology and Cultural Form*. New York: Schocken, 1974. Print.

2

"A STRETCH OF TIME"
Extended Distribution and Narrative Accumulation in Prison Break

J. P. KELLY

As a number of scholars have argued, the accelerated pace of the "network era"[1] has led to a culture in which the present tense has become the dominant temporal order.[2] According to these accounts, culture, technology, and the economy are accelerating at such a pace as to leave us feeling left behind. Within this perpetually accelerating "chrono-digital ecology," as Robert Hassan has described it (237), time is an ever-dwindling resource and without sufficient means to contemplate the past or plan for the future our lives are reduced to nothing more than a series of fleeting present-tense experiences. As Hassan elaborates, "the creation and application of reflexive knowledge and reflexive evaluation becomes increasingly difficult. There is simply less time for it" (237). This chapter is concerned with how this particular temporal mode has shaped popular television narrative. Indeed, evidence of this accelerated temporality can be found not just in the narratives, but also in the production and distribution practices surrounding a number of contemporary series such as *24* (Fox, 2001–2010). Through the use of a real-time hook, recurring temporal cues, split screens, and condensed patterns of distribution, the series embodies this dominant temporal mode in a variety of ways.[3]

According to the logic of network time, acceleration destabilizes narrative linearity. In other words, if we exist primarily in the present, then the past and the future hold less significance. In making these claims, scholars often cite the acceleration (and fragmentation) of other media, for example the evolution of the audio format from vinyl to CD and more recently to mp3 and AAC.[4] In its analogue form, consumers had no choice but to purchase entire albums—a specifically arranged collection of texts that had a clear beginning, middle, and end. However, once music became digital following the introduction of mp3s and Apple's hugely popular iTunes Store, consumers were suddenly free to pick and choose individual tracks. From this perspective, our media diet is increasingly comprised of a shuffled selection of random and unconnected texts—beginnings, middles, and ends start to disappear as we simply consume in the moment.

In this chapter I intend to challenge the assumption that the accelerated temporalities of the network era (and of televisual narrative) invariably lead to the fragmentation of text and a dominance of the present tense, as evident in *24*. On the contrary, through an analysis of Fox's *Prison Break* (2005–2009), I show that the very same (digital) technologies that have supposedly caused this acceleration and fragmentation of time and text can help sustain more enduring serialized and linear narratives. In making this claim, I intend to highlight several key differences in the styles of seriality employed by *24* and *Prison Break*; while the former adopted a format of condensed and self-contained *episodic* season arcs, the latter used a more open-ended model of extended and ongoing *serialized* season arcs. Furthermore, I argue that these narrative differences are fostered by the network's divergent strategies of production and distribution. Indeed, while both series can be considered exemplary network era texts, *Prison Break* represents a different tendency in contemporary U.S. television, one that reverses the distributional logics of *24*, stretching the series out in order to sustain its own particular brand of extended seriality.

SERIALIZED SEASONS AND EXTENDED DISTRIBUTION

Over the course of its four seasons, the narrative arc of *Prison Break* tells a long and complex story that, in many ways, parallels television's own recent shifting temporal regimes. The series begins with the incarceration of structural engineer Michael Schofield following an armed robbery—an intentional act that is part of an elaborate plan to free his wrongfully imprisoned brother, Lincoln Burrows. Primarily set within the confines of the Fox River State Penitentiary, the first season operates within a regular and routinized regime of institutional time. By the second season, Schofield, his brother, and six other inmates break free. Now on the run across various parts of North America, the rigid temporal regimes that had governed the first season gave way. The narrative became increasingly complex, with the action split between the fugitives and a government conspiracy led by a clandestine agency simply called "The Company." The third season continued this narrative arc. Having been captured in the second season finale, the tables were turned as Schofield found himself incarcerated in a Panamanian prison, leaving it up to Burrows to orchestrate his escape. In the fourth and final season, Schofield is freed and heads back to North America, and during this last installment works with his brother to expose "The Company," clearing their names in the process in order to reach a final narrative resolution. Although a rather condensed version of events, this brief synopsis gives some indication of the complexity and scope of the narrative arc that the series developed across its four seasons.

It is this ongoing arc that marks *Prison Break* as distinct from *24*. Whereas *24*'s storylines are contained to individual seasons (due to its limited twenty-four-hour narrative structure), the plot of *Prison Break* is continually deferred. The fundamental temporal difference can be summarized in the following way: while *24* operates under the influence of the seconds, minutes, hours, and days of clock-time (and is distributed with equal haste), *Prison Break* runs according to the days, weeks, months, and years of calendar time (with its distribution drawn out in order to serve this particular narrative temporality). Indeed, just as clocks feature throughout the mise-en-scène of *24*, calendars are the preferred motif of *Prison Break*, providing viewers with a different temporal framework. In order to elucidate these differences I turn now to the institutional and distributional context of *Prison Break*.

Like *24*, the breadth and complexity of *Prison Break* was further evidence of a shift in the production style of television narrative, one that has seen a steady growth of serials in a market largely dominated by episodic programming, particularly within the schedules of network television. While *24* had initially struggled to take off due to its complex and demanding seriality, *Prison Break* was commissioned for this very reason. Originally the series had been pitched to Fox in 2003 by executive producer Paul Scheuring at a time when *24* had just begun to show signs of commercial success. Unfortunately for Scheuring, the network was still dubious about the viability of serialized programming and the pitch was declined. However, by the following 2004–05 season several important factors prompted a shift in the production and distribution strategies of network TV. First, the broadcast ratings and ancillary DVD sales of *24* had increased considerably by this point, indicating a potentially lucrative market for serialized prime-time programming. Furthermore the commercial and critical success of *Lost*'s (ABC, 2004–2010) debut episode on ABC later that season had a significant impact upon Fox's programming strategy. As Scheuring recalled, the network's decision to green light *Prison Break* had been a complete volte-face: "*Lost* had its huge, huge debut and literally the next day [Fox] called wanting to put the *Prison Break* pilot into production" (qtd. in Goldman). Within a short space of time, the foundations had been laid for the production of more narratively complex and temporally innovative programming.

While *Prison Break* might be regarded as an archetypal network era narrative, embodying many of the same tropes of speed and simultaneity that characterized *24*, the series' format and its patterns of distribution were far more varied. *24* was bound by its real-time narrative structure whereas the temporal regimes of *Prison Break* were far less rigid, ranging from compressed time (the narrative often covers long periods of time in a matter of seconds), to real time (the date of Burrow's execution coincides with the approximate date that the first series was due to conclude), to the extension or stretching out of time (primarily through the use of cliffhangers)—a complex temporal structure that is reflected in the series' equally fluid model of distribution. Synchronicity, compression, and immediacy enhanced the narrative experience of *24* but Fox took an entirely different approach in their distribution of *Prison Break*, a series less preoccupied with the present-tense pressures of real time. The primary strategy here was one of disruption and extension versus the compression of *24*'s broadcast window. In particular, each of *Prison Break*'s four seasons were stretched out over a much longer period of time, with numerous delays including midseason breaks that lasted up to several months.

Of course, midseason breaks are a common feature of the U.S. television schedule, usually taking place from mid November to early January in order to make way for the Thanksgiving and Christmas holidays, during which time special programming and feature films occupy a much larger portion of the broadcast schedule. This period of delay allows networks to stretch out their series, ensuring that original episodes are broadcast during all-important sweeps weeks. However, Fox extended this several-week gap to several months, pausing the first season of *Prison Break* in late November and only resuming again in late March the following year. Just as Fox's innovative distribution strategies for *24* were later copied by other networks (for example, ABC with *Lost* and *Alias*, 2001–2006), the extended gaps that punctuate *Prison Break*'s broadcasts seem to have also become a popular strategy of television scheduling. At the beginning of the midseason break in the 2009–10 season, *Variety* noted that several popular prime-time network serials, including *FlashForward* (ABC, 2009–2010), *Glee* (Fox, 2009–Present), and *V* (ABC, 2009–2011), were all following a similar distributional pattern by pausing their runs for several months (Schneider).[5]

Although it will be discussed in greater detail later in this chapter, it is worth mentioning the show's use of midseason and end-of-season cliffhangers, a key narrative device that can shed further light on the network's preference toward extended and intermittent distribution. While *24* adopts a structure of self-contained season arcs (with the notable exception of the second season, which ends with a prequel sequence intended as a segue to the following installment) the narrative arc of *Prison Break* is much more complex and open-ended. *24* essentially resets the narrative with each new season—a format that might best be described as the *episodic* season—whereas *Prison Break*'s plot continues across all four of its installments—a format best described as the *serialized* season.

Admittedly, there are several key storylines and characters that continue across seasons of *24* (such as the recurring appearance of Nina Myers); however, on the whole the series requires very little foreknowledge in order to comprehend each new season. In other words, a viewer could quite easily begin at season two without having watched season one. This is not the case with *Prison Break*, in which the narrative continues across all four seasons. The later into the series that a viewer begins, the more difficult it becomes to follow. In fact, this may have been the reason for the drastic decline in viewing figures for later seasons, and the series' eventual cancellation. Whereas *24* was able to constantly attract new audiences due to its *episodic* season arcs, *Prison Break*'s *serialized* seasonal format made it difficult for uninitiated viewers to join the narrative midway through.

For viewers, the eight-month breaks between *24*'s seasons, which ran from mid-May to mid-January the following year, were far more tolerable given the episodic nature of these largely self-contained narrative arcs. By comparison, *Prison Break*'s cliffhanger finales and multi-season story arcs left audiences desperate to know what was going to happen next. While anticipation can be a powerful marketing tool, a break of eight months might have been detrimental given the narrative complexity and seasonal continuity of *Prison Break*. During such an extended interim, viewers could easily have forgotten many details of the series' rich narrative tapestry. At the end of the second season, for example, the fates of several characters are left unresolved, while the "The Company" remains a prominent threat.

Following the second-season finale, viewers new to season three may have found themselves overwhelmed by the volume and complexity of these various narrative threads. For instance, it may have been unclear as to why Fernando Sucre (Schofield's cell mate in the first season) was desperate to free his former prison guard, Brad Bellick, from a Panamanian prison. However, those who had seen the previous season would have been aware that he was acting under duress—Bellick had taken Sucre's fiancée hostage in the latter part of the second season and would only reveal her whereabouts upon being freed. Similarly, in the fourth season the (re)appearance of agent Paul Kellerman, an employee of "The Company," would only have been a surprise for those who had seen his supposed execution in the second-season finale. In fact, even those who had been watching the series from the start may have struggled to recall the fate of this particular character or where his allegiances lay, with Schofield or The Company.

Rather than having a potentially disruptive eight-month break between seasons (as was the case with *24*), Fox chose to stretch *Prison Break* over the full course of the television year, resulting in a much shorter gap between seasons. The first season, for example, ended May 15, 2005, while the second began August 21, 2006—a gap of just over three months—making it much easier for audiences to recall the previous season while also creating a more sustained sense of narrative continuity. This strategy of extended distribution compressed the gap between seasons but it meant many more intermittent delays throughout the broadcast of the full twenty-two-episode run including a several-month-long midseason hiatus.

As with *24*, Fox employed several strategies to manage the series' narrative demands and to retain audience interest across these frequent interruptions. For the first season, the network decided to premiere *Prison Break* in late August—an unusually early start given that most new seasons tend to debut in late September. According to Fox, this decision was an attempt to get viewers on board early but was also in anticipation of the Major League Baseball play-offs that had already been scheduled for the same Monday night slot for three weeks in October. Rather than premiering the series post play-off to a potentially smaller audience (who by this point may have already been courted by other shows in the same time slot on another network), Fox attempted to get a head start by hooking viewers early on, broadcasting seven of the thirteen already commissioned episodes before the planned October break. However, this presented a problem for the network; how would they retain interest in such a narratively complex show that was due to stop for several weeks?

To keep the momentum of the series, Fox developed several initiatives. First, they aired a special behind-the-scenes episode. This was broadcast exactly midway through the break and included interviews with several cast and crew members, as well as an extended recap of the first seven episodes. By producing this special episode, Fox hoped to refresh the memory of those who had been watching from the start and, by condensing the key narrative details into an easily digestible size, court new viewers. As Max Dawson has argued, such paratextual materials are vital in supporting the vast and complex narrative arcs of "monumental serials" such as *Prison Break*. As is the case with the DVD box set, the availability of individual television episodes via alternative channels (such as VOD and online streaming) and the proliferation of paratextual materials has created a more flexible and accommodating environment in which the linear and serialized narratives of series such as *Prison Break* can thrive. In short, these new distribution opportunities have increased the range of ways that consumers can accumulate narratives, and in the process have enabled more linear, enduring, and complex story arcs.

Whereas distributional compression worked well for *24*, the different narrative structure of *Prison Break* required its own complementary model of distribution. In the remainder of this essay, I want to provide further evidence of this relationship by taking a closer look at the formal composition of the series. In doing so, I intend to highlight the stylistic means through which *Prison Break* created the necessary momentum to maintain audience interest through individual episodes, and across multi-episode and multi-season arcs. Ultimately, I demonstrate that contrary to the logics of network time the series was able to sustain an accelerated and linear narrative arc, a model of storytelling reflected in its own specific industrial and technological context.

TO BE CONTINUED
From Segmentation and Stacking to Narrative Accumulation

In a recent essay, Thomas Hylland Eriksen describes the phenomena of *stacking* and *continuity*—a dichotomy that he argues underpins the temporal regimes of contemporary popular culture. As he explains, "the close cousins of acceleration and exponential growth lead to vertical stacking . . . this means that since there is no vacant time to spread information in, it is compressed and stacked in time spans that become shorter and shorter" (Eriksen 147). In illustrating this tendency, Eriksen refers primarily to the Internet, but argues that this process is affecting almost all media. Indeed, he begins his analysis with reference to *Dynasty* (ABC, 1981–1989), a prime-time serial that predated later narratively complex series such as *24* and *Prison Break*. "*Dynasty*," he explains, "was tailored for the multichannel format. It was produced in the awareness that the viewers would restlessly finger their remote control while watching, ready to switch channels at the first sign of inertia" (Eriksen 141).

From this perspective, texts are profoundly shaped by their industrial, economic, and technological contexts. Facing competition from an ever-expanding broadcast spectrum, Eriksen argues that the writers of *Dynasty* felt compelled to accelerate the narrative in response to the numerous distractions on offer. Following this logic, the particular context of *Prison Break* may provide some insight as to why its narrative moves at an even more accelerated pace. Indeed, in the current mediascape competition is not just from other channels but also from other media such as the Internet. Thus, writers and producers of contemporary U.S. series must try even harder to keep viewers tuned in, and the real-time and accelerated narratives of series such as *24* and *Prison Break* are effective ways of retaining audience attention. In these narratives, every second really does count.

There is other evidence to suggest that the format of prime-time drama is changing in response to this growing competition. The lengthy pre-credit sequences that feature in serials such as *Prison Break*, *Lost*, and *Ugly Betty* (ABC, 2006–2010) are one such example. In the former, episodes begin with short recaps lasting between one to two minutes before moving seamlessly into the narrative. The title sequence only appears after a further seven or eight minutes, by which point the episode is well underway and, as the network hopes, viewers will be less likely to switch channels. If anything then, this kind of narrative acceleration can help retain attention and thus lead to a more structured sense of continuity and linear story arcs.

Although I would agree with Eriksen's central thesis, I would disagree with his conclusion that "information lint destroys continuity" (152). Using *Dynasty* again to illustrate this tendency, Eriksen claims that "the cost of this breathless, accelerated kind of drama is a lack of progression. Like other serials of the same kind," he continues, "*Dynasty* is a story that stands still at enormous speed. *Instantaneous time precludes development*" (142, my emphasis). *Prison Break* has arguably accelerated the pace of storytelling more so, but unlike *Dynasty* tells a story that, to paraphrase Eriksen, moves forward at enormous speed. In *Prison Break*, and several other recent serials including *Lost* and *FlashForward*, there is a clear sense of progression, a well-defined end point toward which the narrative arc moves. Indeed, the entire first season of *Prison Break* hinges upon one very explicit deadline—the execution of Lincoln Burrows. Constant repetition and foregrounding of this deadline occurs throughout most episodes, ensuring the viewer is always conscious of this narrative trajectory. Indeed, much of the pleasure of watching *Prison Break* comes from such continuity, from a constant awareness of this narrative end goal, and from seeing the various developments and delays in Schofield's plan—a pattern of continuity and delay that is evident in both the narrative and distribution of the series.

As noted above, cliffhangers are crucial to the narrative continuity and accelerated pace of *Prison Break* and are also complimentary to the series' pattern of distribution. Although cliffhangers feature in *24*, the series' real-time format prevents them from being used as frequently as in *Prison Break*. End-of-episode cliffhangers are a staple feature, yet the temporal order of *24* means that in-episode cliffhangers (pre-commercial) would undermine the series' real-time conceit. Instead of freezing the action, writers of *24* must let the clock run and allow the story to carry on "'behind the veil' of the commercials" (Peacock 29).

As Josh Lambert points out, "cliffhanger continuity" has been a key feature of the serial going back, in his account of visual media, to early cinema and comic strips. In his analysis Lambert cites one particular moment in *Desperate Desmond*, a serialized comic strip first published in 1910 that was key in innovating this device. The very first installment, he explains, "ends with Claude strapped to the minute-hand of a large elevated clock. The narration under the text concludes, 'Claude will be sheared off at 5:27. Will he fall 900 feet?'" (Lambert 9). This kind of narrative device recalls the various diegetic and non-diegetic temporal cues employed throughout *24* (on-screen clocks, ticking bombs, expository dialogue) as well as the major cliffhangers used in *Prison Break*. As is also the case with both these shows, *Desperate Desmond*'s use of "cliffhanger continuity" was designed to satisfy commercial imperatives (ensuring audiences would continue purchasing the same paper) by foregrounding "the use of break[s] between episodes to create suspense" (Lambert 9). This, in turn, produced a "disjunction between the timescale of the narrative and that of the reader's experience" (Lambert 9), an intentionally engineered delay that enhances suspense, leaving the fate of the protagonist in a state of suspended animation.

Prison Break follows a similar logic, borrowing heavily from this serial convention and, as in *Desperate Desmond*, uses time explicitly to foreground narrative urgency, build audience loyalty, and develop longer narrative arcs. Of course, newspaper comic strips are usually only a few panels in length, while an individual episode of *Prison Break* conveys a much longer period of narrative time and will often include cliffhangers at multiple points. Episodes nearly always end on a note of unresolved dramatic tension producing an overlap intended to bridge the weekly (or sometimes monthly) gaps between installments. A clear example of this occurs in the second episode of the first season, "Allen." In an attempt to gain the help of John Abruzzi, a convicted mobster and fellow inmate whose resources are crucial to execute his escape plan, Schofield finds himself in a rather precarious situation. Having told Abruzzi that he knows the whereabouts of the witness who testified against him, but unwilling to provide full details until they have escaped, the episode ends with Schofield being retained by two of the mobster's henchmen. Abruzzi demands to know the location of the witness, threatening to amputate Schofield's toe. He counts to three, but Schofield holds his tongue, and the episode finishes with the sound of garden shears cutting through his foot. With such a conclusion, or rather lack of conclusion, the viewer is refused narrative closure on several fronts; was Schofield's toe really amputated? If so, is there more punishment to come? And perhaps most important, how will Schofield convince Abruzzi, an essential part of his escape plan, to join forces with him? Just as Claude is left perilously hanging in *Desperate Desmond*, these questions can only be answered by tuning in to the next installment.

As well as at the level of individual episode, the series employs several major cliffhangers at the level of multi-episode arc. For example, the first season was initially conceived of as thirteen episodes that concluded with the successful escape of Schofield, his brother, and several other inmates. However, this arc was altered after the series was commissioned for a full season run. In the new re-drafted version, the thirteenth episode ends with a last-minute complication. Having been derailed several times in the build-up to this episode, Schofield and several other inmates finally commence their escape. Unfortunately a vital weak point in an air vent that the plan depends upon has been repaired leaving the inmates stranded from their cells and Burrows only hours away from his inevitable execution.

To add to the desperation, Theodore Bagwell (a.k.a. T-Bag), a prisoner with a violent past and a particular dislike for Schofield, pulls a shank from his boot and insists that the inmates must continue with their escape—with or without Burrows. This leaves several even more pressing and unresolved questions than those posed in the average episodic cliffhanger: Will Burrows really be executed? Can Schofield think of another way to save him before his time is up? Will T-Bag force the inmates to flee or perhaps even attack them? If they decided to call off the escape, how will the inmates return to their cells unnoticed? To add to the frustration (or perhaps pleasure) of this open-ended narrative, viewers who were watching the original broadcast would have to wait several months for these questions to be answered.

In contemporary television production, the cliffhanger has become a common narrative convention used as a means to keep viewers tuned in through the commercial break or to draw audiences back for the following week. In *24*, for example, individual episodes often end at a climatic moment, with the split-screen refusing closure on multiple narrative threads. However, as noted above, there is little continuity between seasons of *24*. *Prison Break*, on the other hand, develops a single narrative arc over the course of its four seasons, ending each installment on a note of heightened suspense. The finale of the first season, for instance, ends with the eventual escape of the prisoners, but a last-minute reversal of fortune threatens their chances of freedom. Unable to make it to the nearby airfield on time, their getaway plane takes off, leaving the prisoners stranded. The final shot pulls wide to reveal the inmates fleeing across an open field, while the police close in around them. At this point, it seems that there is very little chance of evading the authorities, and the viewer, having invested in the series for almost nine months, is refused any sense of narrative closure. Somewhat paradoxically, it is this kind of disruption that helped *Prison Break* to achieve its continuity and extended linear arc. By deferring narrative closure and pausing the action on a cliffhanger at the end of each season, the series maintains a consistent pace over a longer period of time.

In addition to the cliffhanger, I would argue that *Prison Break* adopted a highly accelerated formal style that was equally key to sustaining its narrative continuity. This was achieved in several ways, particularly through rapid editing, accelerated interstitials, and through the use of a more fragmented narrative style. As Dana Walden, an executive at Fox pointed out, "Where traditional dramas used to be told in 50 scenes, last year you had 'Prison Break,' which averaged about 88 scenes an episode" (qtd. in "TV Navigation"). Given the extra time and money that these additional set-ups required (each new scene had to be re-lit and reframed, a location manager must first scout the site, etc.) the highly segmented structure of *Prison Break* was undoubtedly a conscious decision made in the earliest stages of pre-production. As Walden's comments highlight, *Prison Break* is a highly fragmented text, exemplary of the stacking or segmentation that Eriksen and others have described. However, rather than producing an effect of discontinuity, this textual strategy results in an acceleration of story that actually works to propel the viewer along a structured and linear narrative path. In the case of *Prison Break*, individual segments are not arbitrary pieces of narrative, but are interconnected and overlap in a way that compel and develop the story in a clear and logical way.

CONCLUSION

As I have argued here, industrial and technological conditions are key in sustaining the accelerated and extended story arcs of series such as *Prison Break*. While *Dynasty* existed during a broadcast only period, television has since evolved into a much different medium, one now characterized by greater convenience and more flexible models of distribution. Within this new mediascape, online streaming, digital video recorders, and the DVD box set have made the production of longer narrative arcs a more artistically and economically viable model of storytelling.

I have also described how distribution is tailored to accommodate specific narrative types. *24* epitomizes the dominant network era temporality in which speed and the present tense are the principal forces—a temporality evident in both the series narrative and distribution. Conversely, *Prison Break* demonstrates the possibility for an alternative network era temporality. While the story is equally if not more accelerated, it maintains its momentum and linearity through utilizing increasingly flexible models of distribution. The *serialized* seasons of *Prison Break* build vast and expansive narrative arcs that exceed the individual season, but these are more manageable in an era when the material collection of television has become commonplace. As my description of the series and its distribution shows, accelerated network era narratives are not necessarily condemned to the present tense, but demonstrate a potential for greater narrative longevity.

SUGGESTED EPISODES FOR ADDITIONAL STUDY

24

1:24. "11:00 p.m.-12:00 a.m." Writ. Robert Cochran, Howard Gordon, Michael Loceff, and Joel Surnow. Dir. Stephen Hopkins. May 21, 2002.

Prison Break

1:13. "End of the Tunnel." Writ. Paul Scheuring. Dir. Sanford Bookstaver. November 28, 2005.
1:22. "Flight." Writ. Paul Scheuring. Dir. Kevin Hooks. May 15, 2006.
2:1. "Manhunt." Writ. Paul Scheuring. Dir. Kevin Hooks. August 21, 2006.
4:23. "The Old Ball and Chain." Writ. Seth Hoffman, Nick Santora, and Christian Trokey. Dir. Brad Turner. May 24, 2009.
4:24. "Free." Writ. Zack Estrin, Karyn Usher, and Kalinda Vasquez. Dir. Kevin Hooks. May 24, 2009.

NOTES

1. To avoid confusion, I should clarify my usage of this term. "The network era" refers to a period—as identified by Manuel Castells—roughly beginning in the early 1980s that saw a significant degree of technological development. Although this chapter deals with "television networks," my uses of "network era" and "network time" refer to this broader social phenomenon.
2. For instance, see Castells, 1996; Hassan, 2003; Eriksen, 2007.
3. By the 2004–2005 season, Fox programmed the series to run within a condensed eighteen-week period (compared to its previous thirty-four-week broadcast window)—a strategy that served to emphasise and sustain the show's real-time narrative premise.
4. See Eriksen, 2007.
5. In the case of *Prison Break*, the midseason break was actually longer than the summer break between new seasons.

WORKS CITED

"Allen." *Prison Break*. Fox. August 29, 2005. Television.
"A TV Navigation Guide." *Hollywood Reporter.* September 13, 2006. Print.
Castells, Manuel. *The Rise of the Network Society.* Cambridge, MA: Blackwell, 1996. Print.
Dawson, Max. "Television Abridged: Ephemeral Texts, Monumental Seriality and TV-Digital Media Convergence." *Ephemeral Media: Transitory screen culture from television to YouTube.* Ed. Paul Grainge. London: BFI, n.d. n. pag. Print.
Eriksen, Thomas Hylland. "Stacking and Continuity: On Temporal Regimes in Popular Culture." *24/7: Time and Temporality in the Networked Society.* Ed. Robert Hassan and Ronald E. Purser. Stanford, CA: Stanford University Press, 2007. 141–60. Print.
Goldman, Eric. "Paley Fest: Prison Break." *IGN: UK Edition.* March 13, 2006. Web. March 19, 2010.
Hassan, Robert. "Network Time and the New Knowledge Epoch." *Time & Society* 12.2–3 (2003): 225–41. Print.
Lambert, Josh. "'Wait For the Next Pictures': Intertextuality and Cliffhanger Continuity in Early Cinema and Comic Strips." *Cinema Journal* 48.2 (2009): 3–25. Print.
Peacock, Steven. "*24*: Status and Style." *Reading 24: TV Against the Clock.* Ed. Steven Peacock. London: IB Taurus, 2007. 25–34. Print.
Schneider, Michael. "The Waiting is the Hardest Part; New and Returning Shows are Taking a Lengthy Hiatus." *Variety.* December 11, 2009. Web. March 21, 2010.

3

"IT'S NOT UNKNOWN"
The Loose- and Dead-End Afterlives of Battlestar Galactica and Lost

JORDAN LAVENDER-SMITH

> "So say we all. So say we all. So say we all . . . We're a long way from home. We've jumped way beyond the red line, into uncharted space . . . maybe it would have been better for us to die quickly . . . instead of dying out here slowly in the emptiness of dark space. Where shall we go? What shall we do? 'Life here began out there.' Those are the first words of the sacred scrolls . . . We are not alone in this universe . . . There's a 13th colony of humankind, is there not? . . . It's not unknown. I know where it is. Earth! The most guarded secret we have. The location is only known by the senior commanders of the fleet, and we dared not share it with the public . . . It won't be an easy journey. It will be long and arduous. But I promise you one thing on the memory of those lying here before you: we shall find it. And Earth will become our new home. So say we all. So say we all. So say we all."
> —ADMIRAL ADAMA, *BATTLESTAR GALACTICA* ("PILOT")

I like to think that Ronald D. Moore and the writers of the "reimagined" *Battlestar Galactica* (Sci-Fi Channel, 2003–2009) wrote Admiral Adama's (Edward James Olmos) rousing speech to his fleet as a self-reflexive commencement of the writers' and viewers' "long and arduous" "journey" through the latest manifestation of a TV-III,[1] cult-quality[2] serial—a genre of contemporary television far more popular than these labels might first let on. How does one write a show that continually teases its audience into believing that the truth is out there, that suggests there will be satisfying resolutions to all of the show's mysteries, some desirable endpoint that will structure and give meaning to the "journey"? Adama's speech offers a cleverly rhetorical solution to the problems facing both the leaders in the series and the leaders of the series. The truth is out there: "it's not unknown."

Having learned from the commercial and artistic missteps of David Lynch (*Twin Peaks*, ABC, 1990–1991) and Chris Carter (*The X-Files*, Fox, 1993–2002), the creators of the enigma-packed *Battlestar* and *Lost* (ABC, 2004–2010) were granted the right to end their shows when they wanted to, hoping to convince viewers that the course is known *and* that they will reveal it before viewers stop caring. In "The Peaks and Valleys of Serial Creativity," Marc Dolan rightly suggests that "a narrative that is not intended to come to a predetermined ending cannot . . . be judged by aesthetic protocols generated to evaluate more finite narrative forms" (32). As works of "intentionally finite length," *Battlestar* and *Lost* meet one of Dolan's criteria for what critics usually feel comfortable calling televisual "art." However, unlike the writers of a traditional miniseries, the creators of *Battlestar* and *Lost* certainly did not script every episode before the shows went to air. Perhaps it is too impractical to write a series in its multi-season entirety before it takes off, even if there is a planned end date: What if several members of the cast leave? What if ratings are low from the get-go?

In this chapter I consider a few formal features of *Battlestar* and *Lost*, those that resonate with the series' central themes and that metaphorize the creation and reception of TV-III serials. Along with the logistics of TV production, the very same advanced technologies that allow contemporary writers the opportunity to create shows with such novelistic ambitions also undermine the narrative coherence of these elaborate, plot-heavy epics. Building on and responding to the work of Ivan Askwith, Jennifer Hayward, and Jason Mittell, I suggest that, like *Twin Peaks* and *The X-Files*, *Battlestar* and *Lost*—outstanding as they are—are ultimately failures according to their own narrative terms, failures from which tomorrow's TV serialists have important lessons to learn.

THE PLEASURES OF REFLEXIVITY

Writers of mystery-rich serials are always in the process of returning to previous material, changing the valences of past events because of their present, a present shaped as much by long-term planning as by the winds of reception and logistics, a present that will itself be reevaluated and revised in subsequent episodes. *Battlestar*'s tagline is reflexively apt: "All this has happened before. All this will happen again." Precisely because a show cannot be literally revised if it has already aired, Moore and company take special care to make space in each episode for possible future developments, for backstories that have yet to be written. Accordingly, the "previously on" trope is particularly symbolic of *Battlestar*'s thematic and reflexive concerns. Acting as a terministic screen, the trope delimits and rewrites the relevancies of the show's history, repressing many memories while reliving others, facilitating the very important serial practice of retroactive foreshadowing. One might effectively rephrase "previously on" to "what already did but still might happen on." Perhaps the same can be said about the "previously on" feature of *True Blood* (HBO, 2008–Present) or *Friday Night Lights* (NBC, 2006–2011). The difference for *Battlestar*, as well as for *Lost*, is that the series continually thematizes repeating histories and uncanny recontextualizations. There is no telling whether the speaker refers to the show or the ship when she or he says "Previously on Battlestar Galactica," and this conflation is identical to the one in Adama's speech; it is the simultaneity of theme and reflexivity at the very heart of the show, a show that continually allegorizes its own processes of creation and reception. Further still, *Battlestar*'s "teaser" feature, in which viewers see fast-paced clips of the upcoming episode immediately prior to its presentation, suggests that the show's future (as much as its past) is embedded in its present, that, just like for the ship itself, *Battlestar*'s course is "not unknown."

In the final season of *Lost*, characters continually find themselves in situations that mirror earlier events in the series, from as far back as the first season. Called "callbacks" by fans, these series-long echoes, often quite faint, reward committed viewers as insiders. Steven Johnson writes about this feature of contemporary TV at length in his book *Everything Bad Is Good for You*: "[Watching *Seinfeld* (NBC, 1990–1998)], if you haven't seen the 'Mulva' episode, or if the name 'Art Vandelay' means nothing to you, then the subsequent references—many of them arriving years after their original appearance—will pass on by unappreciated . . . The gap between setup and punch line could sometimes last five years" (85–86). Johnson suggests that such callbacks make viewers smarter, that they require viewers to be active participants in the meaning-making process, bridging the gaps and connecting the dots; of course, such a claim is hard to stand by without cognitive data at hand. Nevertheless, Johnson correctly points out that this feature is increasingly common and that viewers must now dedicate in order to appreciate. It might be difficult, though, to make the case that the callbacks on *Seinfeld* are thematically significant, that they mean something important to the show besides their simple existence, a televisual novelty of the early and mid-1990s worth pursuing for its own sake.

The callbacks on *Lost*, however, are thematically and reflexively organic; they correspond with the characters' and viewers' experiences throughout the run of the series (and beyond). In *Lost*'s final season, the show's major characters exist in two realities, one on the island and one off. The group not on the island has no knowledge of their alternate lives. Just like viewers who left the show in droves during the early episodes of the third season, these alternate-reality characters are disconnected, living episodically in police, hospital, and courtroom dramas. In the series' finale, a chain of events leads each major character in this alternate world toward an epiphanic recall of, essentially, the entire series. And so while the show's callbacks are certainly knowing winks at the audience (as they are on *Seinfeld*), they are also aesthetically justified, foreshadowing and developing the series-long theme of return, of reviewing and working through the past. These scenes constitute the emotional core of the final episode, and viewers are perhaps flattered by the fact that these characters have to catch up, have to download and review their serialized histories—a process with which fans of this heavily plotted serial are deeply familiar. Further still, Damon Lindelof and Carlton Cuse, the head writers and executive producers of *Lost*, anticipate the uncanny sensations likely to accompany the die-hard fan's process of starting over, of purchasing and reviewing the box set or their archived episodes in the hopes of making new connections across the show's long history, reading backshadowing as foreshadowing, actively unknowing the known course of events. Callbacks on *Lost*, then, are thematic shout-outs: they bridge the gap, not just between one diegetic event and another, but between characters and viewers as well. "Life here began out there"—just as the remaining crew of *Battlestar* land safely on Earth, characters on *Lost* finally find themselves as viewers of themselves, at home in the world of the show's audience.

Previously unknown to prime-time serial TV, the sustained thematic reflexivity of both *Battlestar* and *Lost* is profoundly elegant. All of the existential dilemmas these characters face concerning fate, faith, design, etc. resonate deeply for me, but not (for better or worse) because I spend a great deal of time thinking about such things in my daily life; rather, these are the questions I ask when I watch these shows: Is there a plan? Should I believe? What does it all mean? Indeed, when viewers watch one of these shows, they are likely to experience "the weird, mostly happy feeling that it is watching [them] back" (Beck).

THE DIGITAL SERIAL

Battlestar is a complex, finite narrative centered on themes of fate and eternal recurrence, a series for which discerning viewers are all but required to notice foreshadowing. Having completed the series, what are viewers to make of certain features from the miniseries pilot that may have seemed unremarkable the first time around, but that carry a new valence upon a subsequent viewing? In the confidence of a Cylon (the series' cyborgian, threatening "others"), Gaius Baltar (James Callis) says, "no one knows that Cylons look like humans" ("Pilot"). The scene then cuts to Colonel Tigh (Michael Hogan) speaking to Admiral Adama: "So, Cylons look like us" ("Pilot"). The cut facilitates dramatic irony, as Colonel Tigh's statement directly contradicts Baltar's. However, several seasons later, viewers will learn that Colonel Tigh is a Cylon.

Is this ostensibly marginal moment in the pilot, then, a case of long-form foreshadowing? Is it thematically significant that Tigh essentially confesses to something that he does not yet know about himself? Most important, did the creators of *Battlestar* intend viewers to ask these sorts of questions about this moment in the pilot?

On podcasts, Moore continually alludes to the "Bible" he wrote prior to *Battlestar*'s production, or the "sacred scrolls" that map *Battlestar*'s course. Yet Moore also speaks often about "good cans of worms" that open up when he deviates from the backstory (Moore, iTunes 109). Asked if there is a "story behind Adama's pilot handle 'Husker,'" Moore replies, "I'm sure there is. In all honesty, I just made it up. I don't have the backstory yet" (Moore, *In Review*). Similar to how Admiral Adama's crew might have felt had they known that he was indeed lying about the location of Earth, *Battlestar*'s dedicated audience is likely disenchanted by Moore's behind-the-scenes revelations. The serious fan, or the implied viewer, owns and rewatches the DVDs, fitting every piece of the difficult puzzle together. But what if half of the pieces are not pieces at all? A faithful reader who rereads an analogous statement to that of Colonel Tigh's in a novel would probably feel confident that the writer had revised and planned for such a reading, confident that there are interpretive rewards for following through. However, the dedicated viewer rewatching *Battlestar*'s pilot is likely disoriented, knowing full well that the fact that Tigh is a Cylon is not part of his backstory yet. Like much self-consciously "cult" serialized TV, *Battlestar* encourages a kind of paranoid viewing, but it fails to identify just how "forensic" our "fandom" ought to be (Mittell, "*Lost*" 128). Upon review, Tigh's comment in the pilot is an unintended foreshadow, an interpretive impasse that is as regular a feature of the series as "previously on," tempting one to follow the advice that *Lost* offers throughout its final season: "let go." The trouble with this advice, of course, is that the show also encourages viewers to rewatch, to piece together, to purchase to own and hold on tightly.

In light of recent technological developments, consider a passage about "serial ephemerality" from Hayward's outstanding 1997 monograph *Consuming Pleasures*:

> The sheer volume of textual production virtually negates the possibility of reexperiencing earlier installments. Unless we save each day's strip or videotape or buy one of the histories created and marketed as a solution to exactly this problem of serial ephemerality, there is no way to perform the kind of reality check we often run on novels, glancing back through the text to see what we have missed or forgotten. There is also no way to read early cues differently in light of later developments. (135)

DVDs, DVRs, and downloads—the proliferation of digital distribution and storage platforms—render Hayward's insights remarkably archaic: producers of serialized TV series now bank on viewers' ability to reexperience earlier installments; these shows are created, sold, and re-sold with viewers' unfettered digital access to the deep diegeses in mind. And so while it is often the case, as Roger Hagedorn points out, that when "new media technology is introduced commercial exploiters have consistently turned to the serial form of narrative presentation precisely in order to cultivate a dependable audience of consumers" (5), it is also true that the ideal audiences of these contemporary digital serials are all but required to be dependably rabid, to be so deeply familiar with the story that they can hear faint echoes from seasons long past (though not long gone). Additionally, the serial is simply one of the more narratively efficient ways of rewarding viewers' investment in new entertainment technologies. Just as the navigation buttons on the remote control and the proliferation of cable channels in the 1980s and 1990s allowed intertextual allusion to flourish on TV, so too do the pause and rewind buttons and the new portability of content promote the intratextual seriality of today's most acclaimed shows; naturally, both trends reward deep familiarity with and massive consumption of media.

For Robert J. Thompson, *St. Elsewhere* (NBC, 1982–1988) marks the pivot in prime-time seriality, as "never before had a television series maintained this level of intricacy and consciousness of its own history" (91). In the mid- and late 1980s, *St. Elsewhere* began to appear in syndication, and broadcasters quickly learned that audiences had trouble following such an inhospitable narrative. Appearing out-of-order and nightly (turning the weekly appointment into one more likely missed and difficult to reschedule), *St. Elsewhere*'s episodes became just that—episodes standing alone, though characters were remembering events that had not yet been syndicated. The rerun ratings suffered, proving that the most successful shows in syndication are often the episodic one-offs of sitcoms and procedural dramas, in which "episodes may be seen in any order and may be skipped without compromising future comprehension and engagement" (Newman 23). *St. Elsewhere* ends by retroactively imagining the entire series as the daydream of an autistic child, reflexively diagnosing the abnormal qualities of memory and attention to detail that mobilized the show's artistic success, even if they debilitated the show's pre-digital commercial afterlife. Moore, Lindelof, Cuse, and colleagues charter off into the deep, mostly unexplored spaces of heavily serialized prime-time TV, and in so doing tether viewers to the new technological markets that allow such endeavors the success that *St. Elsewhere* could not enjoy, a success beyond the first airing of an episode. These writers also effectively thematize the production and reception of new media seriality, translating the audience's tactile participation in the materials of distribution and access into something abstract and metaphoric, further strengthening its bond to the new media technology.

However, it is clear from the persistent problem of unplanned, dead-end foreshadowing and loose ends that the writers of these shows are not yet able to keep up with Moore's Law, that the technology outpaces the execution, even if it does not outpace the writers' admirably lofty ambitions. Obviously, it is hardly an aim of this chapter to list every unintentional foreshadow or loose end of *Battlestar* and *Lost*. Viewers who have watched these shows understand that they leave countless (and seemingly important) questions unanswered, or that the programs provide answers in ways that betray the original terms of the questions.[3] *Lost* did not have a planned end date until after its third season; nevertheless, the final three seasons, ostensibly planned out, generate just as many unsolved mysteries as the first three. *Battlestar* and *Lost* are a new type of popular TV narrative, one with novelistic aspirations, but one suffering from growing pains, hindered as it is by the very same serial accessibility that allows for its scope. These shows are thoroughly reviewable, but only until their final episodes air.

ETERNAL, DIMINISHING RETURNS

As scholars often do with the intertextual irony of *Seinfeld*, *The Simpsons* (Fox, 1989–Present), or *Buffy, The Vampire Slayer* (The WB, 1997–2001; UPN, 2001–2003), there is obviously a temptation to label the aporiae of contemporary serial TV "postmodernist," to interpret Colonel Tigh's statement in the miniseries as a deconstruction, whether of dramatic irony, foreshadowing, or narrative coherence more generally.[4] One should hesitate to do so, though. Consider another popular genre that has emerged from these same developments in media technology. Like the contemporary TV serial, the "puzzle" film is what Thomas Elsaesser refers to as "DVD-enabled," a type of film "that requires or repays multiple viewings; that rewards the attentive viewer with special or hidden clues; that is constructed as a spiral or loop" (38). The "narrative special effects" of *The Usual Suspects* (Singer, 1995), *Fight Club* (Fincher, 1999), *The Sixth Sense* (Shyamalan, 1999), *Memento* (Nolan, 2000), and *Shutter Island* (Scorsese, 2010) cost little, and the films themselves often become cult classics, big hits on the small screen (Mittell, "Narrative" 35). Costing far less to manufacture than VHS tapes, DVDs became a key revenue stream for studios beginning in the early 2000s. "The real growth in DVDs was in the sell-through market, which barely existed in the VHS era" (Block and Wilson 812); consumers are far more likely to *own* movies on DVD than they ever were to own them on VHS. Of course, DVDs allow lossless playback, instant scene access, and much clearer picture resolution. It is important to note that the people to whom the majority of these puzzle films are marketed were the first generation raised with home video; they are used to revisiting films at their convenience, and so providing them with a challenge—a narrative game perfectly suited to the new technology—has met great success. These films would not have been as successful—many of them would not even exist— without the narrative accessibility that DVDs offer; likewise, the ascendency of the DVD owes much to the pleasures of reviewing these puzzle films.

Still, contemporary puzzle films do not necessarily "indicate the 'messiness of life'" as many of those postmodernist narrative experiments in art cinema do (Panek 86). Unlike, say, *Last Year at Marienbad* (Resnais, 1961), today's experimental narratives are *solvable* puzzles. Even *Mulholland Dr.* (Lynch, 2001), as N. Katherine Hayles and Nicholas Gessler illustrate through a minute-by-minute diagram of the film, is in many senses narratively stable, not "completely indeterminate" as David Bordwell suggests (82). The contemporary puzzle film often foregrounds its interpretability, almost always satisfying close analysis, teaching us what counts and rewarding our diligence. *The Sixth Sense* and *Memento* force first-time viewers to reflect, to turn their attention back to seemingly innocuous details, and repeated viewings and freeze framing afford viewers a conspiracy they can solve.[5]

These puzzle films are not "open" narratives in the postmodernist sense. Rather, they are overdetermined, formally unified, and they successfully convince audiences that the writer knew what the truth out there was before the film went into production. As is the case with the writers and directors of puzzle films, Moore, Lindelof, Cuse, and others employ heavy doses of foreshadowing, callbacks, revelations, and twists toward the goal of textual unity, of rewarding attentive viewers for their choice to "pay painstaking attention" (Johnson-Smith 71). But these writers' canvases are much larger than those of the puzzle film—100 *hours*, not minutes. Those reality checks that make the puzzle film so much fun for re-viewers (and many novels so much fun for re-readers) often lead to dead ends the second time through *Battlestar* and *Lost*. This would not be a problem if the shows had thematized decenteredness, had they ended in chaos and disharmony. Rather, as is the case for first-time viewers of *Battlestar*, one of "*Lost*'s great pleasures is the sense of faith in its narrative design and purpose that the show manages to instill" (Mittell, "*Lost*" 127).

Lost's "insistent claim that 'everything happens for a reason' makes causality an essential structuring device, central to deciphering the most enigmatic aspects of the show" (Askwith 170). Both *Battlestar* and *Lost* try to convince viewers that everything happens for a reason, that faith is a virtue; they continually ask their audiences to identify symmetries and echoes, to revisit the past and connect it to the present, to map out and be familiar with countless plotted events, to treat the shows, in other words, as unified texts, as solvable puzzles. Those are the terms of these shows and these shows fail according to those terms. Needless to say, plenty of "open" texts do not thematize the "messiness of life" so much as embody it.

Perhaps a new hermeneutics is called for. Mittell goes far identifying the critical position from which many viewers enjoy these shows, writing that *Battlestar* "offers narrative coherence not because [the writers] knew what they were doing beforehand, but because the outcome exhibits the illusion of a design—there is a plan, even if it didn't precede its execution" ("Authorship"). Assuming that the course is "not unknown"—neither known nor not known—allows critics to appreciate the execution of such lofty ambitions while acknowledging the logistical hurdles of TV production that inevitably undermine the finished product. The problem, though, is that this discourse often devolves into an academic fandom that consciously looks past loose ends and praises the "journey"—even though most viewers who saw the journey through did so because of all of those cues pointing to coherence. As Askwith points out, the viewer's pleasure is "predicated in large part on the promise of eventual fulfillment and revelation" (169). Imagine trying to put a puzzle together, one with an elaborate, beautiful picture on the front of the box. After countless hours, frantically looking back and forth between the box and the pieces, you begin to realize that the puzzle-as-sold is impossible to put together. At this point, do you want to be told that it is the "journey" of trying to put the puzzle together that matters? Will it impress you that the creators of the puzzle were able to effectively create the "illusion" of a solution? These shows are not intentionally deconstructing serial TV or puzzle narratives. Foreshadowing and twists on *Battlestar* and *Lost* point to an overall design; both shows thematize and promote faith in structural coherence and in everything counting for something; many individual episodes of each series are complicated and coherent narrative puzzles: it is clear that there is nothing the writers of *Battlestar* and *Lost* would have liked more than to create a one-hundred-hour saga that holds up as well on a second viewing as *Memento* or *The Sixth Sense*. The problems here are not hermeneutical; they are creative.

The seriality and forensic fandom of soap operas and professional wrestling—perhaps the two most critically derided genres in TV history—now characterize "quality" on TV. Soaps and wrestling came of age in a technological context that did not allow easy access to a serial's diegetic history. In this environment, the serialist's aim was to stimulate an "endless deferred desire for textual gratification," without ever getting to the "point of not stopping, of desire's saturation" (Hayward 137, 151). As much as *Twin Peaks* and *The X-Files*, technological advancements have provoked contemporary TV serialists to demand end dates from their networks, and, consequently, much of TV is taken seriously today for its formal aesthetics. Making great use of this new medium, *Battlestar* and *Lost* invite, or rather demand, that viewers have unfettered access to the entire diegesis. "Endless deferred desire" has made way for review, for endless engagement with the archive, both during and after a show's run. *Battlestar* and *Lost* artfully thematize these processes of review and renewal. Both shows end dramatically, and with ostensible closure; they end "out there": where life began, where the truth is. However, upon review, the uncanny, revelatory experiences of the characters on the final episode of *Lost* become for the viewer sad reminders of the show's promised epiphanies, cruel illustrations on the back of the puzzle box showing happy people who have made every piece fit. The missteps of the otherwise outstanding series *St. Elsewhere*, *Twin Peaks*, and *The X-Files* taught contemporary serialists important lessons about deliberately writing for advanced distribution platforms, about effectively convincing audiences that the show's course is known, about the necessity of demanding end dates from networks. What will the serial missteps of the contemporary classics *Battlestar* and *Lost* teach tomorrow's writers? I hope, for the pleasures of review at least, that it's not unknown.

SUGGESTED EPISODES FOR ADDITIONAL STUDY

Battlestar Galactica
2:5. "The Farm." Writ. Carla Robinson. Dir. Rod Hardy. 12, August 2005.
2:7. "Home (Part 2)." Writ. David Eick and Ronald D. Moore. August 26, 2005.
3:1. "Occupation." Writ. Ronald D. Moore. Dir. Sergio Mimica-Gezzan. October 6, 2006.
4:10. "Revelations." Writ. Bradley Thompson and David Weddle. Dir. Michael Rymer. June 13, 2008.
4:17. "Someone to Watch Over Me." Writ. Bradley Thompson and David Weddle. February 27, 2009.

Lost

2:7. "The Other 48 Days." Writ. Carlton Cuse and Damon Lindelof. Dir. Eric Laneuville. November 16, 2005.

3:22/23. "Through the Looking Glass." Writ. Carlton Cuse and Damon Lindelof. Dir. Jack Bender. May 23, 2007.

4:1. "The Beginning of the End." Writ. Carlton Cuse and Damon Lindelof. Dir. Jack Bender. January 31, 2008.

4:5. "The Constant." Writ. Carlton Cuse and Damon Lindelof. Dir. Jack Bender. February 28, 2008.

6:1/2. "LA X." Writ. Carlton Cuse and Damon Lindelof. Dir. Jack Bender. February 2, 2010.

6:15. "Across the Sea." Writ. Carlton Cuse and Damon Lindelof. Dir. Tucker Gates. May 11, 2010.

NOTES

1. Timothy M. Todreas identifies the three eras of TV as broadcast, cable, and digital. Mark C. Rogers, Michael Epstein, and Jimmie L. Reeves re-label these eras TV-I, -II, -III, hoping to avoid any platform-specific distinctions that fail to account for the continuity between the eras (for example, many broadcasting and cable practices are still in effect in the digital era, and many aspects of the creation, marketing, and reception of digital-era TV were practiced, though perhaps less extensively, in the broadcast and cable eras).

2. Thompson defines as "quality TV" those shows that have "large ensemble casts," that tend to be "literary and writer-based," that attract "blue-chip demographics," and that are "showered with awards and acclaim" (15). Heavily serialized, narratively complex, and full of mystery, self-consciously "cult" shows in the TV-III era are those that generate what Jason Mittell calls "forensic fandom," encouraging "viewers to parse the show more than simply consume it" ("*Lost*" 128).

3. Countless online pages are dedicated to listing the loose ends of *Battlestar* and *Lost*. See *Screen Rant* http://screenrant.com/lost-finale-explanation-kofi-61464/, *GOR[B]* http://www.gorbould.com/blog/index.php/2009/01/94-unanswered-bsg-questions/, and *TV Without Pity* http://www.televisionwithoutpity.com/show/battlestar_galactica/battlestar_galactica_unanswere.php.

4. For an analysis of TV's abundance of intertextual allusion, and the relation such allusive practices have with postmodernist literature, see David Foster Wallace's "E Unibus Pluram."

5. For more on puzzle films and other cinematic genres emerging in the digital content era, see Berg, "Taxonomy"; Eig, "Mind(fuck)"; Lavik, "Changing Narratives"; and Panek, "The Poet and the Detective."

WORKS CITED

Askwith, Ivan. "'Do You Even Know Where This is Going?': *Lost*'s Viewers and Narrative Premeditation." *Reading Lost*. Ed. Roberta Pearson. London: I. B. Tauris, 2009. 159–80. Print.

Beck, Richard. "Treasure Island." *N + 1*. May 30, 2010. Web. June 1, 2010.

Berg, Charles Ramírez. "A Taxonomy of Alternative Plots in Recent Films: Classifying the 'Tarantino Effect.'" *Film Criticism* 31 (2006): 5–61. Print.

Block, Alex Ben, and Lucy Autrey Wilson. *George Lucas's Blockbusting: A Decade-by-Decade Survey of Timeless Movies, Including Untold Secrets of Their Financial and Cultural Success*. New York: itBooks, 2010. Print.

Bordwell, David. *The Way Hollywood Tells It: Story and Style in Modern Movies*. Berkeley and Los Angeles: University of California Press, 2006. Print.

Dolan, Marc. "The Peaks and Valleys of Serial Creativity: What Happened to/on *Twin Peaks*." *Full of Secrets: Critical Approaches to* Twin Peaks. Ed. David Lavery. Detroit: Wayne State University Press, 1995. 31–50. Print.

Eig, Jonathan. "A Beautiful Mind(fuck): Hollywood Structures of Identity." *Jump Cut* 46 (2003). Web. May 10, 2010.

Elsaesser, Thomas. "The Mind-Game Film." *Puzzle Films: Complex Storytelling in Contemporary Cinema*. Ed. Warren Buckland. Chichester, West Sussex, UK: Wiley-Blackwell, 2009. 14–41. Print.

Hagedorn, Roger. "Technology and Economic Exploitation: The Serial as a Form of Narrative Presentation." *Wide Angle* 10.4 (1988): 4–12. Print.

Hayles, N. Katherine, and Nicholas Gessler. "The Slipstream of Mixed Reality: Unstable Ontologies and Semiotic Markers in "*The Thirteenth Floor, Dark City*, and *Mulholland Drive*." *PMLA* 119.3 (2004): 482–99. Print.

Hayward, Jennifer. *Consuming Pleasures: Active Audiences and Serial Fictions from Dickens to Soap Opera*. Lexington: University Press of Kentucky, 1997. Print.

Johnson, Steven. *Everything Bad Is Good for You: How Today's Popular Culture Is Actually Making Us Smarter*. New York: Riverhead Books, 2005. Print.

Johnson-Smith, Jan. *American Science Fiction TV: Star Trek, Stargate, and Beyond*. Middletown, CT: Wesleyan University Press, 2005. Print.

Lavik, Erlend. "Changing Narratives: Five Essays on Hollywood History." Diss. University of Bergen, 2007. Print.

Mittell, Jason. "Authorship, Intentionality, and Intelligent Design." *Just TV*. March 26, 2009. Web. April 10, 2009.

———. "*Lost* in a Great Story: Evaluation in Narrative Television (and Television Studies)." *Reading Lost*. Ed. Roberta Pearson. London: I. B. Tauris, 2009. 119–38. Print.

———. "Narrative Complexity in Contemporary American Television." *The Velvet Light Trap* 58 (2006): 29–40. Print.

Moore, Ronald D. *Battlestar Galactica* Podcast. *iTunes*. 2005–2009. Web. April 4, 2009.

———. Chatroom Interview. *In Review*. Marc Flemming and Sean Kelly, n.d. Web. May 10, 2009.

Newman, Michael Z. "From Beats to Arcs: Toward a Poetics of Television Narrative." *The Velvet Light Trap* 58 (2006): 16–28. Print.

Panek, Elliot. "The Poet and the Detective: Defining the Psychological Puzzle Film." *Film Criticism* 31 (2006): 62–88. Print.

"Pilot." *Battlestar Galactica* (Miniseries). Perf. James Callis, Mary McDonnell, Edward James Olmos. Creator, Ronald D. Moore. Sci-Fi Channel. December 8, 2003. Television.

Rogers, Mark C., Michael Epstein, and Jimmie L. Reeves. "*The Sopranos* as HBO Brand Equity: The Art of Commerce in the Age of Digital Reproduction." *This Thing of Ours:*

Investigating The Sopranos. Ed. David Lavery. New York: Columbia University Press, 2002. 42–59. Print.

Thompson, Robert J. *Television's Second Golden Age: From* Hill Street Blues *to* ER. New York: Continuum, 1996. Print.

Todreas, Timothy M. *Value Creation and Branding in Television's Digital Age*. Westport, CT: Quorum Books, 1999. Print.

Wallace, David Foster. "E Unibus Pluram: Television and U.S. Fiction." *A Supposedly Fun Thing I'll Never Do Again: Essays and Arguments*. Boston: Little, Brown and Co., 1997. 21–82. Print.

4

ZERO-DEGREE SERIALITY
Television Narrative in the Post-Network Era

NORMAN M. GENDELMAN

The year of 2010 saw the demise of two popular television dramas. While Fox's *24* (2001–2010) entered its eighth and final season, ABC's *Lost* (2004–2010) entered its sixth and, likewise, final season. As historically situated siblings and narrative experiments in televisual structure and style, both programs are serial electronic bodies that enact their own duration and speak to their contemporary "times." If *24*'s renegade antiterrorist Jack Bauer (Kiefer Sutherland) is inverted as a "real-time" interface (a *human* prosthesis in service to electronic technologies of martial automation), *Lost* similarly inverts character-based narrative. It plays out the destinies of its island-bound plane crash survivors as a reverse ensemble of temporal currencies (flashbacks, flashforwards, and flashsideways). Both shows reinvent narrative as explicitly about electronic temporality itself, resisting linear narratives that follow from a centrally conceived protagonist. These two programs suggest that the medium of television—as specifically structured by its real-time consumption—has now become its own "character." Through a close reading of the opening sequences of *24* and *Lost*, this chapter explores what it means for contemporary viewers and shows to be "serial" in terms of both ontological reception (the experience of viewing in time) and epistemological intellection (the articulation of viewing in time).

Both *24* and *Lost* construct narrative codes that confront the electronic present while likewise mapping its displacements. By stylistically and structurally foregrounding, or "plotting," their own contexts—obsessive speed for the former and digressive multiplicity for the latter—these programs are semiotic/experiential modes and electronic "signatures" of our era.

OUTLINING THE TELEVISUAL
Seriality, Mapping, and Materiality

Transitioning away from a previous era's centralized network hegemony, the current "post-network era" is characterized by convergence technology (Lotz

3). Given the explosion of interface technologies of a digital ilk, previously discrete and identifiable media lose their component identity. They become fused and integrated. A television program can be watched on an iPod, video-streamed off the Internet, or shared on a social network site. In terms of time and space, the choice of when and where to watch is as variable as it is dispersed. Be it through digital ON-DEMAND systems, recorded DVR boxes, or packaged DVD sets, technologies now ironically *mediate* television. Viewing is no longer linear. Viewership, likewise, pushes program variability. Both the adeptness with which viewers access and utilize new reception technologies and the specific modes of their usage have forced televisual programming into a more diverse and differentiated output. Jettisoned outside the domestic hub whose sedentariness the broadcast era relied on for its centralized delivery, television is now mobile and differentiated.

Noting this, Jason Mittell outlines an emerging "complex" television narrative whose "experimentation and innovation" challenges the conventional norms of the network era's episodic and serial structures (29). The intertwining of prime-time episodic dramas (their conventional stand-alone rudiments) with daytime soap opera serials (their multiple storylines and contiguous plot unfolding) mark the complex era's character that Mittell calls the "operational aesthetic" (34). Defined by both the intricacy of plot and the reflexivity of structure, shows of this kind are characterized by a Byzantine world foregrounding the *process* of both duration and design.

Not only do *24* and *Lost* share these qualities, they are the very qualities that mark them as "serial." Television narrative in any era takes form as a series that repeats in time. If the serial soap opera consists of multiple storylines and the incessant charge of its day-to-day schedule, it is designated by a quotidian temporal dimension. It approximates the pattern of everyday duration. And if episodic drama is marked by its stand-alone generic tropes, it is no less temporal for its repetition. Given either one's formulaic unfolding, they are structured by their status as series. Therefore, I utilize "seriality" as an umbrella term to emphasize what is centrally temporal about electronic narrative generally and the two shows of this study specifically. *24* and *Lost* push the very rudiments that define them as electronic televisual expressions. They entertain and explore their own condition as time-based electronic media and in doing so, in many ways, extend the theoretical exploration of the cultural theorists and artists who came before them.

During the network era, Fredric Jameson similarly analyzed how broad changes in technology and related corporate structures drive narrative. His analysis focuses on how diffuse electronic systems (computational and televisual) inflect representational fiction. He analyzes cinematic narratives of his time that map or visualize the complexity of late-twentieth-century communications technologies (Jameson 9). For him communication technologies hide themselves within the very *immaterial* of their offering and resist traditional forms of representation. The paradox of Jameson's focus rests on its attempt to articulate a system that is, by its very structure, ephemeral in nature. Due to a computer code's invisibility and network complexity, its logic is hidden (Jameson 9). Corporate technologies that undergird broader social practices resist figural models capable of penetrating, and thereby potentially critiquing, multinational capitalism's operational influence. Given the post-network era's even more nebulous and disparate industrial practices, affixing television drama's ideational purpose proves difficult. Despite his interests in analyzing the material of cultural production, Jameson avoids analyzing televisual narrative directly. As an antidote to his omission, the practices of some contemporary minds, the Soviet avant-garde artists of the early twentieth century, are helpful to turn to because of their explicit attention to form and process.

Organized around a series of disparate but related movements (Zaumism, Suprematism, and Constructivism, respectively) Soviet artists foregrounded aesthetic material to uncover its ideological content. By plying and experimenting with the actual conditions of cultural production, the movements sought to map the process of image-making (Bois et al. 132). The artists insisted on material confrontations that analyzed how a given culture "signs" its own identity. For example, in stressing the two-dimensionality of the picture plane, the conventional square of its framing, or the texture of the paint itself, these paintings suggest that their material makeup *is* their thematic content. By resisting any form/content split, and thereby explicitly addressing the material logic of how art works, the artists pushed the actual *material* of culture to *create* culture (Bois et al. 131). One artist of the movement, Vladimir Malevich, went so far as to evacuate figuration altogether, choosing simply to write the name of the absent subject on a canvas. With such nominalist exercises, Malevich advocated an art of the "zero" in which his paintings sought to push past the limits of transparent representation (Bois et al. 131). However different their material, *24* and *Lost* operate in a similar fashion. By foregrounding their nominal and electronic conditions, the shows approximate Malevich's experiments in achieving a zero degree.

I am not suggesting that early twenty-first-century television drama, which is largely rooted in the capitalist model of Jameson's critique, is in any way similar to Soviet art of a century earlier. And the aim of my chapter is not to situate any kind of parallelism in terms of material usage and intent. I am interested, however, in noting the similarity in their formal dimensions. Much like Malevich's experiments in painting, *24* and *Lost* foreground televisual material and thereby equally map their own formation. Specifically, they work in and through the serial forms of their constructed lineaments. Secondly, in foregrounding said material they express the procedure of making seriality and attempt to discern what electronic repetition implies. By pushing through the logic of their own televisual articulation (their own "naming") as the logic of their own production, they are serial "zero degrees."

These programs not only formally discern the experiences of our own multimedia time, they interrogate them by way of their own self-reflexive structures. While they map a larger subjectivity inflected by the shifting conditions of our era, they no less *materialize* the rudiments of their own operations. Specifically, they emphasize electromagnetic transmission and computer recursion systems. They are conditioned by a dual formal expression: the rhetoric that announces them (their title sequences), and the style of their characterological makeup (their self-reflexive material expression).

MAPPING THE ZERO DEGREE
Real-Time Automation

Before the onset of action, and before the unfolding of its credit sequence, *24*'s title introduces each episode. A black screen opens each episode resembling the screen presence of a computer interface. It seems literally "off." It is then suddenly flash-rendered with audio blips and beeps as a sped-up digital alarm clock flickers the numeric articulations of time, its full-screen red bold italics ticking away in microdot millisecond specs before fixing on an emblazoned "*24*." The title then sparks in nominal diffusion as an inverse peddling display descends into dissipation. As the screen fades back to black, the audio indicates interface "trash" via the crunch of a data erasure. While implying its obsolescence, the flitting numbers also suggest a kind of code logic intrinsic to digital expression—the bits of information that invisibly undergird its expression. But as much as it is an interfacial space, it is also a signature of ephemeral time, a displacement of its collapsed interval.

Regarding the technologies of simultaneity associated with information systems, Paul Virilio notes the contraction of intervals. Dissolving the discrete parameters that situate dialectical boundaries, interfaces make "things and objects perceived . . . infra-thin" where they "lose their weight, their bulk" (Virilio, *Open* 26). The movement that situates distances loses the vast geophysical and concrete register of their association. The electronic interface erases any sense of a striving body traversing an actual ground between two points. What becomes foregrounded is temporal immediacy itself. While the sense of space is all but eroded, the sense of time is intensified by the interface's urgent simultaneity (Virilio, *Open* 25). For Virilio, this marks the efficacy of "real-time," a live moment that claims informational certainty. While indicating a seemingly ever-present reality, it evacuates a living duration of bodies that extend out into space (Virilio, *Open* 26). The image-screen collapses temporal passage into an informational image. It both stresses a *signalectic* logic (a transmission emplaced, accentuated, and characterized by electromagnetic speed), while it no less punctuates an information register expressive of code (a *recursive* rhetoric of bits and bytes representing the actual language of digital code).

The title of every episode of *24* and the unfolding screen action are structured around the introductory digital clock and its literally signifying parameters. But the clock continues to serve as a placeholder and organizer of time for the show. It calls attention to a fixation with clock time. As each episode is titled based on the countdown (the passage of one hour of time) the logic of televisual time is here the actual time in which the interval is erased and re-expanded. Thereby, each discrete episode acts as an extended temporal signifier. As if designating a skeletal outline from the title's signifier, each episode fulfills itself by forming into an embodied macrocosm around its signifying titular subdivisions. These ever-diminishing instants organize and tailor the show's movement. Take, for example, season one's episode "6:00 a.m.–7:00 a.m."

The episode is partitioned into four "chapter" headings. Each part is announced by a digital nomenclature similar to its title sequence. It is literally structured *in* and *as* clock time delineated to the second. Bracketed by way of screen intertitles that begin and end narrative sequences ("6:17:08," "6:29:47," "6:42:54," and "6:54:22"), the clock's audio-visual expression continues the title sequence but with a more emphatic and centralized formal focus. Pausing on well-timed dramatic cliffhangers (corresponding to commercial breaks), the digital intertitles are immediately cut into the screen announcing the sudden suspension, or continuation, of action. A fiery electro-cardio grapheme announces the exact "time" of narrative action while a thumping pulse-synthesized heartbeat threatens thrombosis by way of its overwrought bass-beat phonetic throbs. The show literally expresses the respiration of computational automata.

As the digital clock acts as a discrete interface, plotted action unfolds. True to the repetitive, and yet driven logic of the program, the episodes of season one reveal Jack in the midst of an assassination conspiracy. Compromised into playing double agent because his wife and daughter are being held hostage, Jack is used to aid in the assassination of the man he is obligated to protect, presidential candidate David Palmer. Oddly, Jack's own voice "reads" the show's opening's screen information announcing: "THE FOLLOWING TAKES PLACE BETWEEN 6:00 A.M. and 7:00 A.M. ON THE DAY OF THE CALIFORNIA PRESIDENTIAL PRIMARY." Actor Kiefer Sutherland's non-diegetic omniscient intertitling emplaces Jack as the vocal conduit of the screen itself. Subjectivity is interpenetrated and "read" as interface, as before Jack can even identify himself as "Jack Bauer," he is subordinated to screen logic. He is the show's ventriloquist dummy mouthing clock-time cursives.

Just as Jack's voice miraculously announces the interface from a seemingly disembodied nether-location, his action is introduced via a "screen" environment. Having blackmailed Jack into his service, Gaines (the conspiracy ringleader) works a central control room. Shot in close-up and backgrounded by a plethora of technological gadgetry, he is intercut with extreme close-ups of split-screen video surveillance monitors and computer terminals scrolling coded messages. As Gaines turns to face his video monitor, the camera synchronically tracks toward the monitor narrowing into a tightly framed focus on a moving car. The video frame is then emplaced as the diegetic screen, the car driven by Jack Bauer. In an instant, there is a thematic transition. Media forms are conflated, plot locations are refocused, and the supposed central character is peripherally mated to a screen interface. The protagonist is prescribed and predetermined by the structural and stylistic coefficients of the show, the interface lens that both tells time and surveys action. As no more than screen content, Jack is the subsumed object of the interface's surveilling agency.

Literally in his head, Gaines issues commands via a remote audio implement in Jack's ear. Cutting between the literal interface operator (sedentary and yet multitasking) and the literal interface agent (in action and yet controlled), subjectivity is again foregrounded as technological—immediate and interactive. Between close-ups and medium close-ups, the visual space of the characters' communication is oddly contracted and cloistered. The closeness of their interactivity is uncomfortably intimate. Their dialogue is shared exclusively through the terminal, a paradoxically personalized surveillance. Their proximity parallels the structural barometer of the show's obsessive clock time. The interactive proximity of their communications is organized and monitored by the show's own flickering time indices. The clock-time signifiers create a sympathetic hyperawareness not only between Jack and Gaines, but between the viewer and their own interfaces. The anxiety of real time is the central focus. Where the time signatures organize and announce the action, the action itself is emphasized as an impacted presentness. As the two characters are challenged and motivated by the variety of interfaces that stud the diegetic space, they operate as ciphers to the clock they are quite literally on. As social actors they are no more than subordinate extensions of a real-time instantaneity. Hardly co-present or socially communal, they are exclusively determined by the digitized serial flickers of surveillance technology.

Operated by Gaines, Jack's compromised autonomy is by no means an anomaly in the series. However tele-puppeteered, duplicity and surveillance are the skeletal rudiments of the show. Indeed, by "7AM" an entire series of entangled, multiple, and inverted paranoiac couplings has transpired. The incessant order of betrayal operates to speed the show's plotting. It both multiplies and instantiates new plot dynamics while diffusing and expiating others. With a plot as complex as any information system in need of breaking, Gaines watches Jack, who in turn is watched by Counter Terrorist Unit (CTU) agent Nina, who then garners the jealous attentions of fellow CTU agent Tony, who then unveils CTU systems-analyst Jamey as a double agent, who is then in turn killed by Nina, who is ultimately unveiled as a modern Mata Hari. The motifs of secrecy and betrayal underscore the plot and act to structure the operative logic of electromagnetic code.

At the heart of *24*'s adrenalized nervous system is a contradictory "interfacial," a double bind that articulates the madness of American automation systems. No matter how compressed into two-dimensional interfaces, *24* insists on its own three-dimensional depth. While the screen world implies the obliteration of the distinctions between subject and object, *24* still behaves as if it were a "human" character—an identity its own operational logic denies. It performs as a surveillance system that pretends user interactivity. Discussing surveillance systems that centrally track and trace consumer behavior and military weapons systems, Virilio analyzes their increasing complexity or "mediametric monitoring" that flip perceptual parameters (*The Virilio* 139). Such information systems *produce* worlds. As Jack is the scrutinized object-content of a similar screen, he is no more than its surveillance rat. It is the interface itself that is the agent of action. In ways similar to the Soviet artistic practices of the 1920s, this central focus captures *24*'s zero-degree state. The program foregrounds a real-time immediacy and expresses an automaton logic of "real-time reciprocal telesurveillance—24 hours a day" (Virilio, *The Virilio* 145).

The show also approximates our own disposition, suggesting a way of reading our own era. It registers the impossible logic of automated temporality—a temporality that is inconceivable to perceive, yet is actually able to be expressed through the automated surveillance intelligence of speed and complexity. It expresses "the infinitesimal instant in which the virtual and the real are one and the same for the sensor or the human observer" (Virilio, *The Virilio* 146). The zero-degree twist of *24* is that Jack still thinks he is "human."

MAPPING THE ZERO DEGREE
"Incompossible" Time

While narratively instanced as a very different type of story, *Lost* shares much of the same thematic and formal characteristics as *24*. It is equally concerned not only with time as a televisual experience, but also in expressing technological legibility and orientation. Additionally, the show foregrounds its own nomination implying the difficulty of discerning a "when" and "where." Like *24* it performs serial apperception.

    The title sequence conditions these expectations. More traditionally sandwiched between an introductory action and a first act, it nonetheless emphasizes the show's own signifying process. As the introductory action ends, an echo-chamber audio shot announces a pitch-black screen. The pointillist crack is then enjoined to a slow whining synthesized warble. Beginning as a low eerily elongated note, the warbling is synchronized with a blurry illumination of the word "Lost." Derailed from any distinct linguistic grid or pictorial axis it rotates in a nebulous void, wading through an antigravity outerspace vacuum as an astronautically unhinged sign. The white letters at first seem an effervescent drift, but as they advance they surprisingly solidify. Unlike *24*'s horizontally fronted numerals, *Lost*'s signifiers are unmoored. If *24*'s numbers "come into being" they are nonetheless afforded a conventional grid from which to be deciphered. *Lost*'s nominal cipher, however, rotates laterally in zero-gravity somnambulance. Its otherworldly approach highlights its own foreground and background. *Lost*'s warbling signifier expresses the confusion of its own dimensionality as a linguistic sign. Beginning as an untethered two-dimensional signifier, it pivots, increasing in size and volume until finally coming into focus as a gigantic three-dimensional material obelisk, the angling sway of its graphemes' white solid marble radiances of "L" and "O." And the approach does not stop. As with *24*'s flitting digits, it is continual and incessant in its passage. But unlike the "24," these letters emerge as embodied three-dimensional forms; the paradoxically incandescent bulk of its graphemes seemingly passing through the screen itself. The signifiers "articulate" in both senses of the word. First, the letters express a sensual presence by moving through an oblique nether-sphere. With their unfolding concrete edges and increasingly shrill whine, they approximate the animation of a body in motion. Second, the word means what it *does*. Without a determinant plane on which to rest itself horizontally the word is "lost." It is a signifier adrift.

    Like *24* it expresses a subjectivity instanced by its graphic singularity. Without a conventional title sequence to ground humans as producers/performers of a fictional world, *Lost*'s opening identifies the show as its own character.

Like *24* the stylization and isolation of its title renders it as both machinic process and subjective definition. In creating a "there" from nowhere, the title manifests from a diffuse media sphere. The stark glow of its emergent white begins as if a powered-down artificial screen only to emerge as blocky chiseled ciphers replete with cornices and cast shadows that perform three-dimensionality. But *where* the light source comes from, or *what* the dimensional shifts are, is graphically "up in the ether" of the screen itself. The show announces its own predicament as an electromagnetic serial—its own spatial-temporal condition "lost." The show's opening charts the actual form of the show.

Like *24*, the title sequence acts as a skeletal microcosm to the show's action. It repeats being "lost" as an extensive structural embodiment and a manifestation of its thematic meaning. But unlike *24*, the movement of the term determines a dimensional shift in its graphic register. Its temporal signature is different. Transitioning from a conventional two-dimensional screen title, its motion becomes embodied. In other words, the word as a foregrounded signifier in time is what *moves* the show. Unlike the fleeting and charged intensity of *24*'s blipping millisecond automation of time—a digital clock's homogenized numbers—*Lost*'s signifying body unfolds. It expresses physical movement in time, and thereby is subject to change.

As mentioned, *Lost* concerns the lives of a group of plane crash castaways who are stranded on an island seeking various ways to get off. In this way it is no different from the 1960s comedy *Gilligan's Island* (CBS, 1964–1967). However, it is not the particularity of story that marks the show, but the operational logic of its structure. What gives *Lost* its particular disorientation is its form. It is a serial that multiplies and splices time signatures by interweaving and bifurcating them into a "complex" of narrative webs. While the first three seasons register plot as flashbacks particular to a given character, the remaining seasons experiment with flashforwards and flashsideways while still juggling and foregrounding different characters to different episodes. All its seasons are organized by a plot that specifically revolves around time as intersubjectivity. In this way the serial impacting frenzy that characterized *24* and drove its overstimulated intensifications (the density of its mise-en-scènes, the stylization of its screen effects, the rapidity of its plot arcs) is here formally built around more expansive macro-structures. If the titular sequence of *24* is about a temporal contraction, *Lost*'s title sequence is about temporal passage—about how serial temporality dilates.

The show implies a differential subjectivity open to constant modification and expansion. *Lost* enacts a "complex" seriality by way of its *necessity* for invention. If a serial show unfolds in an ever-more labile time, then constant variability is its *operating logic*. And by way of contrast, if *24*'s Jack is a screen conduit for the show's own foregrounded "characterization" it is important to look at *Lost*'s only character who motivates his own temporal juxtapositions: Desmond Hume.

Desmond operates as *Lost*'s hinge. Unlike any other character during the show's run, Desmond is the only one whose multiple-time flashes are overtly motivated. His exposure to a flood of electromagnetic waves at the end of season two enables him to see snatches of the future. Additionally, he experiences both a flashsideways (due to an experiment that further unlocks his seer mechanics) *and* a series of flashbacks. Season four's "The Constant" foregrounds this "talent."

The episode is structured around a series of flashbacks and reciprocal flashforwards initiated by both Desmond's ability and the island's own peculiar traits. Helicoptered to a freighter off the island's coast, Desmond's own electromagnetic currency is somehow triggered by the approximate bearing. An initial series of flashbacks jettison Desmond's consciousness to and fro in time from the island in 2004 to Glasgow in 1996. Losing his "present" memory in the first flashback, his consciousness affixes to the unfolding plotting of his past. Unhinged and flailing in the present, he desperately tries to find a "constant" that will successfully suture him between times.

Elisions in the narrative times are stitched by way of well-rendered editing techniques. If Desmond's hand grips a helicopter seatbelt in 2004, a fluid graphic match shows him gripping a bed in a military barracks with the same hand in 1996. If he is doing pushups in 1996, a cut-on-action shows him rising in rhythmic tandem in 2004. But as the intervals between the edits increase these seamless continuities lose their ground. The increased length of the narrative 2004 world muddies the eye-line-matches that synch him back into 1996. As viewers see him in extreme close-up eyeing a doctor examining him in 2004, a cut to an extreme close-up of his hand raising a dropped coin in 1996 feels disjointed and random even though the edit is perfectly matched as a cut-on-action. And as the edits continue, it becomes more difficult to "read" these bifurcations. If Desmond performs a discontinuous doublet, the structure itself toys with dissolving continuity logic altogether. Desmond (as well as the variable times he flips to and the characters he comes across) is reapproximated and newly configured with each scene. As events are constantly repositioned, the repetition compulsion intrinsic to seriality is pushed, foregrounded by its reinstantiation as different. Gilles Deleuze would call such plotted experimentation "incompossible."

In his analysis of Robbe Grillet's work, Deleuze notes that the novelist/screenwriter's penchant for "giving narration a new value" consists of "the distribution of different presents to different characters, so that each forms a combination that is plausible and possible in itself, but where all of them together are "'incompossible'" (101). Although he is specifically discussing the film *Last Year at Marienbad*, whose structural trifurcations produce a wellspring of variable and interrelated plot repetitions, Desmond's return to the past similarly marks a "repetition [that] distributes its variations on three presents" (Delueze 101). And this mirrors the three parallel arcs of action that Desmond intercepts. In touch with the island survivors, while on the freighter with others, he returns to and remakes a past-as-present. Time here is not impossible: it is the affective and ontological condition of the "same" as different. If the "incompossible" differentiates and multiplies a seemingly intractable and unwavering instant it is here characteristic of televised seriality. Desmond's passage actualizes the condition of televisual experience and renders it legible. Like the cursive warped passage that opens each show, his temporal movement is the *character* of television. Desmond articulates the show's own logic while approximating a post-network ontology. By emphasizing the serial straits of different viewing positions as temporal platforms (the freighter deck in 2004, his army barracks in 1996, and the labile temporal interface itself), the show renders the dispersive flux of a post-network transition.

CONCLUSION
Apocalyptic Endgames and Infinite Regress

As serial expressions of post-network television, *24* and *Lost* nominate themselves. By inscribing their own condition as two-dimensional interfaces with a distinct and noteworthy duration, they extend their signified condition into subjective presence. They symptomatically articulate not only a medium in transition but the broader parameters of a culture steeped in information systems. By aping serial "lives" they thematize an interface culture that influences as it acts. In this regard, it is worth briefly commenting on the implications of their expression.

As complex electronic maps they express both the automated information landscapes of Jameson's network era and Mittell's post-network condition. But, central to my argument is that they do so by pushing the very logic of electronic media. Just as the Soviets of the early twentieth century explored the constructed rationale of their aesthetic world, both *24* and *Lost* are noteworthy for demonstrating the ideational parameters of their historical condition.

24 performs the culture's ever-increasing tendency toward speed. As it foregrounds and wallows in the logic of military automation systems, the show expresses a real-time acceleration that endlessly recycles its own self-destructive endgame. *24* imagines both an eradication of time/space parameters and an incessant escalation of real-time apocalyptic scenarios. *Lost* delimits the changing condition of a medium whose own mediation is in question. Unable to assuredly express its own technologic as an electronic vehicle, it spools into an endless series of plotted trajectories and points of view. And while its invention is noteworthy for potentially generating variable ways of thinking and conceiving difference, it nonetheless proffers a flipside. It suggests an infinite sense of expansion without end. It seems incapable of conceiving limits. While *24* highlights its obsession toward annihilating time into ever-finer real-time instants, *Lost* seems incapable of conceiving what limits might look like. If electronic culture is an embodied life-blood, then what does it mean that one program signifies as an uncontrollable automation that relentlessly obliterates time, while the other careens into endless scenarios without end? Perhaps it is time to think more "serially" about the logic of a post-network era.

SUGGESTED EPISODES FOR ADDITIONAL STUDY

24

1:7. "6:00 a.m.—7 a.m." Writ. Andrea Newman. Dir. Bryan Spicer. January 8, 2002.
2:6. "Day 2: 1:00 p.m.—2.00 p.m." Writ. Elizabeth Cosin. Dir. Jon Cassar. December 3, 2002.
5:2. "Day 5: 8:00 a.m.—9:00 a.m." Writ. Evan Katz. Dir. Jon Cassar. January 15, 2006.
5:23. "Day 5: 5:00 a.m.—6:00 a.m." Writ. Howard Gordon and Evan Katz. Dir. Jon Cassar. May 22, 2006.

Lost

1:1. "Pilot." Writ. Damon Lindelof. Dir. J. J. Abrams. September 22, 2004.
3:1. "A Tale of Two Cities." Writ. J. J. Abrams and Damon Lindelof. Dir. Jack Bender. October 4, 2006.
4:5. "The Constant." Writ. Damon Lindelof and Carlton Cuse. Dir. Jack Bender. February 28, 2008.
4:13. "There's No Place Like Home: Part 2." Writ. Carlton Cuse and Damon Lindelof. Dir. Jack Bender. May 29, 2008.

WORKS CITED

"6:00 a.m.–7:00 a.m." *24*. Writ. Joel Surnow, Robert Cochran, and Andrea Newman. Fox Television. January 8, 2002. Television.

Bois, Yve-Alain, Hal Foster, Rosalind Krauss, and Benjamin H. D. Buchloh. *Art Since 1900: Volume 1 1900–1944*. New York: Thames & Hudson, 2004. Print.

"The Constant." *Lost*. Prod. J. J. Abrams, Jeffrey Lieber, and Damon Lindelof. ABC. February 28, 2008. Television.

Deleuze, Gilles. *Cinema 2: The Time Image*. Trans. Hugh Tomlinson and Robert Galetta. Minneapolis: University of Minnesota Press, 1989. Print.

Lotz, Amanda D. *The Television Will Be Televised*. New York: New York University Press, 2007. Print.

Jameson, Fredric. *The Geopolitical Aesthetic: Cinema and Space in the World System*. Bloomington: Indiana University Press, 1992. Print.

Mittell, Jason. "Narrative Complexity in Contemporary American Television." *The Velvet Light Trap* 32.58 (Fall 2006): 29–40. Print.

Virilio, Paul. *Open Sky*. Trans. Julie Rose. New York: Verso, 1997. Print.

———. *The Virilio Reader*. Ed. James Der Derian. Malden: Blackwell Publishers, 1998. Print.

5

"PLAY IT AGAIN, SAM . . . AND DEAN"
Temporality and Meta-Textuality in Supernatural

MICHAEL FUCHS

In his article "Narrative Complexity in Contemporary American Television," Jason Mittell argues that due to numerous contextual factors, such as increased media savvy on the part of the recipients, "television's reputation as a producer's medium, where writers and creators retain control over their work," and numerous technological advancements, "American television of the past twenty years will be remembered as an era of narrative experimentation and innovation, challenging the norms of what the medium can do" (31, 29). Indeed, the present volume is testament to the fact that one of the most widely found types of narrative experimentation is connected to questions of temporality. This may seem a little surprising, since due to the "spatial turn" that took the humanities by storm in the 1990s, our current, (post-)postmodern era is often associated with the privileging of space over time. Still, one must not ignore that the postmodern aesthetic is defined by a temporality that is neither oriented toward a utopian future nor toward a more innocent past, but is rather redirected to the present. In the postmodern conception of time, "[f]uture and past form a covalent bond with the present so that temporality as such becomes non-directional, non-linear, and non-singular" (Eckhard and Hölbling 94). Fredric Jameson attributes this conception of time, a "perpetual present," to the loss of a sense of history that characterizes late capitalism, an era in which "our entire contemporary social system has little by little begun to lose its capacity to retain its own past" (125). Therefore, and as Walter Benjamin already argued in the late 1930s, traditional historiography, that is, to conceive of the past as static, must be challenged. He proposed a dynamic model of history in which the past constantly interacts with the present: "The true picture of the past flits by. Only as a picture, which flashes its final farewell in the moment of its recognizability, is the past to be held fast" (Benjamin 695).[1] Thereby, Benjamin foreshadowed the contemporary temporal logic by conceiving of history as a sudden moment of standstill in which the "then" merges with the "now."

THEN AND NOW

The pilot episode of *Supernatural* (The WB, 2005–2006; The CW, 2006–present) opens with the camera showing a night sky with no traces of civilization at first. A title card indicates the setting: "Lawrence, Kansas; 22 years ago." What is of special interest within the context of this collection is, of course, the temporal marker: "22 years ago." At this early point of the narrative, the viewers possess no additional knowledge of the series' temporal setting and thus very likely assume that the following events took place twenty-two years before the real-world present of the first broadcast of the show, that is, in 1973. This assumption proves true a couple of episodes later, and throughout its first five seasons.[2] *Supernatural* emphasizes that it takes place in the present—even the very present of the original broadcast. The most telling example in this context is "Lazarus Rising," the first episode of the fourth season. In the episode, Dean Winchester, one of *Supernatural*'s main characters, rises from the dead after having died at the end of the previous season. After he has freed himself from his grave in a scene that is reminiscent of numerous zombie movies—albeit taking place in bright daylight—he walks around until he finds a gas station. He takes a newspaper and realizes that it is Thursday, September 18, 2008, not coincidentally the day the episode was originally broadcast. As the episode moves along, the audience learns that Dean has been in Hell for about four months, triggering a meta-awareness on the viewers' part, since these four months are exactly the period of time that has passed between the end of season three (May 15, 2008) and the start of season four.

To return to the pilot episode, it is noteworthy that the opening of the episode establishes a structure that is continued throughout *Supernatural*; each episode starts with a brief summary of the past, before the focus of attention turns to the present. Past and present events are visually separated by title cards indicating "then" and "now."[3] These paratextual hints draw the viewers' attention to the fact that they are watching a constructed and fictional visual narrative but at the same time aid viewers' immersion into the narrative and suggest a rather clear differentiation between past and present. In the diegesis, however, the borderlines separating past and present are blurred, often resulting in a kind of "continuous present" that Gertrude Stein longed to achieve in her fiction (411).[4] In "Route 666," for example, a black ghost truck is killing African Americans and whites who supported the civil rights movement. After her daughter has been attacked by the ghost truck, Mrs. Robinson, a white woman who dated a black man back in the 1960s, informs Dean and his brother Sam that "[t]here were rumors—people of color disappearing in a truck" ("Route 666"). This sentence triggers a series of jumps between present and past. In the present, Mrs. Robinson tells the Winchesters about some crucial past happenings, and this narration is intercut by rather brief flashbacks during which the audience hears Mrs. Robinson's present narration, but sees past events. I am far from suggesting that a voice-over introducing and overlaying a flashback sequence is revolutionary—indeed; it is anything but. In fact, contemporary television programs are more likely to not, or at least much more subtly, indicate shifts in time. Still, through the combination of verbal and visual text during the voice-over, the viewers are situated in three spatiotemporal locations at the same time—the "real," physical location from which they watch the show, the diegetic present elicited by the voice-over narration, and the diegetic past elicited by the visuals. This bridging of the space-time-continuum is, of course, not a groundbreaking development, yet it is characteristic of the moving image (be that television or film)[5] and sequential art. Thus, the scene described above not only juxtaposes the present moment to the past violence that caused it, but it also conveys the idea that past violence can continue to reverberate throughout time. Indeed, the ghost of a man whose disappearance and death have been a town secret for a couple of decades haunting the present provides a textbook example of Sigmund Freud's notion of "the return of the repressed" (257).[6] Given the racial context of the episode's story, this quickly turns into the return of the repressed racialized American past.

Another episode that is intriguing for its merging of past and present in a different way is "Mystery Spot." In this *Groundhog Day*-esque episode, Sam wakes to the tune of "Heat of the Moment" by Asia, gets dressed and then, together with his brother Dean, goes to a diner to have breakfast, before Dean dies—only for Sam to wake to the tune of Asia again and relive the day and, more importantly, Dean's death time and again, finding himself stuck in a time loop. To a certain extent, the structure of the episode mirrors a video game, as Sam tries to save Dean but repeatedly fails. After going through the motions numerous times, Sam realizes that it is a trickster who is "making reality out of nothing, sticking people into time loops" ("Mystery"). Although Sam figures out this part, he believes that the trickster figure does it for the sake of "killing Dean over and over again" ("Mystery"). When Sam confronts the Trickster, it turns out that even though he has played the game for who knows how long, he has not been able to decode the central rule of the game—it is not about saving Dean, but accepting that he cannot save his older brother. Dean does not die and the next morning, Sam wakes to the tune of—fittingly—"Back in Time" by Huey Lewis and the News, and soon realizes that he has escaped the time loop. Apart from the fact that past, present, and future become one in the time loop, the episode concentrates rather obviously on destiny—in this case the death of Dean, who sold his soul to a demon in exchange for Sam's resurrection. As was already indicated earlier in the chapter, Dean does, in fact, die at the end of season three, but, as I have argued elsewhere, "for the Winchester boys, death is not an end" (Fuchs 51). Both of them have died a number of times so far, but they have not stayed down for long in any of these cases. Of course, the very fact that the Winchesters simply will not die also impacts conceptions of time, since the meaning of death as the final point in one's life, as the end, is questioned, if not taken ad absurdum.

To come back to the question of "now" and "then," it is in episodes in which memories, visions, or dreams are visually manifested and turn into objects that can be actively engaged with and even altered that the question of temporality becomes even more interesting. In "Dream a Little Dream of Me," Bobby, a father figure to the Winchesters, is in a coma in a Pittsburgh hospital. As the brothers soon discover, he is locked inside his dream world. With the help of some African dream root, Sam and Dean pull a Freddy Krueger, enter Bobby's dreams, and rescue him from his "resurrected" wife. In the end, Sam defeats the episode's villain, Jeremy, who has killed a doctor studying dreams while dreaming, in Dean's dream. In this episode, dreams are not merely visual remnants of the past or visual manifestations of wishes and desires, but malleable objects. As a result, dreams become "a means of effective present action, precisely when the body is immobilized or otherwise constrained from its normal active role" (Miller 177). This idea is taken to its extreme in "Dark Side of the Moon," in which Sam and Dean are shot and killed in the opening minutes of the episode before going on a journey to find God—that is, taking present actions while their bodies are dead and their lives supposedly past—and returning to planet Earth. On their search for God, they literally step into their memories. Interestingly, it was none other than Henri Bergson who portrayed the act of remembering as stepping into what he calls "pure memory," the accumulation of all past experience. According to Bergson, a French philosopher well known for his theories on time and consciousness, forgetting is impossible in the realm of pure memory, since forgetting does not mean losing the data stored, but rather merely forgetting how to access it (139–41). He furthermore believed that pure memory could be accessed by choice (Bergson 139–41). The depiction in *Supernatural* is different in this latter respect, because it becomes obvious rather quickly that the Winchesters do not choose what places of memory to (re)visit, as they even see moments of their respective lives that make the other brother feel bad. Thus, *Supernatural* is closer to the Proustian notion of "mémoire involontaire," formulated in his *A la Recherche du Temps Perdu*, which suggests certain stimuli can evoke recollections of the past without any conscious effort.[7]

Fig. 5.1 2010 Dean (*right*) meets 1996 Sam (*left*) in "Dark Side of the Moon"

TRAVELING THROUGH TIME AND SPACE

While one may argue that even the revisiting of past memories mentioned above constitutes instances of time traveling, television—and *Supernatural* in particular—presents further examples of time travel. In her monograph *Window Shopping: Cinema and the Postmodern*, Anne Friedberg states that

> cinema functions as a machine for virtual time travel in three ways: first, as a theatrical "set piece," set in a period in the past or in the future; second, in its capacity, through montage, to elicit an elliptical temporality; and third, in its ability to be repeated, over time, imparting to each spectator a unique montage-consciousness. (103)

Even though I am not suggesting that film theory can be simply absorbed by television studies, Friedberg's observations have some validity in the context of television: like in film, fictional television programs can take the viewers into the past, the future, or an altogether different reality; just as in film, editing influences viewers' perception of time; and finally, and which is maybe more important for television than film, there is the factor of "rewatchability," a crucial element when it comes to processes of cultification. While the televisual apparatus can serve as a virtual time-traveling device for the audience, the idea of time traveling frequently appears in contemporary television. In many ways, time-traveler narratives are most explicit in their play with time and its normally divided compartments of past, present, and future, since the deviation from linear time not only occurs on the level of discourse—to employ narratological terminology—but primarily on the level of story. Whereas the Very Young Man in H. G. Wells's *The Time Machine* dreamed of "a machine [. . .] [t]hat shall travel indifferently in any direction of Space and Time, as the driver determines," *Supernatural*'s Sam and Dean Winchester need no machines—rather; it is angels who zap them through space and time (6).

To date, there have been three episodes in which the Winchester brothers actually travel through time. In "In the Beginning," Dean is sent back to 1973 to meet his parents, who at that point in time are about five years younger than their son returning from the future. After having arrived in the unknown past, Dean is determined to keep his mother from making a decision that will change her life and the lives of those that she loves for good, even if that may jeopardize his present life and undo all his good deeds. Apart from the fact that the idea of changing the past to change the present (or future) for good relies on a paradoxical assumption—if Dean were to change the past and thus the present, he would live a different life, and thus (unless one takes a quantum-theoretical approach to the problem) his present persona would not return to 1973 to change his family's fate—*Supernatural* puts strong emphasis on destiny, continually underlining that Sam's and Dean's lives are part of the divine plan. Thus, it is not highly surprising that while Dean succeeds in changing the past a little, the bigger picture, and as a result the present, remains unchanged. Similarly, in "The Song Remains the Same," the angel Anna goes back in time to 1978 to kill the Winchesters' parents before Sam is born, and the brothers are sent after her to keep her from doing so. When thinking about how to approach their parents, who in this past are younger than their children, the following dialogue ensues:

DEAN: What exactly are we gonna march up there and tell 'em?
SAM: Uhm. The truth?
DEAN: What? That their sons are back from the future to save them from an angel gone terminator? Oh, come on, those movies haven't even come out yet!" ("The Song")

While the wallowing in intertextual references in this brief scene could be interpreted along the lines of questions of temporality, with the weight of past popular culture artifacts impacting present ones such as *Supernatural*, Dean raises a good point: how can Sam and Dean explain that they are visitors from the future? This question turns even a little trickier when Mary, their mother, recognizes Dean as a hunter whom she met in 1973 the day her parents

Fig. 5.2 Dean Meets His Future (and his past) in "The End"

died. Like in "In the Beginning," nothing really changes. However, this time around, Sam and Dean need the helping hand of the walking and talking deus ex machina Michael (the archangel), who not only destroys Anna and clears the Winchester parents' minds of the events that have just taken place, but also informs Dean that his and Sam's bloodlines go back to Cain and Abel, already hinting at Dean's destiny. Toward the end of the dialogue, Dean's fate is then more explicitly addressed when Michael says: "Think of the million little choices that you make and how each and every one of them brings you closer to your destiny. . . . It's a plan that has played itself out perfectly. Free will is an illusion, Dean" ("The Song").

In contrast to the travels to the past in the two episodes just discussed, "The End" shows Dean arriving five years in the future. He finds a post-apocalyptic scenario in which a virus has spread over the entire planet, turning human beings into zombie-like creatures hungering for human flesh. He learns that Lucifer (the fallen angel) has taken Sam's body, and Dean's future self begs him to give his body to Michael to fight Lucifer. A little later, Dean witnesses how Lucifer—in Sam's body—kills his future self. Lucifer refuses to kill the time-traveling Dean, telling him that "[w]hatever you do, you will always end up here. Whatever choices you make, whatever details you alter, we will always end up here" ("The End"). While the angels believe that this travel to the future has changed Dean's mind and he has accepted his destiny, that is, to give his body to Michael, Dean thinks different, telling the angel Zachariah that he "learned a lesson alright, just not the one you wanted to teach" ("The

End"). What Dean learned is that by following his current path, on which he and Sam have separated, he will not be seeing Sam again until 2014. Thus, he decides to join forces with Sam again instead of giving in to the Divine Plan. Or, to put it more generally, "the time traveler . . . achieve[s] an insight . . . not available to him or her before risking the encounter with the other in time" (Miller 176).

Despite the repeated emphasis that all of Sam's and Dean's lives are part of the Divine Plan, slated to become tools in a fight between Michael and his younger brother Lucifer, the final battle between the two of them does not end as planned. Sam succeeds in locking up both Lucifer and Michael in an infernal cage. Free will is not an illusion. Moreover, in the same way that the departure from the standard notion that death equals the end has implications for the conceptualization of time, so does the fact that the Divine Plan's end—which would have resolved all problems—has been altered. Michael and Lucifer were not allowed to square off on the battlefield, thereby delaying the end, the temporal marker that seemed so fixed in time.[8]

"TIME IS FLUID"

As has been shown above, *Supernatural* employs various deviations from chronological time, many of which I can only mention in passing. In addition to those discussed above, there are several episodes opening with the episode's climactic moment before showing how that very situation came about; the episode "Tall Tales" employs the structure of a frame narrative; "It's a Terrible Life" takes place in an alternate reality, a different space-time-continuum, in which Sam and Dean do not know each other; "What Is and What Should Never Be" also depicts an alternate reality, but one entirely constructed inside of Dean's mind; "Changing Channels" metaleptically sends the Winchesters through a series of realities of intradiegetic TV shows, effortlessly hopping through spaces and times; and "Monster at the End of This Book" introduces a meta-textual twist that suggests that the Winchesters' lives are reenactments of the events unfolding in the pulp novel series *Supernatural* (of course), written by a prophet named Chuck, who has visions about the brothers' lives, thus adding a second spatiotemporal universe—the one in the pulp novels—to the first five seasons of the series.

What all of these re-configurations of linear time have in common is that through these departures from linear storytelling, *Supernatural* "call[s] attention to the constructed nature of the narration" (Mittell 35). Additionally, nonlinearity highlights that past, present, and future "are categories of historical consciousness which are constructed at the level of the apprehension of history as a whole. More specifically, they are categories of historical totalization in the medium of cultural experience" (Osborne ix). In other words, not only is the narrative the audience is watching a cultural construct, but so are the notions of linear time that the show critiques. Indeed, following Vivian Sobchack one can argue that while in former times there used to be a differentiation between subjective and objective time, this differentiation has largely faded today: "Temporality is now constituted and lived paradoxically as a *homogeneous experience of discontinuitiy*" (156, emphasis in original). By underscoring differences from chronological time, the traditional—dare I say "naturalized"—concept of chronological time is made visible and turned into an object of intellectual inquiry. As one of Alan Lightman's propositions regarding alternate realms of time reads:

> In this world, time is a visible dimension. Just as one may look off in the distance and see houses, trees, mountain peaks that are landmarks in space, so one may look out in another direction and see births, marriages, deaths that are signposts in time, stretching off dimly into the far future. And just as one may choose whether to stay in one place or run to another, so one may choose his motion along the axis of time. Some people fear traveling far from a comfortable moment. They remain close to one temporal location, barely crawling past a familiar occasion. Others gallop recklessly into the future, without preparation for the rapid sequence of passing events. (133–34)

It is the notion of the connection between time and space that comes to the fore in the quote above that I want to close this chapter with. While the collection at hand emphasizes temporal concerns, it is at least since Mikhail Bakhtin's idea of the chronotope gained acceptance in Western humanities back in the 1980s that there has been a tendency to regard time and space as intrinsically linked. Andreas Huyssen has since argued that "to separate time and space [would be] at great peril to a full understanding of . . . postmodern culture. As fundamentally contingent categories of historically rooted perception, time and space are always bound up with each other in complex ways" (12). Indeed, if "time is fluid," as the angel Castiel tells Dean Winchester in the episode "In the Beginning," then space must be just as malleable. And if we learn our lessons from *Supernatural*—a fictional TV series about angels, demons, vampires, werewolves, of all things—then both space and time are pliable.

SUGGESTED EPISODES FOR ADDITIONAL STUDY

Supernatural

1:1. "Pilot." [a.k.a. "The Woman in White"]. Writ. Eric Kripke. Dir. David Nutter. September 13, 2005.
1:9. "Home." Writ. Eric Kripke. Dir. Ken Girotti. November 15, 2005.
1:17. "Hell House." Writ. Tray Callaway. Dir. Chris Long. March 30, 2006.
1:20. "Dead Man's Blood." Writ. Cathryn Humphris and John Shiban. Dir. Tony Wharmby. April 20, 2006.
1:21. "Salvation." Writ. Sera Gamble and Raelle Tucker. Dir. Robert Singer. April 27, 2006.
1:22. "Devil's Trap." Writ. Eric Kripke. Dir. Kim Manners. May 4, 2006.
2:1. "In My Time of Dying." Writ. Brad Buckner, Eric Kripke, and Eugenie Ross-Leming. Dir. Kim Manners. September 28, 2006.
2:9. "Croatoan." Writ. John Shiban. Dir. Robert Singer. December 7, 2006.
2:18. "Hollywood Babylon." Writ. Ben Edlund. Dir. Philip Sgriccia. April 19, 2007.
3:8. "A Very Supernatural Christmas." Writ. Jeremy Carver. Dir. J. Miller Tobin. December 13, 2007.
3:13. "Ghostfacers." Writ. Ben Edlund. Dir. Philip Sgriccia. April 24, 2008.
4:5. "Monster Movie." Writ. Ben Edlund. Dir. Robert Singer. October 16, 2008.
4:9. "I Know What You Did Last Summer." Writ. Sera Gamble. Dir. Charles Beeson. November 13, 2008.
4:10. "Heaven and Hell." Writ. Eric Kripke. Dir. J. Miller Tobin. November 20, 2008.
4:13. "After School Special." Writ. Daniel Loflin and Andrew Dabb. Dir. Adam Kane. January 29, 2009.
4:20. "The Rapture." Writ. Jeremey Carver. Dir. Charles Beeson. April 30, 2009.
4:22. "Lucifer Rising." Writ. and Dir. Eric Kripke. May 14, 2009.
5:1. "Sympathy for the Devil." Writ. Eric Kripke. Dir. Robert Singer. September 10, 2009.
5:9. "The Real Ghostbusters." Writ. Eric Kripke and Nancy Weiner. Dir. James L. Conway. November 12, 2009.
5:19. "Hammer of the Gods." Writ. Andrew Dabb, Daniel Loflin, and David Reed. Dir. Rick Bota. April 22, 2010.
5:21. "Two Minutes to Midnight." Writ. Sera Gamble. Dir. Phil Sgriccia. May 6, 2010.

5:22. "Swan Song." Writ. Eric Gerwitz and Eric Kripke. Dir. Steve Boyum. May 13, 2010.

6:4. "Weekend at Bobby's." Writ. Andrew Dabb and Daniel Loflin. Dir. Jensen Ackles. October 15, 2010.

6:5. "Live Free or Twihard." Writ. Brett Matthews. Dir. Rod Hardy. October 22, 2010.

6:15. "The French Mistake." Writ. Ben Edlund. Dir. Charles Beeson. February 25, 2011.

6:17. "My Heart Will Go On." Writ. Eric Charmelo & Nicole Snyder. Dir. Philip Sgriccia. April 15, 2011.

6:18. "Frontierland." Writ. Andrew Dabb, Daniel Loflin, and Jackson Stewart. Dir. Guy Norman Bee. April 22, 2011.

6:20. "The Man Who Would Be King." Writ. and Dir. Ben Edlund. May 6, 2011.

6:21. "Let It Bleed." Writ. Sera Gamble. Dir. John Showalter. May 20, 2011.

NOTES

1. My translation of "Das wahre Bild der Vergangenheit huscht vorbei. Nur als Bild, das auf Nimmerwiedersehen im Augenblick seiner Erkennbarkeit eben aufblitzt, ist die Vergangenheit festzuhalten."

2. Season six, which started on September 24, 2010, takes place about a year after the events closing the previous season, and is thus set about one year in the future.

3. In the first season, a voice-over usually introduces the past events with the line "previously on *Supernatural*," before an insert indicating the spatial setting takes us to the present events. Furthermore, there are some episodes without the "then" and "now" title cards; there are episodes that open with a title card that reads "The road so far" (mainly the season finales and premieres, but there are some others, too), and there are a few episodes that feature a foreshadowing "soon" sequence at the very end. Due to *Supernatural*'s high degree of self-consciousness and the games that the writers play with the viewers, one might expect these teasers to not happen diegetically, but—unlike, e.g., *Arrested Development* (Fox, 2003–2006)—the depicted events do happen in the story world, even if the teasers, of course, withhold vital information.

4. Ulla E. Dydo has pointed out that since "Stein offers few theoretical terms to her often bewildered readers, they cling to the two words ['continuous present' and 'prolonged present'], hoping for distinctions that may not have been clear to Stein herself" (93). Liesl M. Olson has outlined the concept of the continuous present as follows: "In 'Composition as Explanation,' Stein coins the phrase 'continuous present' . . . to describe her . . . attempt to escape chronological narrative . . . . The 'continuous present' might be understood as resisting moments of temporal stasis, or what Stein called the 'prolonged present'" (356). For a recent discussion of the concept, see Katz (2010).

5. I am tempted to add video games to this list. However, there is an emerging scholarly debate as to whether video games can be regarded as moving images. For a discussion, see Meskin and Robson (forthcoming).

6. "Wiederkehr des Verdrängten" in the original. Freud suggested that memories and feelings that are hidden away (repressed) have a tendency to resurface (return) in a different form, usually in dreams or manifested through psychological symptoms.

7. The first chapter of William Faulkner's *The Sound and the Fury* is structured according to the same principles.

8. As most people reading this chapter will probably know, Eric Kripke had planned to bring the series to a close with the end of season five, yet The CW contracted the series for another year. Thus, the story of the extra-compositional Author-God does not pan out, just like the story of the diegetic God.

WORKS CITED

Benjamin, Walter. "Über den Begriff der Geschichte." 1939. *Gesammelte Schriften I*. Vol. 2. Frankfurt/Main: Suhrkamp, 1974. 691–704. Print.

Bergson, Henri. *Matière et Mémoire: Essai sur la Relation du Corps à l'Esprit*. Paris: PUF, 1939. Print.

"Changing Channels." *Supernatural: The Complete Fifth Season*. Writ. Jeremy Carver. Dir. Charles Beeson. Warner Home Video, 2010. Blu-Ray.

"Dark Side of the Moon." *Supernatural: The Complete Fifth Season*. Writ. Andrew Dabb and Daniel Loflin. Dir. Jeff Woolnough. Warner Home Video, 2010. Blu-Ray.

"Dream a Little Dream of Me." *Supernatural: The Complete Third Season*. Writ. Sera Gamble and Cathryn Humphris. Dir. Steve Boyum. Warner Home Video, 2009. Blu-Ray.

Dydo, Ulla E. *Gertrude Stein: The Language That Rises, 1923–1934*. Evanston, IL: Northwestern University Press, 2003. Print.

Eckhard, Petra, and Walter W. Hölbling. "Postmodern Chronotopoetics: An Introduction." *Landscapes of Postmodernity*. Ed. Petra Eckhard, Michael Fuchs, and Walter W. Hölbling. Vienna: LIT, 2010. 93–97. Print.

"The End." *Supernatural: The Complete Fifth Season*. Writ. Ben Edlund. Dir. Steve Boyum. Warner Home Video, 2010. Blu-Ray.

Faulkner, William. *The Sound and the Fury*. 1929. Franklin, PA: Franklin Library, 1979. Print.

Freud, Sigmund. "Die Verdrängung." 1915. *Gesammelte Werke*. Vol. X. Frankfurt/Main: Fischer, 1999. 248–61. Print.

Friedberg, Anne. *Window Shopping: Cinema and the Postmodern*. Berkeley and Los Angeles: University of California Press, 1993. Print.

Fuchs, Michael. "Trapped in TV Land: Encountering the Hyperreal in *Supernatural*." *Simulation in Media and Culture: Believing the Hype*. Ed. Robin DeRosa. Lanham, MD: Lexington, 2011. 47–55. Print.

Huyssen, Andreas. *Present Pasts: Urban Palimpsests and the Politics of Memory*. Stanford, CA: Stanford University Press, 2003. Print.

"In the Beginning." *Supernatural: The Complete Fourth Season*. Writ. Jeremy Carver. Dir. Steve Boyum. Warner Home Video, 2009. Blu-Ray.

"It's a Terrible Life." *Supernatural: The Complete Fourth Season*. Writ. Sera Gamble. Dir. James L. Conway. Warner Home Video, 2009. Blu-Ray.

Jameson, Fredric. "Postmodernism and Consumer Society." *Postmodern Culture*. Ed. Hal Foster. London: Pluto, 1985. 111–25. Print.

Katz, Adam. "From Habit to Maxim: Eccentric Models of Reality and Presence in the Writing of Gertrude Stein." *Anthropoetics* 15.2 (2010): n. pag. Web. February 25, 2011.

"Lazarus Rising." *Supernatural: The Complete Fourth Season*. Writ. Eric Kripke. Dir. Kim Manners. Warner Home Video, 2009. Blu-Ray.

Lightman, Alan. *Einstein's Dreams*. New York: Warner, 1993. Print.

Meskin, Aaron, and Jon Robson. "Videogames and the Moving Image." *Revue Internationale de Philosophie*. N.d. n. pag.

Miller, Tyrus. *Time-Images: Alternative Temporalities in Twentieth-Century Theory, Literature, and Art*. Newcastle: Cambridge Scholars, 2009. Print.

Mittell, Jason. "Narrative Complexity in Contemporary American Television." *The Velvet Light Trap* 58 (2006): 29–40. Print.

"The Monster at the End of This Book." *Supernatural: The Complete Fourth Season*. Writ. Julie Siege. Dir. Mike Rohl. Warner Home Video, 2009. Blu-Ray.

"Mystery Spot." *Supernatural: The Complete Third Season*. Writ. Jeremy Carver and Emily McLaughlin. Dir. Kim Manners. Warner Home Video, 2009. Blu-Ray.

Olson, Liesl M. "Gertrude Stein, William James, and Habit in the Shadow of War." *Twentieth-Century Literature* 49.3 (2003): 328–59. Print.

Osborne, Peter. *The Politics of Time: Modernity and Avant-Garde*. London: Verso, 1995. Print.

"Pilot." *Supernatural: The Complete First Season*. Writ. Eric Kripke. Dir. David Nutter. Warner Home Video, 2010. Blu-Ray.

Proust, Marcel. *A la Recherche du Temps Perdu*. 1913–1927. Paris: Gallimard, 2002. Print.

"Route 666." *Supernatural: The Complete First Season*. Writ. Eugenie Ross-Leming and Brad Buckner. Dir. Paul Shapiro. Warner Home Video, 2010. Blu-Ray.

Sobchack, Vivian. "The Scene of the Screen: Envisioning Photographic, Cinematic, and Electronic 'Presence.'" *Carnal Thoughts: Embodiment and Moving Image Culture*. Berkeley and Los Angeles: University of California Press, 2004. 135–62. Print.

"The Song Remains the Same." *Supernatural: The Complete Fifth Season*. Writ. Sera Gamble and Nancy Weiner. Dir. Steve Boyum. Warner Home Video, 2010. Blu-Ray.

Stein, Gertrude. "Composition as Explanation." 1926. *Modernism: An Anthology*. Ed. Lawrence S. Rainey. Malden, MA: Blackwell, 2005. 407–12. Print.

"Tall Tales." *Supernatural: The Complete Second Season*. Writ. John Shiban. Dir. Bradford May. Warner Home Video, 2010. Blu-Ray.

Wells, Herbert George. *The Time Machine*. 1895. London: Heinemann, 1965. Print.

"What Is and What Should Never Be." *Supernatural: The Complete Second Season*. Writ. Raelle Tucker. Dir. Eric Kripke. Warner Home Video, 2010. Blu-Ray.

PART II

HISTORICIZING THE MOMENT
How the Cultural Climate Impacts Temporal Manipulation on the Small Screen

6

TEMPORALITY AND TRAUMA IN AMERICAN SCI-FI TELEVISION

ARIS MOUSOUTZANIS

The last decade has witnessed the emergence of a number of American sci-fi TV shows that have demonstrated an increasing experimentation with temporality, such as *Lost, Flashforward, Alias, 24, Fringe*, and *The Sarah Connor Chronicles*, among others. This chapter will approach the complex temporal structure of these shows by focusing on the fact that they often concentrate on a major event that structures their entire narrative. Nonlinear temporality may then be seen as related to a preoccupation with the topic of psychological trauma, which has been receiving increasing attention during the last fifty years in diverse disciplines and media representations to the extent that has led scholars such as E. Ann Kaplan to argue for the emergence of a "trauma culture" or even to what Roger Luckhurst refers to as a "trauma paradigm." As a psychopathology that constantly returns patients to the incident they experienced, which they relive in nightmares or hallucinations, trauma is characterized by a temporal structure that is nonlinear and repetitive, and fictions of trauma often attempt to convey that aspect of the disease by experimenting with narrative structure.

The emergence of a subgenre of "trauma sci-fi," however, should not be seen merely as a response to contemporary social issues and political crises. In this chapter, I will be arguing that trauma sci-fi television should be seen as a very self-conscious, "metatextual" television genre that reflects on certain aspects of the nature, function, and history of the medium of television itself. The fact that often the major event within these programs involves a technological accident or breakdown only highlights further such an approach. More specifically, these shows illustrate three aspects of the relationship between television, temporality, and trauma: first, the structural equivalences between trauma and the new media, whose ability to challenge conventional perceptions of time and space has been seen as similar to the structure of traumatic temporality; second, the history of the medium of television itself, which is often theorized in terms conceptually similar to that of trauma, such as "discontinuity," "rupture," and "conflict" between older and new media; and third, the fact that television serves by now as the major site where collective tragedy and historical trauma are witnessed, experienced, or even registered as traumatic in the first place.

CULT TELEVISION AND TRAUMA CULTURE

Originally theorized during a period ranging roughly from the 1860s to the 1930s, the psychopathology of traumatic neurosis was largely ignored by official psychiatric circles until they started receiving pressure by activist groups within the climate of the late 1960s, such as feminists and Vietnam veterans, who were urging for further attention to issues such as sexual harassment and combat neurosis, respectively. Research on the subject that took place as a response to these campaigns eventually led to the inclusion of the term "posttraumatic stress disorder" (PTSD) in the *American Diagnostic and Statistical Manual for Mental Disorders* in 1980, which led to a series of fierce debates among members of psychiatric communities on the nature of traumatic memory in the 1990s, now called the "Memory Wars."[1] These debates were taking place at the same time with a growing preoccupation in the humanities with the question of representation of atrocious historical events such as the Holocaust, which led to the emergence of "trauma theory." Contemporary media were both responding to and participating in this widening interest in trauma, as may be seen in the increasing popularity of TV genres such as the talk show, the real-life police show, and court television. This trend was also emerging at the same time with an increasing fascination with images of violence and destruction from the late 1970s onward, in film genres such as the horror movie or the sci-fi blockbuster, which were also followed by recurrent debates on Internet pornography, pedophilia, and the violence in the media. By the late 1990s, trauma seemed to be, according to Kirby Farrell, "both a clinical syndrome and a trope . . . a strategic fiction that a complex, stressful society is using to account for a world that seems threateningly out of control" (2).

The emerging media culture of trauma, however, did not restrict itself to the above genres and debates. Trauma has actually acquired a central place in a significant number of cult TV shows at the level of plot and narrative structure. The embeddedness of these shows in trauma culture becomes evident when bearing in mind that the same cultural moment that witnessed the Memory Wars and the emergence of trauma studies was also the period of the original broadcasting of a television show that was highly influential to later cult TV series, David Lynch's *Twin Peaks* (ABC, 1990–1991). Lynch's show, set in the small fictional Washington town of Twin Peaks, followed the investigation of the murder of homecoming queen Laura Palmer while presenting the ways in which the investigation gradually revealed a dark underworld of crime, prostitution, drug trafficking, and domestic abuse lurking beneath the surface of an idyllic small-town community. As with the rest of Lynch's work, the show lends itself to psychoanalytic readings, specifically from the perspective of the theories of Jacques Lacan. In a world where human subjects are immersed in a universe of signifiers (what Lacan terms the Symbolic register), perceptions of everyday "reality" are nothing but "a fragile, symbolic cobweb" which, however, "can at any moment be torn aside by an intrusion of the real" (Žižek, *Looking* 17). The register of the Real, however, should not be mistaken for "reality," but rather refers to the overwhelming, the unrepresentable, whatever cannot be integrated in the Symbolic and yet always emerges "in the form of that which is *unassimilable* in it—in the form of the trauma, determining all that follows, and imposing on it an apparently accidental origin" (Lacan 55, emphasis in original). In presenting the ways in which Laura's death disrupted the harmonious life of Twin Peaks, the show faithfully followed the dictates of "Lynch's 'ontology,'" according to which, for Slavoj Žižek, "the universe is a palpitating slime that continually threatens to blow up the settled frame of everyday reality" ("Grimaces" 59).

Twin Peaks, however, was a narrative whose temporal structure was, to a large extent, conventionally linear. Nevertheless, Lynch's decision to work on a television series came out of his interest "in the way in which a television serial could at once slow down and open out narrative time compared to the confines of film" (Luckhurst 199). The show's final episode refused to provide closure to most of the storylines and left the main character, FBI agent Dale Cooper, trapped in the timeless realm of the Red Room. Cooper was also found to be trapped there already in the prequel film, *Fire Walk with Me* (1992), to welcome Laura's spirit there after her death, even if in the real world he had not yet arrived to Twin Peaks. "The series must end, with Cooper trapped, in order for Laura to be killed in the film and for the story to start all over again in a hellish loop" according to a "cyclical logic" that "suspends any narrative drive" (Luckhurst 202).

The focus on a major event around which the entire narrative circulates was a defining feature of the next important series in the history of cult television, Chris Cater's *The X-Files* (Fox, 1993–2002). FBI agent Mulder's investigations of alien abductions and government conspiracies were propelled by his witnessing of his sister's alleged abduction by extraterrestrials when he was a child, an incident that the show persistently restaged over the years in numerous flashback scenes shot in different directing styles, each time adding new details to the scene or removing earlier ones. Narrative repetition, in these cases, may be seen as following the rhythms of traumatic temporality: one common post-traumatic symptom is the constant reenactment of the traumatic incident in patients' nightmares or hallucinations. Sigmund Freud termed this symptom the "repetition compulsion" to refer to "a clear indication [of a] fixation to the moment of the traumatic accident" whereby the patients "have not finished with the traumatic situation" but "were still faced by it as an immediate task which had not been dealt with" ("Fixation" 274, 275). Repetition is therefore part of an effort to assimilate and master an incident originally too overwhelming to register in the psyche.

The most common narrative device to convey that aspect of the disease is, as in the case of *The X-Files*, that of the "intrusive flashback trope," which is often used as "a way of signaling and exploring the return of trauma" (Turim 207). The most representative show in this context would be J. J. Abrams's *Lost* (ABC, 2004–2010), which experimented with narrative temporality even further in ways that invite a reading from the perspective of trauma theory.[2] Trauma was one of the major themes of the show in its early stages, often discussed directly by various characters as they were trying to cope with the experience of having survived a plane crash. Furthermore, the show was compulsively returning to "the scene of the accident" either by including scenes taking place before or during the plane crash in individual flashbacks or by staging other technological accidents on or off the island. The character flashbacks themselves can easily be read from this perspective, as most of the backstories dealt with stories of loss, mourning, and guilt that the characters had to deal with on the island in order to overcome the past. Furthermore, in later seasons the show engaged with trauma in more sophisticated ways that affected the organization of its temporal structure in its introduction of "flashforwards." The intrusive flashback is generally employed to convey the second important aspect of trauma often discussed for its implications for temporality, termed by Freud as *Nachträglichkeit* (translated as "belatedness" or "deferred action"): individuals who experience a traumatic event often appear unaffected by the incident and only develop symptoms after a period of "latency," usually lasting a few weeks, when they are exposed to a second situation that triggers memories of the earlier event. But whereas conventional attempts to convey traumatic belatedness within narrative resort to the flashback in order to signal "the return of the repressed," at the same time, these attempts miss a major implication of belatedness, the reversal of ordinary causality: the trauma is experienced only when it is remembered, in the future, in a temporal structure that reverses the relationship between cause and effect. As Ned Lukacher explains,

Deferred action demands that one recognize that while the earlier event is still to some extent the cause of the later event, the earlier event is nevertheless also the effect of the later event. One is forced to admit a double or "metaleptic" logic in which causes are both causes of effects and the effects of effects. (35)

From this perspective, the "flashforwards" of *Lost* may be seen as a literal narrativization of this implication of traumatic belatedness for temporality. This reading is encouraged by the fact that the show introduced scenes from the future by focusing on the character of Desmond Hume, who developed a precog ability as a result of his exposure to electromagnetism after an industrial accident. This narrative gesture further associates nonlinear temporality with technologically induced trauma.

These are only three major television shows whose engagement with trauma has affected the organization of their temporal structure, and they have been largely influential to other series. Essentially a linear narrative with occasional flashbacks, *The 4400* (CBS, 2004–2007) was nevertheless a show that adopted the theme of abduction to follow the ways in which 4,400 individuals from different times and places across the globe were dealing with "a life interrupted"—to use the phrase featuring in the show's opening titles—after having been abducted and returned to present-day Seattle with supernatural abilities. *The Sarah Connor Chronicles* (WB, 2008–2009), another program with nonlinear features, expanded on the mythology of the *Terminator* franchise precisely by focusing on trauma as one of its major themes as, particularly during season two, several different characters were trying to cope with their experiences of murder, death, torture, and survival. Episodes focusing on the two major characters who traveled back from the future to the present, Kyle Reese and the female Terminator Cameron, included "future flashbacks"—memories from their own past while living still in the future—that were presenting the traumatic impact of being tortured by cyborgs or even transformed into a cyborg, respectively. The flashforward became the central tenet of Brannon Braga and David S. Goyer's *Flashforward* (ABC, 2009–2010), which was following the ways in which different individuals' lives were affected by a "blackout" experienced around the world on October 6, 2009, for two minutes and seventeen seconds during which everyone experienced visions of their lives on April 29, 2010. This show not only followed a nonlinear structure but was also very focused on the relationship between the internal time of narrative progression and the external time of scheduling and broadcasting. NBC's recent short-lived series *The Event* (2010–2011) originally followed this trend, as its first few episodes were progressing in a nonlinear sequence of scenes, all of them revolving around a major incident: the disruption of a press conference with the U.S. president by an airplane which is just about to crash to the conference when it suddenly disappears into a vortex in midair. The choice of the show's writers to introduce a new show in this manner only highlights further the appeal and popularity of the trend of "trauma sci-fi."

TELEVISION HISTORY, NEW MEDIA, AND TRAUMA

An exclusively historicist interpretation of these shows would read this increasing interest in trauma against contemporary social concerns and political crises, such as domestic violence and sexual abuse in the case of *Twin Peaks*, post–Cold War anxieties on the political integrity of U.S. governments in *The X-Files*, or discourses of globalization, which is increasing theorized in terms of disaster, shock, and crisis, in *Lost*.[3] Such an approach, however, would not explain why the engagement with trauma affects the organization of temporality. This aspect may be interpreted instead through an approach that sees these shows not only as symptomatic of contemporary socio-political concerns, but also as self-reflective of the history of television itself, which is often theorized in terms conceptually similar to that of trauma, such as "rupture," "heterogeneity," and "conflict" between the medium of television and older or newer forms of media. Such an approach would interpret nonlinear narratives both in terms of their preoccupation with trauma and as a result of novel ways of producing and consuming programming by new digital media technologies. An approach that pays a combined attention to textual analysis and technological and industrial transformation therefore allows one to perceive the relations between television and trauma in both conceptual and historical terms.

The periodization of television history by Jimmie Reeves, Mark Rodgers, and Michael Epstein is particularly useful, whereby they distinguish between the era of TV I (1948–1975), associated with the "network era" or "broadcast era," TV II (1975–1995), the "cable era," and TV III (1991–present), the "digital era," if only because major shows in the tradition of trauma sci-fi have an important place for each period: *Twin Peaks* marks a turning point from TV I and TV II; *The X-Files* is one of the most representative texts of TV II, even as it signals the shift to TV III, whereas *Lost* may be seen as a show paradigmatic of the era of TV III. The chapters in the first section of this collection address the impact of technological development on nonlinear narrative in detail, which is why this discussion will highlight only the extent to which the historical development of television across the three eras is marked by processes and theorized in terms such as "discontinuity," "disjuncture," or "rupture" between the medium itself and older or new media: radio, in the case of TV I; the video cassette recorder, the remote control, and the personal computer, in the case of TV II; the Internet, mobile technologies, and digital media in the case of TV III. Operating on Fordist principles of mass production, most shows produced during the era of TV I belonged to genres such as the soap opera, the situation comedy, and the crime show, interrupted by thirty-second advertisements that provided the dominant form of economic support for the networks. Narrative interruption was therefore integral to the medium since its inception not only because of the inclusion of commercials but also because genres such as the soap opera deny closure by definition for the perpetuation of their narrative in an "unstable, reversible, and circular movement" that, according to Sandy Flitterman-Lewis, "embeds interruption into the very heart of the discursive structure" (222). The advent of the video recorder and the personal computer during the TV II era disrupted established linear conceptions of televisual temporality even further. Back in the mid-1980s, the journalist Tom Shales described television in an *Esquire* article as "the national time machine" and the VCR as popularizing "a new form of exercise called time shift" (68, 67). The contemporary appeal of replays, remakes, and time-travel films during this time was due to the fact that "[w]e are not amazed at the thought of time-travel because we do it every day . . . Television, where it's always now, is almost always some other time as well" (Shales 67). For Shales, the "phrase that almost sums the Eighties up" (67) was *Back to the Future*, a film exemplary of the arguments pursued in this chapter: the main character Martin McFly travels back to the 1950s and "saves his father from the traumatic bullying that would otherwise make him the emasculated, harried patriarch of the 1980s" (Farrell 370). The film features the same scene repeated in both timeframes, where Marty's family watches an episode of *The Honeymooners*: "These characters seem subjected to a sort of repetition compulsion, doomed to neurotic closed loops until Marty intervenes to rewrite the script" (Gordon 374). Robert Zemeckis's film is thus representative of the connections between television, temporality, and trauma discussed in this chapter, even as it joins a list of popular fictions associating time travel, technology, and trauma, of which series like *Lost* is only one of the most recent examples.

Lost, however, is a show iconic of the era of TV III, during which new media technologies and practices such as the Internet, mobile phones, online streaming, and downloading has brought about a diffusion and mobilization of the television experience that has challenged established perceptions of time in ways that parallel the structure of traumatic temporality. Jason Mittell has demonstrated the ways in which the production of increasingly complex television narratives is a result of the emergence of new media and changes in the industry, such as the decrease of broadcast network audiences with the dominance of cable and satellite, and new technologies and methods of recording and playback such as DVRs, downloading, and online streaming. More generally, Andreas Huyssen had diagnosed a contemporary "crisis of temporality" precisely as a result of "the interface of technological change, mass media, and new patterns of consumption, work, and global mobility" (21). This "crisis," however, is largely marked by the advent of the new media, whose temporal structures operate in ways that correspond to both major aspects of traumatic temporality outlined above. Compulsive repetition has been seen as an integral aspect of "postmodern media." Theorists such as Jean Baudrillard have suggested that the endless proliferation of images and signs has generated a depthless universe of simulation where everything is reproducible ad infinitum. Traumatic belatedness, too, may be seen as an integral aspect of the "media image," which, for Allen Meek, "is always both displaced in relation to the event it records *and* its literal trace" (13). The nonlinear structure of these shows may therefore be seen as reflecting these structural analogies between traumatic temporality and the temporality of television in the age of the new media.

However, there is a last way in which these shows may be seen as self-referential of the medium of television. This final explanation, which I turn to in the last section of this chapter, relates to the very question of mediation, representation, and broadcasting of trauma in the era of TV III.

TRAUMA TELEVISION / TELEVISING TRAUMA

Trauma is essentially about mediation—or the lack of it. In *Beyond the Pleasure Principle*, Freud invoked a metaphor of the human psyche as an amoeba-like organism coated with a "protective shielding" that is pierced by an overwhelming incident: trauma is therefore "a situation in which the outside goes inside *without mediation*" (Matus 423, emphasis added). In early-twenty-first-century Western industrialist societies saturated with mediated images and signs, "trauma increasingly serves as a model for deep memory in a mass mediated culture" (Meek 9). Trauma is then the Real that disrupts the Symbolic cobweb of mediated representations, or what counts as "authentic" in the Baudrillardian universe of simulation. As Allen Meek explains, "it is as if the idea of trauma has assumed a place that is somehow commensurate with the proliferation of visual media in our lives" (7). Accordingly, the nonlinear, traumatic temporality of these shows should be seen as self-reflective not only of structural or historical relations between television and trauma but also of the very nature of representation of disaster and crisis in the medium in the era of TV III. The proliferation of scenes of plane crashes in shows like *Lost*, *The Event*, and *Fringe* might be read as a symptom of the aftermath of 9/11 when "our gaze was transfixed by the images of the plane hitting one of the WTC towers" and "we were all forced to experience . . . the 'compulsion to repeat' . . . we wanted to see it again and again; the same shots were repeated *ad nauseam*" (Žižek, *Welcome* 11–12). As the biggest media event, 9/11 stood as exemplary of the ways in which crisis is broadcast in terms of "a disarray of competing and contradictory accounts" and "obsessive repetition of the same" that is "only gradually corralled into a meaningful, strongly shaped media story, slowly edited back into conformity with News discourse as the initial crisis recedes" (Luckhurst 79). The genre of the media event offers, for Mary Anne Doane, "evidence of television's compulsion to repeat" and is thus highly representative of a medium that "organizes itself around the event" (231, 223). "The major category of television is time," according to Doane, insofar as it "deals not with the weight of the dead past but with the potential trauma and explosiveness of the present" (222). It is in this sense that, for her, "television is a kind of catastrophe machine, continually corroborating its own signifying problematic—a problematic of discontinuity and indeterminacy which strives to mimic the experience of the real, a real which in its turn is guaranteed by the contact with death" (Doane 234).

The recent shift of focus in the genre of media events is further indicative of this dialectic between television and trauma. Whereas, in 1992, Daniel Dayan and Elihu Katz were classifying media events in terms of ceremonies, contests, and conquests, by 2007 Katz and Tamar Liebes were arguing that the focus has now shifted to disaster, terror, and war, not necessarily because there has been an increase in the occurrence of these events, but because the proliferation of media technologies make these events more visible at a global scale. Contemporary catastrophes are therefore extraordinary because of what Hayden White has called a "revolution in representational practices . . . and the technologies of representation made possible by the electronic revolution. . . . Modern electronic media 'explode' events before the eyes of viewers" (23). There is a sense in which contemporary media, and television in specific, "do not just mirror those experiences; in their courting and staging of violence they are themselves the breeding ground of trauma" (Kaplan and Wang 17). The preoccupation with trauma in this set of television shows discussed above must therefore be seen as symptomatic of a cultural moment where disaster and crisis is witnessed, experienced, even registered as traumatic in the first place primarily through television.

It may be seen as quite ironic that, even if they have relied on any possible resource provided by new technologies for the production and consumption of their narrative, many of these shows are quite technophobic, and not only for the compulsive restaging of plane crashes and car accidents mentioned above. Abduction narratives like *The X-Files* often provide fantasies of technological breakdown: abductions are marked by electrical failures in the car, power surges in televisions, clocks stopping. The abductee is often implanted with microchips that monitor their biological and mental functions, thus literally being transformed into a cyborg, a transformation also rendered traumatic in the backstory of Cameron in *The Sarah Connor Chronicles*. Technology in *Lost* was also always either a source of disaster and trauma, depicted as malfunctioning, dated, decaying, or a means of surveillance. This sense of irony is, however, dispelled when paying attention to the view of the industrial accident not as an aberration but as a *measure* of technological progress. Wolfgang Schivelbusch's discussion of the proliferation of railway accidents in Victorian Britain that led to the first official theorizations of trauma made him suggest that "the more efficient the technology, the more catastrophic its destruction when it collapses. There is an exact ratio between the level of the technology with which nature is controlled, and the degree of severity of its accidents" (133). In the era of the digital revolution, this symbolic function of the industrial accident has gained a renewed currency:

> Where the accidental was once the essence of meaninglessness, today the accident must be recognized as the unavoidable shadow of technology, the expression of the unconscious underpinnings of technological expansion. Accidents are the predictably unpredictable traumatic effects that have taken ever-greater importance with the explosion of technology as an unavoidably immersive aspect of everyday life. (Malater 891)

Such an approach would thus consider the compulsive restaging of technological accidents as only symptomatic of the technological revolution of which these shows are the product of. Even if Reeves, Rodgers, and Epstein proclaim TV III to be "probably the final moment in the age of television" (8), these are probably the most self-consciously televisual narratives ever. And in presenting their stories in increasingly complex temporal frames, they reflect on the ways in which our own experience of time is being reconfigured by our engagement with new media technologies and television itself.

SUGGESTED EPISODES FOR ADDITIONAL STUDY

The Event
1:4. "I Haven't Told You Everything." Writ. Nick Wauters. Dir. Jeffrey Reiner. October 22, 2010.

Flashforward
1:1. "No More Good Days." Writ. David S. Goyer and Brannon Braga. Dir. David Goyer. September 28, 2009.

Fringe
1:1. "Pilot." Writ. J. J. Abrams, Alex Kurtzman, and Roberto Orci. Dir. Alex Graves. September 9, 2008.
2:1. "A New Day in the Old Town." Writ. J. J. Abrams and Akiva Goldsman. Dir. Akiva Goldsman. September 17, 2009.
2:3. "Fracture." Writ. David Wilcox. Dir. Bryan Spicer. October 18, 2009.
2:18. "White Tulip." Writ. J. H. Wyman and Jeff Vlaming. April 15, 2010.

Lost
1:1. "Pilot." Writ. Jeffrey Lieber, J. J. Abrams, and Damon Lindelof. Dir. J. J. Abrams. September 22, 2004.
2:15. "Maternity Leave." Writ. Dawn Lambertsen-Kelly and Matt Ragghianti. Dir. Jack Bender. March 1, 2006.
3:8. "Flashes Before Your Eyes." Writ. Damon Lindelof and Drew Goddard. Dir. Jack Bender. February 14, 2007.
3:22. "Through the Looking Glass." Writ. Carlton Cuse and Damon Lindelof. Dir. Jack Bender. May 23, 2007.
4:5. "The Constant." Writ. Carlton Cuse and Damon Lindelof. Dir. Jack Bender. February 28, 2008.
5:16. "The Incident." Writ. Carlton Cuse and Damon Lindelof. Dir. Jack Bender. May 13, 2009.

Sarah Connor Chronicles
2:4. "Allison from Palmdale." Writ. Toni Graphia. Dir. Charles Beeson. September 29, 2009.
2:8. "Mr. Ferguson Is Ill Today." Writ. Daniel Thomsen. Dir. Michael Nankin. November 10, 2008.
2:9. "Complications." Writ. John Wirth and Ian B. Goldberg. November 17, 2008.

NOTES

1. For more information on the memory wars, see the works by Brewin, Crewes, and Loftus and Ketcham.
2. A more detailed discussion of temporality and trauma is pursued in my article on *Lost*.
3. For the associations between disaster and globalization, see the works by Hardt and Negri, Kalaidjian, and Klein.

WORKS CITED

Baudrillard, Jean. *Simulacra and Simulation*. Trans. Sheila Faria Glaser. Ann Arbor: University of Michigan Press, 1994. Print.

Brewin, Chris R. *Posttraumatic Stress Disorder: Malady or Myth?* New Haven, CT: Yale University Press, 2003. Print.

Crewes, Frederick C. *The Memory Wars: Freud's Legacy in Dispute*. New York: New York Review of Books, 1995. Print.

Dayan, Daniel, and Elihu Katz. *Media Events: The Live Broadcasting of History*. Cambridge, MA: Harvard University Press, 1992. Print.

Doane, Mary Anne. "Information, Crisis, Catastrophe." *Logics of Television: Essays in Cultural Criticism*. Ed. Patricia Mellencamp. Bloomington: Indiana University Press, 1990. 222–39. Print.

Farrell, Kirby. *Post-Traumatic Culture: Injury and Interpretation in the Nineties*. Baltimore: Johns Hopkins University Press, 1998. Print.

Flitterman-Lewis, Sandy. "Psychoanalysis, Film, and Television." *Channels of Discourse, Reassembled: Television and Contemporary Criticism*. Ed. Robert C. Allen. 2nd ed. London: Routledge, 1992. 203–46. Print.

Freud, Sigmund. "Fixation to Traumas—The Unconscious." *The Standard Edition of the Complete Psychological Works of Sigmund Freud*. Ed. and trans. James Strachey et al. Vol. 1. London: Hogarth Press, 1963. 274–80. Print.

———. "Beyond the Pleasure Principle." *The Standard Edition of the Complete Psychological Works of Sigmund Freud*. Ed. and trans. James Strachey et al. Vol. 18. London: Vintage, 2001. 4–64. Print.

Gordon, Andrew. "*Back to the Future*: Oedipus as Time Traveller." *Science Fiction Studies* 14.3 (1987): 372–85. Print.

Hardt, Michael, and Antonio Negri. *Empire*. Cambridge, MA: Harvard University Press, 2000. Print.

Huyssen, Andreas. "Trauma and Memory: A New Imaginary of Temporality." *World Memory: Personal Trajectories in Global Time*. Ed. Jill Bennett and Rosanen Kennedy. Hampshire: Palgrave Macmillan, 2003. 26–29. Print.

Kalaidjian, Walter. "Incoming: Globalization, Disaster, Poetics." *South Atlantic Quarterly* 106.4 (2007): 825–48. Print.

Kaplan, E. Ann. *Trauma Culture: The Politics of Terror and Loss in Media and Literature*. New Brunswick, NJ: Rutgers University Press, 2005. Print.

Kaplan, E. Ann, and Ban Wang. *Trauma and Cinema: Cross-Cultural Explorations*. Hong Kong: Hong Kong University Press, 2008. Print.

Katz, Elihu, and Tamar Liebes. "'No More Peace!': How Disaster, Terror and War Have Upstaged Media Events." *International Journal of Communication* 1 (2007): 157–66. Print.

Klein, Naomi. *The Shock Doctrine: The Rise of Disaster Capitalism*. London: Penguin, 2007. Print.

Lacan, Jacques. *The Four Fundamental Concepts of Psycho-Analysis*. Ed. Jacques-Allain Miller. Trans. Alan Sheridan. Harmondsworth: Penguin, 1979. Print.

Loftus, Elizabeth, and Katherine Ketcham. *The Myth of Repressed Memory: False Memories and Allegations of Sexual Abuse*. New York: St. Martin's, 1994. Print.

Luckhurst, Roger. *The Trauma Question*. London: Routledge, 2008. Print.

Lukacher, Ned. *Primal Scenes: Literature, Philosophy, Psychoanalysis*. Ithaca, NY: Cornell University Press, 1986. Print.

Malater, Evan. "David Cronenberg's Benevolent Pathology: Technology, Trauma, and the Perverse Social Link in *Crash*." *Psychoanalytic Review* 94.6 (2007): 887–901. Print.

Matus, Jill L. "Trauma, Memory, and Railway Disaster: The Dickensian Connection." *Victorian Studies* 43.3 (2001): 413–36. Print.

Meek, Allen. *Trauma and Media: Theories, Histories, and Images*. London: Routledge, 2010. Print.

Mittell, Jason. "Previously On: Prime Time Serials and the Mechanics of Memory." July 3, 2009. Web. November 6, 2010.

Mousoutzanis, Aris. "'Enslaved by Time and Space': Determinism, Traumatic Temporality, and Global Interconnectedness." *Looking for* Lost: *Critical Essays on the Enigmatic Series*. Ed. Randy Laist. Jefferson, NC: McFarland, 2011. Print. 43–58.

Reeves, Jimmie L., Mark C. Rogers, and Michael M. Epstein. "Quality Control: *The Daily Show*, the Peabody and Brand Discipline." *Quality Television: Contemporary American Television and Beyond*. Ed. Janet McCabe and Kim Akass. New York: Palgrave Macmillan, 2007. 79–97. Print.

Schivelbusch, Wolfgang. *The Railway Journey: Trains and Travel in the 19th Century*. Trans. Anselm Hollo. New York: Urizen, 1979. Print.

Shales, Tom. "The Re Decade." *Esquire* 105.3 (1986): 67–72. Print.

Turim, Maureen. "The Trauma of History: Flashbacks Upon Flashbacks." *Screen* 42.2 (2001): 205–10. Print.

White, Hayden. "The Modernist Event." *The Persistence of History: Cinema, Television, and the Modern Event*. Ed. Vivian Sobchack. London: Routledge, 1996. 17–38. Print.

Žižek, Slavoj. "Grimaces of the Real, or When the Phallus Appears." *October* 58 (1991): 59. Print.

———. *Looking Awry: An Introduction to Jacques Lacan Through Popular Culture*. Cambridge: MIT Press, 1991. Print.

———. *Welcome to the Desert of the Real*. New York: Verso, 2002. Print.

7

THE FEAR OF THE FUTURE AND THE PAIN OF THE PAST
The Quest to Cheat Time in Heroes, FlashForward, *and* Fringe

MELISSA AMES

> To be mired in the past is to be unable to think and act the future; conversely, to be unanchored in the past ... is also to have no way to see or make a future.
> —ELIZABETH GROSZ (*THE NICK OF TIME* 116)

Fictional narratives have traditionally depended on a narrative time that is linear in nature. This temporal structure "carries with it the implication of an arrow of time, pointing from the past to future and indicating the directionality of sequences of events" (Davies 34). Although this has been the narrative norm for a majority of fictional texts across media, a great many tales have arisen that question and/or disrupt this directionality. One thematic motif that participates in such narrative disruption is the "do-over." The last several decades have found this theme increasing in popularity in the American culture realm and it has amplified further since the September 11 attacks. Although this theme has existed across mediated divides, the medium that embraced it most readily (even if not always as overtly) is television. The last televisual decade has seen an acceleration of this theme and the prevalence of it in shows that specifically deal with post-9/11 material makes it worthy of analysis.

In the years following the attacks on the World Trade Center and the Pentagon, cultural products have been sites for interrogating the trauma that 9/11 caused for U.S. citizens. Although these cultural concerns were played out in both nonfictional and fictional spaces across media, this essay argues that televisual narratives in particular provide great insight into societal concerns during the start of this century. They do this in a unique space that repackages these concerns from "reality" and displaces them into the safe comforts of "fiction" where they can be repeatedly addressed with more favorable results. Although this underlying motif of fear is often developed through the subject matter of various television programs (e.g., the wave of rescue/salvation shows), it is also amplified in series that foreground time. I analyze three contemporary fictional narratives that often remediate the tragedy of 9/11: ABC's *FlashForward* (2009–2010), NBC's *Heroes* (2006–2010), and Fox's *Fringe* (2008–Present). These programs include experimental temporality and center their plots on anxieties concerning time: the longing to correct mistakes of the past, the panic of living in a hypersensitive present, and the fear of the premediated future. These shows suggest that the fear viewers feel as a nation post-attack unconsciously resurfaces and seeks resolution in narrative spaces through repetition and that the consumption of these narratives is a means by which viewers "work through" the lingering emotional trauma caused by the attacks.[1]

While a vast array of American programs from the twenty-first century could be studied due to their thematic obsessions with salvation, this essay actually avoids this broad focus. Instead of focusing on this larger motif, I consider how this salvation theme morphs into personal quests: individual quests of redemption/rescue. Three individual episodes, all aired during 2010, will be analyzed. Within each, main characters from the three programs—*Heroes*, *Fringe*, and *FlashForward*—wrestle with personal demons, rage against the ticking time clocks that shape their own destinies, and attempt to manipulate time to "save" themselves and loved ones. The analysis of these episodes reveals an interesting commonality: each program includes an allusion to a cultural archetype or myth that carries with it a warning. The message appears to be that although the desire to change the past or control the future is perhaps unavoidable, extreme efforts to do so will only result in harm to any who attempts such feats. It is a message that delivers fear to both characters and viewers alike.[2]

THREE SNAPSHOTS OF TELEVISION POST-9/11

It is not hard to classify *Heroes*, *Fringe*, and *FlashForward* as post-9/11 television. Besides the fact that each premiered after the attacks, they each contain apocalyptic storylines that quite obviously point back to the national tragedy.

Heroes

Created five years after the attacks, Tim Kring's drama, *Heroes*, revolves around a plot where seemingly ordinary individuals realize they have supernatural powers. Although the post-9/11 relevance remains throughout all four years of the program's run, the first season clearly sets up this focus. During the final episode of the first season, all of the characters' paths cross so that they can collaboratively prevent a national tragedy from occurring—one foreshadowed throughout the season's run. When studying this fictional tragedy, the allusions to 9/11 cannot be overlooked.

The first mention of this pending disaster comes in the form of a character's painting of a New York cityscape in flames. This disaster finally becomes "reality" toward the end of the season when, "in 'Five years Gone,' *Heroes* presents an alternative future vision not only of the characters' world but also of the series itself . . . The episode reveals a dystopia that is yet to come" (Porter, Lavery, and Robson 149). The echoes of 9/11 are not subtle. In this episode, as the president speaks to a sober crowd in the ruins of the city, beneath a banner reading "America Remembers," the scene is reminiscent of memorials stationed at Ground Zero years after September 11. This episode highlights the cultural fascination with the theme of the "do-over." Arguably, this postexplosion scene is shared with viewers so that they might hope (along with the main characters) that it can still be prevented. The timing of this episode is also important. In it the characters are viewing a time *five years* in the future— one that if they could go back in time *just five years* (and some do have this power), they could change. Also significant is the fact that viewers are watching the episode *five years* after the attacks of September 11, 2001.

As the series progresses the desire to turn back the hands of time gets linked less to longing to undo societal wrongs or national catastrophes but instead becomes more linked to the individual choices (and their consequences) made by the various characters.

Fringe

In 2008 Fox launched yet another narrative to explore the concerns of a nation battling an invisible enemy called "terror." Created by J. J. Abrams, Alex Kurtzman, and Roberto Orc, *Fringe* focuses its plot around the FBI "Fringe Division," agents operating under the supervision of Homeland Security. At the heart of this show lies an eclectic team headed by Olivia Dunham (Anna Torv), an FBI agent with enhanced supernatural skills leftover from being part of a childhood experiment; Dr. Walter Bishop (John Noble), a mad scientist figure and former government researcher who understands of the capabilities existing on the periphery of science; and his son, Peter Bishop (Joshua Jackson), a potential/eventual love interest to Olivia and investigative sidekick.

Originally the program was concerned with investigating "the pattern"—a series of unexplainable, and often catastrophic, events caused by fringe science attacks. The perils from which the characters save society hint at mass concerns about the possible use of biological warfare and new technology.

Like *Heroes*, this program ended its first season with an obvious moment of wish fulfillment when it presented viewers with a parallel universe in which the Twin Towers had not been destroyed on 9/11. In season two this storyline is continued as some of the supernatural feats they uncover (and prevent) include travel that disrupts the normal space-time continuum.

FlashForward

Brannan Braga and David Goya adapted Robert J. Sawyer's 1999 science fiction novel to create a program about a mysterious event that caused a blackout wherein the entire human population lost consciousness for two minutes and seventeen seconds. During this brief time period, all unconscious persons had visions of their lives six months later. A team of Los Angeles FBI agents assembled the Mosaic, a database system that compiled the visions of all who volunteered what they saw through an online Web site. These tentative future visions laid the foundation for their investigation as they attempted to not only discover how this event was possible but how it could be prevented in the future.

Although the larger goal of the investigative team is to protect society at large, many of the agents actually have personal motivation for trying to unravel the future before it occurs. In fact, many want to prevent the future they saw (or did not see) from occurring. The main character, Mark Benford (Joseph Fiennes), hopes to prevent his future in which he is under attack and about to die on the fated day of April 29, while his wife, Dr. Olivia Benford (Sonya Walger), is in bed with another man, Lloyd Simcoe (Jack Davenport), someone partially to blame for the science behind the global event. Mark's partner, Demetri Noh (John Cho), is on a quest to prevent the future from occurring as predicted specifically because he did *not* have a vision during the two-minute blackout—an anomaly that has proven to mean only one thing: he will be dead.

THE STRUCTURE AND IDEOLOGY OF TIME-TRAVEL NARRATIVES

Although each of these programs includes elements of time travel through various motifs or individual episodes, this focus on temporal play would likely not be considered a defining feature of most of the shows. Most would categorize *Heroes* as a televisual version of the comic genre, *Fringe* as a variation of the police procedural, and *FlashForward* as a post-*Lost* type of prime-time drama. However, their overarching thematic concerns with the implications of time travel, or controlling time more generally, make them interesting bedfellows in the loose category of "time travel narratives." As such, they follow some of the same structures of similar narratives that came before them: the characters in these programs almost always attempt to either "manipulate foregone events" or "thwart such attempts" to do so (Wittenberg 66). Therefore, like most time travel stories, their goal in "temporal revisionism is quite often to leave events and plots just as they were, or else to restore them to what they *should have been*" (Wittenberg 66, emphasis added). In these three episodes, many of the characters aim to do the latter: ensure a desired alternate future, the future that *should be*. The moral implications of this desire will be analyzed further in the following sections of this essay.

The relatively standard plot structure of the time travel narrative is often the result of the common ideological function that such fictions serve. With ties to the science fiction genre, these narratives provide "the necessary distancing effect" needed

> to be able to metaphorically address the most pressing issues and themes that concern people in the present. If the modern world is one where the individuals feel alienated and powerless in the face of bureaucratic structures and corporate monopolies, then time travel suggests that Everyman . . . is important to shaping history, to making a real and quantifiable difference to the way the world turns out. (Redmond 114)

As post-9/11 narratives, these programs metaphorically address the concerns viewers have after the attacks of September 11 by reworking them into small-screen fictional narratives. In their plots that suggest that one person can make a difference (and perhaps undo time), these shows provide viewers with the hope that they, too, have control in a seemingly out-of-control world. However, the suggestion that everyone has the ability to control his destiny is undermined by the ways the programs weave cautionary tales into their plots.

AN OVERVIEW OF THREE INDIVIDUAL EPISODES

Each of these programs showcases a desire to change the past or future, which, in and of itself, may not be extraordinary. However, they also include characters with the power to actually accomplish such feats—those who *can* travel through or manipulate time. On a larger scale, as each program revolves its action around a group of officials aiming to protect the people (the FBI in both *Fringe* and *FlashForward* and various governmental special task forces in

Heroes), each quite obviously seems to echo concerns from 9/11. But as each series progresses, the longing to undo the past or future becomes more entrenched in the individual storylines of characters attempting personal (rather that national) salvation.

"The Garden of Forking Paths"

In *FlashForward*, Demetri's pending death and the predicted collapse of Mark's marriage are the two central storylines that involve the theme of "fearing the future." This discussion will focus solely on the former narrative arc. "The Garden of Forking Paths" is set on March 15, the day of Demetri's anticipated death. This episode follows immediately after one in which he was abducted and focuses on his colleagues' efforts to find him before his future hypothetical plight becomes real. Viewers first see Demetri as a captive in a nondescript warehouse bound to a chair with an elaborate mechanical set-up positioning Mark's gun (the weapon predicted to kill him) at his head. Demetri's captor, Dyson Frost, a villain connected to the blackout, later explains that beyond being rigged to fire if disarmed, the mechanism also contains a backup timing device. Frost also points out an elaborate chalk flowchart positioned on the wall behind Demetri, calling it his "Garden of Forking Paths." This chart documents all the possible futures Frost has seen through years of engineering smaller flashforwards. It focuses on key decision points and days that alter the future path—one being this specific day when both of them are slated to die. Through this scenario, Frost hopes to prevent the future from occurring as it did in his many flashforwards, although he is convinced that by the day's end one, if not both, of them will be dead.

The episode then shifts primarily to Mark's efforts to save Demetri. In the previous episode Frost had delivered clues concerning Demetri's whereabouts to Mark's young daughter, Charlie, cryptically concealed in riddles: he told her that his favorite Dr. Seuss book was *One Fish, Two Fish, Red Fish, Blue Fish* (this clue eventually prompts Mark to know the proper way to disarm the colored wires attached to the firing mechanism) and he gave her a photograph of a painting by Jean-Auguste-Dominique Ingres titled *Oedipus and the Sphinx* (this clue allows Mark to find where Demetri is located because the street address matches the painter's name). Before these clues can become evident Mark first engages with Frost, only to watch him die by the hands of another villain. In his last breath Frost admits that he provided Charlie with all of the information needed to save Demetri. Racing against the clock, Mark decodes the riddles and arrives at the warehouse with only minutes to disarm the contraption. With his hand on the gun viewers are led to believe that the future cannot be prevented and that Demetri will, in a sense, die (as predicted) by Mark's hand. However, Mark manages to disarm the motion sensors and tilts the gun just as it fires, barely missing Demetri's head. The rescue triggers a sprinkler system aimed directly at Frost's chart and the two agents watch helplessly as the clues melt away. The most ominous piece of information lingers in Mark's memory. It was the event at the end of the probability lines, simply written as "The End" and dated December 12, 2016. For them, the future remains something to be afraid of.

"The White Tulip"

In *Fringe*'s second season viewers learn a secret hinted at throughout much of season one: that a terminal illness ended Peter's life when he was a young boy. Desperately attempting to find a cure, Walter had been spying on his alternate self, a version of him in the other universe who was slightly more skilled at science and was also attempting to accomplish the same task—to save *his own* son. When the other Walter failed to notice that he had, indeed, created a cure for the disease, Walter realized that the second Peter would also die. Walter decided to cross over to the other universe, abduct that Peter, and nurse him back to health. Although he had intended to return him, he was never able to do so and instead Peter lived out the remainder of his life not knowing that any switch had been made.

An episode toward the end of this season, "The White Tulip," is devoted to the guilt Walter feels for these actions. This episode starts with him writing a letter to his son confessing his past mistake. His determination to deliver this letter is interrupted as both he and Peter are called to a crime scene investigation in which a train has arrived at a station with all of its passengers dead. Walter later determines that all of the persons died instantaneously when their body cells were drained of energy. The closest thing they have to a witness is a teenage pickpocket who saw one living man depart the train. The team discovers that he is Alistair Peck, an astrophysics professor at MIT. Walter determines that Peck has found a way to apply the Theory of Relativity—a feat that would require massive amounts of energy. When they attempt to apprehend him at his apartment for the murders, Peck remarks that they are not permanently dead and then disappears. Viewers see him again aboard the commuter train as they did at the start of the episode where he disembarks and walks past the pickpocket. The only difference is this time he tells the boy: "sorry you have to go through this all again" ("The White"). After Peck is out of sight, again, the teenager discovers all the corpses on the train. The episode starts over with slight variations in the investigation.

In this second version they meet a colleague of Peck's at MIT who informs them that he was obsessed with creating wormholes that would allow time travel. Through her they discover that Peck's fiancée, Arlette, was killed in a car crash ten months earlier. After realizing that the unfinished chapter in Peck's book, titled "The Arlette Principle," refers to time travel, Walter realizes that Peck is attempting to time-travel back ten months—an act that would kill thousands of people. When they next discover Peck he is in his lab. Going in before the SWAT team, Walter warns Peck of the team's presence and then tells him that they know of his plans. Walter explains that the time-jump he is attempting will kill thousands of people. Peck, rather than address this immediate concern, explains his desire to attempt this in the first place. On the day his fiancée died they had had a fight. It was also on this day that he realized how to apply his theories of time travel while he sat in an empty field. Peck then tells Walter that he plans to jump directly to that field to avoid killing anyone. Walter, who realizes Peck cannot jump further than twelve hours, points out the error in his calculations. As the FBI team rushes in Walter warns Peck that he will not be able to live with the consequences of bringing back a loved one who was intended to die. He explains what he did with Peter and the burden he has felt, commenting that he keeps looking for a sign of forgiveness: a white tulip. Immediately after this conversation, Peck escapes.

The episode then begins a third time. Peck has time traveled back to his apartment, killing all of his neighbors in the process. The investigative team, possessing no knowledge of the previous two attempts to solve this crime, again closes in on Peck at his office at MIT as he writes a letter addressed to his colleague, Carol. Just as the FBI break in, Peck teleports back into the past to the empty field on the day of his fiancée's death, thanks to Walter's calculations. Viewers see him running to her car and getting in, sobbing. As he tells her that he loves her, a car hits and kills them both. Months later, Carol finds Peck's letter in his files. In it is an envelope addressed to Walter Bishop with instructions that it be sent to him on a specific date in the future. She follows through with his wishes and the letter arrives unmarked to a Walter who would have no recollection of ever engaging with Peck (since their encounter has no longer happened). He opens up this letter right after having burnt the one he had written to confess to his son. Inside this envelope is s single drawing: a white tulip. His eyes fill up with tears and the episode comes to a close.

"Brave New World"

This *Heroes* episode revolves around the romantic story arc of Hiro Nakamura (Masi Oka) and Charlie Andrews (Jayma Mays). Seen initially in the first season, Charlie is a waitress in Midland, Texas. Like many of the characters on the show she has a gift: enhanced memory skills. However, unlike most of the characters, her gift comes at a cost. When Hiro meets her she is currently dying from a blood clot in the brain. Although the two quickly become friends, their bond is short lived as she is soon after murdered by Sylar, the key villain of the series. In an attempt to undo this tragedy, Hiro travels back in time and meets Charlie again a few months earlier. The two fall quickly into a relationship and Hiro is forced to prove his powers to her by stopping time, restarting it after he has made and hung one thousand origami cranes all about her.³ Hiro urges her to escape with him but she declines his offer, telling him of her disease. Hiro inadvertently travels back into the future before he could complete his time-travel salvation mission leaving her in the past to die once again.

The storyline remains in the backdrop until the fourth season when Hiro attempts to save her once again, traveling back in time with a new villain at his side, Samuel. They arrive just as Sylar is about to kill Charlie. Hiro prevents it, forces Sylar to fix her brain with his new healing powers, and then lets Sylar go free even though he knows the damage he will cause in the future. Instead of being grateful for this rescue, Charlie is angry with Hiro. Having accepted her fate, Charlie scolds him: "Hiro, 300,000 people die every single day—young, old, there are accidents, murders—why am I any different?" She further questions how he could set Sylar free knowing that he would go on to kill so many people. Hiro claims that it was their "happily ever after," proclaims his love, and eventually Charlie forgives him. However their happiness is thwarted as soon she is kidnapped by another time traveler and dropped into a time and place unknown to Hiro whose rescue attempts thereafter would be futile. The loss of Charlie and the ethical questions she pitched haunt Hiro in the coming months. The show dedicates one episode to his guilt in "Pass/Fail," where Hiro experiences a dreamlike state where he stands on trial for his actions.

The episode discussed here brings closure to this storyline. While Hiro is hospitalized a nurse arrives and hands him an origami crane with the message, "Hiro, is it really you? Come and find me" ("Brave"). Hiro enters a hospital room to find an aged Charlie. He learns that when she was kidnapped she was dropped off in 1944 during World War II. Hiro responds, "I'm so sorry, Charlie. This was all my fault. I led the evil butterfly man right to you. It was because I loved you that he sent you away" ("Brave"). Their conversation reveals that Hiro is still not finished trying to undo the past.

> CHARLIE: Don't beat yourself up, Hiro. I would have waited for you but by the time you were born I was middle aged. I'm just so happy I got to see you before . . .

HIRO: You're not well . . . I can fix this, Charlie . . . It's simple, I'll be waiting for you in 1944. When you pop out onto that snowy street corner I'll take you right back to the (diner) where I left you.
CHARLIE: I'd be young again.
HIRO: And we can finally build a life together.
CHARLIE: That sounds nice. But Hiro, I already had a life—a wonderful life. 65 years is a long time. ("Brave")

Charlie further explains why she cannot accept his offer: "Hiro, after the war I married a wonderful man. I had four children. I now have seven beautiful grandchildren. We had a home, friends, cherished memories, a life. If I was to go back now and live a different life what would happen to all of that?" ("Brave").

Hiro's best friend, Ando, calls him away and he watches through the hospital window as her family happily enters the scene. Hiro smiles and says, "It is over. The damsel has found her happy ending. My hero's journey has come to an end" ("Brave"). He bows, blows a kiss, and walks away.

SYMBOLS, ALLUSIONS, AND THEMES
Beware Those Who Attempt to Master Time

All three of the episodes summarized above contain symbolic allusions that carry the same didactic message: changing the past/future is something to regret. In *Heroes*, Hiro refers to the man who instigated the kidnapping of Charlie, who used time travel to fulfill his own selfish needs, as "the butterfly man." In that same episode, while he is concocting his scheme to travel back to 1944, he has a brief conversation with Ando that again returns to this motif: Ando comments, "There's no such thing as stepping on a small butterfly," and Hiro responds, "All I'm doing is righting a terrible wrong" ("Brave"). The scientific principal they are referring to, the butterfly effect, is a metaphor related to chaos theory, an idea that small factors in the initial condition of a complex system may produce large variations in the long-term behavior of the system. It has been a common trope in the fictional work of time travel, creating "what if" scenarios. The phenomenon specifically refers to the idea that a butterfly's wings might create tiny changes in the atmosphere to the point that it could even alter the path of a tornado. Their allusion to the butterfly effect quite obviously suggests that Hiro's actions might (continue to) disrupt the future rather than heal it.

The allusions in the other two episodes receive less attention. In *FlashForward*, the most important allusion is the painting given to Mark's daughter by Frost: Jean-Auguste-Dominique Ingres's *Oedipus and the Sphinx*. The painting focuses on Oedipus's actions which inadvertently brought about the death of his parents—the very fate he was trying to avoid. Within the episode this allusion causes the agents to wonder if they themselves are following in a similar path, if their rescue efforts may actually be contributing to rather than preventing Demetri's death. Finally, in *Fringe*, the drawing of the white tulip that closes the episode symbolizes forgiveness, suggesting that changing the past requires forgiveness.

All three of these symbolic references point to the negative consequences that accompany attempts to alter time.[4] The programs reinforce this by pairing all such attempts with death. Hiro's choice to save Charlie brought about the deaths of many. Peck's time-travel attempts cause accidental death and even when he finally masters his quest, he is unable to save his fiancée and dies beside her. In the *FlashForward* episode, the mention of Oedipus points to choices that ultimately lead to death. This may seem counterintuitive to the celebratory episode itself, which suggests momentarily that fate can be altered. However, the Oedipus tale is very well aligned with the program as a whole as it proves repeatedly that fate cannot be avoided as all the characters' attempts to avoid death ultimately fail.[5]

CONCLUSION

Each of these episodes showcases characters who are haunted by their past actions and who live in fear of what is to come. Therefore, their present temporal states are preoccupied and determined by that of their past and future ones. The characters are frozen in the present and unable to move forward freely into the future without fear until the guilt they feel is resolved. Friedrich Nietzsche believed that "too strong an immersion in the past is an illness, a debilitation, an inhibition to life, for it prevents our active living in the present" (Grosz 116). Such a fixation on the past results in an inability to digest that past, move on from it, and be rid of it; the past, instead, dominates and haunts the present (Grosz 116). These storylines validate this sentiment, and as figures in post-9/11 texts, the characters within them may represent citizens at large who are also frozen in a temporal pocket, unable to move beyond the past, reliving it over and over through the consumption of remediated versions of the very past that haunts them. In some ways these programs may be conceived as spaces in which viewers unconsciously work through the emotional trauma remaining after the attacks—especially fears dealing with time: the past, the future, and the present that is dependent on them both (the past and future). These three episodes also indicate that we may be able to learn from our mistakes and craft a better future accordingly—that our past truly can be a "resource for overcoming the present, for bringing about a future" (Grosz 257). They may even go as far as suggesting that each person has the ability to control his or her own destiny, as individual characters in these shows are shown to have the ability to help craft the futures they desire. However, as the cultural allusions in the three analyzed episodes suggest, these shows also simultaneously urge viewers to steer clear of hopes that they might fully control the future or undo the past altogether. In their efforts to show characters who have successfully manipulated time, *FlashForward*, *Fringe*, and *Heroes* clearly highlight the personal conflicts, rather than successes, that stemmed from these acts.

SUGGESTED EPISODES FOR ADDITIONAL STUDY

FlashForward

1:1. "No More Good Days." Writ. David S. Goyer and Brannon Graga. Dir. David S. Goyer. September 24, 2009.

1:16. "Let No Man Put Asunder." Writ. Seth Hoffman and Quinton Peeples. Dir. Bobby Roth. April 15, 2010.

1:20. "The Negotiation." Writ. Byron Balasco, Quinton Peeples, and Deborah J. Ezer. Dir. Leslie Libman. May 13, 2010.

1:21. "Countdown." Writ. Lisa Zwerling and Seth Hoffman. Dir. John Polson. May 20, 2010.

1:22. "Future Shock." Writ. Timothy J. Lea and Scott M. Gimple. Dir. John Polson. May 27, 2010.

Fringe

1:1. "Pilot." Writ. J. J. Abrams, Alex Kurtzman, and Roberto Orci. Dir. Alex Graves. September 9, 2008.

1:19. "The Road Not Taken." Writ. Jeff Pinkner, J. R. Orci, and Akiva Goldsman. Dir. Fred Toye. May 5, 2009.

2:13. "What Lies Below." Writ. Jeff Vlaming. Dir. Deran Sarafian. January 21, 2010.

2:15. "Jacksonville." Writ. Ashley Miller and Zack Stentz. Dir. Charles Beeson. February 4, 2010.

2:16. "Peter." Writ. Jeff Pinkner, J. H. Wyman, Josh Singer, and Akiva Goldsman. Dir. David Straiton. April 1, 2010.

2:22. "Over There: Part I." Writ. J. H. Wyman, Jeff Pinkner, and Akiva Goldsman. Dir. Akiva Goldsman. May 13, 2010.

2:23. "Over There: Part II." Writ. J. H. Wyman, Jeff Pinkner, and Akiva Goldsman. Dir. Akiva Goldsman. May 20, 2010.

3:1. "Olivia." Writ. J. H. Wyman and Jeff Pinkner. Dir. Joe Chappelle. September 23, 2010.

3:7. "The Abducted." David Wilcox and Graham Roland. Dir. Chuck Russel. November 18, 2010.

3:10. "The Firefly." Writ. J. H. Wyman and Jeff Pinkner. Dir. Charles Beeson. January 21, 2011.

3:14. "6B." Writ. Glen Whitman and Robert Chiappetta. Dir. Tom Yatsko. February 18, 2011.

3:18. "Bloodline." Writ. Alison Schapker and Monica Breen. Dir. Dennis Smith. March 25, 2010.

3:21. "The Last Sam Weiss." Writ. Monica Breen and Alison Schapker. Dir. Tom Yatsko. April 29, 2011.

3:22. "The Day We Died." Writ. Akiva Goldsman, J. H. Wyman, and Jeff Pinkner. Dir. Joe Chappelle. May 6, 2011.

Heroes

1:1. "Genesis." Writ. Tim Kring. Dir. David Semel. September 25, 2006.

1:9. "Homecoming." Writ. Adam Armus and Nora Kay Foster. Dir. Greg Beeman. November 20, 2006.

1:10. "Six Months Ago." Writ. Aron Eli Coleite. Dir. Allan Arkush. November 27, 2006.

1:23. "How to Stop an Exploding Man." Writ. Tim Kring. Dir. Allan Arkush. May 21, 2007.

2:7. "Out of Time." Writ. Aron Eli Coleite. Dir. Daniel Attias. November 5, 2007.

2:9. "Cautionary Tales." Writ. Joe Pokaski. Dir. Greg Yaitanes. November 20, 2007.

3:1. "The Second Coming." Writ. Tim Kring. Dir. Allan Arkush. September 22, 2008.

3:2. "The Butterfly Effect." Writ. Tim Kring. Dir. Greg Beeman. September 22, 2008.

3:4. "I am Become Death." Writ. Aron Eli Coleite. Dir. David Von Ancken. October 6, 2008.

3:8. "Villains." Writ. Rob Fresco. Dir. Alan Arkush. November 10, 2008.

3:14. "A Clear and Present Danger." Writ. Tim Kring. Dir. Greg Yaitanes. February 2, 2009.
3:23. "1961." Writ. Aron Eli Coleite. Dir. Adam Kane. April 13, 2009.
4:8. "Once Upon a Time in Texas." Writ. Aron Eli Coleite and Aury Wallington. Dir. Nathaniel Goodman. November 2, 2009.

NOTES

1. Each of the programs analyzed is loosely related to the genres of science fiction and fantasy. While both genres have historically been understood as escapist modes or fictions of wish fulfillment, research has indicated that their subject matter may often play an important role in how victims of trauma construct their narratives.

2. Television has long been associated with the catastrophic and the affect of fear. See Mellencamp and Doane on how televised news coverage works to both instill and relieve anxiety in viewers. This article, inspired by their works and the affect theory of Silvan Tomkins (see Sedgwick and Frank), suggests that fictional programming works in a similar way.

3. In Japanese custom it is thought that the person who could fold 1,000 cranes would have his greatest wish fulfilled. As most of these time-traveling attempts are in fact attempts at wish fulfillment, this symbol seems quite relevant.

4. These shows are not the first to explore the moral issues of temporal manipulation. NBC's *Quantum Leap* (1989–1993) dealt heavily with this theme.

5. This is best shown in two linked episodes, "The Gift" and "Course Correction," in which, despite the often heroic or altruistic efforts of various characters to prevent deaths predicted by the flashforward, those predicted to die do so (even if delayed for a short while). The program hints that Demetri is an exception rather than the rule and suggests that he still may not be safe.

WORKS CITED

"Brave New World." *Heroes*. NBC. February 18, 2010. Television.
"Course Correction." *FlashForward*. ABC. May 6, 2010. Television.
Davies, Paul. *About Time: Einstein's Unfinished Revolution*. New York: Simon & Schuster, 1995. Print.
Doane, Mary Ann. "Information, Crisis, Catastrophe." *Logics of Television*. Ed. Patricia Mellencamp. Bloomington: Indiana University Press, 1990. 222–39. Print.
"Five Years Gone." *Heroes*. NBC. April 30, 2007. Television.
"The Garden of Forking Paths." *FlashForward*. ABC. April 22, 2010. Television.
"The Gift." *FlashForward*. ABC. November 5, 2009. Television.
Grosz, Elizabeth. *The Nick of Time: Politics, Evolution, and the Untimely*. Durham, NC: Duke University Press, 2004. Print.
Mellencamp, Patricia. "TV Time and Catastrophe, or *Beyond the Pleasure Principle* of Television." *Logics of Television*. Ed. Patricia Mellencamp. Bloomington: Indiana University Press, 1990. 240–66. Print.
"Pass/Fail." *Heroes*. NBC. January 18, 2010. Television.

Porter, Lynnette, David Lavery, and Hillary Robson. *Saving the World: A Guide to Heroes.* Toronto: ECW Press, 2007. Print.

Redmond, Sean, ed. *Liquid Metal: The Science Fiction Film Reader.* London: Wallflower Press, 2004. Print.

Sedgwick, Eve Kosofsky, and Adam Frank, ed. *Shame and Its Sisters: A Silvan Tomkins Reader.* Durham, NC: Duke University Press, 1995. Print.

"The White Tulip." *Fringe.* Fox. 15 April 15, 2010. Television.

Wittenberg, David. "Oedipus Multiplex, or The Subject as a Time Travel Film: Two Readings of *Back to the Future.*" *Discourse* 28.2&3 (2006): 51–77. Print.

8

LOST IN OUR MIDDLE HOUR
Faith, Fate, and Redemption Post-9/11

SARAH HIMSEL BURCON

In *Understanding Media*, Marshall McLuhan credits Edgar Allan Poe with offering "an incomplete image or process" in his stories in order to "[involve] his readers in the creative process"; Poe, claims McLuhan, "grasped at once the electric dynamic as one of public participation in creativity" (430). Like Poe, but moving forward in time approximately 150 years, the producers of television's *Lost* (ABC, 2004–2010) also offer "an incomplete image" to involve the viewer in the creative process. During its six-season run, *Lost* attracted a cult-like following, in part because of its plot, and in part because of its narrative development. *Lost* tells the story of the survivors of Oceanic 815, a plane that crashes into a mysterious island: this is an island inhabited by polar bears, "others," and a smoke monster; this is an island that allows a paralyzed person to regain his mobility; this is an island where people move back and forth in time. The list of mysteries grows longer with each subsequent episode, with viewers being quick to point out that each season brings with it more questions than answers.

Many of the questions put forward on the program are posed in the form of symbols. *Lost* is rife with symbols—religious, philosophical, and scientific among these—that point to important themes, two of which are free will versus destiny and faith versus reason. In addition to using symbols to highlight these themes, *Lost* also uses flashbacks, flashforwards, and flashsideways for the same purpose. Television shows throughout the twentieth (and into the twenty-first) century have, for the most part, been arranged in chronological order. This changed significantly, however, when *Lost* aired in 2004. This chapter explores the aforementioned themes, as well as the intertwined theme of good versus evil, by analyzing *Lost*'s format and narrative content. Ultimately, this essay discusses how the audience of *Lost* creates meaning from the program, rather than having meaning thrust upon them. The many fan Web sites associated with the show attest to the fact that this program engages its viewers by presenting questions and ultimately encouraging viewers to try to determine the answers. Some of these inquiries deal with the ability or inability of humans to "do-over" events. That is, *Lost* interrogates whether it is possible to somehow alter the past or the future, and theorizes the ramifications these hypothetical do-overs would have for the future and/or the past. Most people would hold that there is no possible way to alter the past because it is already lived. Oceanic 815 survivor, John Locke, however, tells viewers early in the series that "everyone gets a new life on the island" ("In Translation"). The notions of free will/destiny and faith/reason are hinted at within this brief statement, as will be discussed at greater length later in the chapter. This essay problematizes what these concepts might mean to the survivors of *Lost*, and more largely, to humanity.

The September 11, 2001, attacks prompted many Americans to speculate on these very themes; after this historical event, many examined their faith and speculated on the primordial issues of predestination and free will. There were many questions and few answers following the tragedy, a tragedy that people fervently wished could be "done-over" or "done away" with. Hence, it seems that it was not a coincidence that *Lost* considered such uncertainties along with the rest of the American population. Both the form (the use of flashbacks, flashforwards, flashsideways, and the unfathomable endings to episodes) and the content (the storylines themselves) of the program, then, paralleled the struggles Americans were facing at the start of the twenty-first century.[1]

The self-reflexive nature of *Lost* is not surprising. Steven Johnson argues that television today offers more thought-provoking material than television in the past. This is not only due to more intricate storylines but also to more narratively complex television. Johnson further highlights the fact that, in the past, shows have worked against this type of complexity because a perplexed audience was not a happy audience: "if the show didn't make complete sense the first time around, that was it. There were no second acts" (167). Hence, thirty years ago, producers wished to ensure that television was not too complex, lest they lose viewers because they simply did not understand the program. Today, however, with instantaneous replay options available through DVD players, TiVo, On Demand, and the Internet, people no longer have to wait to "get it." And many would argue that now, part of the joy of television watching is working to understand the meaning of a show, rather than "getting it" from the start. *Lost* caters to this new televisual preference and certainly falls into the category of the narratively complex, and it is this complexity that has drawn and maintained viewers throughout the greater part of the first decade of the new millennium.

IN THE BEGINNING THERE WAS LIGHT

Lost begins its pilot episode with a close-up of Dr. Jack Shepherd's eye slowly opening and taking in its new surroundings. Upon opening his eyes, Jack immediately becomes aware of the chaos surrounding him, chaos that will soon consume his life. The viewer notes that he is in a bamboo grove, the first of many symbols in a show filled with them. According to Chinese philosophy, bamboo symbolizes enlightenment (Tollefson). This symbol, accompanied by the opening of Jack's eye and his "seeing light," work together to represent this enlightenment, another major motif in *Lost*. As the show nears completion, the audience learns of a different sort of "light," one that emanates from the "source" of the island. Light can be interpreted as a religious symbol; Psalms 4:6 reads, "Many, Lord, are asking, 'Who will bring us prosperity?' Let the light of your face shine on us." Light is also, of course, thematically contrasted with darkness, both of which represent the ancient dualism of good and evil.[2]

The bamboo in this opening sequence also suggests strength and resilience. From the beginning of the show, then, the viewer might associate these traits with Jack, especially as they manifest themselves in different ways throughout the series. Upon awakening in the bamboo grove, Jack runs toward the commotion and learns what has happened: the flight he was on never landed in Los Angeles after taking off from Sydney. Rather, it crashed into an island, leaving forty-eight passengers to survive on an island where nothing was as it seemed. Along with the unusual plot comes an intriguing narrative style. Early into the series the audience recognizes that this program is different from others—especially given its extensive use of flashbacks nearly from the onset, and toward the end of the series, its integration of flashforwards and flashsideways—and that it almost requires strength and resilience from its audience as well, as viewers are forced to keep up with a narratively complex, "smart" television program like none before it.

Although at first these narrative structures appear to be needed as they "fill in the blanks" of unclear segments of the storyline—providing character backstories, for example—soon the audience realizes that even though some blanks get filled, many remain open. But it is this very structure that viewers learn to accept and, later, to crave. As Jason Mittell argues, *Lost* mimics "puzzle films," which "[invite] audiences to play along with the creators to crack the interpretive codes to make sense of their complex narrative strategies" (38). Thus, in a show like *Lost*, the viewer is active and always wanting "to enjoy the machine's results while also marveling at how it works" (Mittell 38). Indeed, this complex temporal structure invites the viewer to "crack" the code, thus enhancing the joy of viewing; and certainly the flashbacks and flashforwards contribute to these efforts. Additionally, I argue that these past/present pairings also work together to develop the show's thematic content and immerse viewers in the philosophical and theological debates the characters struggle with both on and off the island. In order to further explore these themes and how the narrative structure works to develop these themes, I examine four episodes as they relate to free will/destiny and faith/reason: "White Rabbit," "House of the Rising Sun," "Across the Sea," and "The End."

DOWN THE RABBIT HOLE

"White Rabbit" begins with flashbacks that offer important background information on Jack's formative years as the son of a prominent surgeon. Certainly much can be said about this father/son relationship;[3] however, the discussion here will be limited to an utterance of Jack's father that resonates with Jack throughout his life. In the first flashback, the viewer watches as Jack makes the choice to become involved in a fight to help a friend being attacked by a bully. After Jack briefly tells his father about the incident, Dr. Shepherd offers the following response:

> I had a boy on my table today. He had a bad heart. It got real hairy, real fast. And everybody's looking at your old man to make decisions. And I was able to make those decisions because at the end of the day, after the boy died, I was able to wash my hands and come home to dinner. You know, watch a little Carol Burnett, laugh till my sides hurt. And how can I do that . . . ? Because I have what it takes. Don't choose, Jack, don't decide. You don't want to be a hero, you don't try and save everyone because when you fail . . . you just don't have what it takes. ("White")

Later in this same episode, Jack echoes his father's words after Locke tells him he needs to lead the survivors:

> LOCKE: . . . they need someone to tell them what to do.
> JACK: Me? I can't.
> LOCKE: Why can't you?
> JACK: Because I'm not a leader. [. . .] I don't know how to help them. I'll fail. I don't have what it takes. ("White")

Locke then asks Jack why he is there in the jungle, and Jack responds that he is chasing what appears to be the ghost of his dead father, which must be, according to Jack, a hallucination. Locke, however, disagrees with the hallucination theory because he believes the island is special. Locke continues, significantly:

> I'm an ordinary man, Jack. . . . I'm not a big believer in magic. But this place is different. It's special. . . . Is your white rabbit a hallucination? Probably. But what if everything that happened here, happened for a reason? What if this person that you're chasing is really here? ("White")

Locke, a man of faith (unlike his famous namesake, who called for individuals to employ reason in their search for truth), alludes to destiny in this monologue. Jack, however, as a surgeon and a man of reason, is not entirely convinced of this predestined journey until the end of the series.

TWENTY-FIRST-CENTURY EDEN

In the next episode, "House of the Rising Sun," Jack leads a group to fresh water. When Jack and another main character, Kate, arrive at the caves, they discover two skeletons, one of which holds two stones, one white and one black—clearly a reference to good and evil. Locke dubs them their "very own Adam and Eve" ("House"). At this point, the notions of free will/destiny and faith/reason are more clearly articulated.

Not unimportantly, this episode houses a flashback concerning two other main characters, Sun and Jin. The young Korean couple are unhappily married due to Jin's oppression of Sun and his involvement with her father's corrupt business ventures. The flashbacks show Sun contemplating leaving her husband and beginning a new life. Given the fact that Sun and Jin are young, childless, and one of only two married couples on an island where people are forced to begin their lives fresh, they may represent the biblical Adam and Eve. This flashback, then, further amplifies the theme of free will/destiny in that Sun's decision of whether or not to remain with Jin affects her life at the same time that it impacts the lives of anyone associated with her. Furthermore, this episode demonstrates how *Lost* utilizes temporal shifts not simply as a strategy to develop character but as thematic devices as well. The connection between the "Adam and Eve" corpses and Sun and Jin as symbolic modern-era Adam and Eve representatives shows that the "past" moment is always thematically relevant to the "present"; hence, the flashbacks reinforce the overall message of the episode in particular and the series in general.

Adam and Eve disobeyed God's command when they ate from the Tree of Knowledge. Many would say this disobedience signaled that Adam and Eve exercised free will *rather than* faith in and obedience to God. William Walker, however, in his analysis of John Milton's *Paradise Lost*, which portrays Adam and Eve's fall from grace, speaks to the idea of reason and faith working together rather than being separate. Walker's overarching claim is that, for Milton, faith and reason are not mutually exclusive: "For Milton's God does not ask of his creatures endowed with reason that they believe in him independently of that faculty" (143). For example, in book three "[t]he first major occasion for this presentation [of reason, faith, and human freedom]" occurs because it is here that God declares "he made man free and that this freedom is a precondition for their ability to prove to him their 'true allegiance, constant Faith or Love'" (Walker 146–47). For, if he had not created man free,

> what praise could they receive?
> What pleasure I from such obedience paid,
> When Will and Reason (Reason also is choice)
> Useless and vain, of freedom both despoil'd,
> Made passive both, had serv'd necessity,
> Not mee. (qtd. in Walker 146–47)

Walker interprets Milton's verse to mean that obedience, in God's eyes, is "an action that may look like forced obedience" (147) but in reality, it is not so. "What makes it different from the 'obedience paid' God dismisses is that it is freely performed, that it is an exercise of freedom" (Walker 147). Hence, "God does not segregate reason from this kind of obedience. On the contrary, the freely performed obedience God requires of Adam and Eve involves not only the will but also reason . . . Free obedience, God also suggests, is obedience that is *chosen*" (Walker 147–48, emphasis in original). In *Lost*, reason and faith are intertwined, much as they are in *Paradise Lost*. Drawing this parallel between *Lost* and *Paradise Lost* is significant for at least two reasons. First, the very titles of the television show and the epic are suggestive of 9/11 (although, obviously, the latter was written long before 9/11): *Lost* and *Paradise Lost* demonstrate what Americans felt, collectively, after 9/11. The paradise that was once America—complete with its freedoms, its sense of individuality, its righteousness (in the sense that, after 9/11, we came to understand that we were not as well liked as we had once believed), and its sense of security (being relatively unaffected by terrorism and fear)—had been lost. The Homeland Security Advisory System and heightened security at airports and other public areas are palpable examples of this fact.

It is not by accident that *Lost* makes use of religious themes to highlight fears and problems faced by society; indeed, people often look to religion to explain various events in their lives, both positive and negative; *Lost* simply amplifies this tendency. After 9/11, religious discourse, for better or worse, became, in a sense, a renewed part of America's national identity. John Murphy argues that President George W. Bush used religious discourse in the immediate aftermath of 9/11 not only to help Americans heal, but also to "dominate public interpretation" of the attacks and, ultimately, to formulate "the appropriate response to them" (607). In particular, Bush used epideictic rhetoric: "appeals that unify the community and amplify its virtues" (Murphy 609). Murphy remarks that Bush's initial use of this rhetoric to legitimize the response to the terrorist attacks and the ensuing war in Afghanistan was understandable given the fact that the American population was simply struggling to understand how such a tragedy could have occurred on American soil. In the speech Bush gave during the evening of September 11 he quoted the 23rd Psalm, which "[shaped] the meaning of 9/11 as a passage through the valley of the shadow of death yet simultaneously [assured] us that the Lord was with us" (Murphy 611). (Interestingly, an episode of *Lost*'s second season is titled "The 23rd Psalm"). However, it was on September 14 during a memorial service that Bush truly "crafted our interpretation of the attacks" (Murphy 611).

Bush began his September 14 speech with: "We are here in the middle hour of our grief. So many have suffered so great a loss, and today we express our nation's sorrow" (qtd. in Murphy 611). Murphy comments on Bush's "deft management of time ('middle hour')," remarking that it "crafted the response of the audience; we mourned the past and looked to the future as we stood in the present" (Murphy 611). This mention of "time" is especially significant. September 11 has now become, sadly, one of those periods in history when people remember exactly what they were doing and where they were when the attacks occurred. Further, in the days following the attacks, people—especially those who had lost loved ones—were experiencing, in a strange sense, three different "times" at once: they were contemplating the past and fervently wishing to "do over" this point in history; they were living in an extremely unpleasant, unpredictable present; and they were looking to some "Other"—God, each other, the president—to help them move forward and into the future. However, I would argue that we have not moved forward, and narratives like *Lost* reveal that we are *still* in the "middle hour" of our grief: we are past the initial tragedy of the attacks but not yet "past" them in terms of resolution.

President Bush ended his speech with a quote from Romans 8:38: "neither death nor life nor angels nor principalities, nor powers nor things present nor things to come nor height nor depth can separate us from God's love" (Bush).

This letter of Paul to the Romans "detailed the rebellion of humanity against God's Lordship, a terrible sin for which Jesus Christ redeemed all those who accepted his sacrifice" (Murphy 612). Redemption, therefore, is key. In 2000, Bush declared that "*the nation* had lost its moral compass and wasted the opportunity afforded by prosperity" (qtd. in Murphy 623, emphasis in original). Moreover, "Bush also believed that *his generation* had lost its way . . . The boomers had embraced bad values, a process that culminated in Bill Clinton, and [he] offered redemption" (Murphy 623, emphasis in original). In the September 14, 2001, speech, the president announced that "And in our grief and anger we have found our mission and our moment" (Bush). Bush's speech suggested

> That as a nation, as a generation, and as individuals, we once were lost and now were found. That was, perhaps, why God allowed these terrible events . . . Given the redemption story that he had lived and now offered to the nation, no other man was so fitted to be America at this time. We had indeed finally found our mission and our moment—and our man. (Murphy 623–24)

As many critics and fans have pointed out, redemption is also a major theme in *Lost*. All of the survivors of the plane crash come to understand that on this island they can begin again—they can, indeed, "do over" their lives because nobody there knows their past. Hence, the island itself becomes their savior. In light of the political situation in America at the time, *Lost* questioned—and prompted the viewers to question—what redemption means. Further, *Lost* inadvertently questioned, by way of its narrative content (the many instances of good versus evil) and through its use of flashbacks, flashforwards, and flashsideways (which allowed characters to see "what might have been" or "what might be"), whether the war on terror might really be a battle "for the nation's soul" (Murphy 624).

GENESIS
Adam and Eve, Cain and Abel

A creature of vengeance, rather than redemption, the "smoke monster"—which, as its name implies, is a shapeless, vicious entity, and an obvious reference to Satan, or evil—makes its first appearance in the pilot episode. Seasons later, in "Across the Sea," it is revealed that the smoke monster was once a person. He was known first as the "Boy in Black," and as a grown man, "The

Man in Black" (MIB).⁴ Significant here is this anonymity; called simply "Man in Black," this person/thing symbolizes potentially interchangeable evil figures from past mythologies: Satan, the Devil, Beelzebub, Lucifer, the Islamic Jinn, and so forth. It is not until season six that the audience learns more about him and his brother, Jacob, the protector of the island: the boys were born on the island, having been brought there by their pregnant mother, Claudia, whose ship wrecked two thousand years prior to the "present" (yet another biblical reference to Jesus). Claudia gives birth to twin sons with the help of a woman who lives on the island; the woman kills her and raises the boys as her own. As teenagers they begin questioning this woman about the existence of "others" on the island, to which she responds that the others are dangerous and that only they are good. She follows up this ominous warning by blindfolding them and taking them across the island to a secret location, a cave which radiates a bright light. Similar to God's admonition to Adam and Eve not to eat of the Tree of Knowledge, the boys' mother presents her sons with a temptation-ridden dictate: despite having brought them to this magical location, she tells them they must never enter it.

As time passes temptation surfaces yet again when the boys see that the others are building a civilization on the island. Their mother repeats her cautionary advice to stay away from them. Jacob, who later is shown to represent "destiny," listens, but his brother, the island representation of "free will," does not. In fact, the audience finds that as an adult the MIB lives with the "others" on the island in the hopes of being able to use their technology and the island's powers, the light source which he has re-discovered, to escape it. He shares this information with his brother, who in turn informs their mother.

This leads to a confrontation. The mother and the MIB argue, he refuses to rethink his plans, and the woman knocks him unconscious. Perhaps knowing her time is limited, she rushes off to her other son and tells Jacob that he is in charge of protecting the light, which she claims represents "Life, death, rebirth . . . the source, the heart of the island" ("Across"). The mother follows up with a plea, "Just promise me. No matter what you do, you won't ever go down there . . . It'd be much worse than dying" ("Across"). In a ritualistic manner, Jacob's mother pours liquid into a cup for Jacob to drink, saying that he now must protect the source and find a replacement when he no longer can. After he drinks, she tells him, "Now you and I are the same" ("Across").⁵

At this point the MIB awakens, finding the village destroyed, assumedly by his mother. After returning home from her exchange with Jacob, she is murdered by the MIB in retaliation for the death of his people. Jacob returns and, seeing what his brother has done, attacks him, brings his body to the cave and throws him toward the mouth of it. The MIB is sucked into the source and shortly thereafter the Smoke Monster appears from it, disappearing into the jungle. Jacob retrieves his brother's body and carries him home. After placing two jewels—one black, one white—into a pouch, Jacob lays his mother and brother side by side, placing the pouch in his mother's hand. They are the "Adam and Eve" to whom Locke refers in season one.

This episode makes an interesting use of temporal play in that it exists as an extended flashback: almost the entire episode takes place in the distant "past." Further, in ways predicting the epiphany moments that will close the show—when the characters in the alternate reality "remember" their past lives on the island (revisiting along with the viewers, earlier scenes from the show)—the episode ends with the juxtaposition of images from this particular episode (the distant past) in which Jacob lays his family members to rest, and the episode from season one (the more immediate past) in which Jack, Kate, and Locke first encounter "Adam and Eve" in the cave. This juxtaposition, which eventually allows for narrative closure, at the same time works to *delay* resolution due to this merging of the present with the past. That is, the "present" for the viewer (of "Across") is actually the distant past. The episode ends by transporting viewers to their own "viewing past"—a scene they first encountered six years prior. Hence, the temporal play in this episode works to develop the thematic content of the show as a whole.[6]

REVELATIONS

Throughout the first five seasons—all embedded with layered temporality—the audience learns that all of the characters on the island are flawed in some way. Extending this thematic, the sixth season suggests that these characters are all seeking redemption for their past mistakes, in a way echoing President Bush's dictate that this quest should be one tackled nationwide. In the final episode of *Lost*, containing flashsideways, viewers see these characters as they "might have been" if they had made different choices. This episode, and indeed the entire season, relies on these flashsideways—a purgatory in which characters, now dead, must work out their problems in order to move forward, to cross over. The audience later realizes that although some of the survivors went on to live their lives after getting off the island, the most important part of their lives was the time they had spent together. This narrative structure reinforces this fact.

During the regular timeline taking place on the island, and not the flashsideways taking place supposedly post-island back in the states, the viewer watches as Jack, who has been chosen by Jacob to protect the island, tries to get to the light source in order to fix it, and thus save the world. Kate asks him why he took the job, to which Jack responds that he "was supposed to" ("The End"). He continues: the "island's all I've got left. It's the only thing in my life I haven't managed to ruin." Kate tellingly replies, "You haven't ruined anything. Nothing is irreversible" ("The End"). Jack, showing the resilience foreshadowed in the pilot episode, is determined to go down into the cave alone, knowing that he will not survive. Once again, he explains that this is what is supposed to happen, clearly a reference to destiny. In a surprising move, he names Hurley—the good-natured castaway often utilized for comic relief—as the next protector after his death. He then modifies the protection ritual, and viewers watch it unfold for the third time (the first time being between Jacob and his mother, the second between Jacob and Jack, and now this final exchange between Jack and Hurley). Jack fills an Oceanic bottle with water from the stream, offers it to Hurley, and, after Hurley drinks, utters the echoed line, "Now you're like me" ("The End"). Before Jack is lowered into the source—where he ultimately repairs the light, redeeming himself in this role of martyr for the island—he tells Desmond, a character whose path crossed his both on and off the island, that he will "see him in another life." This is a line repeated throughout the series; "another life," significantly, hints at another temporality and, indeed, another universe.

At the end of the final episode, the following exchange takes place between Hurley and Ben, the former leader of the "others":

HURLEY: Jack's . . . gone . . . isn't he?
BEN: He did his job, Hugo.
HURLEY: It's my job now . . . What the hell am I supposed to do?
BEN: I think you do what you do best. Take care of people. You can start by helping Desmond get home.
HURLEY: But how? People can't leave the island.
BEN: That's how Jacob ran things . . . Maybe there's another way. A better way. ("The End")

The line "maybe there's another way. A better way" suggests that people can—and should—exercise reason at the same time that they have faith. Thus, Ben advocates many ways to fulfill one's destiny, which further articulates that blind faith or unquestioning obedience to the past, just as Milton's God illuminated, is not always the best way.

PARADISE REGAINED?

Television shows prior to the first decade of the twenty-first century worked to tie up loose ends, if not at the end of an episode, then at least at the end of its run. *Lost*, however, did not offer its viewers any such ending. Just as the American climate was still marked with uncertainty by the end of the program's run, so was the narrative closure of *Lost* marked with uncertainty. Just as viewers struggled to make sense of the world around them, *Lost*, through its six-year run, tried to make sense of that very same world that had changed beyond recognition. The narrative structure of *Lost*, added to the many questions posed within the series, and its allusions to philosophy, religion, and psychology, all add up to a program that corresponded to the general population's feeling of apprehension in the face of a new era, one that could not be "done over." Indeed, this was—and perhaps still is—our middle hour, a time in which Americans were situated in an unstable present at the same time that they grieved for a lost past and looked forward to a brighter future.

SUGGESTED EPISODES FOR ADDITIONAL STUDY

Lost
2:1. "Man of Science, Man of Faith." Writ. Damon Lindeloff. Dir. Jack Bender. September 21, 2005.
2:3. "Orientation." Writ. Javier Grillo-Marxuach and Craig Wright. Dir. Jack Bender. October 5, 2005.
2:7. "The Other 48 Days." Writ. Carlton Cuse and Damon Lindelof. Dir. Eric Laneuville. November 16, 2005.
2:23. "Live Together, Die Alone." Writ. Carlton Cuse and Damon Lindelof. Dir. Jack Bender. May 24, 2006.
3:1. "A Tale of Two Cities." Writ. J. J. Abrams and Damon Lindelof. Dir. Jack Bender. October 4, 2006.
3:20. "The Man Behind the Curtain." Writ. Elizabeth Sarnoff and Drew Goddard. Dir. Bobby Roth. May 9, 2007.
4:1. "The Beginning of the End." Writ. Carlton Cuse and Damon Lindelof. Dir. Jack Bender. January 31, 2008.
4:5. "The Constant." Writ. Carlton Cuse and Damon Lindelof. Dir. Jack Bender. February 28, 2008.
4:12. "There's No Place Like Home, Part 1." Writ. Carlton Cuse and Damon Lindelof. Dir. Stephen Williams. May 15, 2008.

4:13/14. "There's No Place Like Home, Parts 2 and 3." Writ. Carlton Cuse and Damon Lindelof. Dir. Jack Bender. May 29, 2008.

5:1. "Because You Left." Writ. Carlton Cuse and Damon Lindelof. Dir. Stephen Williams. January 21, 2009.

5:15. "The Variable." Writ. Edward Kitsis and Adam Horowitz. Dir. Paul Edwards. April 29, 2009.

5:16/17. "The Incident, Parts 1 and 2." Writ. Carlton Cuse and Damon Lindelof. Dir. Jack Bender. May 13, 2009.

6:01/02. "LA X, Parts 1 and 2." Writ. Carlton Cuse and Damon Lindelof. Dir. Jack Bender. February 2, 2010.

6:9. "Ab Aeterno." Writ. Melinda Hsu Taylor and Greggory Nations. Dir. Tucker Gates. March 23, 2010.

6:16. "What They Died For." Writ. Edward Kitsis and Adam Horowitz and Elizabeth Sarnoff. Dir. Paul Edwards. May 18, 2010.

NOTES

1. J. Wood also speaks to the theme of how *Lost* works out the concerns of the 9/11 tragedy.

2. For a more in-depth look at symbolism in *Lost*, see Christian Piatt's work.

3. For an in-depth analysis of father/son relationships on *Lost*, see Melissa Ames's article.

4. The obvious biblical versions of Jacob and The Man in the Black (MIB) are Adam and Eve's sons, Cain and Abel (Genesis 4:1–15 tells the story of the pair). Other famous brothers include Ishmael and Isaac (Genesis 16–17); Esau and Jacob (Genesis 25:19–26); Perez and Zerah (Genesis 38:27–30), and, of course, Joseph and his brothers (Genesis 37–50): all of these siblings' tales are beset with references to deceit, murder, and/or good versus evil.

5. Drinking the liquid suggests the drinking of Christ's redemptive blood during a Christian mass.

6. See also Jesse Kavadlo regarding time travel in season five. Significantly, Kavadlo claims that time travel is a type of "wish fulfillment . . . a way to rewrite and re-right the past in order to alter the present" (237).

WORKS CITED

"Across the Sea." *Lost*. Dir. Tucker Gates. ABC. May 11, 2010. Television.

Ames, Melissa. "Where Have All the Good Men Gone?: A Psychoanalytic Reading of the Absent Fathers and Damaged Dads on ABC's *Lost*." *Journal of Popular Culture*. N.d. N. pag.

Bush, George W. "Remarks at the National Day of Prayer & Remembrance." Episcopal National Cathedral, Washington, D.C. September 14, 2001. Speech.

"The End." *Lost*. Dir. Jack Bender. ABC. May 23, 2010. Television.

Holy Bible. Ed. Reverend John P. O'Connell. Chicago: The Catholic Press, 1950. Print.

"House of the Rising Sun." *Lost*. Dir. Michael Zinberg. ABC. October 27, 2004. Television.

"In Translation." *Lost*. Dir. Tucker Gates. ABC. February 23, 2005. Television.

Johnson, Steven. *Everything Bad Is Good for You: How Today's Popular Culture Is Actually Making Us Smarter*. New York: Riverhead Books, 2006. Print.

Kavadlo, Jessa. "We Have to Go Back: Lost After 9/11." *Looking for* Lost: *Critical Essays on the Enigmatic Series*. Ed. Randy Laist. Jefferson, NC: McFarland, 2011. Print.

McLuhan, Marshall. *Understanding Media: The Extensions of Man*. Ed. Terrence Gordon. Corte Madera, CA: Gingko Press, 2003. Print.

Mittell, Jason. "Narrative Complexity in Contemporary American Television." *The Velvet Light Trap* 58 (2006): 29–40. Web. September 2010.

Murphy, John M. "Our Mission and Our Moment: George W. Bush and September 11th." *Rhetoric & Public Affairs* 6.4 (2003): 607–32. Web. December 26, 2010.

Piatt, Christian. *Lost: A Search for Meaning*. St. Louis: Chalice Press, 2006. Print.

"Pilot." *Lost*. Dir. J. J. Abrams. ABC. September 22, 2004. Television.

Tollefson, Pam. *Chinese Significance of Plants*. March 10, 2010. Web. December 26, 2010.

Walker, William. "On Reason, Faith, and Freedom in *Paradise Lost*." *SEL* 47.1 (2007): 143–59. Print.

"White Rabbit." *Lost*. Dir. Kevin Hooks. ABC. October 20, 2004. Television.

Wood, J. *Living* Lost: *Why We're All Stuck on the Island*. New Orleans, LA: Garrett County Press, 2007. Print.

9

"NEW BEGINNINGS ONLY LEAD TO PAINFUL ENDS"
"Undeading" and Fear of Consequences in Pushing Daisies

KASEY BUTCHER

The ending of *Pushing Daisies* (ABC, 2007–2009) looked much like the beginning. Mirroring the first scene of the series, the camera pans out on Digby the golden retriever running through a field of yellow daisies as the narrator (Jim Dale) notes, "At that moment, in the town of Coeur d'Coeurs, events occurred that are not, were not, and should never be considered an ending. For endings, as it is known, are where we begin" ("Kerplunk"). The parallel structure and optimistic ending of the series, in contrast with the abrupt manner in which it ended, facing struggles through a writers' strike and an untimely cancellation, gesture toward the central conflict of the series. Through the mysteries and secrets that make up the plot of each *Pushing Daisies* episode, the characters' major conflict is a persistent tension between pessimism and optimism, or hesitation and risk taking, and the fear of consequences that accompany such. In this conflict, as the characters struggle to find a balance between their hopes and their fears, they are in stride with the political atmosphere of the time, overlapping not only with the 2007–2008 writers' strike, but also with the build up to the 2008 market crash and the rhetoric of the Obama campaign within the broader discourse of the 2008 presidential election. In this way, the larger-than-life world of *Pushing Daisies* reflects the political anxieties of its time as well as the interaction between the audience and other media in a hyperconnected age.

"I DON'T BELIEVE IN REINCARNATION"
Genre, Anxiety, and Do-Overs

In the "Pie-lette," PI Emerson Cod (Chi McBride) says he does not believe in reincarnation because "the planet's falling apart. Right now, it's the children's problem. We reincarnate, it's our problem." The premise of *Pushing Daisies* (hereafter *Daisies*), however, is couched firmly in the consequences of a do-over. Ned (Lee Pace), a pie maker with the ability to touch "dead things" and bring them back to life, revives his childhood sweetheart, Charlotte "Chuck" Charles (Anna Friel), giving her a second start at life. On the surface, *Daisies* is a candy-colored, fast-talking supernatural dramedy, but beneath the potential of "undeading" and bringing justice to murder victims lurks anxiety about the consequences of one's actions, as well as about the responsibility that comes with a fresh start. Ned's gift comes with limitations. If he touches someone he has "undeaded" a second time, the person dies again forever, and if he keeps someone alive for longer than a minute someone else drops dead. Ned dreads what would happen if people found out about his gift and insists on keeping it a secret. Despite this fact, he uses his gift to help Emerson solve murder mysteries in order to keep his business, The Pie Hole, afloat. Although *Daisies* deals primarily with murder mysteries and romance, the series is most concerned with the consequences of a person's actions and the push-pull between pessimistic hesitancy and optimistic risk taking.

The period during which *Daisies* was produced and aired was one of growing anxiety over the economy and the presidential election, which became a media circus as candidates used unprecedented amounts of new media (Facebook, Twitter, YouTube, etc.). Similarly, popular entertainment of the time offered increasingly complicated and innovative narrative frameworks, remixes of genre conventions (as in the rise of reality TV) (Mittell xi–xiii, 200–201), and warrior dramas coping with the trauma of September 11 (Dixon 1–4).

Hitting stride with both the rhetoric of optimism and the anxiety of its time, the aesthetic of *Daisies* is heavily infused with both retro throw-back and elements of *film noir*. The bright color scheme of the clothing and exterior sets throw the dim interior lighting and crime-drama storylines into stark contest. Dale Ewing Jr. claims, "The stylistic gloom of *film noir* afforded an appealing paradigm of disorder. At the surface of life, America reflected an innocent appearance, but this was only repression, which is a breeding ground for all sorts of irrationalities and fears" (63). Similarly, the over-the-top murders, *femme fatales*, and playfully sharp narration of *Daisies* only heighten the sense of anxiety surrounding the consequences of Ned's actions, as well as of the actions of the murderers.

Further, Ken Hillis argues that the ambivalence of *film noir* originally reflected an uncertainty about postwar identity and deep doubts about the ability to achieve the American Dream (3). Therefore, it makes sense that *Daisies*, along with other shows of the period, such as *Veronica Mars* (WB, 2004–2007) and a plethora of forensic or cop dramas, would incorporate elements of *noir* at a time when the economy cast doubts on the financial prospects of many Americans and national identity post-9/11 was still an issue, especially during the contentious election. As much as it plays with genre conventions, however, *Daisies* is not true *noir*, which features "romantic pessimism as a kind of slap in the face of American naïveté and innocence" (Ewing 63). Instead, in *Daisies noir* is mixed with more nostalgic vintage visuals, heightening the tension in the series between pessimism and optimism. For example, the past, usually depicted as a happier time, always looks like the 1950s with perfectly maintained kitchens and yards. Further, Chuck's personal style draws on iconic looks from the 1960s through the 1990s, with her bright clothing matching her attitude (Rochlin). While the nostalgic elements of the show align with the optimistic characters' view that having a fresh start comes with a world of opportunities, the *noir* elements highlight the potential for history to repeat itself—that maybe having a fresh start does not actually free a person from his or her past.

The blending of nostalgic and *noir* motifs speaks to the ideological implications of the show. The noir elements implicate reactions to the aftershock of the September 11 terrorist attacks and a growing distrust of the government, of Wall Street, and uncertainty about the economic and political future of the country. The nostalgic elements overlap with political discourses that emphasize "traditional" American values or the presentation of the Obamas as heirs to the Kennedys' Camelot (Venkataraman). Further, the retro styling of the show, along with plots and dialogue that make reference to contemporary technology and culture create a sort of timelessness that lends the show an ability to play out anxieties without being tied directly to the events surrounding them. *Daisies* can reflect contemporary discourses without literally having to recreate current events.

According to John Fiske in *Television Culture*, the characters on television are more than just individuals, they are also "encodings of ideology," and the way television encodes meaning for the viewer comes through intertextuality, in which one text is "necessarily read in relationship to others and that range of textual knowledge is brought to bear upon it" (9, 108). The viewer of the television program is not meant to read each episode as a singular text, but rather as a part of a series and the discourse surrounding the series (vertical intertextuality) and also in relationship to the other programs circulating at the same time, such as other TV shows, news media, film, and so forth (horizontal intertexuality). According to Fiske, then, narratives are written using the knowledge of the viewing culture and texts only really make sense when they work within, rework, and re-present the discourses already encoded in this culture (*Television* 115–16). Thus, *Daisies* works on a visual level because of the way it draws on a variety of genres from fairytale to *film noir* in ways that the audience can recognize and on an emotional level because it plays out popular discourses in a more distanced medium than the nightly news.

In the twenty-first century, however, the rise of new media increasingly affected the way audiences consumed television. The increased use of online streaming through network Web sites and other venues such as Hulu, along with the ability to download shows to handheld devices, partly worked to diminish the experience of television audiences watching shows together. Instead of water-cooler standbys watched at the same time, audiences are split temporally so that viewers are increasingly watching what they want, when they want, and where they want (Lotz 35–36). In this way, television usage has shifted from providing an "electronic public sphere" in which it reached a massive, largely heterogeneous audience, to providing more opportunities for subcultural forums. Amanda Lotz asserts that in this way the electronic public sphere exists on a continuum so that large media events, such as the Super Bowl, *American Idol*, or Obama's thirty-minute prime-time ad (during which, coincidentally, *Daisies* aired), still operate to reach a large audience, but other programming reaches a more self-selected, like-minded group (42–43). It could be argued that this "subcultural forum" explains the cult-appeal of programming such as *Daisies* and *Arrested Development* (Fox, 2003–2006) despite poor ratings and early cancellations.

Perhaps the genius inspiring *Daisies*' cult following is that the diverse narratives it draws on do not always resolve in the way the audience may expect. For example, Emerson is the noir touchstone of the show, a parody of the hardboiled PI, but he also has a soft spot, visualized through the motif of his knitting in season one and his creation of a pop-up book in season two (Rochlin). But he knits gun holsters and money cases and creates a pop-up book about a little detective, blurring the distinctions between the *noir* and nostalgic visual cues. The innocence of the nostalgic elements of the show is often undermined (pop-up books can become murder weapons), as are the *noir* elements.

To achieve this complex web of visuals and emotions, the series also engages in temporal play through flashbacks that present both relevant history from the primary characters' lives and key details to the murder mysteries they investigate. Thus, *Daisies* layers time in such a way that the past is never very far away for the viewer (or in the memory of the characters) and the consequences or causality always appear imminent, which is further demonstrated through the narrator's exact accounting of time, down to the second. Therefore, the viewer is asked to keep track of all the layers of the plot as well as the overlaps between different aesthetic cues. For the humor of *Daisies* to fully work, the writers assume that the audience sees the irony in the knitting PI or the homage to classic *noir* movies such as *The Birds* ("Bitter Sweets") or *Vertigo* ("Bitches").

The use of do-overs also plays with narrative time as it both interrupts time and presents multiple layers of the story simultaneously. Usually when a character is brought back from the dead, he is unaware that he has been killed and that time has passed him by. Still, once the victim realizes what has happened, she fills the investigators in on the details surrounding her death, the narration of which is often accompanied by a flashback and/or parallel narration unveiling pertinent details to the case. In this way, the viewer is presented with multiple layers of narrative time concurrently, creating frame texts that allow the murder victims, through their one minute of "new life," to actively participate in bringing their killers to justice. This use of time intersects with both the *noir* and the retro elements of the show and intensifies the tension between optimism and pessimism as not everyone is given the fresh start Chuck is given—the majority of people only get one minute back from the dead.

The temporal play of the do-over and "undeading" thus connects these two aesthetics. The *noir* drives the ambivalence and disorder that motivate the wish to try again and the nostalgia provides a perpetual sense that, as gloomy as the situation may be, things were once good. Here "undeading" is also key. For some characters, like Emerson, new life just means new responsibilities, but for others it means a whole world of opportunity and a responsibility to live more fully.

FIRST TOUCH, LIFE
Optimism and Pessimism in Pushing Daisies

This tension between pessimism and optimism drives the main story arcs of the series. Over the course of twenty-two episodes, Ned and Chuck have several long-term conflicts, at the heart of which is a tug-of-war between Chuck's optimism and impulses toward action and Ned's pessimism and fear of the consequences action might have. Ned fears both the consequences of someone from Chuck's past recognizing her and of Chuck learning his secret that he accidentally killed her father when he brought his own mother back to life. Additionally, the pair must constantly be alert to the consequences that would occur if they ever should touch again; thus they are forced to forever engage in a "ballet of avoidance" ("Bzzzzzzzzz!"). In the second season, Chuck begins to rebuild her life, moves into Olive's apartment, and considers getting her own job outside of the Pie Hole. Because she previously stayed close to home to care for her aunts, Chuck views her own "undeading" as a liberating opportunity and is eager to make the most of it. As she puts it, "I suppose dying is as good an excuse as any to start living" ("Pie-lette"). Chuck's desire to enjoy her fresh start in life causes Ned to worry needlessly that they are drifting apart.

In "Circus Circus," when Ned's worry over Chuck's behavior reaches its peak, the murder the team investigates mirrors his anxiety. The episode begins with a flashback to Ned trying to start anew by leaving boarding school, an experience after which he ultimately concludes that "new beginnings only lead to bitter ends" ("Circus"). Then, when investigating the mass murder of clowns in a traveling circus, Emerson, Ned, and Chuck discover that the murderer is Pierre, an acrobat who killed the clowns because they were planning to unionize and he feared the consequences this would have for his circus workplace. Pierre's reflection, "I just wanted everything to stay the same. Is that so terrible?" ("Circus"), echoes Ned's own feelings about Chuck moving out of his apartment. While Pierre goes to jail, Ned comes around to the idea of Chuck moving on with her life. Although the episode seems to come out on the side of change and progress, in true *Daisies* fashion, it is more complex than that. As Emerson returns Sweet Nicky Heaps, a teen who ran away to the circus, to her mother, Mrs. Heaps exclaims, "I don't know who she is anymore, she's completely changed" ("Circus"). Emerson instructs her to "love what's there," but his comments are complicated by his regret over losing his own daughter and wondering if she "had changed too much to ever be found" ("Circus"). The episode is just one example of the way change and fear of change are an undercurrent of the series.

Meanwhile, Chuck's aunts Lily (Swoosie Kurtz) and Vivian (Ellen Greene) mirror the tension between Ned and Chuck. Throughout the duration of the series runs a subplot in which Chuck tries to get her grieving aunts, once famed synchronized swimmers who now have "matching personality disorders" ("Pie-lette"), out of their house and back into the water. Aunt Lily (secretly Chuck's mother) falls into a deeper depression after Chuck's death. Aunt Vivian, however, looks for a way to move on, prepared to take the plunge back into life, pushing for the duo to start swimming again. She cannot really get started, however, without Lily, whose reluctance does not stem just from her depression. Deeply protective, Lily is afraid of Vivian getting hurt, and her fear of acting is caused by her fear of the consequences of Vivian's actions and remorse over the consequences of actions in her own past. This "sibling yin-yang" further emphasizes the binary between optimism and pessimism established in the series, heightening within the narrative a similar pattern played out in the media coverage of the presidential election.

Further, the narrator's exposition of details or secrets with his catchphrase, "the facts were these . . . ," punctuates each episode. This device, which Steven Johnson calls a "flashing arrow" heightens the tension surrounding the action and consequences within any given episode (73). While Johnson describes flashing arrows as "narrative handholding," reducing "the amount of analytic work you need to make sense of a story," *Daisies* uses the arrows ironically, directing the audience toward all the relevant details, but also commenting on the events with word play and sarcasm so that the audience feels in on a joke with the narrator (74). For example, in "Dummy" he observes: "As Olive considered how much she loved Digby for paying attention to her when the Pie Maker would not, Digby considered how much he loved salt." Moreover, the narrator's account of the exact timing of events, knowledge of all the details, and recounting of how they interact sets up the cause-and-effect rhythm of the series, legitimizing the hesitancy of characters like Ned and Lily. The voice-over and focus on causality are also *noir* staples, important to the mysteries on the show. Often on *Daisies*, small actions end in disastrous results; and in small details Emerson, Ned, or Chuck usually find the key to solving their cases. For example, in "Dim Sum Lose Some," the team investigates the death of a cook who lost his daughter's hand in marriage during a complicated game using Chinese food in lieu of cards. In the end, a dog solves the mystery by sniffing a suspect's pockets revealing that he was hiding food that allowed him to cheat. The narrator's commentary on the plot makes explicit that these seemingly unimportant actions or small details are crucial in both investigation and life.

While the audience has the narrator's help in navigating the twists of the plot, the personal baggage each character brings to the story is more complicated. As each episode begins with a scene from a character's past, the show asks the audience to keep track of how these stories are folded into the main narrative. Further, these secrets from the past influence the hesitancy of the characters to act in present situations. These overlaps in the characters' individual stories, themes, and anxieties are common to the series as a whole and are strengthened by the use of flashback and the temporal play of "undeading." Conversely, the development of an increasingly complicated social network full of secrets also intensifies the temporal play. Secrets are often expressed in current time, but explained in flashbacks. As the secrets compound, the moments of stalled or layered time in which the critical details are recounted become more important to remember. Because the flashbacks often include information that the audience is privy to but the other characters are not, the social network also underscores anxiety about people not being who they seem to be, an anxiety that was also an undercurrent in the 2008 presidential election.

PUSHING DAISIES AND CIRCULATING POLITICAL DISCOURSES

While *Daisies* does not feature politicians or explicitly discuss politics, through intertextuality and transmediation the viewer can pick up on how the show mirrors the political discourses circulating at the time, overlapping with the rhetorical "risk taking" of the Obama campaign, in which Americans were asked to be optimistic despite an array of major national challenges. Specifically, the show's tension between optimism and pessimism reflects these political attitudes as portrayed in mainstream media and the larger-than-life fictional plots covered an array of issues that were at the forefront during the period, including corrupt corporations ("Dummy"; "Bzzzzzzzzz!"), labor issues ("Circus"), the plight of small business owners ("Pie-lette"; "Bitter Sweets"), and greedy insurance companies ("Corpsicle").

In the 2008 campaign, one plagued by the above issues, the race ran largely as a competition between the images both of the political parties and the candidates themselves, and how those images were constructed and interpreted. As the candidates positioned themselves in strategic narratives, their opponents offered counternarratives, using the very same images, but interpreting them in different ways (Buck-Morss 150–53). The public was thus faced with the task of individually determining how to interpret the images and platforms of the candidates.

Specifically, starting as early as when fundraising for the primaries began, the rhetoric of the Obama campaign focused on hope and change, connecting back to his 2004 Democratic National Convention speech and subsequent book, *The Audacity of Hope*. In response, the opposition framed this hope as naivety and cited his lack of experience as support. Throughout the entire race, the tension was consistently between the portrayal of the Obama campaign as a movement for the optimistic renewal of the American Dream (Kephart and Rafferty 6) and the portrayal of John McCain and the other Republican candidates as holding firmly to "traditional" American ideals, even as McCain positioned himself as a maverick interested in action rather than speech (Kellner 711). Despite their divergent depictions of the state of the country, Marilyn Lashley argues that the public voted largely on personality, rather than on key issues. The candidates, capitalizing on this, built their platforms by spinning personal narratives meant to sway voters (Lashley 364–65). While Republicans largely based their spin on the cultural identity of the opponent, focusing on

Obama's religious affiliations and questioning his citizenship (Lashley 366), the Clintons attempted to spin Obama's image into that of a "fairytale" figure without real-life solutions (Phillips).

Another significant part of molding candidate imagery was the creation of media spectacle, especially in the primaries, and over the course of the race Barack Obama became a "master of the spectacle," using a European tour, a half-hour television spot, and new media to create a buzz around his grassroots campaign (Kellner 708). The rhetorical strategy behind the spectacle hinged on his slogan "Yes We Can!" The slogan became the central theme of the campaign, presenting Obama as the candidate most in-touch with the American spirit of hope and optimism (Kephart and Rafferty 6–7). Media events, however, are not so much about the event itself as about the narrative *about* the event (Fiske, *Media* 4). Consistently, through the use of spin and spectacle, the candidates used the media in an attempt to present themselves as the best leader for the country, whether through the promise of hope and change or through a maverick's clear-headed action (Kellner 711).

While it may not be possible to argue that *Daisies*' writers were directly influenced by the presidential election as they wrote the show, the question of intent may be a moot point. When looking at the show, especially the fall 2008 season, considering intertexutality and transmediation, the relationship between politics and popular entertainment carries more resonance. This complex relationship between creating both a relevant narrative connected to popular discourses and a unique narrative that moves the viewer as an individual is a challenge for both television writers and campaign managers. Henry Jenkins writes, "Popular culture can generate a fair amount of effortless emotion by following well-trod formulas, but to make us go 'wow,' it has to twist or transform those formulas into something marvelous and unexpected" (3). Perhaps what *Daisies* and the political atmosphere in which it was run most obviously have in common is the reworking of old tropes toward the goal of "wowing" the public. While *Daisies* played with the conventions of film *noir*, fairytale, romance, comedy, and drama to create a larger-than-life, retro world, the discourse of the 2008 election worked with the common conventions of American politics—promise of change, hope in the American Dream, and imagery of liberty. As these "narratives" ran at the same time, the observant viewer may have picked up on the overlapping messages that ran throughout the campaign and *Daisies*. Amid the tension over bank collapses, bailouts, an ongoing war, and political spin that presents opponents as not-as-they-may-seem, *Daisies* and its complex narratives draw attention to the ways in which fear of consequences, misunderstandings, and secrets can be worked out and overcome, at least within the safe confines of fiction.

SECOND TOUCH, DEAD AGAIN FOREVER
The Writers' Strike and the End of Pushing Daisies

While *Daisies* reflects political discourses, the show's run also directly interacted with the 2007–2008 Writers Guild of America strike. The strike began on November 5, 2007, and lasted until February 12, 2008, during which production of network television series was halted as Screen Actors Guild actors also refused to cross the picket line. The writers went on strike over DVD residuals and compensation for the distribution of their work through new media. At its heart, the strike dealt with the consequences of new technology's impact on entertainment, especially television. Although Webisodes and viewing TV episodes on the Internet were both tremendously popular, the writers asserted they were not fairly compensated for their work as distribution through these novel means began (Cieply and Barnes).

ABC and *Daisies* executives decided to end the first season with the last episode produced after the strike began, "Corpsicle." The rationale was that the show would not air against *American Idol* and, starting in March 2008, the cast and crew could spend the interim on new episodes and the show could come back stronger in the fall. In some ways, the strike offered *Daisies* a new start. At the end of "Corpsicle," the reconciliation between Ned and Chuck was still shaky after Ned confessed his responsibility for her father's death. Meanwhile, scent expert Oscar Vibenius was suspicious of Chuck, whom he thought smelled of death, and was determined to discover her secret. Vibenius's story was left a cliffhanger, but the cliffhanger was never returned to. When *Daisies* returned on October 1, 2008, Ned and Chuck's relationship had been repaired and Vibenius was never mentioned again. Instead, momentum shifted to the revelation of other secrets and to Chuck's request for Ned to undead her father, who has been buried for twenty years. The narrative time gap exaggerates the gap created by the strike. Instead of picking up where the show left off, time moved forward as it had in real life, but the audience was not made privy to the events during this lapse. Under other circumstances, the complete and unexplained abandonment of a plotline would probably be an issue, but given the long break between seasons, no one seemed to notice or care if they did. *Daisies* prepared to take advantage of this new beginning.

Instead, however, a painful end was in store. Although the show had a cult following and was critically acclaimed, the second season never really gained any momentum in the ratings and, likely because of high production costs, was canceled by November 30, 2008. Adding insult to injury, ABC waited nearly six months before airing the last three episodes.

Perhaps the show's untimely end after the new beginning provided by the writers' strike reflects Ned's idea that "new beginnings only lead to painful ends." The tenor of the series' close, however, is positive, with Digby running through the daisies and the narrator gesturing toward the cyclical nature of life. Through all the conflicts over change and the consequences of the characters' actions, for better or worse, the series seems to end on the side of Chuck's optimism and readiness to take action. Though it ended in the spring of 2009, months after the presidential inauguration, it would have been interesting to see how the show would have developed as the politics of hope and change that got President Obama elected faced further challenges. As the election ended, Obama's presidency began amid the continued economic downturn, war, a much-contested health care reform, and the beginnings of the Tea Party movement. Although *Pushing Daisies* had ended, for the political culture surrounding it, the conflict over change and hope was just beginning.

SUGGESTED EPISODES FOR ADDITIONAL STUDY

Pushing Daisies
1:3. "Fun in Funeral." Writ. Bryan Fuller. Dir. Paul Edwards. October 17, 2007.
1:5. "Girth." Writ. Katherine Lingenfelter. Dir. Peter O'Fallon. October 31, 2007.
2:3. "Bad Habits." Writ. Gretchen J. Berg and Aaron Harberts. Dir. Peter O'Fallon. October 15, 2008.
2:8. "Comfort Food." Writ. Douglas Petrie. Dir. Peter Lauer. December 3, 2008.
2:9. "The Legend of Merle McQuoddy." Writ. Dara Resnik Creasey and Chad Gomez Creasey. Dir. Lawrence Trilling. December 10, 2008.

WORKS CITED

"Bitches." *Pushing Daisies*. Writ. Chad Gomez Creasey and Dara Resnik. ABC. November 14, 2007. Television.
"Bitter Sweets." *Pushing Daisies*. Writ. Abby Grenwater. ABC. November 28, 2007. Television.
Buck-Morss, Susan. "Obama and the Image." *Culture, Theory & Critique* 50.2–3 (2009): 145–64. Print.
"Bzzzzzzzz!" *Pushing Daisies*. Writ. Bryan Fuller. ABC. October 1, 2008. Television.

Cieply, Michael, and Brooks Barnes. "Writers Say Strike to Start Monday." *New York Times*. November 2, 2007. Web. September 30, 2010.
"Circus Circus." *Pushing Daisies*. Writ. Peter Ocko. ABC. October 8, 2008. Television.
"Corpsicle." *Pushing Daisies*. Writ. Lisa Joy. ABC. December 12, 2007. Television.
"Dim Sum Lose Some." *Pushing Daisies*. Writ. Davey Holmes. ABC. October 29, 2008. Television.
Dixon, Wheeler W. *Film and Television After 9/11*. Carbondale: Southern Illinois University Press, 2004. Print.
"Dummy." *Pushing Daisies*. Writ. Peter Ocko. ABC. October 10, 2007. Television.
Ewing, Dale E., Jr. "'Film Noir': Style and Content." *Journal of Popular Film and Television* 16.2 (1988): 61–69. *Academic Search Complete*. EBSCO. Web. December 15, 2010.
Fiske, John. *Media Matters: Everyday Culture and Political Change*. Minneapolis: University of Minnesota Press, 1994. Print.
———. *Television Culture*. London: Methuen, 1987. Print.
Jenkins, Henry. *The Wow Climax: Tracing the Emotional Impact of Popular Culture*. New York: New York University Press, 2007. Print.
Johnson, Steven. *Everything Bad Is Good for You: How Today's Popular Culture Is Actually Making Us Smarter*. New York: Riverhead, 2005. Print.
Kellner, Douglas. "Media Spectacle and the 2008 Presidential Election." *Cultural Studies Critical Methodologies* 6th ser. 9 (2009): 707–16. Print.
Kephart, John M., and Steven F. Rafferty. "'Yes We Can': Rhizomic Rhetorical Agency in Hyper-Modern Campaign Ecologies." *Argumentation and Advocacy* 46 (2009): 6–20. Print.
"Kerplunk." *Pushing Daisies*. Writ. Gretchen J. Berg and Aaron Harberts. ABC. June 13, 2009. Television.
Lashley, Marilyn. "The Politics of Cognitive Dissonance: Spin, the Media, Race (and Ethnicity) in the 2008 Presidential Election." *American Review of Canadian Studies* 39.4 (2009): 364–77. Print.
Lotz, Amanda D. *The Television Will Be Revolutionized*. New York: New York University Press, 2007. Print.
Mittell, Jason. *Genre and Television: From Cop Shows to Cartoons in American Culture*. New York: Routledge, 2004. Print.
Phillips, Kate. "The Clinton Camp Unbound." *New York Times*. January 8, 2008. Web. December 15, 2010.
"Pie-lette." *Pushing Daisies*. Writ. Bryan Fuller ABC. October 3, 2007. Television.
Rochlin, Margy. "Clothes Make the Show: Robert Blackman: 'Pushing Daisies.'" *New York Times*. June 5, 2009. Web. December 10, 2010.
Venkataraman, Nitya. "Camelot Crowns Obama for 'the Future.'" *ABC News*. January 29, 2008. Web. December 15, 2010.

PART III

THE FUNCTIONS OF TIME
Analyzing the Effects of Nonnormative Narrative Structure(s)

10

"DID YOU GET PEARS?"
Temporality and Temps Mortality in The Wire, Mad Men, and Arrested Development

GRY C. RUSTAD AND TIMOTHEUS VERMEULEN

Critically acclaimed and thriving commercially, *Mad Men* (AMC, 2007–Present) has been the subject of widespread debate. It has attracted the attention of television scholars, philosophers, cultural historians, commentators and columnists, newspaper critics, ad executives, fashion designers, and bloggers, to name but a few. There are books, journals, essays, magazine entries, newspaper articles, and thousands of blogs devoted entirely to *Mad Men*. In this chapter, we aim to explain at least some of the appeal *Mad Men* has for critics and viewers alike by concentrating on the textual and temporal nature of one scene that has generated much discussion: the "pear scene."

The scene at stake, which takes place toward the end of the season-four episode "The Rejected," depicts two elderly people arguing about groceries. As an old man stands in the doorway, an old woman slowly walks toward him from across the hallway. "Did you get pears?" he asks her. The woman does not reply. "Did you get pears?" he asks again. Then, impatiently, "did you get pears?" Finally, the old woman agitatedly replies, "we'll discuss it inside," after which they both step inside, closing the door behind them. After they close the door, the scene cuts to the other side of the hallway, just in time to see the show's main character, Donald Draper (John Hamm), step inside his apartment and close the door behind him.

Critics have called the scene anything from a microcosm of the series as a whole to a metaphor for Don's state of mind at this moment. Bloggers have variously pondered it as a consideration of the emerging generational conflict (the scene is set on the cusp of the sixties, after all), as a contemplation of the changing relationship between public and private, and as a commentary on, respectively, institutionalism, etiquette, or a particular mindset. As one critic bemusedly put it: "if anyone knows what the real deal was with the pears discussion at the end, let me know" (Sassone). What seems to have confused most critics and bloggers is that the scene has no apparent meaning for, and cannot be explained in terms of, either the episode's plot or the series' narrative arc. Its actors play no further part in either the episode or the series, and its action has no function for the development of any one storyline. As a number of bloggers frustratedly scoffed: who cares whether she got pears?

This chapter will explain why critics and bloggers have cared whether the woman got pears, and why we think one *should* indeed care. Drawing on the work of the French art philosopher Jacques Rancière, and to a lesser extent that of Gilles Deleuze and Felix Guattari, along with extensive textual analysis, this chapter will argue that the so-called pear question opens one's eyes and mind (and stomach) to an aesthetic that is increasingly common in contemporary "Quality Television"—one that has largely gone by unnoticed. We have elsewhere discussed the implications this aesthetic has for the televisual mise-en-scène. We will here concern ourselves primarily with its particular narrative inferences, especially with respect to narrative time. Besides the pear scene, this essay will also take a cursory glance at a few similar "non-narrative" moments in the HBO police procedural *The Wire* (2001–2008) and FOX's situation comedy *Arrested Development* (2001–2003). The choice for the combined discussion of these three programs is threefold: they illustrate that the particular aesthetic and poetic exemplified by the pear scene are increasingly present across networks, channels, and genres; they show how the pear scene inflects the nature of genre; and, most important, they demonstrate how the pear question influences serial television's seriality or temporality.

FROM AN EPISTEMOLOGY OF THE WORD . . .

There is widespread consensus that television is currently undergoing fundamental changes: commercially, technologically, but certainly also aesthetically. Although few agree on what these changes entail exactly, it seems safe to suggest that they inform the ways in which programs are produced, distributed, and broadcasted; influence the ways in which programs are structured; inflect the way programs look; and transform the ways in which programs are viewed. One phrase frequently used to describe these changes is "Quality Television."

"Quality Television" is a problematic phrase, which can refer to different debates in different contexts. As Sarah Cardwell has pointed out, for example, "quality" has a significantly different meaning in the United States and the United Kingdom. In the former, the term "quality" infers an aesthetic or generic category, whereas in the latter, it appears to be invoked primarily to describe bourgeois taste and middle-class value judgments. To make matters even more complicated, however, the two meanings are often used interchangeably. Questions of aesthetics are answered in terms of taste, and, vice versa, questions of value judgment are mistaken for inquisitions into genre(s). Other chapters in this book discuss this category of "Quality Television" in more detail. It therefore suffices here to summarize it simply as the correlation between an elaboration of mise-en-scène characterized by an attention to detail and a narrative intensification characterized by flexi-narratives (Nelson 32–33), narrative complexity, and narrative compression (Mittell 29–32).

Unsurprisingly, *Mad Men*, *The Wire*, and *Arrested Development* are often cited as prime examples of "quality television." After all, each of these programs is extraordinarily attentive to the particular qualities and sensibilities of the image, each thrives on complicated flexi-narratives, and each features multiple characters each with his or her own well-developed personal life story. Yet as may already be apparent, scenes such as the above described pear scene cannot be understood in terms of this vernacular. If one were to read the pear scene in terms of Jason Mittell's notion of narrative complexity, for example, one would have to consider it a compression or problematization of a plotline. One would have to assume that although it seems meaningless now, it will eventually be signified when its narrative logic is revealed. As Mittell puts it himself: "we may be temporarily confused by moments of *Lost* or *Alias*, but these shows ask us to trust in the payoff that we will eventually arrive at a moment of complex but coherent comprehension" (37). But the pear scene's narrative logic is never revealed; one will never arrive at that moment of coherent comprehension: one will never find out whether the woman got pears, or whether any one of the central characters would ever get to eat them, or if any one of them would get diarrhea, or die, because of them.

In fact, the scene's narrative and mise-en-scène suggest that the pear question disintegrates the episode and/or series' plotlines. For one, the scene's narrative is structured around the enigma of the pear question (has the old lady bought pears?) rather than around any one of the episode's or series' plotlines. For another, the scene's narrative is structured around an enigma none of the episode's or series' plotlines can or will resolve. Further to that, the scene's mise-en-scène concentrates on two people that are peripheral to any of the other plotlines rather than the one character central to them. The couple dictates the editing, they direct the camera, they are in the center of the frame, they are in focus, and they dominate the soundscape ("Did you get pears?"). The protagonist Don, on the contrary, is nearly invisible, out of focus, and silent. Indeed, the elements that conventionally structure narrative—plot, event, and character—literally dissipate into the details of the image.

In Mittell's terms, thus, the pear question is, or rather, can only be extra- or non-narrative.

Of course, one might argue that we have hypothesized Mittell's positions beyond their initial or intended parameters. Yet that is precisely the point. The problem with most interpretations of (quality) television is that they take the nature and form of television serials for granted. They each assume that plots are invariably structured around events, and that images not in support of those events are excessive, or "an oddity." Thus, if the plotlines of "The Rejected" entail, among others, the marriage of one character and the divorce of another, the arrival of one baby and the departure of another, the bringing in of one client and the letting go of another, the hiring of one secretary and the firing of another, the images that do not seem to further any one of those specific plots can only ever be symbolic or transitory if they are not to be interpreted as surplus.

It is not unthinkable, however, that some narratives are not structured solely around plots, events, and characters. Indeed, an increasing number of art philosophers, literary scholars, and film critics have begun to reconceive narratives as diverse as those of Picasso, Flaubert, Dostoyevsky, Ozu, Antonioni, and Akerman in terms of the unplottable, the uneventful, and the uncharacteristic. As the film critic Andrew Klevan writes with respect to Ozu's cinematographic masterpiece *Late Spring* (1949):

> By structuring the narrative in terms of blocks, the film's story does not progress in a linear manner. The film understands that everyday life cannot be represented by a fluent, ongoing narrative, marching forward, orientated teleologically towards a resolution. The landscape shots repeatedly situate the characters' activity in terms of a larger world and cycle continuing around them, precisely establishing the importance of family relationships through this perspective. *This contrasts with a viewpoint which must establish significance from the momentum provided by a sequence of events. The shots which do not ostensibly further the plot are, in fact, crucial to the film's narrative.* They inflect the viewer's perspective on the human incidents, and so they are *not* breaks in the narrative or moments in which merely to ponder the scene just finished. (144, emphasis added)

The pear question equally enables one to begin to rethink televisual narratives along the same lines. These scenes can be viewed not as excessive breaks in narrative or moments in which to ponder the scene just finished, but as essential inflections of one's perspective on the fictional details of everyday life.

... TO AN ONTOLOGY OF THE IMAGE

In his recent works on the history and nature of aesthetics, most notably *The Politics of Aesthetics* and *The Future of the Image*, Rancière distinguishes between three discourses of art: the Aesthetic regime, the Representative regime, and the Ethical regime. For argument's sake, this discussion will concentrate only on the distinction between the Aesthetic and the Representative regimes. The Aesthetic regime is a reinterpretation of (post)modernist notions of art; the Representative regime compares to the Aristotelian poetics of mimesis (i.e., plot, event, agent) (Rancière, *Politics* 22).

In *The Future of the Image*, Rancière discusses the nature of what he terms the "image." It is important to note that for Rancière an image is not "exclusive to the visible ... [T]here are images which consist wholly in words" (*Future* 7). Rancière suggests that each image can be defined by the "relationship between the sayable and the visible" (*Future* 7). With the sayable (the Representative regime) he means signifying practices. By the visible (the Aesthetic regime) he means presence. Rancière thus perceives the image as the interplay between signifying practices and what (and how it) is shown.

Rancière maintains that in Representative images the sayable tends to dictate and direct the visible. In such images plots, events, or characters define and delineate the extent to which the world, the everyday, or a subject is, quite literally, *ex-posed*. Most classical Hollywood films (and fictional television shows) would fit into this regime. In Aesthetic images, however, Rancière suggests the sayable is subsumed by the visible. In these images, the plot does not determine what is visible; instead, it becomes just one of many potential plotlines each of which is present in its own right.

Returning to the pear scene, it likewise "does not make visible." Or, at least, it does not make visible along the lines of the representative categories. That is to say, it does not define, determine, and direct what and how viewers see along the lines of plot, event, and character. The old couple and their pear argument might become important for the plot, but then again, they might not. They just happen to be *there* in the hallway and the scene. The pear scene imposes presence. It imposes plot *and* place, event *and* everyday, character *and* subject equally. What one might expect to be the plot (say, Don's existential loneliness) disperses into place. Let us briefly explain what we mean by this.

What one might anticipate to be the event (Don coming home alone) dissipates into the rhythms of the everyday. The sequence draws as much attention to time passing as to time stilled: that is to say, it provides a chronological account of what many would consider a diegetic atemporality—a moment in fictional, narrative, or onscreen time without a narrative past or future. One never learns the background story for the man's insatiable lusting after pears nor if he ever gets them. The pear question might be a happening for the two elderly people, but for Don, and for viewers, there is no relevance or rationale for what happens; it just happens. The scene does not represent a happening, but presents a "happens to." The scene does not feature active characters pushing the boundaries of their environment, but instead merely presents the inaction of subjects as they are being pulled into their surroundings. It relocates Don from his well-defined, representative role as an agent within the plotted event to a less definable, social, personal, and physical persona.

The pear question might not immediately inflect the narrative, but it does influence one's interpretation of the fictional world from which that narrative springs. Indeed, the reason one needs to care about whether the woman got pears lies in the influence it renders on one's interpretation of the context and source of the narrative. That is to say, crucially, that the pear scene opens one's eyes to the situatedness of situations, that might or might not become relevant (for the plot) in the future, the larger social reality from which plotlines may or may not emerge. To explain more clearly: the pear scene draws attention to the fact that the events and happenings in the lives of Don Draper and his co-workers are only one possible story the narrative might focus on.

Indeed, what the pear scene begins to reveal, is that the differences between "Quality Television" and what one is apparently expected to call non-quality television might be reconceived of as distinctions between the Aesthetic regime and the Representative regime. *Mad Men* and, say, *Desperate Housewives* (ABC 2004–Present) are not merely two different variations on the same image. They are two different *kinds* of images, Representative and Aesthetic, each with its own aesthetic ontology, relational and internal logic, and laws of time and space. Each, also, to return to the question we began this chapter with, requests and requires another audience engagement. *Desperate Housewives* requests the viewer to be part of a storyline, an event, an interaction between characters; *Mad Men* requires the viewer to immerse him or herself in the world in which such a storyline may or may not come into existence and make sense. It is not unlikely the widespread critical devotion has something to do with this.

S(PEAR)TIME
From Temporality to Temps Mortality

It is something of a cliché among historians, literary scholars, and narratologists that when one discusses narrativity, one cannot but discuss temporality as well. If one discusses the former, one cannot but implicate the latter, and vice versa. On the one hand, literary scholars tend to argue that narrative is always temporal.[1] On the other hand, narratologists assert that temporality cannot but be narrative. As Paul Ricoeur writes in the introduction to his canonical essay "Narrative Time," "I take temporality to be that structure of existence that reaches language in narrativity and narrativity to be the language structure that has temporality as its ultimate referent. Their relationship is therefore reciprocal" (169). Interestingly, most scholars agree that narrative and temporality meet in the plot, in the causal ordering and chronological sequencing of events and their agents. Ricoeur suggests that plot *makes* events into a (causal) story, and that events can only be part of a plot when they are temporal and contribute to the development of plot (170). He implies, thus, that without plot, events are neither events in the Aristotelian sense of the word nor temporal.

If one understands narrative time in the manner that Ricoeur conceptualizes it (or Mittell, or Nelson), the pear scene is atemporal. It is, to paraphrase Seymour Chatman, *temps mort*: dead time (*Antonioni* 125–26). With *temps mort* Chatman means moments in film or fiction that are coterminous with the narrative yet do not contribute to it—moments that take time, but do not make time (i.e., that have no function whatsoever in the furthering of plot). Chatman uses an example from Antonioni's *Red Dessert* (1964) where the main characters walk off screen, but instead of cutting away with them, the camera lingers on the "empty" cityscape (*Coming* 54). One can think here of unnecessarily extended transition shots, late cuts, early cuts, and so forth, or indeed, the pear scene. However, Ricoeur's understanding of narrative time still stems, simplistically put, from what one may ultimately call Aristotelian understanding of narrativity: it is structured around plots, which in turn are structured around events, which in turn are enacted by agents. As demonstrated above, *Mad Men* is structured around plots, events, and agents, but at the same time around place, subjects, and the uneventful. If narrative and temporality are as closely related as Ricoeur suggests, another narrative form will thus yield another temporality. The Representative image and the Aesthetic image will doubtlessly each infer another temporal configuration.

So how can one conceptualize a narrative time structured around what are essentially *temps morts*: dead times? It seems a contradiction in terms. But the difference between life and death is not that time stops. It is rather that time continues at a different pace, takes on another meaning. The difference between a Representative temporality and an Aesthetic *temps mortality*, between *Desperate Housewives* and *Mad Men*, can be explained by the distinction between what Deleuze and Guattari have termed the *arborescent trace* and the *rhizomatic map*.

Deleuze and Guattari describe the difference between the trace and the map as follows: "The tracing has organized, stabilized, neutralized the multiplicities according to the axes of significance and subjectification belonging to it. It has generated, structurahzed the rhizome . . ." (13). The map on the contrary

> . . . is open and connectable in all of its dimensions; it is detachable, reversible, susceptible to constant modification . . . A map has multiple entryways, as opposed to the tracing, which always comes back to the same. (12–16)

Very simplistically explained, imagine the difference between a Google map one can pan and scroll as one pleases and the Route Planner one gets using the Get Directions option: linear, predetermined, and fixed step-by-step directions that bring the user from one point to another. In other words, in the trace, the sayable dominates the visible. Its distribution is hierarchical, its connections are causal: it selects, it prioritizes, it emphasizes; signification precedes and determines connections. On the map, on the contrary, the sayable is subsumed by the visible. Its distribution is democratic, the connections coincidental in the most literal sense of the word: no element is more important than others, and every one point can be connected to any other point.

If one understands the Aesthetic image in terms of the rhizomatic narrative, one can begin to grasp its temporal inferences. The rhizome, by its very nature, replaces the closedness, the going somewhere of the trace (the Route Planner directions), with an openness (panning and scrolling), a going potentially everywhere of the map. That is to say, by not allowing one trace to be more significant than others, by presenting the trace *and* the map, the event *and* the everyday, the situation of character *and* the situatedness of a subject equally, the Aesthetic image as rhizome always already suspends closure of whatever kind. Indeed, in Aesthetic television, suspense stems, paradoxically, not from withholding information, but from overextending data. Everything could potentially become part of the plot.

If one understands the pear scene in terms of a map rather than a trace, or rather, as a map *and* a trace, one can understand it is not atemporal, but rather expressive of another kind of narrative temporality. The pear scene exposes—and exemplifies—a temporality that is first synchronous (in the sense that everything happens at once), and then diachronic (in the sense that the audience will need to narrativize it in order to understand it); for the scene simply *imposes* a map of possible traces—of possible events that might, but likely will not, become actual (the resolution of the pear question, the engagement between the elderly people, the interaction between the elderly people and Don)—on which a fleeting fragment of a trace of an actual event (Don's loneliness) also happens to be visible.

The phrase "pear scene" does not necessarily denote only this particular scene. It could also denote scenes or even images of apples. Or of oranges. Or of something else altogether. As we have discussed elsewhere, there are many "pear scenes" in *Mad Men*. It could be the lingering reaction shot of a random secretary drinking a glass of wine[2] or the prolonged take of Don unzipping his pants, urinating, zipping his pants, and washing his hands.[3] Or any scene indeed that narrativizes the ostensibly non-narrative; any shot that infers a temporality that is enigmatic (unfolding one scene at a time) because it can not necessarily be explained in terms of plot.

SOME FINAL OBSERVATIONS ON *THE WIRE* AND *ARRESTED DEVELOPMENT*

This chapter has so far concerned itself with one series or, indeed, one episode, and, more or less, one scene only. Yet a short stroll through America's contemporary televisual landscape reveals a wealth of pear scenes, of shows structured around narrativized moments of narrative discontinuity.

The Wire's season-three episode "Reformation" features a particularly telling shot. One of the season's many plotlines involves one gangster, Lamar (Deandre McCullough), chasing another gangster, Omar (Michael K. Williams). At one point in "Reformation" Lamar's chase leads him to a gay bar Omar tends to frequent. As Lamar prowls about, the camera momentarily lingers, "kills time," and unexpectedly exposes police commissioner Bill Rawls (John Doman).

Rawls's cameo is almost imperceptible: he is only onscreen, in frame, for about two seconds, and remains in the background. In addition, Rawls's sexuality remains a narrative blind spot. It never comes to inflect the narrative nor at any point affects Rawls's persona. As *The Guardian*'s critic Mark Smith puts it:

> And of course we have Rawls' surprising appearance—surprising only because you expect to recognize gay characters on TV from their behaviour. But it doesn't always work like that in real life so why should it in Television. Raises the question though: why even show him in there at all? (151)

By momentarily killing narrative time, *The Wire* opens up another, extra-diegetic temporality. It discloses a worldliness, a situatedness, and a subjectivity that never come to inflect plot, event, or character, but from which plot, event, and character nonetheless materializes. Rawls's sexuality is never problematized; but that is not to say that his public displays of chauvinist behavior and fetishization of heterosexual intercourse do not acquire another meaning for those watching.

The Wire plays hide and seek with the conventions of the police procedural. In a police procedural like *Law and Order* (NBC, 1990–2010), there is a distinct plot that defines and delineates what is seen (a dead body), and what is not (yet) seen (the killer). Each episode features another crime and killer. *The Wire*'s serialized plot, however, is subsumed by the sheer presence of the world, and everything becomes equally visible: from the reality of capitalism to the reality of political decision making, from a speculative press to a failing school system, and from the police brass to the drug addicts. *Law and Order* is concerned with a trace: a crime. *The Wire* is concerned with the map on which that trace, among many other traces, exists: Baltimore, the declining great American city.

Similarly, on paper, *Arrested Development* is a single camera, family sitcom about the dysfunctional Bluth family, but on screen it has much more in common with the absurdist comedy of, say, Monty Python than *Two and a Half Men* (CBS, 2003–Present). The show's supposed plots are always inter- and undercut by "non-narrative" cutaways, sideways, and flashbacks, and it is from these *temps morts*, these "arrested developments," that its comedy often stems.

One incident in the last episode of the season "Development Arrested" is particularly illustrative here. George-Michael (Michael Cera) is desperately looking for his ex-girlfriend Ann. He looks for her in town, at school, and finally her home. When he tries her home, her uncle informs him she is not there, either. The moment George-Michael leaves, however, a young boy wrestles his way past the uncle and runs away. One might have expected Ann to show up, but instead a boy who remains unidentified and whose act at no point inflects the narrative enters the frame. The narrative stops, but the world from which that narrative emerges does not. And this is funny. Indeed, *Arrested Development*'s comedy stems precisely from the problematic relationship between the universal logic of the trace and the inexplicable multiplicity of the map.

In season three's "Mr. F," one of the characters is browsing the Internet. In the corner of the screen a small faux-advertisement for the *Arrested Development* DVD box set appears. The ad reads: "All good people watch the best show on TV. Buy the DVD and merchandise." The image of the screen is only visible for about two seconds and the viewer will probably only notice it on the second or third viewing. The viewer is forced to pause the episode if he or she wants to be able to see (read) the entire meta-joke—it is quite literally a temporal inference of plot.

CONCLUSION

There is undoubtedly a lot more to be said about the structure of programs like *Mad Men*, *The Wire*, and *Arrested Development*, as there will be about the ontology of "pear scenes." But we hope that, by means of our necessarily somewhat satiated and schematic attempt to begin to come to terms with them, we have opened up some pathways into the matter. The pears discussion demonstrates that *Mad Men* and others cannot be understood in terms of the Representative image but should be conceived of as Aesthetic; that they do not make visible a trace, but impose a map; that in them everything is present, but nothing representative yet; and that although time may stand still narratively on occasion, it always progresses in terms of the world from which narratives cannot but emerge.

SUGGESTED EPISODES FOR ADDITIONAL STUDY

Arrested Development
3:5. "Mr. F." Writ. Richard Day and James Vallely. Dir. Arlene Sanford. November 7, 2005.
3:13. "Development Arrested." Writ. Richard Day and Mitchell Hurwitz. Dir. John Fortenberry. February 10, 2006.

Mad Men
1:3. "Marriage of Figaro." Writ. Tom Palmer. Dir. Ed Bianchi. August 2, 2007.
1:12. "Nixon vs. Kennedy." Writ. Lisa Albert, André Jacquemetton, and Maria Jacquemetton. Dir. Alan Taylor. October 11, 2007.
2:3. "Three Sundays." André Jacquemetton and Maria Jacquemetton. Dir. Tim Hunter. August 17, 2008.
4:4. "The Rejected." Writ. Keith Huff and Matthew Weiner. Dir. John Slattery. August 15, 2010.

The Wire
1:4. "Old Cases." Writ. David Sinom and Ed Burns. Dir. Clément Virgo. June 23, 2002.
3:10. "Reformations." Writ. David Simon and Ed Burns. Dir. Christine Moore. November 28, 2004.

NOTES

1. Susan Stanford Friedman, for example, writes in *A Companion to Narrative Theory* that "narrative exists in time" (193). And H. Porter Abbott writes that "narrative is the principal way in which our species organizes its understanding of time" (3).
2. The scene can be seen in the season-one *Mad Men* episode "Nixon vs. Kennedy."
3. The scene can be seen in the season-one *Mad Men* episode "Marriage of Figaro."

WORKS CITED

Abbott, H. Porter. *The Cambridge Introduction to Narrative*. Cambridge: Cambridge University Press, 2002. Print.

Cardwell, Sarah. "Is Quality Television Any Good? Generic Distinctions, Evaluations and the Troubling Matter of Critical Judgement." *Quality TV: Contemporary American Television and Beyond*. Ed. Kim Akass and Janet McCabe. London: Taurus & Co., 2007. 19–34. Print.

Chatman, Seymour. *Antonioni, or, The Surface of the World*. Berkeley and Los Angeles: University of California Press, 1985. Print.

———. *Coming to Terms: The Rhetoric of Narrative in Fiction and Film*. Ithaca, NY: Cornell University Press, 1990. Print.

Deleuze, Gilles, and Felix Guattari. *A Thousand Plateaus: Capitalism and Schizophrenia*. Minneapolis: University of Minnesota Press, 1987. Print.

"Development Arrested." *Arrested Development: Season Three*. Prod. Mitchell Hurvitz. 20th Century Fox Television, 2006. DVD.

Friedman, Susan Stanford. "Spatial Politics and Arundhati Roy's *The God of Small Things*." *A Companion to Narrative Theory*. Ed. James Phelan and Peter J. Rabinowitz. Oxford: Blackwell Publishing, 2005. 192–205. Print.

Klevan, Andrew. *Disclosure of the Everyday: Undramatic Achievement in Narrative*. Trowbridge: Film Flicks Books, 2000. Print.

Mittell, Jason. "Narrative Complexity in Contemporary American Television." *The Velvet Light Trap* 58 (2006): 29–40. Print.

"Mr. F." *Arrested Development: Season Three*. Prod. Mitchell Hurvitz. 20th Century Fox Television, 2006. DVD.

Nelson, Robin. *TV Drama in Transition: Forms, Values and Cultural Change*. Basingstoke: Macmillan, 1997. Print.

Ranciére, Jacques. *The Politics of Aesthetics: The Distribution of the Sensible*. Rockhill: Tr. Gabriel, 2004. Print.

———. *The Future of the Image*. London, NY: Verso, 2007. Print.

"Reformations." *The Wire: Season 3*. Prod. David Simon and Ed Burns. HBO, 2007. DVD.

"The Rejected." *Mad Men*. AMC. November 24, 2010. Television.

Ricoeur, Paul. "Narrative Time." *Critical Inquiry* 7.1 (1980): 169–90. Print.

Sassone, Bob. "'Mad Men'—'The Rejected' Recap." *TVSquad*. August 16, 2010. Web. January 15, 2011.

Smith, Mark. "Episode 10—'Reform, Lamar, Reform.'" *The Wire Re-Up. The Guardian Guide to the Greatest TV Show Ever Made*. Ed. Steve Busfield and Paul Owen. London: Guardian Books, 2009. 150–52. Print.

11

TEMPORALITIES ON COLLISION COURSE
Time, Knowledge, and Temporal Critique in Damages

TONI PAPE

> "I've been thinking a lot about God. Heaven and hell. [. . .] The nine circles of hell are for the unrepentant who try to justify their sins. [. . .] Everyone in hell has knowledge of the past and the future, but not of the present. It's a twisted joke because, after the final judgment, time ends. And all of us, burning in hell, will know nothing for all eternity."
> —DANIEL PURCELL, *DAMAGES* ("LOOK")

If what Daniel Purcell, one of the protagonists in *Damages* (FX, 2007–Present), describes is a twisted joke in itself, an additional turn of the screw consists in the fact that his statement about ignorance produced by an obsession with the past and the future applies directly to the television show *Damages* itself. This *mise en abyme*, that is, a passage *within* a narrative that reflects the narrative as a whole, is the moment in which *Damages* most explicitly lays out its narrative program. For a few seconds, the show puts its cards on the table and lets the viewer *know* that its experiments with time are closely related to the issue of knowledge. The viewer may at this point realize that the narrative has been playing the very same twisted joke on him or her for the last twelve episodes of the season: *Damages* lets its audience know about a narrative past and a narrative future and, yet, the spectator has no idea of what *is going on*. In this way, the TV show takes a stand on the kind of "truth" and knowledge which can be produced or withheld by time or, rather, by a *concept* of time. But just as the viewer may pay attention to this scene and recognize in it a reflection on the complicities of narrative, time, and knowledge, he may be more plot driven, and disregard the scene as prosaic and curiously wait for the next twist in the story. The point is that the twists and turns are—strictly speaking—not in the *story*, that is, the events told, but in the *discourse*, that is, the telling of these events. To overlook this distinction is to overlook how the narrative discourse of *Damages* plays with time and, consequently, with knowledge.

In this chapter, I argue that *Damages* performs a critique of the modern, scientific notion of homogeneous, chronological time. This critique consists in demonstrating that this scientific, objective time, in which "all is given," sets certain limits to the production of knowledge. As we will see, the deletion of the experiencing subject on the conceptual level allows "modern time" to undo knowledge just as easily as it produces it. Narrative that is based on this notion of time is thus complicit in "the making and unmaking of ignorance" (Proctor and Schiebinger iii). For, as *Damages*'s Daniel Purcell reminds us, if time ends—and, according to a number of philosophers discussed below, the modern notion of time has already sublated the lived experience of time in favor of a scientific concept that bears peculiar resemblance to "eternity"—we will know nothing at all.

DAMAGES
Temporalities on Collision Course

Damages is about a New York–based law firm run by Patty Hewes (Glenn Close). In each season, Hewes and Associates act as the plaintiffs' lawyers in a major class action against a corporate enterprise. The series presents the work of lawyers in civil litigation as that of knowledge management: information must be procured or held back, that is, both the defendants' and the plaintiffs' attorneys need to acquire knowledge without letting the opposing party know what they know. Needless to say that neither of the two parties is innocent, Patty being as much of a manipulator as her corporate adversaries are. *Damages* is thus not about truth and justice, but about law, knowledge, and power. In itself, this is not particularly original or surprising.

The originality of *Damages* resides in the way the story of scheming lawyers is told and, more importantly, in the meaningful relation between the story told and its discursive articulation. Each season of *Damages* begins "in the future," a future that is significantly linked to violence and death.[1] After thus giving away the end of the story, after determining the season's *telos*, the narrative goes back to what happened "six months earlier." The entire season then traces the process of regaining this point of time in the future that the initial prolepsis[2] represented. In this sense, *Damages* shares an obsession with the future that is common in modern thought. Mark Currie identifies a tendency in contemporary culture to anticipate an "endpoint" from which one "look[s] back" at the present instead of attempting to make sense of it *as present (About* 33). *Damages* does exactly this when it offers viewers the ending—or a preliminary version of it—before it actually starts telling the story.

Everything that is subsequently viewed necessarily acquires meaning with respect to the foretold ending. In this way, *Damages* can be seen as the symptom of "a generalised future orientation" the result of which is that "the present becomes increasingly focused on the question of what it will come to mean" (Currie, *About* 22). Scholars such as Jean-Pierre Dupuy and Slavoj Žižek have detected this discursive strategy, which closely links knowledge production to a specific concept of time, in a variety of social spheres. Future orientation builds on anxiety, sanctions policies, and thereby forms contemporary societies. The stakes of what Currie terms the "anticipation of retrospect" are thus by all means political (*About* 14).

Consequently, this particular phenomenon deserves a closer examination in a volume entitled *Time in Television Narrative* because it allows linking a series like *Damages* to current concerns in other areas of study such as sociology. In addition, television series *themselves* have become increasingly occupied with the notion of future and with the impact that narrating and therefore *knowing* the future may have on a shared imaginary. TV shows such as *Life on Mars* (BBC, 2006–2007) and *FlashFoward* (ABC, 2009–2010) resemble *Damages* in that they also set a determined future as the aim of the story at the very beginning of the narrative. Moreover, as law, detective, or crime shows, all of these series are linked to the themes of violence and death. The stance they take on futurity seems to be informed by the idea that *knowing* the *future* is dangerous.

This analysis focuses on *Damages*, particularly its second season, for yet another reason: *Damages* is not only a "symptom" of futurity, but also a critique of it. The show is certainly complicit in exploiting narrative time in order to produce or prevent knowledge. Yet, the overall narrative scheme, as well as the negotiation of the topics of knowledge and power in the story, suggests that *Damages knows* about the uses and abuses of its underlying concept of time for the production of knowledge. This implicit reflection comes to the fore in season two of *Damages*; for it is here that the past ("six months earlier") and the future ("six months later") are most clearly "articulated to each other" in the sense that they are bound not only to meet but also to collide (Currie, *About* 97). While the story elements from "six months earlier" are told forward, the events taking place "six months later" gradually (and disproportionately slowly) regress into the past. Consequently, the discontinuity between the two time levels is overcome when the progressing past and the regressing future eventually clash in the last episode of season two. It is only when continuity is thus established that the narrative produces reliable knowledge. Taking my cue from this observation, I will try to unpack the philosophy of time that is inscribed in *Damages*'s narrative temporality.

"WHAT'S PRESENT IS PROLOGUE"
Narrative and the Philosophy of Time

As previously mentioned, the second season of *Damages* presents two temporal trajectories that are bound to meet, one directed forward and one in backward direction. In order to establish a link to Currie's reflections on time in *written* narrative, I would like to suggest that (a) the forward-moving main narrative of *Damages* corresponds to the forward movement of the events as lived by the fictional characters and that (b) the second timeline starting at the end and moving backward provides a perspective from which we can understand retrospectively, by virtue of the proleptic knowledge that this perspective offers. These two movements are epistemically incommensurate; in a most general way, this is what *Damages* knows about narrative temporality and modern time.

For the purpose of demonstration, let me move into the domain of literature for a brief moment to consider the aspect of knowledge that is only secondary in Currie's approach itself. (The benefit of such contrastive intermedial analysis is that it enables a clearer elaboration of the proleptic structure of *Damages*'s audiovisual narrative in contrast to the specificities of written narrative.) In a recent paper, Currie sums up his fundamental observations concerning prolepsis and time in narrative:

> [T]here are grounds on which prolepsis might be thought of as a distinctly modern temporal structure in the novel, partly because it corresponds to a temporal experience outside of the novel which can be clearly linked with contemporary conditions. It may be that prolepsis in the first person narrative is nothing more than a function of retrospect, as Genette claims, but in other forms (such as third person impersonal narration) there is a kind of *backward movement* that it imports into a narrative, in the sense that *it installs in the present a future moment from which that present is understood in retrospect*, thereby *joining the forward motion of time to the backward motion of explanation*. ("Expansion" 359–60, emphasis added)

What I want to contest here is the idea of the "joining" of the forward and the backward movements, that is a joining of lived experience and of retrospective understanding, for this relation between "the forward motion of lived experience and the backward motion of explanation" is vital to an investigation into the relations between (narrative) time and knowledge (Currie, "Expansion" 360). The notion of the "joint" suggests an *interlinkage* of the two movements through prolepsis. This notion, which is, if not pronounced, suggested at least, becomes problematic if one shifts one's analytical focus to the issue of knowledge. Currie acknowledges that the narrative model of time and the lived experience of time are ontologically incompatible.[3] Yet, it seems that Currie bypasses the epistemological implications of this observation, which shows in the fact that he considers first-person narration *un*problematic in this respect "because of its avowedly retrospective character" (Currie, "Expansion" 360); since the narrator and the protagonist are the same person, forward and backward motion necessarily "join." This, however, discards too easily the intuition according to which the narrating "I" and the narrated "I" are *epistemically* unequal. The character who lives a story (narrated "I") can never know as much as the character who tells the story (narrating "I") knows. It is this irreducible epistemic gap between the narrating "I" and the narrated "I" that necessitates a theoretical disjunction of living forward and understanding backward (Currie, "Expansion" 357). The temporal distance between the narrating "I" and the narrated "I" may stretch across decades or only hours. Accordingly, the epistemic distance will be larger or smaller. But it can never be erased for one cannot experience and at the same time narrate what one is experiencing.[4] Consequently, the irreducible *temporal* interval between the story and the discourse of a *written* narrative always implies an *epistemic* gap between the forward movement of lived experience and the backward movement of understanding/explanation. In this sense, it is impossible in *verbal* narrative to "understand forward."

This, of course, may seem quite obvious and would be banal if there were not a decisive difference between verbal and audiovisual narration. Film narration is usually considered to be present-tense narration.[5] And therefore, one might argue, a *forward* movement of lived experience should be able to *join* the *forward* movement of narration, of meaning production, of understanding. However, film is different in a different way. What *Damages* shows by virtue of its two approaching (but initially distant) temporalities is that audiovisual narrative can have several time levels that are all articulated in present tense. The problem then is that *everything* is the present. Or, to put it another way, while *everything is present* in *Damages*, there is no "real" present, only relations. Neither of the two temporal movements in *Damages* is ontologically privileged: It could be argued that the forward narrative is the present and that the backward narrative is the future of this present; one might just as easily claim that the forward narrative is the past of the backward narrative that is the present. The important thing to note is that one cannot decide between the two. In *Damages*, "all is given" at the same time and, thus, the show seems to allow its viewers privileged, ultimate knowledge (or, in any case, knowledge of the *ultimo*). To use Elizabeth Grosz's suggestive formulation: The basic narrative scheme of *Damages* is "a matter of unfolding an already worked out blueprint" (110–11).

This leads me further into the problem of modern time and time philosophy. The concept of time that underlies *Damages* has been under attack at least since Henri Bergson. Most recently, Bliss Cua Lim has reassessed this modern concept of "empty homogeneous" time and described it "as spatialized, abstract, chronological, measurable" (18). Time is spatialized in all representations that humans have produced of it: the clock face, the timeline, the calendar, and so on This spatialization of time reached its conceptual apex in Einstein's Relativity theory, in which time is described as and proven to be the fourth dimension of space. As it is split up into equal units, time becomes unified and therefore measurable. In human imagination, this has led to so-called untensed views of time known as the block universe in modern physics and B-theory in the philosophy of time:[6]

> B-theory [. . .] is an *untensed* view of time that rids itself of the ontological priority of the now and therefore of the tensed notions of past and future. For B-theory, the idea of a now that moves along a timeline is too egocentric, too psychological, too subjective to properly describe temporal sequences. [. . .] B-theory views time in terms of relations, such as being earlier than or later than, and explains the ordinary tensed view of time through these relations. (Currie, "Novel" 322, emphasis in original)

It should be clear by now that this relational block view of time in which "all is given" in terms of "earlier than" or "later than" is the concept of time that *Damages* relies on. The important distinction to make then is between this notion of modern, physical, impersonal time on the one hand and the lived experience of time on the other. Since Bergson, whose philosophy addresses this conceptual opposition under the labels of abstract time versus concrete duration (*durée*) (98), thinkers such as Gilles Deleuze and Gayatri Spivak (among many others) have acknowledged this distinction in their own theoretical set-ups. While their perspectives and philosophical interests may diverge a great deal, they systematically criticize what Lim calls "modern time consciousness" for its excision or marginalization of the experiencing subject (10). In his monograph *Bergsonism*, Deleuze agrees with Bergson that our experience of time is fundamentally distinct from spatialized time and concludes:

> But we must [. . .] be delighted that the *Whole* is not given. This is the constant theme of Bergsonism from the outset: The confusion of space and time, the assimilation of time into space, make us think that the whole is

given, even if only in principle, even if only in the eyes of God. [. . .] In any event, time is only there now as a screen that hides the eternal from us, or that shows us successively what a God or a superhuman intelligence would see in a single glance. (104, emphasis in original)

To conceive of time in spatial terms and to consider that *in theory* the "*Whole*" must always already be given, is to misconceive the experience of time for at least two reasons: First, it measures the immeasurable and suggests that we can know and therefore control that which is *in practice* unknown to us, that is, the future. Secondly, in order to suggest this, this conception of time must exclude the experiencing and knowing subject so that the inconvenient aspect of human contingency and the ensuing questions (such as "measured *for whom*?" or "knowable *to whom* really?") need not be confronted.

Neither Bergson nor Deleuze wants to do away with modern, scientific time. Rather, their stake is to unmask this notion of time as a *theory* of time, that is, as a set of propositions meant to explain certain phenomena and to produce a certain knowledge. By uncovering the discursive character of modern time, these thinkers intend to denaturalize a temporal regime whose validity has largely remained unquestioned. Once modern time has been acknowledged as a convention, it is possible to evaluate its productivity and, more important in this context, its *limitations* on productivity within a knowledge economy. Modern, scientific time has incontestably contributed to a more efficient reorganization of modern societies; scientific advances in various domains have drawn on this concept of time. Yet, against the background of the above time philosophies and in the interest of elaborating the temporal critique inscribed in *Damages*, it is more urgent to ask how modern time can be complicit in the *un*making of knowledge and the making of ignorance.

"EVERYONE IS LOOKING TO PLAY AN ANGLE"
The Making and Unmaking of Ignorance

After these theoretical considerations, I would like to return to *Damages* and elaborate which kind of temporal critique is inscribed in it. In order to pass the stretch between time philosophy and crime/law fiction, I would like to briefly address Spivak. In her essay "Time and Timing: Law and History," she takes on Hegel's opposition between European (i.e., historical) and Indian art. Spivak's vast theoretical and philosophical repertoire is here supplemented by the terms "Time" and "timing," in which I rediscover the opposition that I have described earlier:

I will assume that one common way of grasping life and ground-level history as events happening to and around many lives is by fleshing out "time" as sequential process. This I have called "timing." I will assume, further, that this feeling for life and history is often disqualified, for the sake of a dominant interest, in the name of the real laws of motion of "time." This version of "time" I have called "Time." (Spivak 99)

Spivak associates Time and Law. And, indeed, modern time consciousness imagines a set of laws by which time functions. Such an assumption of natural rules that govern time is convenient enough for the modern scientist as it effaces his or her part in constructing that concept of time.

Damages's critique consists in constantly reminding us of Time's discursiveness. It knows that to adhere to a notion of time articulated in a set of laws is to adhere to a scientific dictum. *Damages* shows that "Time graphed as Law manipulates [. . .] timing in the interest of cultural-political explanations" (Spivak 102). In other words, the show demonstrates that, as law, time is a powerful tool that can be used and abused to one's interest. The show achieves this by means of a persistent correlation of its twisted, yet law-abiding temporal structures with the twisted logic of civil litigation. More precisely, the story of legal scheming continuously points to the "temporal scheming" of the narrative itself. While, within the story, the show *explicitly* criticizes the legal system, the narrative discourse *implicitly* performs a critique of modern time.

The TV series suggests that, like modern time consciousness that supersedes subjective time experience, criminal and civil law have a "sublated" other, too—namely, justice (Spivak 108). As time is dissected into intervals and units, justice is codified in articles, clauses, and paragraphs, and thus becomes law; once established, this code is self-sufficient and may diverge from an individual or consensual sense of justice. *Damages* relentlessly points to this gap between justice and law:

> ELLEN: Kids got a really basic sense of justice [. . .]. And then, as we get older, it gets all screwed up.
> TOM: I don't think so. I think you get older, you realize the world is unfair and that mommy and daddy can't make everything okay. If you want justice, you gotta fight and claw and do whatever you have to to get it.
> ELLEN: You've been working for Patty way too long. ("Burn")

In Tom's words, a "screwed-up" notion of justice serves to legitimize a professional conduct that allows "whatever" means to an end. With respect to this suggested gap between law and justice, the show's title is even more telling:

as "damages," a legal term from civil law, indicates, the measure for justice is money. Civil litigation then functions as an institutionalized discursive means by which justice is quantified in economic terms and ultimately made commensurable. If each civil crime has a price, then all of them are effectively comparable. The correlation in *Damages* between "Time as Law" and civil law consequently consists in their equivalent status as authoritative discourses that originate from human experience (both individual and collective) but that are subsequently separated from their experiential foundation. This disjunction allows the computation of time and justice in mathematical and economic terms, respectively.

In this capacity, these discourses acquire authority by regulating the accessibility of knowledge. *Damages*'s story presents a group of characters who, *all* of them, have at least one hidden agenda.[7] In this intricate network of intrigue, knowledge management is the main strategy to achieve one's goals. As an FBI (double) agent says to the protagonist Ellen Parsons: "The smart move is to keep the information in your back pocket" ("London"). All of the characters keep information in various pockets and try to obtain the secret knowledge of others or to eliminate those who know too much. Inasmuch as the characters' motivation is to prevent the production and accessibility of knowledge, *Damages* presents them, and most of all the lawyers among them, as "friends of ignorance" who are complicit in spreading disinformation (Proctor 2).

Following my argument concerning the correlation between legal and temporal regimes in *Damages*, the knowledge management on the story level must be related to the discourse level, which does to the viewer as the show's characters do to one another. It becomes clear then that *Damages*'s experiments with modern time are as complicit in the making and unmaking of ignorance as the show's deceitful characters are. The adoption of its conspicuous temporal scheme allows the narrative to have *all* story elements at its disposal at *all* times. While the temporal *relation* between these elements is marked (six months earlier/later), the different parts of the story remain epistemically disjunct. The narrative pretends to give additional knowledge of the future when, in fact, it keeps the information that is necessary for *understanding* the story in its back pocket. In this way, *Damages* bases narrative temporality on a modern concept of time that enables it to *provide information* for the purpose of *undoing knowledge* and *creating uncertainty*. So when, at the beginning of season two, Patty warns her young employee: "Oh, you have to be careful, Ellen. Everyone is looking to play an angle," the viewer would do well to feel concerned, too ("Burn"). Just as everyone is playing angles on one another within the show, the show itself is constantly playing angles on the viewer, and this by virtue of its underlying concept of modern time.

This last argument concerning an implied temporal critique in *Damages* stands or falls with the assumption of a correlation of the legal regime on the story level with the temporal regime of the narrative. This correlation is most blatant at the moment when the forward and backward temporalities eventually collide in the last episode of season two. For, unlike written narrative understood as the articulation of a forward living *through* a retrospective understanding, *Damages* as film narrative can consume the gap between its two trajectories. And indeed, the temporal and epistemic interval between them is closed, if only eight minutes before the season's end when the viewer learns that Patty, shortly before entering Ellen's hotel room in which the backward narrative takes place, has been stabbed and severely wounded ("Trust"). One last time, the viewer has to reconfigure the bits and pieces of knowledge provided earlier and reinterpret the narrative accordingly.

This moment of collision achieves three things. First, it establishes temporal continuity between the two formerly disconnected narrative trajectories. Second, the backward-moving future narrative that the audience *knows* since the first episode becomes *intelligible* for the first time. This first coincidence is telling: *Damages* unmakes ignorance and produces reliable knowledge at the exact same instant when it disavows its relational "all is given" view of time in favor of continuity and contextuality. In other words, it is at the very moment the spectator seizes the *becoming* of things that these things become *intelligible*, truly knowable to him or her. By virtue of this intelligible becoming, *Damages* makes a case against teleological retrospect and for understanding forward. Third, the reestablishing of continuity and intelligibility opens toward the final scenes of the season in which something like justice is granted: The criminals that Patty's law firm pursues are arrested.

The term collision is also used here to highlight the fact that the meeting point of the two temporal trajectories is a moment of violence. As was mentioned above, the production of continuity and knowledge coincides with a physical assault on Patty. This is noteworthy as this crucial moment presents an attack on the character who stands at the very center of a network of intrigue and corruption and who personifies a problematic legal system. Hence, it is only when this legal order is suspended through a violent act that continuity, knowledge, and justice can surface. From this perspective, the pivotal scene of Patty's violent stabbing can then be seen as simultaneously undoing the systemic violence of the temporal, epistemic, and legal regimes that underpin the larger part of the series up to this moment.

Admittedly, the continuous ending of the narrative makes up only 10 minutes of the entire 560-minute season. Furthermore, of course, the arrest of three culprits out of an entire cast of schemers is not exactly what one calls poetic justice. Ultimately then, the television series cannot escape the contiguity of its temporality nor that of its setting in the lawyer milieu. It cannot escape the complicity between narrative, time, and knowledge. Yet, from within these constraints, *Damages* manages to level a critique at both Time and Law by measuring each of them against (a semblance of) their inconvenient others: the lived experience of time, knowledge, and justice. As far as modern time is concerned, *Damages* does certainly not sublate "[t]hat apparently benign subordination of 'timing' (the lived) into 'Time' (the graph of Law)" (Spivak 117). But it is successful in drawing attention to this subordination and points to its epistemic limits: Within the wider analytical framework of temporal regimes underlying social orders, these narrative temporalities can be read as a performed temporal critique. *Damages* substitutes the enthralling obsession with the future for an intelligible presentism that avoids anxiety and speculation. The show *shows* what Daniel Purcell *tells* us in his remark quoted at the beginning of this chapter: The orientation toward, or even obsession with, pasts and futures leads to the neglect of the meeting point between the two, which, in the lived experience of time is the present. It is only through such an interface, such a reference point, link, or joint between the past and the future that these temporal categories become intelligible to begin with. *Damages* thus relativizes the authority of the future and relegates it to the present as intelligible becoming.

SUGGESTED EPISODES FOR ADDITIONAL STUDY

Damages
1:1. "Get Me a Lawyer." Writ. Todd A. Kessler, Glenn Kesser, and Daniel Zelman. Dir. Allen Coulter. July 24, 2007.
1:10. "Sort of Like a Family." Writ. Mark Fish and Jeremy Doner. Dir. Timothy Busfield. October 2, 2007.
1:11. "I Hate These People." Writ. Adam Stein. Dir. Ed Bianchi. October 9, 2007.
1:13. "Because I Know Patty." Writ. Todd A. Kessler, Glenn Kesser, and Daniel Zelman. Dir. Todd A. Kessler. October 23, 2007.
2:1. "I Lied Too." Writ. Todd A. Kessler, Glenn Kesser, and Daniel Zelman. Dir. Todd A. Kessler. January 7, 2009.
3:1. "Your Secrets Are Safe." Writ. Todd A. Kessler, Glenn Kesser, and Daniel Zelman. Dir. Todd A. Kessler. January 25, 2011.
3:13. "The Next One's Gonna Go in Your Throat." Writ. Todd A. Kessler, Glenn Kesser, and Daniel Zelman. Dir. Todd A. Kessler. April 19, 2010.

4:1. "There's Only One Way to Try a Case." Writ. Todd A. Kessler, Glenn Kessler, and Daniel Zelman. Dir. Todd A. Kessler. July 13, 2011.

NOTES

1. At the beginning of season one, the protagonist and Patty's young protégée Ellen Parsons escapes from a crime scene. In season two, a "vindictive" Ellen fires two shots at a yet unknown opponent. The beginning of season three has Patty involved in a hit-and-run.

2. In narrative studies, the term "prolepsis" has first been used and theorized by Gérard Genette. In his systematic description of temporal orders in narrative, he reserves the term for "any narrative maneuver that consists of narrating or evoking in advance an event that will take place later" (Genette 40). A more common expression for prolepsis is "flashforward." See also Currie, *About Time* 29–50.

3. "It is more rational to think of the narrative, the already-there-ness of its future, and its tangible block view of its own universe, as a model which exactly fails to represent the ontological conditions of human being" (Currie, *About Time* 21).

4. This, of course, does not mean that authors have not tried to do this. However, as Hempfer shows in his analysis of several examples, *first*-person narration in *present* tense is markedly experimental and, as I have tried to indicate, logically problematic. It is precisely for its "unnatural" feel that this specific narrative perspective is often explored in texts that draw attention to their own discursiveness and "constructedness."

5. A useful survey of scholars who argue that film narrative is present-tense narration can be found at the beginning of Dagle.

6. On the topic of "untensed" views of time, see Currie, "Expansion," 364. Concerning the "block universe," see Currie, "Novel," 323.

7. A few examples may suffice to give an impression of the situation (spoiler alert!): Patty Hewes's employee Ellen Parsons who wants to take down Patty for trying to kill her (in season one); Ellen's lover Wes, who, secretly investigating her, is an informant for a corrupt policeman; Walter Kendrick, the CEO of an indicted multinational company, who hides the toxicity reports of his company's products *and* manipulates the energy market; the afore-mentioned Daniel Purcell, who worked for Kendrick but turns his back on him and leaks the toxicity reports to Patty, *and* thinks he killed his wife (but did not); Claire Maddox, Kendrick's head attorney, who finds herself in the uncomfortable situation of working for Kendrick and sleeping with Purcell.

WORKS CITED

Bergson, Henri. *Time and Free Will: An Essay on the Immediate Data of Consciousness.* Mineola, NY: Dover Publications, 2001. Print.
"Burn It, Shred It, I Don't Care." *Damages.* FX. January 14, 2009. Television.
Currie, Mark. *About Time: Narrative, Fiction and the Philosophy of Time.* Edinburgh: Edinburgh University Press, 2007. Print.
———. "The Expansion of Tense." *Narrative* 17.3 (2009): 353–67. Print.
———. "The Novel and the Moving Now." *Novel* 42.2 (2009): 318–25. Print.

Dagle, Joan. "The Question of the Present Tense." *Narrative Strategies: Original Essays in Film and Prose Fiction*. Ed. Syndy Conger and Janice Welsh. Macomb: Western Illinois University Press, 1980. 47–59. Print.
Deleuze, Gilles. *Bergsonism*. New York: Zone Books, 1988. Print.
Dupuy, Jean-Pierre. *Pour un catastrophisme éclairé: Quand l'impossible est certain*. Paris: Seuil, 2004. Print.
Genette, Gérard. *Narrative Discourse: An Essay in Method*. Ithaca, NY: Cornell University Press, 1980. Print.
Grosz, Elizabeth. *Time Travels: Feminism, Nature, Power*. Durham, NC: Duke University Press, 2005. Print.
Hempfer, Klaus W. "(Pseudo-)Performatives Erzählen im zeitgenössischen französischen und italienischen Roman." *Romanistisches Jahrbuch* 50 (1999): 158–82. Print.
Lim, Bliss Cua. *Translating Time: Cinema, the Fantastic, and Temporal Critique*. Durham, NC: Duke University Press, 2009. Print.
"London, Of Course." *Damages*. FX. March 18, 2009. Television.
"Look What He Dug Up This Time." *Damages*. FX. March 25, 2009. Television.
Proctor, Robert. "Agnotology: A Missing Term to Describe the Cultural Production of Ignorance (and Its Study)." *Agnotology: The Making and Unmaking of Ignorance*. Ed. Robert Proctor and Londa L. Schiebinger. Stanford: Stanford University Press, 2008. 1–33. Print.
Proctor, Robert, and Londa L. Schiebinger, eds. *Agnotology: The Making and Unmaking of Ignorance*. Stanford: Stanford University Press, 2008.
Spivak, Gayatri Chakravorty. "Time and Timing: Law and History." *Chronotypes: The Construction of Time*. Ed. John B. Bender and David E. Wellbery. Stanford: Stanford University Press, 1991. 99–117. Print.
"Trust Me." *Damages*. FX. April 1, 2009. Television.
Žižek, Slavoj. *In Defense of Lost Causes*. London, NY: Verso, 2008. Print.

12

FREAKS OF TIME
Reevaluating Memory and Identity through Daniel Knauf's Carnivàle

FRIDA BECKMAN

Many things are hard to understand in Daniel Knauf's award-winning series *Carnivàle* (HBO, 2003–2005).[1] Characters share dreams, communicate without speaking, and have memories of events they could not have attended. The grotesque and confusing nature of this American TV series, suggested by one critic to be fit for those who thought David Lynch's *Twin Peaks* was too simple to follow, forced its producers to cancel the planned six seasons after only two seasons (twenty-four episodes) (Rouch). The series is set in the United States during the first half of the 1930s and features a traveling carnival making a living by setting up their entertainment in various small towns in the American Midwest. Apart from an invisible "Management" who makes all the big decisions, a family of "cootch" dancers, and a blind man with mysterious powers, the carnival also includes various "attractions" such as a pair of Siamese twins, a giant, a dwarf, a reptile man, a bearded lady, a Tarot reader, and a snake charmer. These characters are just some of the "freaks" of the show. But the freakiest thing about the series is not these characters, but the fact that the more regular temporal structure of narrative events involving the carnival characters is complemented by what seems to be another more elusive temporal structure. As the series progresses, it becomes increasingly clear that some of the characters—most importantly its protagonists, a young man named Ben Hawkins, whom the carnival picks up along the way, and Brother Justin, a man in a parallel and seemingly unconnected storyline—are connected to, and also connected by, a spatiotemporal context that is larger, more frightening, and much harder to define.

Before attempting to untie some of the temporal complexity of *Carnivàle*, it needs to be explained that *Carnivàle* offers two main temporal axes. To begin with, the show provides what may be called the diegetic time of the fictional universe into which the viewer is invited. This narrative time develops along what could be termed the temporal-content axis. Next, there is the temporality built into the medium of audiovisual representation in general, and the serialization of television programming in particular. This is a set of temporal conditions that affect and include the viewer's capacity to comprehend the narrative, such as the length of each session and the separation between episodes. This could be classified as the temporal-formal axis. While the former axis is a rather unusual way of dealing with time, the latter is, to a large extent, a genre-specific feature that Knauf's series has in common with numerous other serialized TV shows. The latter has also been under interrogation more generally lately in terms of what Steven Johnson calls a "structural transformation" of serialized television programming (66). Increasingly, contemporary TV series offer a narrative complexity that demand considerable cognitive work on behalf of the audience. Multiple narrative threads and plotlines in combination with gaps for the viewer to fill in makes it necessary for the viewer, not just to remember, but to analyze (Johnson 62–66). While narrative complexity can certainly be found in other media, too, not the least in the more reputed field of literary fiction, multistranded serialized television, as Kristin Thompson notes, puts a genre-specific pressure on the viewers' cognitive capacity as any narrative complexity needs to be untangled over a number of interruptions, including those of commercials, between episodes, and even seasons (ix). *Carnivàle*, this chapter shows, not only portrays a formal complexity of multiple storylines, but also conveys a highly complex relation between two different temporalities within the temporal-content axis. These two temporalities intersect in the narrative structure as well as in the bodies of the characters in intricate and challenging ways. This means that the viewer of Knauf's series is invited, not just to keep track of multiple strands of narrative, but also to inquire into the relation between identity and temporality. Thereby, this essay suggests, narratological examinations of the ways in which TV series challenge the viewers' cognitive capacity need to be complemented with more philosophical analyses of the questions that television programming increasingly pose. Because *Carnivàle* raises enough questions about temporality and identity to fill a whole book, this essay is meant to be a tentative suggestion of how some of these questions may begin to be answered. It focuses on the relation between temporality and identity in two main ways relating to causality and narrative and to memory and personal identity. Considering these two ways in which time is expressed in *Carnivàle*, we see that somewhere in the intersection between the temporal-formal axis, toward which this essay merely gestures, and the temporal-content axis, on which this essay focuses, emerges new ways of understanding TV programming in the twenty-first century as well as new ways of understanding constructions of identities in relation to both the past and the present.

THE TWO TEMPORALITIES OF *CARNIVÀLE*

A first key to the temporal set up of the series can be found in the initial speech given at the beginning of the first episode of the first series.

> Before the Beginning, after the great war between Heaven and Hell God created the Earth and gave dominion over it to the crafty ape he called Man. And to each generation was born a Creature of Light and a Creature of Darkness . . . and great armies clashed by night in the ancient war between good and evil. There was magic then. Nobility. And unimaginable cruelty. And so it was until the day that a false sun exploded over Trinity, and man forever traded away wonder for reason. ("Milfay")

Apart from noting the multiple emphases on issues of time—before, after, forever—viewers increasingly understand that Ben and Justin, the two main characters, represent these creatures of light and darkness, that they are what the DVD commentary describes as "avatars" born into a specific generation but part of an "ancient" war. In one way, these two characters could not be more different. Ben is a lonely and dirty young man without a clear place and identity and, initially, without family or friends. Justin is an increasingly powerful man of God who is respected by many people. At the same time, however, something keeps them together. The fact that they are avatars entails that they have access to the two very different temporalities suggested in the above quote. These two temporalities are positioned as something approaching a finite time and an infinite one, one of specific generations and one of endless repetition. This in itself may not be so remarkable.

What is remarkable is rather the fact that Knauf lets these two temporalities intersect through the bodies of the series' two key characters, which, in turn, affects the bodies of many of the others as well.

The first and more predictable temporal dimension of *Carnivàle* is what appears as a recognizable and regular development of narrative time according to the rules of causality. That causality is central to how narrative development is commonly presented as well as understood is reflected in narrative theory. Ever since Aristotle, it has been argued that events in narrative are "radically correlative" and, more than that, causative (Chatman 45). Classical narrative builds on the distribution of events according to more or less explicit connections between cause and effect and even if some modern authors work to discard causality as a main feature of their narratives, narrative theory, Seymour Chatman argues, needs to take into account the reader's tendency to connect events according to the principle of causality (47). Chatman cites

Roland Barthes, who differentiates between plots that are resolved—built on the hermeneutics of the unfolding of events—or revelatory—concerned with revealing characters' thoughts and feelings with a state of affairs that is already present. While the sense of temporal continuity is more dominant in the former type of plot, both kinds rely largely on some kind of causal relations (Chatman 48). More recently, and along the same lines, Shlomith Rimmon-Kenan builds on the narrative theories of Barthes and Chatman to suggest that a narrative event either advances the action or expands, maintains, or delays it (16). As narrative theory suggests, then, the fictional event remains closely linked to the causal development of the narrative. Such causality is also particularly important in narration in television. A linear causality, Thompson states, is often used in Hollywood to keep time and space intelligible (23). In serial television, it is especially important that the viewer comprehend the logic of diegetic time across its various temporal-formal disruptions (Thompson 36). Commonly, we are thus only able to witness one outcome of any one event and this outcome is typically predicted according to causality. In *Carnivàle*, this kind of narrative time is seen in the daily lives of the characters, their professional chores, and personal involvements.

At the same time, however, a second and more unpredictable temporality emerges. Ben has a gift that allows him to heal people and even bring them back to life from the dead. This is in effect a retracing of temporal development that entails a disturbance of the causal continuity that the characters otherwise inhabit. Ben can heal people and even bring them back to life, but he cannot "give" life, which means that the life he gives to the one he heals has to be taken from something or someone else that is living. As Ben himself puts it, "All I do is move life. I move it from one body to another" ("New"). Thus, for example, he can grant the wishes of a mother praying for her dead son's life after a terrible accident and take the mother's life, thereby giving life back to the son. Ben's capacity to heal or revive life is achieved, not through medical treatment belonging to a belief in reason but through the wonder of his own capacity to complement a natural course of events based on the laws of a causal temporality with another more ungraspable temporality in which he can retrace events that have already happened. This temporality is profoundly linked to Ben himself. While his actions seem to disrupt causality, his special powers are also a way of explaining these disruptions within the linearity of the narrative. While this disobedience to causality is thus to some extent naturalized through his powers, it nonetheless forces events to move according to his logic rather than to the more conventional logic of causal, physical development.

With Ben's gift of moving life viewers are thus invited to visualize two alternative temporal structures. The temporal shifts that occur through what is in effect a reversal of time complicate the notion of the narrative event. Through Ben, it becomes possible to argue that causality can be seen as causality simply because we are usually prevented from getting a glimpse of alternative outcomes to any one event. Given enough space, a large number of philosophical conceptions of time could be tested against the fact that the viewers of *Carnivàle* get to witness a temporality that is otherwise hidden from them including, for example, those of Baruch Spinoza, Henri Bergson, and Friedrich Nietzsche. One example, which to some extent is a negotiation between these three philosophical approaches and therefore appears as a good starting point, can be found in the philosophy of Gilles Deleuze. Building at least partly on Spinoza's understanding of univocity, Bergson's comprehension of the virtual, and Nietzsche's theroretization of the eternal return, Deleuze works to question time as a dialectical movement and to theorize temporality beyond causality.

If causality can be seen as a relation between the real and the possible, that is, where the outcome of events can be estimated according to a causal extension of the present, the Deleuzean conception of time opens for a more unpredictable shifting between corporeal and incorporeal layers of time. Time, Deleuze puts it, "must be grasped twice, in two complementary though mutually exclusive fashions" (*Logic* 8). Instead of one causal and linear development, we have to account both for the "living present" of actual bodies, what he calls the actual and for an incorporeal time that shadows physical existence and that holds the past and the future; that is, the virtual. The actual and the virtual are in turn related to a large ontological claim of univocity, a claim that opposes the idea of different and hierarchical levels of being. Instead of making an ontological distinction between the real and the unreal and between the human and the transcendent, Deleuze finds that that everything is equally real. This is a non-hierarchical view of the world in which no being transcends the other and where everything coexists although everything is not always represented. This means that time, too, exists in layers where one layer is actualized in the present and one exists as a virtual dimension of past and future. *Carnivàle* offers an interesting version of such a comprehension of time.

SPACE, REPETITION, MEMORY, AND INHERITANCE

One example of how corporeal and incorporeal temporalities affect the characters in the series can be seen in the way Ben's "moving of life" echoes in the spatiotemporal set up of the series as a whole. It is, of course, in the very nature of a carnival to be constantly on the move and this spatial activity is built into the series since almost every episode features a new setting as the party moves to new locations. Initially, the exhausting recurrence of setting up the carnival—the tents, the Ferris wheel, the Merry-go-round—for one night, only to take it all down and "shake some dust" afterward, gives this spatial movement a practical and very physical temporal quality. It is a circular movement in space, one followed up by a temporally predictable pattern based on a day's work. Before they picked up Ben, then, the carnival followed a certain route, thus keeping space and time linked in a circular and regular movement. As Ben joins, however, Management demands that the carnival take new routes that break their spatial pattern. Management shares with Ben a prediction of an explosion of the "false sun"—a weapon that will kill millions—and tells him he must break the chain of events that are "unfolding as we speak" and thus change a causality that has already been put in motion ("Los Moscos"). Ben must stop the future and is implored not to run from his destiny. The regular temporal structure of the carnival is thus disturbed by a seemingly incomprehensible timeline according to which Ben is forced to move. This causes much frustration as the characters are forced to go to unexpected and inhospitable places and to watch what seems like a workable routine be dismantled in favor of an exasperating schedule that forces them to move, not according to their own common temporal and spatial circuit but in accordance with a much larger but nevertheless invisible cycle of time moving according to generational avataric struggle in the aforementioned "ancient war between good and evil" ("Milfay").

A more specific example of how the two temporalities come to intersect in the bodies of characters can be seen in episode nine of the second season. After a terrible accident with the Ferris wheel where several children die, Jonesy, the man responsible for the Ferris wheel, is tarred and feathered by the locals. The tarring and feathering of Jonesy is anchored in the cause and effect of the narrative in that he is seen as the cause of the children's deaths and gets his punishment for it. It is also anchored in the temporal setting of the series, which, although it is set in the dust-bowl era, repeatedly plays with the time in which such punishments took place—the American frontier. In a spectacular scene where Ben sits alone by Jonesy's body in the desert, waiting for enough vultures to flock to enable him to "move life" from them to Jonesy, a causal chain would suggest that time is running out for Jonesy. Instead, as Jonesy is on the verge of dying from his burns, Ben rescues him and he recovers, not only from his (nearly) fatal burns, but also from the limp he has had during the whole series. This scene may be one example of what the critics saw as the unbearable slowness of the series.[2] This particular scene is prolonged, which gives us the sense that time has literally slowed down. After the previous action-packed scenes of the actual tarring, and what in a more conventional causal development should have been the death of Jonesy, viewers get to wait, with Ben, for the frightening birds to arrive. What is important in this scene, apart from a stunning visual aesthetics, is not the narrative event in the sense of a progression of narrative causality but rather a careful and detailed rendering of an event in which finite and infinite temporality intersect. If we read this through Deleuze, we can understand this event as a shift between the actual dimension of reality and the virtual layer in which causality does not apply. The most crucial thing here is that by breaking the causal chain, Ben not only reverses time but he also reveals that what seems to be actual—in this case Jonesy's burns—is also virtual. The results of Jonesy's burns (his death) can be retraced and another route of time can be taken. In *Carnivàle*, the actual, physical event does not function as a definitive marker of linear time since it can be undone and thereby disengaged from the temporal axis to which it seemed to belong.

That the two temporalities in *Carnivàle* coexist is suggested by a number of other events, reaching from minor comments to larger turning points. One example includes a scene toward the end when Ben arrives at Justin's house to kill him. Justin's foster father, Reverend Norman Balthus, is completely unsurprised at seeing him and gestures with his eyes to give Ben Justin's location. It is as if he has been expecting exactly this to happen ("Outside"). Another example is when Ben is about to be buried alive by a group of hobos in the woods who say, "Bury him deep. Not like that last one" ("Ingram"). While it remains unspoken who this "other one" is, it is clearly someone with special powers just like Ben who managed to get out. Repeatedly, there is a sense that the characters are situated at one particular point in space and time while also being stuck in a larger dimension of repetition of which they are unable to get an overview. In fact, it seems like the carnival is traveling into a universe of repetition, where all things have already happened or are just about to happen and where most individuals are trying to keep up with reality as events are repeating themselves. If Ben's moving life and the sense of repetition constitute two examples of a time out of joint in *Carnivàle*, a third example can be seen in the way in which characters share dreams, memories, and predictions. The most potent example of this is found in what is arguably the most central scene of the whole series. In the very beginning of the first episode, the viewer is thrown straight into a terrifying scene where someone is chasing or being chased through deep grass. One of the men in this dream sequence has a tattoo of a tree on his back and chest. Ben awakes and the viewer realizes the chase was only a dream. Or was it? Without the classical signposting that clearly signals its status as a dream, the scene remains hard to define. Indeed, since it is the first event that the viewers see after the brief introductory speech by Samson, it initially makes the viewer take it as diegetic reality. The temporary reassurance that this has been a dream caused by Ben's waking up is soon disturbed, however, by the fact that the scene recurs in different contexts throughout the series.

As the series continues, viewers not only see this as a recurring dream for Ben but they also realize that Justin is having the same dream ("Lincoln"). Additionally, and most crucially, the end of the last episode of the second season features this chase through the grass as it is actually happening—Ben is being chased by Justin, who has the tree tattoos on his back and chest. That this scene opens as well as closes the series and also recurs within it in the minds of different characters means that the status of this event in terms of a causal chain must be questioned. That Justin has this tattoo has already become clear to the viewer in an earlier episode, which seems like a good example of what Thompson calls a "dangling cause" (21). A dangling cause is a common technique to maintain causality in serial television while at the same time separating cause and effect over time (Thompson 20–21). By giving some information or starting an action that is not given a resolution until later in the film or series, Thompson explains, the dangling cause enables multiple plotlines while at the same time maintaining maximum clarity (21). As for Justin's tattoo, viewers already know that the image is important and they already know that the person with the tattoo is crucial to the narrative. This way, the tattooing of Justin in episode two of the second season anticipates what is to happen later, all in accordance with television techniques of causality. However, such techniques are insufficient in accounting for the instance of the tattoo as it fills a much more complex temporal function than this in at least two ways.

To begin with, Justin gets the tattoo well *after* Ben's dreams of the man with the tattoo. This can only be described if we can accept that these dreams are dreams of the future. If so, we have a temporal warp here since this should mean that he is dreaming about, or remembering, an event that is yet to come. Secondly, the narrative also seems to suggest that this event has already happened exactly like this before. The fact that Justin gets his tattoo after viewers have seen Ben's dreams of the man with the tattoo presents the possibility that Justin is purposefully reenacting a previous event. Also, viewers realize that it has been Ben's father that they have seen running through the grass in Ben's dreams. This could mean that Ben is destined to reenact the same event as his father. With either of these two options—that is, the shared dream of the future or the shared repetition of the past—the series gives a sense that everything already exists in the shape of a circle of time and that Ben and Justin have access to a layer of time in which past and future exist virtually. Their present, in terms of their final struggle, is but an actualization of a virtual layer of past and future time in which events have always happened or will always happen.

A fourth way in which *Carnivàle* opens up questions of double temporalities is through the notion of inheritance and eternity, of limited life spans in combination with a repetition of roles. At the end of the last season, after the inevitable fight between Ben and Justin in the tall grass, it seems as if Ben has won. He has stabbed Justin at the center of the tattoo and Justin is dead. However, Sofie, another central character in *Carnivàle*, chases through the grass to find Justin and kneels down beside him. As the tall grass all fades around them, viewers understand that Sofie, too, is an avatar. In an earlier episode viewers have seen it written on a mirror that "Sofie is the Omega," and numerous clues suggest that she is special, but only at the very end does this makes sense ("Alamogordo"). That Sofie is the Omega opens up important questions regarding both the temporal-content and the temporal-formal axis of *Carnivàle*. From the point of view of content, the identification of Sofie as the Omega has a strong temporal connotation as it is a way of suggesting that she is the last one in a series. If Sofie is the Omega and as such the last of her kind, does this mean that there has also been an Alpha, as well as another twenty-four avatars before her?

This presumption is supported both by the choice of the notion of the "Omega" and also by the fact that the importance of generations and inheritance is strong in the series as a whole in two main ways. To begin with, Ben's father is an avatar. During almost the entire series, Ben is trying to find his father, and in a surreal set of scenes where Ben is stuck in the old mines of Babylon, he meets him for the first time. When Ben tells him he knows who he is, the father replies "But do you know what it means?" ("Babylon"). What it means, of course, but that neither Ben nor the viewer knows at this point, is that Ben, too, is an avatar. Secondly, we realize at the very end that Sofie is, in fact, Justin's daughter, which explains how she was given her powers.[3] Interestingly, then, the sense of repetition, shared memory, and a virtual layer of time that *Carnivàle* has presented and which has been analyzed through Deleuze also has to be fit into a very specific and decidedly corporeal time frame. The idea of a specific number of generations of avatars is in many ways suggestive of an actual, physical chronology of life span and inheritance. This would mean that Ben, Justin, and Sofie are simultaneously connected to both the actual and the virtual. More than that, not only the avatars themselves but also the temporal system of repetition in its entirety is tied up with physical facts such as aging and generational succession. As we have seen, this dual belonging is also passed on to the people they heal in the reversal of time suggested above. The temporalities that converge in the bodies of the characters in *Carnivàle* are thus finite and infinite concurrently.

This doubling of time through the conflating importance of beginnings and endings, and of finite and infinite is also mirrored in the temporal-formal axis. Positioning Sofie as the new avatar would have been the directors' opening toward the third, aborted, season, the "cliffhanger" that would have opened the seemingly final struggle between Ben and Justin toward new adventures. However, as the series was forced to close down, questions about the Omega are never answered. This way, the open-ended temporality of the series appears not only thematically in the temporal-content axis but also in the extended format of the temporal-formal axis of the TV series as such. The "answers" are delayed, not only until later episodes or even to the added DVD commentary, but also to the "sheet" released later to frustrated viewers. In this sense, the eternal is built into the format of the series in the sense that its premature cancellation withholds what may have been a conclusion. There is a sense, then, in which not only the series as a whole but its ending, too, points toward two temporalities. On the one hand, the actual and very practical facts of withdrawn funding and premature closure mean an end to the series. At the same time, questions of temporal-formal and temporal-content may be said to merge as the canceling of the show also means that the end is endlessly deferred. The last of the avatars, and with her possibly the end of avataric time, is left in a constant state of beginning, or even before the beginning, if we are to believe Samson's initial speech at the very opening of the series. The moment when man trades away magic for reason and the false sun explodes never happens.

CONCLUSION

Interestingly, much critical response to *Carnivàle* was in terms of complaints of the lack of narrative progression. There is a limit, as one reviewer wrote, to "just how much slowly unfolding sadness viewers can take" (Hawrileski). Admittedly, a narrow focus on narrative development may create frustration, at least to a TV audience used to more causally constructed action. But if viewers are prepared to look beyond the main narrative, as this chapter has tried to suggest, they will find a great density of winding and unwinding temporal threads. Where many other contemporary TV series offer the viewer cognitive challenges by way of multiple plotlines, as Johnson and Thompson show, Knauf's series focuses rather on the challenges of deciphering the logic of multiple temporalities. A slight shift of focus, then, is all that is needed to discover that *Carnivàle* is not so much about narrative representation as it is about temporal perspectives. In *Carnivàle*, actual corporeal bodies and actions constantly need to be weighed against the role of a virtual and seemingly impersonal layer of time. By having characters retrace temporality, relive events, and share pasts and/or futures, the portrayal of time and space challenges not only the notion of a continuous, causal temporality, but also the idea of individual subjectivity since memories (the past) and predictions (the future) are not tied to one single body and mind. Rather, there is a repetition of events traveling across generations adding to the notion of individual memory an impersonal loop of virtual memory. If representation, as Deleuze suggests, is about single perspective and thus about false depth—about mediation that shows but does not change anything—it is also possible for art to express multiple perspectives, entangled points of view, and coexisting moments that deform representation (*Difference* 67). When contemporary television programming can achieve this, as is the case of *Carnivàle*, it approximates this view of art as it favors unpredictable change over conventional expectations and active thinking over passive reception.

SUGGESTED EPISODES FOR ADDITIONAL STUDY

Carnivàle

1:4. "Black Blizzard." Writ. Daniel Knauf and William Schmidt. Dir. Peter Medak. October 5, 2003.
1:7. "The River." Writ. Daniel Knauf and Toni Graphia. Dir. Alison Maclean. October 26, 2003.
2:4. "Old Cherry Blossom Road." Writ. Daniel Knauf, Dawn Prestwich, and Nicole Yorkin. Dir. Steve Shill. January 30, 2005.
2:7. "Damaskus, NE." Writ. Daniel Knauf, John McLaughlin, and William Schmidt. Dir. Alan Taylor. February 20, 2005.

NOTES

1. While Daniel Knauf is the creator of the series as a whole, it has a larger number of directors and writers for the different episodes. For the sake of simplicity, and without wishing to diminish the importance of these directors and writers, I will refer to Knauf to denote the collective of makers of *Carnivàle*.

2. Phil Gallo suggests, for example, that the series "takes a leisurely approach toward getting to the point."

3. However, it does not fully explain it as the *Carnivàle* mythologist Michael Strang suggests that only first-born sons can be avatars and that women can only be vessels of avataric blood. This is the case, for example, of Justin's sister Iris, who has no powers herself (DVD commentary). When Sofie heals her father, however, this patriarchal circle is broken.

WORKS CITED

"Alamogordo, NM." Dir. Jack Bender. *Carnivàle*. HBO. January 16, 2005. Television.
"Babylon." Dir. Tim Hunter. *Carnivàle*. HBO. October 12, 2003. Television.
Bible. New Revised Standard Version. Oxford: Oxford University Press, 1995. Print.
Chatman, Raymond Benjamin. *Story and Discourse: Narrative Structure in Fiction and Film*. Ithaca, NY: Cornell University Press, 1980. Print.
Deleuze, Gilles. *Difference and Repetition*. 1968. Trans. Paul Patton. London: Continuum, 2004. Print.
———. *The Logic of Sense*. 1969. Trans. Mark Lester and Charles Stivale. London: Continuum, 2004. Print.
Gallo, Phil. "Carnivale Review." *Variety*. September 11, 2003. Web. July 10, 2010.
Havrileski, Heather. "Gutsy-or Just Gusty?" *Salon.com*. November 1, 2003. Web. July 6, 2010.
"Ingram, TX." Dir. John Patterson. *Carnivàle*. HBO. January 23, 2005. Television.
Johnson, Steven. *Everything Bad Is Good for You: How Popular Culture Is Making Us Smarter*. London: Penguin Books, 2005. Print.
"Lincoln Highway, UT." Dir. Rodrigo Garcia. *Carnivàle*. HBO. March 6, 2005. Television.
"Los Moscos." Dir. Jeremy Podeswa. *Carnivàle*. HBO. January 9, 2005. Television.
"Milfay." Dir. Rodrigo Garcia. *Carnivàle*. HBO. September 14, 2003. Television.
"New Canaan, CA." Dir. Scott Winant. *Carnivàle*. HBO. March 27, 2005. Television.
"Outside New Canaan." Dir. Dan Lerner. *Carnivàle*. HBO. March 20, 2005. Television.
Rimmon-Kenan, Shlomith. *Narrative Fiction: Contemporary Poetics*. 1983. London: Methuen, 2002. Print.
Rouch, Matt. "Roush Riff." *TV Guide*. January 10, 2005. Web. July 5, 2005.
Thompson, Kristin. *Storytelling in Film and Television*. Cambridge, MA: Harvard University Press, 2003. Print.

13

THE DISCOURSE OF *MEDIUM*
Time as a Narrative Device

KRISTI MCDUFFIE

> A high school teenager naps in a classmate's car. She wakes up in a neighbor's home, babysitting. The next moment, she is outside the home, talking to her mother amidst police cars and ambulances. Suddenly she finds herself at her high school again, but not as a teenager—she is a teacher who has a husband and a child. In a matter of minutes, she has lost ten years of her life.
> —*MEDIUM*, EPISODE SUMMARY ("TIME KEEPS ON SLIPPING")

This sequence of scenes sounds like it comes from a television show with a complex narrative like *Lost* (ABC, 2004–2010), but it is just another episode of *Medium* (CBS, 2005–2009; NBC 2009–2011), the seven-season series about a woman with a gift. Allison Dubois (Patricia Arquette) is a medium who sees visions of the past, present, and future. These visions, along with other paranormal elements, emerge within various temporal structures that are used throughout the series to further episodic narratives. The flexible way time is used in the show creates new narrative possibilities for plot structures and for what Sarah Kozloff calls discourse, the way the story is told (69). This chapter explores how time is used in varied, flexible ways throughout the series and how this use of time makes *Medium* unique within its genre. *Medium* has formulaic elements that align with its genre of an episodic crime drama, but its paranormal devices employ narrative time to engage issues often left to other genres, such as the ethics of changing the future and morality. Ultimately, though, audiences may not fully embrace this model of contemporary programming.

The investigation of time and narrative in *Medium* is best understood within the context of its genre. *Medium* is an episodic, paranormal crime drama or, as Jason Mittell calls *Medium*, a "crime drama with a paranormal twist" (221). The main character Allison Dubois is a psychic who receives visions, normally through her dreams, and usually about murders. She uses these visions to help the Phoenix, Arizona, district attorney's office solve crimes. As is common to the crime genre, most episodes contain stand-alone plots revolving around a particular crime, such as a murder or a missing person. Although this premise makes *Medium* an episodic crime drama, *Medium* complicates this premise with paranormal aspects that are more common in the science fiction genre. These paranormal devices include the aforementioned dream sequences, along with visions Allison receives by touching, or catching a glimpse of, a person or object. For example, in one episode she receives visions through a video camera ("Ghost"). Other sporadic paranormal events include Allison hearing music over and over again in her head ("The Song"), seeing symbols above people's heads to represent love matches ("The Match"), and hearing an imaginary buzzer when someone lies ("Truth"). Paranormal devices are, therefore, relatively constant throughout the show and provide the means for time manipulation.

The paranormal elements added to the episodic crime drama make *Medium* unique among similar programs. Although there is a litany of crime dramas, from the *CSI* franchise (CBS, 2000–Present) to *Numb3rs* (CBS, 2005–2010), most do not employ paranormal elements. Alternately, most paranormal programs such as *Fringe* (Fox, 2008–Present) fall under the science fiction category and tend to be less formulaic. An episodic crime drama that might be akin to *Medium* is *The Mentalist* (CBS, 2008–Present), which follows Patrick Jane (Simon Baker), a consultant with the California Bureau of Investigation in solving crimes. Jane is not a true medium, however; he is just skilled at reading people. The show does not actually employ paranormal elements. The program that is most often compared to *Medium* is *Ghost Whisperer* (CBS, 2005–2010), since both shows profile actual mediums. Melinda Gordon (Jennifer Love Hewitt) can see ghosts who have not yet crossed over. She helps the spirits gain closure on earth so that they can enter into the "light." Although the closure sometimes relates to the way the person died, it is more often driven by familial relationships. Thus, while *Ghost Whisperer* is episodic, it is not a crime drama, nor does it employ fluid time techniques in its narrative.

Supernatural (The WB, 2005–2006; The CW, 2006–Present) is a better, but imperfect, comparison to *Medium*. *Supernatural* follows two brothers, Dean and Sam Winchester (Jensen Ackles and Jared Padalecki), as they travel around the United States disintegrating ghosts, demons, and nasty creatures of American folklore. This show is more or less episodic, but, like *Ghost Whisperer*, it is not a crime drama. Its alignment with *Medium*, as will be explained in greater detail later in this essay, rests on the fact that it is a paranormal drama and employs some similar time techniques. Within the show, Dean connects these programs with his intertextual allusion, "Hey, Sam, who do you think is a hotter psychic, Patricia Arquette, Jennifer Love Hewitt, or you?"

("Asylum"). Overall, the lack of a similar program to *Medium* illustrates how the show differentiates itself from the overwhelming number of crime dramas on television today. The differentiation emerges from the way the program utilizes time to capitalize on the narrative possibilities made available with paranormal elements.

GENRE AND NARRATIVE THEORY

In order to further explore how *Medium* differs from other contemporary programming, it is important to turn to narrative and genre theory to see how the program both conforms to and confronts generic standards. *Medium* is classified as episodic because each episode is relatively self-contained. Each episode has a fully resolved storyline about a crime, and it requires no prior knowledge of the series or characters to be understood. By definition, episodic series use the same characters and setting each week for their fully contained stories (Kozloff 90–91), and these characters return to their status-quo equilibrium by the end of the episode (Mittell 228). This structure is not rare, as most crime dramas would be classified as episodic. Episodic programs stand in contrast to serial narratives, where storylines spread over several episodes, a single season, or even a series' entire run (Kozloff 91). The serial format was first "mastered" in soap operas, but has since expanded to prime-time dramas beginning with *Hill Street Blues* (NBC, 1981–1987) (Johnson 68). Recent series such as *Lost*, which interweaves storylines over entire seasons, are contemporary manifestations of this structure. Although these definitions of episodic and serial programming may seem clear-cut, many shows fall somewhere in the middle of this continuum. For example, many shows have large story arcs based on relationships, but still have distinguished plotlines for each episode, such as *The Good Wife* (CBS, 2009–Present). The overall arc in *The Good Wife* focuses on Alicia Florrick's (Julianna Margulies) personal life, while each episode focuses on a particular legal case. Mittell calls storylines that weave throughout episodic series "runners," claiming that runners rarely become the main plotline of any given episode (231). In *The Good Wife*, Alicia's attraction to her boss is a runner because it creates tension throughout multiple episodes, but it rarely becomes the main plot of any given episode.

As a result of these genre constraints, episodic crime dramas are often extremely formulaic. For example, most episodes of *CSI* begin by showing a crime or the moments before a crime. Then the scene cuts to the investigators arriving and working on the crime scene. This crime is the primary narrative thread, although there is usually a secondary narrative interwoven throughout the episode about a second crime or about one of the character's personal lives. Although this formulaic structure might seem limiting, Jonathan Bignell explains that viewers experience pleasure through watching formulaic plots unfold:

> Popular television series rely on recurrent narrative patterns where, as Umberto Eco (1990) argued, formulas produce pleasure for the viewer by rewarding predictive activity. So the pleasures of a specific narrative, such as setting up an enigma that will subsequently be resolved, produce a second kind of pleasure at the level of the series as a whole through repetition of narrative patterns and the programme's conformity to viewer expectations. (170)

This theory accounts for some of the popularity of the *CSI* franchise—fans take pleasure in the formulaic unfolding of the solving of the crime. *Medium* also takes advantage of this opportunity for pleasure by utilizing formulaic elements, but it uses narrative time to maneuver within formulaic parameters and accomplish more than most episodic crime dramas.

As mentioned earlier, one of the formulaic parameters for *Medium* includes the use of dream sequences. Each episode begins with a dream, which feels "real" to both Allison and viewers. Allison then normally wakes up in a panic and the episode cuts to the opening credits. After a commercial break, Allison tries to make sense of the dream, usually beginning as she and her husband Joe (Jake Weber) are feeding their three daughters breakfast. This focus on Allison's home and family life keeps the show grounded in realism that is not always present in paranormal dramas. This repetitive structure—the regular juxtaposition of the fast-paced dream sequences that open each episode with the slower-paced scenes from Allison's familial routine which temporarily stall the action—also showcases the way the program plays with time in terms of narrative delivery. While most television programming purposely omits mundane activities, such as characters sleeping, *Medium* relies on these as part of temporal play. For example, there may be multiple sleeping scenes within a given "day," since Allison usually needs to go to sleep again so that she can have more dreams to unfold the mystery. Occasionally she can dream during naps or receive visions while awake, but for the most part, Allison sleeps many times during a single episode due to the program's reliance on her dreams to forward the main mystery, and hence plot, of the episode.

The way that *Medium* transcends these formulaic limitations is best understood through the lens of narrative theory. As Kozloff notes, most shows on television are narratives or rely on narrative structures (69). Furthermore, most shows tend to have linear narratives that follow chronological order, with some programs adding flashbacks and flashforwards to help explain the current narrative. According to her theorization, narratives can be "split into two parts: the *story*, that is, 'what happens to whom,' and the *discourse*, that is, 'how the story is told'" (Kozloff 69, emphasis in original). Returning again to the most dominant of the contemporary episodic crime dramas, in a *CSI* episode, the *story* is that someone has been murdered and crime scene investigators determine who committed the crime. The *discourse* is how that story is revealed to viewers, such as how much of the murder is shown and which lab procedures are demonstrated. Since episodic programs are so formulaic and viewers have limited investment in both the characters and the weekly plot, discourse becomes more important than story. For any given *CSI* episode, viewers know that the crime scene investigators will find the perpetrator—the interesting part is *how* the investigators will do so. As Bignell explains, viewers experience pleasure by watching the familiar process unfold. Viewers also participate in that process by predicting outcomes.

Medium is similar to *CSI* in that the crime will almost certainly be solved by the end of the episode (unless it is part of a multi-episode arc), although the definition of "solved" depends on the episode. In some episodes, *Medium* follows the traditional crime drama plotline of starting with a murder and then showing the process of finding the murderer. Yet rather than being the standard format, this is only one possible structure, as *Medium* takes advantage of multiple plots and discourses. Other episodes revolve around preventing murders, finding missing people, or something else entirely. Some sample episodic plot structures are: Allison dreams about a murder and subsequently figures out who committed the crime ("Jump"); Allison dreams about a future murder and prevents that murder ("There Will"); Allison dreams about a seemingly random event, such as a suicide, and connects that event to a present-day murder ("The Reckoning"); and Allison dreams of past events and helps solve a present-day crime ("The Other"). The dreams are sometimes incredibly personal for Allison, although they still help her solve present-day crimes. For instance, in one episode, Allison dreams that her youngest daughter, Marie, dies of leukemia at age twenty ("Second") and in another, she dreams that she is alone in the future because her entire family has been murdered ("Bring"). In these examples, discourse becomes more important than story. Viewers probably know that Allison will be able to stop her family from being murdered in the future—the interesting part is watching *how* Allison prevents it. In all of these episodes, the visions are devices that facilitate the manipulation of time within the narrative to enable these discourses.

THE DISCOURSES OF *MEDIUM*

The discourse and plot variation in *Medium* are best illustrated through specific episode analysis. Dreams and other paranormal elements are some devices used for narrative time, and alternative realities are another. Episodes invoke a hyper use of time when characters live in an alternate reality, and these episodes are often the most innovative and interesting. In "Time Out of Mind," the episode begins with Allison in a mental institution, presumably waiting to see someone. However, it soon becomes clear that Allison is actually institutionalized and the staff thinks she is a woman named Beverly. Allison wakes up, so viewers and Allison alike realize she was just dreaming. The next scene follows the standard sequence of Allison having breakfast with her family. But it turns out Allison is still stuck in Beverly's world when she goes to work and it is still 1959. The third time Allison wakes up, she remains in the present. In this episode, then, the show is not overtly about a murder or even a crime. The conflict is that Allison is moving through time and has to figure out why and how to stop. Through more dreams, visions, and even watching old film reels of the real Beverly over the rest of the episode, Allison figures out the link between her visions of Beverly in 1959 and the current murder case the DA is working on. The use of time in this episode is deliberately confusing for both Allison and viewers. Neither Allison nor viewers are aware of which narrative material is real versus dream until Allison wakes up for the third time. While many television programs are confusing to viewers (often deliberately so), it is less common to have episodic crime dramas misleading the characters themselves. In *Medium*, the time manipulation is not just enhancing the viewing experience; it is impacting the characters' experience and furthering the narrative. Furthermore, discourse becomes more important than story once again because the process of Allison solving the mystery is highlighted more than the mystery itself.

Another recurrent use of time is the inclusion of scenes from Allison's past in order to complement current plot events. In "Sweet Dreams," Allison dreams about herself as a teenager (Jessy Schram), and these dreams help Allison solve the crime she is working on in the present. Similarly, in "But for the Grace of God," Allison's oldest daughter, Ariel (Sofia Vassilieva), dreams of her mother's past—giving viewers a reprise of teenage Allison—and these dreams allow Ariel to help Allison solve a present crime. The most overt use of teenage Allison scenes is in "The Boy Next Door." The episode begins with Allison getting her family ready for school and work in the morning, and at the end of the scene, a teenage Allison wakes up from the dream. Viewers know that this is a reversal of the formulaic story structure in that the "present" story is teenage Allison and the dreams are future Allison. The scenes alternate between an adult Allison, who runs into an old high school friend while trying to solve a murder, and teenage Allison, who meets this same friend in her "present." Teenage Allison learns though her dreams that this friend commits the future crimes. While adhering to the traditional formulas of dream sequences, the episode reverses the narrative by having the teenage Allison dream of the future, grown Allison, rather than the other way around. This episode both plays with and conforms to the formulaic structure that viewers are used to while creating an original plotline. Viewers experience pleasure by watching the familiar structure unfold and by achieving insider status from recognizing the reversal of the standard structure.

In addition to entertaining and rewarding regular viewers, temporal structures are also used by the program to create moral dilemmas. In "Raising Cain," Allison dreams of a missing child in the present and a young man in the future. She helps find the missing child based on her dreams and eventually realizes that the boy's parents tried to kill him because they thought he was evil. Future dreams show that the child does, indeed, grow up to be a murderer. The juxtaposition of time in the visions creates a moral dilemma for Allison because Allison has to weigh the current crime committed by the parents to the future crime potentially committed by the child. Narrative time thus creates a unique space to address morality because the characters have options that are not often available in real life. Allison knows how the future might turn out, so she has to decide whether and how to use that knowledge. Eventually, the dilemma solves itself when Allison has a dream that the boy turns out to be a high school valedictorian rather than a murderer. The use of time in this episode thus complicates the main conflict of finding the boy and figuring out who tried to hurt him by adding a moral dilemma and the question of whether the future can be altered. Unfortunately, the resolution of this specific episode allows Allison to avoid confronting the moral dilemma head-on.

The morality theme emerges many times because Allison must confront her responsibility and ability to change the future often. Allison has many conversations with her husband, Joe, throughout the series to consider this very question, and some episodes deal with this notion explicitly. In "Then . . . And Again," District Attorney Manuel Devalos (Miguel Sandoval) and Allison are shot and killed by a recently released convict whom Devalos wrongly convicted of killing his wife five years before. Allison suddenly wakes up five years in the past and must convince Devalos (who does not know her) that he should not convict an innocent man. This episode is not using a flashback—Allison is actually living her life five years in the past. Allison is not able to change the past, though; Devalos moves forward with the conviction. The only resolution is that when Allison wakes up again in the present, she warns Devalos of the danger and Devalos can only right the wrong in the present by making reparations. The episode thus contemplates the possibilities of changing the past and the future, and it is done through Allison's movement in time. Allison's agency in creating change is surprisingly limited in this episode when she cannot change the past. In some episodes Allison is able to change the future, such as by preventing a murder or kidnapping based on a dream, but in other episodes, such as this one, she cannot. Her limited agency serves to keep her and the episode grounded with a shade of realism, one that is highlighted in the series finale when Allison is unable to alter Joe's death ("Me"). This realism thus solidifies *Medium*'s categorization as a crime procedural, rather than a science fiction narrative, because justice emerges from Allison's efforts in "real" time, even though these efforts are influenced by paranormal elements.

A particularly creative episode that showcases an exaggerated use of time is "Time Keeps on Slipping," which contained the complex temporal structure summarized at the start of this chapter. Ariel is the main character in this episode and she lives her life in fast-forward. This is the sequence presented at the start of this chapter: Ariel's day starts off normal, but after she takes a nap in a classmate's car, she keeps jumping ahead in her life, where she is married and had a daughter of her own. Ariel is not simply having visions of a future—she is living her future and is as confused about the time loss as viewers are. Viewers experience Ariel's confusion, and eventually, both Ariel and viewers come to understand how her experience will help her solve a present-day crime. This episode, and others that invoke alternate realities, build upon the scaffolding that *Medium* built through its use of narrative time. Without that scaffolding, this episode would seem too farfetched; with the scaffolding, viewers know this alternate reality is a technique used to solve a crime at the end of the episode. Time is central to the way *Medium* functions, and this episode, among the last of the series, capitalizes upon and celebrates the narrative time used throughout the series.

This scaffolded use of time allows the discourse variations that make *Medium* more flexible than other episodic crime programs. Some serial narratives like *Lost* employ time and narrative techniques, but episodic programs are rarely able to use such techniques due to their formulaic premises. *Quantum Leap* (NBC, 1989–1993) is an episodic program that was explicitly about time travel (Sam Beckett [Scott Bakula] travels to a new time and place each episode). Yet once again, *Quantum Leap* is not directly comparable to *Medium* because it is not a crime drama. Furthermore, *Medium* is unique in the way it uses visions from the past and the future within its discourse. Flashbacks that give important backstory are common in television narratives, and flashforwards are becoming more common. *FlashForward* (ABC, 2009–2010), for example, is about a worldwide blackout in which virtually everyone on earth views slightly over two minutes of their lives six months into the future. The show then centers on the characters' drive to figure out why the flashforwards occurred and how to prevent future flashforwards. The question of changing the future becomes the primary tension in the show, and this tension can be difficult to maintain during a season-long network show. In *Veronica Mars* (UPN, 2004–2006; The CW, 2006–2007), the entire first season is littered with flashbacks in order to show Veronica's (Kristen Bell) life before the death of her best friend in order to help Veronica figure out who killed her. While these flashbacks are useful in adding depth and "showing" vital information rather than "telling," the show remains anchored in the past with a limited ability to move forward. In these other shows, the flashbacks enhance the viewing experience by enabling backstory and character development. By its hyper use of narrative time, such as episodes where characters experience alternate realities, *Medium* avoids the limitations that can occur with the use of traditional flashbacks and flashforwards. The characters themselves have flashbacks and flashforwards through dreams and visions. The visions are part of the discourse by contributing to and furthering the solving of the crimes.

It is true that there are other programs that utilize time in this way; however, other programs do so to a different effect. *Supernatural*, for instance, is similar to *Medium* as a paranormal drama that uses narrative time devices. In one episode, Sam relives the same day over and over again until he figures out how to keep Dean alive ("Mystery"), similar to the *Medium* episode where Allison relives the same day over and over again until she solves the mystery ("Be Kind"). In another episode of *Supernatural*, Sam and Dean appear in an alternate life, where instead of being hunters of nasty creatures, they are corporate drones ("It's a Terrible"). This setup is similar to the *Medium* episode where Allison finds herself married to her high school sweetheart and living a financially improved life until, as usual, it becomes clear how the alternate reality helps solve a present crime ("Twice"). The difference between *Supernatural* and *Medium*'s use of these gimmicks is that *Supernatural* takes a postmodern, metacognitive approach that often laughs at itself and uses different episodic structures for parody. For example, *Supernatural* has a mock episode of *Ghost Hunters* ("Ghostfacers") and a mock 1950s-style episode of *Dracula* ("Monster"). In contrast, *Medium* usually uses narrative time without such strong metacognition and parody. It remains soberly rooted in its investigation of disturbing crimes. Furthermore, since *Medium* already has substantial flexibility in its narratives, these episodes that overtly engage with time emerge organically within the show's structure. The time play in all episodes creates a foundation for the more substantial time exploitation that happens in the episodes described earlier. The drastic use of time in those episodes becomes more palatable given the premise of time utilization overall.

CONCLUSION

Overall, this investigation illustrates how *Medium* engages its paranormal elements to utilize narrative time and expand discourse possibilities within its formulaic premises. Yet despite *Medium's* innovative storytelling, the viewing public does not seem to support this type of program wholeheartedly. Although the fact that *Medium* lasted seven seasons indicates that it achieved quite a degree of success, it was not a blockbuster show. NBC canceled *Medium* after its fifth season in 2009, and CBS picked it up in order to accompany *Ghost Whisperer* on Friday nights. *Medium* lasted only half a season in 2011 after *Ghost Whisperer* went off the air. This cancellation, which occurred when similar shows such as *CSI* spinoffs still prosper, indicates that audiences might not fully embrace this experimental use of time. This temporal play, although expected by a loyal viewer of *Medium*, might make it unpredictable and outside the safe confines of the crime drama for casual viewers. While *Medium* fans can find pleasure in its formulaic plot structure, casual viewers might find the use of narrative time too confusing to find consistent pleasure in the discourse the way that they find pleasure in *CSI's* more predictable discourse. Although *Medium* does have a problem that will eventually be resolved, the path is so variable that it may reduce viewers' predictive ability and pleasure in watching the process unfold. Furthermore, although this analysis shows that *Medium* is innovative in which genre conventions it uses and exploits, a mass audience might resist *Medium's* use of genre. A paranormal crime drama that manipulates time may not be formulaic enough for crime drama devotees, nor edgy enough for science fiction fans. *Medium* may, quite simply, be doing too much.

During at least one point in the series, *Medium* gives a nod to its use of narrative time. In a voice-over at the end of "Then . . . And Again," Allison vocalizes traditional notions about time. She says, "Time is priceless, yet it costs us nothing. You can do anything you want with it, but you can't own it. You can spend it, but you can't keep it. And once you've lost it, there's no getting it back. It's just . . . gone." In its use of narrative time within episodes, *Medium* shows that in fictional television, at least, these clichés do not hold true. Time can be regurgitated, relived, maneuvered, lost, and recovered—at least in the name of entertaining television.

SUGGESTED EPISODES FOR ADDITIONAL STUDY

Medium
1:1. "Pilot." Writ. and dir. Glenn Gordon Caron. January 3, 2005.
1:3. "A Couple of Choices." Writ. Glenn Gordon Caron and Michael Angeli. Dir. Jeff Bleckner. January 17, 2005.
1:8. "Lucky." Writ. David Folwell. Dir. Peter Werner. February 21, 2005.
3:7. "Mother's Little Helper." Writ. Moira Kirland. Dir. Vincent Misiano. January 3, 2007.
3:17. "Joe Day Afternoon." Writ. Ken Schefler. Dir. Aaron Lipstadt. April 4, 2007.
3:22. "Everything Comes to a Head." Writ. Ken Schefler. Dir. Ronald L. Schwary. May 16, 2007.
4:5. "Girls Ain't Nothing But Trouble." Writ. Moira Kirland. Dir. Vincent Misiano. February 25, 2008.
5:4. ". . . About Last Night." Writ. Ken Schefler. Dir. Aaron Lipstadt. February 23, 2009.
6:5. "Baby Fever." Writ. Jordan Rosenberg. Dir. Vincent Misiano. October 30, 2009.
6:6. "Bite Me." Writ. Robert Doherty and Craig Sweeny. Dir. Aaron Lipstadt. October 30, 2009.
6:12. "Dear Dad . . ." Writ. Geoffrey Geib. Dir. Aaron Lipstadt. January 15, 2010.
6:16. "Allison Rolen Got Married." Writ. Heather Mitchell. Dir. David Paymer. March 12, 2010.
7:6. "Where Were You When . . . ?" Writ. Jordan Rosenberg. Dir. Peter Werner. October 29, 2010.
7:9. "The People in Your Neighborhood." Writ. Arika Lisanne Mittman, Jordan Rosenberg, and Denise Thé. Dir. Peter Werner. November 19, 2010.

WORKS CITED

"Asylum." *Supernatural: The Complete First Season*. Warner Home Video, 2006. DVD.
"Be Kind, Rewind." *Medium: The Third Season*. CBS Paramount, 2007. DVD.
Bignell, Jonathan. "Seeing and Knowing: Reflexivity and Quality." *Quality TV: Contemporary American Television and Beyond*. Ed. Janet McCabe and Kim Akcass. London: I. B. Tauris, 2007. 158–70. Print.
"The Boy Next Door." *Medium: The Third Season*. CBS Paramount, 2007. DVD.
"Bring Me the Head of Oswaldo Castillo." *Medium: The Fifth Season*. CBS Paramount, 2009. DVD.

"But for the Grace of God." *Medium: The Fourth Season*. CBS Paramount, 2008. DVD.
"Ghost in the Machine." *Medium: The Third Season*. CBS Paramount, 2007. DVD.
"Ghostfacers." *Supernatural: The Complete Third Season*. Warner Home Video, 2008. DVD.
"It's a Terrible Life." *Supernatural: The Complete Fourth Season*. Warner Home Video, 2009. DVD.
Johnson, Steven. *Everything Bad Is Good for You: How Today's Popular Culture Is Actually Making Us Smarter*. New York: Riverhead Trade, 2005. Print.
"Jump Start." *Medium: The Complete First Season*. CBS Paramount, 2006. DVD.
Kozloff, Sarah. "Narrative Theory and Television." *Channels of Discourse, Reassembled: Television and Contemporary Criticism*. 2nd ed. Ed. Robert C. Allen. Chapel Hill: University of North Carolina Press. 67–100. Print.
"The Match Game." *Medium*. CBS. October 1, 2010. Television.
"Me Without You." *Medium*. CBS. January 21, 2011. Television.
Mittell, Jason. *Television and American Culture*. New York: Oxford University Press, 2010. Print.
"Monster Movie." *Supernatural: The Complete Fourth Season*. Warner Home Video, 2009. DVD.
"Mystery Spot." *Supernatural: The Complete Third Season*. Warner Home Video, 2008. DVD.
"The Other Side of the Tracks." *Medium: The Complete First Season*. CBS Paramount, 2006. DVD.
"Raising Cain." *Medium: The Complete Second Season*. CBS Paramount, 2006. DVD.
"The Reckoning." *Medium: The Complete Second Season*, CBS Paramount, 2006. DVD.
"Second Opinion." *Medium: The Third Season*. CBS Paramount, 2007. DVD.
"The Song Remains the Same." *Medium: The Complete Second Season*. CBS Paramount, 2006. DVD.
"Sweet Dreams." *Medium: The Complete Second Season*. CBS Paramount, 2006. DVD.
"Then . . . And Again." *Medium: The Fifth Season*. CBS Paramount, 2009. DVD.
"There Will Be Blood . . . Type B." *Medium*. CBS. April 9, 2010. Television.
"Time Keeps on Slipping." *Medium*. CBS. May 7, 2010. Television.
"Time Out of Mind." *Medium: The Complete Second Season*. CBS Paramount, 2006. DVD.
"Truth Be Told." *Medium: The Fifth Season*. CBS Paramount, 2009. DVD.
"Twice Upon a Time." *Medium: The Complete Second Season*. CBS Paramount, 2006. DVD.

PART IV

MOVING BEYOND THE TELEVISUAL RESTRAINTS OF THE PAST
Reimagining Genres and Formats

14

MAKING SENSE OF THE FUTURE
Narrative Destabilization in Joss Whedon's Dollhouse

CASEY J. MCCORMICK

INTRODUCTION
Genre and Format

In demarcating the characteristics of science fiction (SF), most scholars, critics, and fans position the genre first and foremost as the narrative of the future. Speculative scenarios, futuristic settings, and a general otherworldliness have driven SF narratives since the genre's inception. As many SF scholars are beginning to realize, however, the conventions of the genre are changing as technology continues to catch up with the old SF imagination. In other words, we no longer need to look to the future to find SF tropes, because we live in that future right now. Nowhere is this thematic shift more evident than in contemporary television. In a recent roundtable discussion on the future of SF television, part of a conference organized by the media studies journal *Flow TV*,[1] I posited that there is an evolution occurring within the genre that is comprised of four basic elements: mainstream appeal, generic hybridity, non-alien antagonists, and temporal immediacy. As SF broke out of its niche cable market (particularly after the rebranding of Sci-Fi Channel to the less generically loyal SyFy), it had to adapt its format for larger network audiences. One way in which SF television accomplished this task was by packaging SF stories within more familiar narrative frameworks. *Fringe* (FOX, 2008–Present), for example, resembles the structure of the crime-solving procedural, though its content is clearly SF. *Lost* (ABC, 2004–2010) relies heavily on traditional soap opera devices to protract its narrative across six seasons of increasingly SF plots, and *Heroes* (NBC, 2006–2010) depends on the cultural pervasiveness of comic book mythos to convey its inherently SF story. These recent examples illustrate the broader move to hybridize the SF genre and make its narratives palatable to a mainstream audience. These shows also reflect the evolution of contemporary postmodern narratology as it gets manipulated by the increasingly sophisticated televisual format.

In this chapter, I will use another recent broadcast network SF series, Joss Whedon's *Dollhouse* (FOX, 2009–2010), to examine the new direction of both the SF genre and television narratology more generally. The contemporary narrative is highly self-aware, interconnected with other narrative counterparts, and hyperlinked to postmodern culture at large. It is posthuman in nature, because it is deconstructed, temporally complex, nonlinear, and multisubjective. I argue that *Dollhouse* functions as a prototype for this posthuman narrative due to its engagement with cognitive theories that reflect both narrative and thematic concerns. The recent application of cognitive science to literary and media studies is indicative of a fundamental merger of science and the humanities, a union that underlies *Dollhouse*, my own research, and critical theory of the twenty-first century.[2] In his 2008 study *Posthuman Metamorphosis: Narrative and Systems*, Bruce Clarke writes that "narratology is well en route to . . . the self-consistent epistemological constructivism of systems theory" (33). Indeed, the production of meaning is now a hyper-aware process of mapping the relationships among diegetic events and interpreting complex narrative formats to construct new models for narrative semiotics.

Dollhouse may not have produced the ratings expected of a prime-time broadcast series, but the ample critical attention it has garnered recently is evidence of its prowess as a unique and intriguing experiment in SF television narrative. The two 12-episode seasons, each capped off with an "Epitaph," have spawned numerous online discussion forums, an installment in the Smart Pop book series, and a special issue in *Slayage*, the online Whedon studies journal. The show's bold engagement with contemporary neuroscience and ethics provides fertile ground for explorations of the moral, psychological, and ontological implications of the story. While its unique narrative format has found some attention, no one has yet attempted a thorough analysis of the show's narratology. This chapter looks at how *Dollhouse* represents an evolution within SF television, arguing that the temporal structure of the narrative manipulates genre conventions to produce a complex layering of plots and interpretations. An engagement with particular episodes, informed by a production history plagued by network struggles, reveals the effects of destabilized temporality on both the narratological and thematic presentation of the series.

SEASON ONE
Narrative Hybridity

Dollhouse is primarily a story about the de(con)struction of identity, specifically the humanistic, Cartesian model of mind/body dualism and the pseudo-secular concept of the soul. By depicting a world identical to our own (save a few particular technological advancements), the diegesis engages directly with contemporary issues. In secret facilities in major cities throughout the world, the corrupt megacorporation Rossum (an allusion to Karel Capek's 1921 play about robot rebellion) operates dollhouses that serve the whims of the extremely wealthy and powerful. The scientists behind the dollhouses have acquired the technology to build, distort, transfer, and erase personalities from human subjects in a matter of minutes. The dolls are "volunteers" who sign well-paid five-year contracts to shelve their own personalities on a hard drive. Clients willing to pay an exorbitant fee then rent the dolls, who are imprinted with made-to-order personalities and participate in specially designed "engagements." When the dolls are not actively engaged, they remain in the dollhouse, their brains in a *tabula rasa* state. The show focuses on the story of the Los Angeles dollhouse and its inhabitants, and it is set in the present day. Season one of *Dollhouse* makes use of various narrative devices, from the embedded episodic stories of the dolls' engagements, to the retelling of the same story from multiple perspectives ("A Spy"). The episodic narratives that dominate the first season were Whedon's answer to FOX's demand that the show appeal to a mass audience (the unaired pilot demonstrates that the initial vision of *Dollhouse*'s narrative progression was quite different). Much like the police procedural content of the first two seasons of *Fringe*, *Dollhouse* embeds various familiar genre narratives within the stories of the doll/protagonist Echo's engagements. In the first five episodes, viewers see recognizable stories such as: a child kidnapping/negotiation, a "Most Dangerous Game"-style survival thriller, a pop star stalker/fan murder plot, a rare artifact museum heist, and an infiltration of a religious cult. This proliferation of familiar narratives becomes part homage and part satire, since the characters (dolls) are deliberately fabricated to play stereotypical roles.

These seemingly self-contained engagement narratives also function to slowly provide clues concerning the larger thematic intentions of the series. The narrative "[f]ocalization complexifies the category of narration by distinguishing a separate, embedded layer of narrative function" (Clarke 31). The engagement plots at first seem to be the primary diegesis of the narrative, while the dollhouse itself appears relegated to a metadiegetic narrative position.[3] In this way, the first season takes an ambiguous place on the continuum of televisual formats, as outlined by Jason Mittell in *Television and American Culture*. Applying Mittell's designations of format, *Dollhouse* is simultaneously an "episodic series," because some episodes appear to possess completely self-contained stories; an "episodic serial," because it also employs multi-episode story arcs; and a "serial narrative," because it has an "ongoing diegesis that demands viewers to construct a storyworld using information gathered from their full history of viewing" (230). The tendency for progressive television series to defy narrative categorization is evidence of the broad move toward hybridized posthuman narratology. In *Dollhouse*, as complicated as the first season's narrative structure certainly seems, the series gets infinitely more complex with the addition of the "secret thirteenth episode"[4] and the ensuing second season.

"EPITAPH ONE"
Temporal Confusion

When Whedon saw *Dollhouse* likely facing cancellation at the end of the first season, he commissioned his brother Jed and sister-in-law Maurissa to write the teleplay of the story that would become "Epitaph One," a post-apocalyptic narrative that jumps forward ten years from the action of the first season. In season one, the Rossum Corporation and its technology claim to offer personal fulfillment for the individual and scientific progress for the community, but the certainty of a vague and darker purpose underlies the entire narrative. "Epitaph One" reveals the ultimate repercussions of Rossum's actions when political/military entities use the imprint technology as large-scale biological weapons. The result is the technoapocalypse:[5] as Topher, the dollhouse's top techno-scientist describes, "One robo-call to a city . . . And an entire army in a single instant in the hands of any government . . . Millions programmed to kill anyone who is not programmed to kill." The potential for such a disaster was first mentioned in the sixth episode ("Man"), but it is safe to assume that Whedon would have prolonged the bleak revelation across many seasons had he enjoyed a different production/network situation. Instead, believing the thirteenth episode to be the last of the series, Whedon ventured to expose the ultimate telos of the story while he still had the chance. In narrative terms, "Epitaph One" acts as what Gerard Genette calls an "external anachronism" (27), since it departs from the *Dollhouse* narrative proper and follows a new set of characters—survivors of the technoapocalypse. The aesthetics of the setting, the temporal moment, and the post-apocalyptic narrative all evoke a sense of "Epitaph One" as a genre piece, and indeed it does return to conventions that the series itself had previously evaded (most basically, temporal setting). Still, despite the intentionally derivative generic format, the episode embeds substantial revelations that refer back to the initial narrative and the familiar characters.

The band of survivors (called "Actuals" because they have not been imprinted and therefore retain their original personalities) stumble upon the abandoned LA dollhouse while evading Butchers—hyper-violent victims of remote imprinting. When the Actuals discover the imprint chair, they are able to sort through catalogued memories to piece together the story behind the technoapocalypse. The episode is thus a flashforward comprised of flashbacks, which are still flashforwards from the temporal realm in which viewers left the characters in episode twelve. This complex temporal structure demonstrates Clarke's observations that "[T]he flip-flop effect of narrative framing . . . draws it most powerfully into the neocybernetic discussion of forms and operational boundaries" (104). As systems theoretical narratology understands events to be spatially and temporally interrelated, the disjointed presentation of flashback scenes in this episode makes any linear understanding impossible, demanding an atemporal interpretation instead. As Mieke Bal remarks in her seminal work *Narratology*, "It is not always possible or relevent to reconstruct the chronological sequence . . . these matters are intentionally confused, the chronological relations expressly concealed" (79). The intentionality of the temporal confusion of "Epitaph One" was a deliberate means of leaving the narrative accessible for revisitation and continuation. The episode offers no real conclusion or diegetic satisfaction, ending with two of the survivors and an imprint of protagonist Echo leaving the dollhouse in search of Safe Haven, a place where supposedly people have found a way to withstand remote imprinting. The epitaph thus resists its definition as a vehicle for closure, priming the narrative to continue into a pleasantly unexpected second season. Even if viewers knew what would eventually transpire as a result of the Rossum Corporation's agenda, the necessary feeling of lack of closure prolongs the viewers' dedication to the story, begging the question, *how do we get there?*

SEASON TWO
Diegesis and Metadiegesis

"Vows," the first episode of season two, capitalizes immediately on the plethora of knowledge revealed in "Epitaph One," beginning a season-long metadiegetic inside joke among writers and viewers of the show. The narrative returns temporally to the "present" moment, but incorporates actual scenes from the "Epitaph One" flashbacks and introduces new plotlines that are directly informed by knowledge of future events. For example, one of the most astonishing revelations of "Epitaph One" is the depiction of the genius scientist Topher suffering from guilt-induced pyschosis as a result of his role in the technoapocalypse. In "Vows," one of the dolls torments Topher and questions his control over the technology, and he replies, "I know what I know." This line is a direct quote from the mentally disintegrated Topher of the future, so its (p)reiteration at this moment is particularly emotionally haunting for the viewer. From the beginning of the season, then, the writers are committed to directly confronting the diegetic gaps created by "Epitaph One." As the season progresses, the writers reveal several ethical turning points for Topher, thus filling in the explanation behind his eventual insanity, although without ever completely closing the temporal gap. Bal surmises that "often omitted events are brought to the fore in other parts of the text. Thus ellipsis—the omission of an element that belongs in a series—gains its power of signification" (217). The missing narrative pieces, therefore, form an absent presence in the story and inform the viewers' interpretation of each event. Another major revelation from "Epitaph One," that former FBI agent and Rossum Corporation enemy Paul Ballard would become Echo's handler, is explained in this first episode. The relatively quick resolution for this diegetic gap demonstrates an urgency on the writers' part to validate their depiction of the future. From the start, the writers make it clear that they are using "Epitaph One" as a narrative guide to season two, meanwhile encouraging viewers to do the same.

Bal posits that "playing with sequential ordering is not just a literary convention, it is also a means of drawing attention to certain things, to emphasize, to bring about aesthetic or psychological effects, to show various interpretations of an event, to indicate the subtle difference between expectation and realization" (81). Season two of *Dollhouse* utilizes this technique to a new extreme, compounded by the self-aware nature of the narrative that the temporal structure demands. In her essay on collaborative narrative and ontology in *Dollhouse*, Julie Hawk posits that the show's "multi-authored storytelling . . . fosters the development of characters who themselves have authorial agency. The narrative proper . . . is refracted through the lens of its method of creation and is thereby diffracted in such a way as to create self-similar patterns (or fractals) in both narrative content and the narrative form" (2–3). While Hawk focuses her argument on the posthuman construction of Echo's subjectivity, the same phenomenon of refraction and diffraction occurs with Topher and, indeed, the rest of the characters. This dispersal of narrative agency is not only a result of collaborative storytelling, but also a direct effect of the unconventional temporal structure and the resulting metadiegesis of the second season.

With the unique and paradoxical temporal position of season two, *Dollhouse*'s writers built an intensely metadiegetic narrative. On the one hand, there is the diegesis of the episodes themselves, but there is also a metadiegesis comprised of the events of the season *in conjunction with* the knowledge acquired from "Epitaph One." This metadiegesis is further complicated by the fact that "Epitaph One" never actually aired on American television. Ostensibly, a viewer who did not purchase season one on DVD or download the episode could be watching season two without the crucial knowledge of the future—so, in truth, there are actually three diegetic levels at play during this season. I acknowledge this point not only to show the multiplied narrative levels present in the show, but also to raise the question of textual boarders in television more generally. If "Epitaph One" never aired,[6] does it count as part of the text? *Of course it does*, and as the cult fandom atmosphere of television viewing (particularly prevalent in the SF genre) continues to grow, the boundaries of televisual text will expand concordantly. Evidence of this paratextuality can be seen in the narrative significance of the Webisodes from Ron Moore's *Battlestar Galactica*, or the various interactive online media communities available to fans of almost every popular show. Therefore, I will focus on the perspective of the informed *Dollhouse* viewer, taking for granted the cult following of Whedon's shows and assuming that a committed fan would have found a way to view "Epitaph One."

In the third episode of season two, "Belle Chose," Topher attempts to perform a remote brain wipe for the first time. This event seems minor, or at least not out of the ordinary, when considered plainly within the diegesis. The viewer's knowledge of "Epitaph One," however, indicates the extreme significance of this moment in terms of the eventual weaponization of the imprint technology and Topher's direct role in its creation. While brainstorming possible methods of wiping a missing active doll, Topher ponders, "Victor would need to have a phone, I'd need to have a tone, I'd have to get him to answer the phone . . . Do you have his number?" This scene evokes the earlier (but later) scene from "Epitaph One," when an insane Topher reflects back on the catalyst of the technoapocalypse—a robotic phone call. Moments like these throughout the first season function as what Genette calls "completive anachronisms," which "function to fill in a previous or later blank (ellipsis) in the narrative" (27). While these scenes do allow the viewer to close diegetic gaps, they also perform a metadiegetic function of recalling and reimagining the content of "Epitaph One." Clarke observes, "In both the narrative and systemic instances, one discerns interpenetration, a double-feedback loop" (31). The perpetually reflexive nature of season two demonstrates this model in a particularly self-aware fashion, allowing the confused temporal structure to produce multiplied meanings and even meaning within the structure itself.

In "How Cancellation Told the Story of *Dollhouse*," Luciana Hiromi Yamada da Silveira discusses the differences between the first and second season in relation to the creators' knowledge of impending cancellation. She writes, "The storytelling style of the series changed. *Dollhouse* could no longer afford to drop bread crumbs—each scene in each episode seemed to exist only because it contributed something important to the main arc" (154). While I agree that the probability of cancellation certainly played a major role in the content of season two, Yamada da Silveira seems to neglect the more internal explanation for these obvious narrative changes. The revelations from "Epitaph One" inherently and permanently destabilized the show's narrative format as well as the diegetic content. Once the narrative telos was laid bare, the only way to keep the show compelling was to offer episodes that would remystify and problematize the viewers' prior knowledge. Therefore, each episode of the second season is designed to force viewers to readjust their interpretation of the entire narrative. In her essay, "Not (Yet) Knowing: Epistemological Effects of Deferred and Suppressed Information in Narrative," Emma Kafalenos points out that

> [r]eaders construct fabulas as they read. Each version of fabula that readers construct during the process of reading is a configuration. Readers interpret events as they are revealed in relation to the configuration they have assembled at that stage in their reading. As the fabula one creates, grows and extends, the configuration in relation to which one interprets events expands. Interpretations shift as one reads *because* the configuration changes. (52, emphasis in original)

The *Dollhouse* writers take full advantage of this phenomenon of textual interpretation by playing heavily on the expectations set forth in "Epitaph One." The televisual format is especially conducive to this kind of incremental reconfiguration, which is why we are now seeing the most innovative and complex narrative structures in television shows.

In "The Attic," perhaps the most narratively self-conscious episode of the season, the spatiotemporalworld of "Epitaph One" collides with the story of the dollhouse in 2009 and creates a somewhat tragic metadiegetic moment. In this episode, Echo enters a digitally constructed dream world where prisoners of the Rossum Corporation are forced to endure their worst nightmare perpetually (meanwhile, their bodies are linked up to a giant computer mainframe that harnesses their brain power). The Attic is thus a virtual grid of narrative loops, a visual manifestation of systems theory approach to storytelling. While most of the prisoners are unaware of their state in the virtual realm, some, like Echo, are able to become aware and escape their loops (i.e., you can only escape the story by realizing that you are a character in it). As Echo navigates her fellow prisoners' nightmares, she eventually meets Rossum Corporation cofounder Clyde, who was betrayed by his partner and trapped in the Attic. Upon entering Clyde's consciousness, Echo is met with a chaotic post-apocalyptic landscape identical in aesthetic to the setting of "Epitaph One."

Viewers learn that Clyde's nightmare loop was performing statistical analysis on the eventual results of the brain imprinting technology, and that all but 3 percent of his scenarios include the "end of civilization," the depiction of which is projected in the post-apocalyptic setting of his nightmare world. Since viewers know that Clyde's prediction is absolutely true, Echo's insistence on her ability to prevent the apocalypse produces a moment of stark dramatic irony for the viewer. In "*Dollhouse*'s Future History Machines," Kirsten Strayer notes, "While our heroes strove to prevent Clyde's prophecy from coming to pass, we knew that it was the inevitable future" (181). By reminding the viewer of the inescapability of *Dollhouse*'s apocalyptic telos, this episode sets up the final two installments of the narrative proper as ultimately ironic. Indeed, the triumphant image of Echo blowing up Rossum's headquarters in "The Hollow Men" is immediately counteracted by a brief flash to the post-apocalyptic future, with the protagonists gunning down imprinted Butchers. The writers make no attempt to close the temporal gap between the impending apocalypse and the events of season two, leaving myriad questions unanswered and many aspects of the narrative timeline unclear.[7]

"EPITAPH TWO"
Posthuman Narratology

In the final episode of the series, the narrative jumps back (and forward) to the post-apocalyptic diegesis with "Epitaph Two: Return." Picking up where "Epitaph One" left off, this episode represented the chance for the *Dollhouse* creators to conclude the narrative with some sort of finality. The episode format for this "Epitaph" is quite different than its predecessor, but it contains equally interesting narrative elements. Instead of using flashbacks to fill in the missing history, viewers learn about some of the events of the past ten years in a more personal, character-driven way. Whereas the main *Dollhouse* characters played only peripheral roles in "Epitaph One," here they are the center of the story. Throughout the episode, the main characters engage in a relatively simplistic narrative practice—alluding to significant events that occurred in the unnarrated years. Still, these tidbits are mostly vague and produce more questions than answers. Bal observes that "the vagueness of the chronology is, at times, just as significant as its painstaking representation" (218). Again, the writers produce meaning through temporal and diegetic confusion. Also in the episode, there are several season-two referential moments, like when the Echo imprint remarks of human civilization, "We are lost, but we are not gone." This is a direct quote from "Vows," when a newly self-aware Echo used the same words to describe the dolls. Then, when Echo confronts Rossum executive Mr. Harding at the company's post-apocalypse headquarters, he taunts her with the proposition that perhaps it was her actions against Rossum (only one episode, but ten years earlier) that caused the technology to spiral out of control. At that suggestion, Echo promptly shoots Harding in the head (a futile gesture, since his personality is backed up on a hard drive), but the viewer cannot help but wonder if there is truth in Harding's statement.

"Epitaph Two: Return" is a technoapocalyptic redemption story. In his mentally disintegrated state, Topher devises a way to "bring back the world" by reversing the effects of the mass imprinting and restoring everyone's original personalities. Of course, the device needed to accomplish this task is a massive explosive, and it can only be activated manually. So, Topher performs the ultimate act of self-sacrifice in order to make amends for his involvement in precipitating the technoapocalyptic disaster. The show then ends in a remarkably posthuman fashion. Topher's device restores personalities to their rightful owners, but civilization is still in shambles, and the survivors have lost years of their lives with no memory of the things that they have done (or the people they have killed). The redemption narrative is therefore only questionably redeeming: the elements are there (death of main characters, self-sacrifice, hopeful music), but a nagging feeling of loss persists in the final moments. As I have demonstrated throughout this chapter, *Dollhouse* consistently resists easy answers, so this unsettling conclusion is narratively appropriate. "Epitaph Two: Return" confronts the viewer with the message that humankind may prevail—but only after devastating hardship—and it will be permanently altered, dejected, and destabilized.

CONCLUSION

I have chosen to focus here on *Dollhouse*'s narrative structure, for the most part allowing the thematic implications of the show to speak for themselves. However, the connections among narrative, theme, and message are what make posthuman narratology exciting, so a brief notation of this interrelationship is worth addressing. Clarke writes:

> [I]t may be said that narratives connect to worldly systems not in their putative representational verisimilitude—especially if the narrative communication at hand is fantastic, speculative, or science-fictional—but in the ways that, at their deepest levels of abstraction, they allow the construction of functional homologies to real processes of life, mind, and society. (35)

Here, Clarke stresses the reciprocal relationship between narrative forms and social reality, a connection that drives *Dollhouse*—and most other interesting contemporary fiction. The purpose of the posthuman narrative is not merely to represent life, but instead to engage actively with it, to recognize the vast web of experience and integrate into that web in a functionally real manner. Clarke's systems theory approach to narrative focuses on patterns of meaning-making in a culture of narrative saturation. He posits that "meaning is the self-generated medium of the self-referential self-maintenance (autopoiesis) of minds and societies out of the systemic recursion of their own forms" (25). In *Dollhouse*, Echo and the other dolls attempt to construct meaning out of discordant memories, while the viewers must also produce meaning out of temporal disjunction and intentional narrative deception. As a genre, SF has always employed daring and progressive narrative techniques in order to provide political and social commentary. Today, however, in a culture inundated with technological progress and advancements in every field of science, SF narrative demands a posthuman path. *Dollhouse* is indicative of this generic evolution, and its structural complexity informs both the semiotic potential of the televisual format and the increasing popularity of stories that challenge assumptions, hybridize genres, and reconfigure narrative temporality to explore a postmodern conception of time, space, and meaning.

SUGGESTED EPISODES FOR ADDITIONAL STUDY

Dollhouse
1:8. "Needs." Writ. Tracy Bellomo. Dir. Felix Alcalá. April 3, 2009.
2:5. "The Public Eye." Writ. Andrew Chambliss. Dir. David Solomon. December 4, 2009.
2:6. "The Left Hand." Writ. Tracy Bellomo. Dir. Wendey Stanzler. December 4, 2009.
2:11. "Getting Closer." Writ. and Dir. Tim Minear. January 8, 2010.

NOTES

1. Flow Conference 2010: A Critical Discussion of Television and New Media. September 30–October 2. See http://flowtv.org/conference for a list of panels and links to participants' position papers.
2. See "Narratology in the Twenty-first Century: The Cognitive Approach to Narrative," by Monika Fludernik for an overview of how cognitive science is currently affecting the study of narrative.

3. I will use "diegetic" and "metadiegetic" throughout this chapter to indicate primary and secondary narrative levels. While some use these terms exclusively in relation to narration practices, I feel that in the televisual format, these terms deserve a broader interpretation.

4. FOX had already paid for thirteen episodes, but they were only going to allow *Dollhouse* to air twelve of them. There was a great deal of Internet buzz about the mysterious episode thirteen. For more on the network struggles with this episode, see the Paleyfest *Dollhouse* interview (available on DVD).

5. This term is fairly self-explanatory, but for an in-depth study of the cultural politics of the technoapocalypse, see Daniel Dinello's *Technophobia: Science Fiction Visions of Posthuman Technology*. While I find his conclusions somewhat reductive, the study is useful in examining the pervasiveness of technoapocalyptic narrative.

6. "Epitaph One" did air in some other countries, but it was only available as a DVD extra in the United States.

7. A short comic book called *Epitaphs*, which takes place at the moment of the robo-call that begins the apocalypse, was included in the season two Blu-Ray packaging. Whedon's publishing company Dark Horse recently announced that it would run a short series that will continue the motif.

WORKS CITED

"The Attic." Writ. Maurissa Tancharoen and Jed Whedon. Dir. John Cassaday. *Dollhouse*. Fox Broadcasting Company. December 18, 2009. Television.

Bal, Mieke. *Narratology: Introduction to the Theory of Narrative*, 3rd ed. Toronto: University of Toronto Press, 2009. Print.

"Belle Chose." Writ. Tim Minear. Dir. David Solomon. *Dollhouse*. Fox Broadcasting Company. October 9, 2009. Television.

Clarke, Bruce. *Posthuman Metamorphosis: Narrative and Systems*. New York: Fordham University Press, 2008. Print.

Dinello, Daniel. *Technophobia! Science Fiction Visions of Posthuman Technology*. Austin: University of Texas Press, 2006. Print.

"Dollhouse: Cast and Creators Live at Paleyfest." The Paley Center for Media, 2010. DVD.

"Epitaph One." Writ. Maurissa Tancharoen and Jed Whedon. Dir. David Solomon. *Joss Whedon's Dollhouse: Season One*. Twentieth Century Fox Home Entertainment, 2009. DVD.

"Epitaph Two: Return." Writ. Maurissa Tancharoen, Jed Whedon, and Andrew Chambliss. Dir. David Solomon. *Dollhouse*. Fox Broadcasting Company. January 29, 2010. Television.

Fludernik, Monika. "Narratology in the Twenty-first Century: The Cognitive Approach to Narrative." *PMLA* 125.4 (2010): 924–30. Print.

Genette, Gerard. "Order, Duration, and Frequency." *Narrative Dynamics: Essays on Time, Plot, Closure, and Frames*. Ed. Brian Richardson. Columbus: Ohio State University Press, 2002. Print.

Hawk, Julie. "Hacking the Read-Only File: Collaborative Narrative as Ontological Construction in *Dollhouse*." *Slayage: The Journal of the Whedon Studies Association* 8.2–3 (2010): 1–20. Web.

"The Hollow Men." Writ. Michelle Fazekas, Tara Butters, and Tracy Bellomo. Dir. Terrence O'Hara. *Dollhouse*. Fox Broadcasting Company. January 15, 2010. Television.

Kafalenos, Emma. "Not (Yet) Knowing: Epistemological Effects of Deferred and Suppressed Information in Narrative." *Narratologies: New Perspectives on Narrative Analysis*. Ed. David Herman. Columbus: Ohio State University Press, 1999. 33–65. Print.

"Man on the Street." Writ. Joss Whedon. Dir. David Straiton. *Joss Whedon's Dollhouse: Season One*. Twentieth Century Fox Home Entertainment, 2009. DVD.

Mittell, Jason. *Television and American Culture*. New York: Oxford University Press, 2010. Print.

"A Spy in the House of Love." Writ. Andrew Chambliss. Dir. David Solomon. *Joss Whedon's Dollhouse: Season One*. Twentieth Century Fox Home Entertainment, 2009. DVD.

Strayer, Kirsten. "*Dollhouse*'s Future History Machines." *Inside Joss' Dollhouse: From Alpha to Rossum*. Ed. Jane Espenson. Dallas: Benbella Books, 2010. 175–87. Print.

"Vows." Writ. and dir. Joss Whedon. *Dollhouse*. Season Two, Episode One. Fox Broadcasting Company. September 25, 2009. Television.

Yamada da Silveira, Luciana Hiromi. "How Cancellation Told the Story of *Dollhouse*." *Inside Joss' Dollhouse: From Alpha to Rossum*. Ed. Jane Espenson. Dallas: Benbella Books, 2010. 147–58. Print.

15

WHY *30 ROCK* ROCKS AND *THE OFFICE* NEEDS SOME WORK
The Role of Time/Space in Contemporary TV Sitcoms

COLIN IRVINE

INTRODUCTION

The relatively new and yet robust subgenre of situation comedies taps into all that technology has to offer narratives and, with viewer participation, stretches the limits of time and space. These sitcoms, or at least some of the more recent, sophisticated ones such as *Arrested Development* (Fox, 2003–2006), *The Office* (NBC, 2005–Present), and *30 Rock* (2006–Present), link in complex ways many and varied imagined worlds with that of the less elastic and more finite real one associated with the viewer. In this regard, these sitcoms constitute a new chronotope, to borrow a term from Mikhail Bakhtin, who explains that the chronotope represents literally "time space" and thus illustrates the "interconnectedness of temporal and spatial relationships that are artistically expressed in literature" (85). He extrapolates on this contention in a statement that broadens the scope of his analysis and further anticipates the era of the television narratives, stating: "The chronotope in literature has an intrinsic generic significance. It can even be said that it is precisely the chronotope that defines genre and generic distinctions" (Bakhtin 84–85).

Though true of novelistic literature in general, this assertion about the role of time/space in determining the generic distinctions of sitcoms is especially accurate. In fact, the refined, often subtle ways sitcoms—again, with the viewers' help—weave together references and allusions from various times/spaces is precisely what makes them what they are: *situation* comedies. Individual episodes, shows, and scenes—each with their "fleshed out" chronotopes—become more rather than less stable and coherent as they fold into themselves references from numerous other texts and from the world beyond the narrative borders.

In light of this contention that the situation comedy represents an emerging, evolving chronotope, I would argue that sitcoms, at their core, involve three essential components, each of which allows them to tap into the elastic nature of narrative time: (1) a similar but separate constructed world that draws upon the real, familiar one in often ironic, humorous ways; (2) frequent references to the world specific to the viewer and his or her time/space, and; (3) a connection (or connections) that tether these worlds together (Hutcheon 1–6). The *situation*, accordingly, involves a braiding together of all three components. And while there are many situations within the fictional realm that those characters residing there are involved in that do not include the viewer, these internal events tied to the narrative are not essential to the situation comedy's aesthetic makeup or its success and survival.

In order for somebody looking in from the outside—from the realm of the real—at the imagined world to find an event or statement to be funny, that event or statement must have relevance in the realm of the real while at once being in step with what is unfolding in the realm of the imagined. By contrast, those inside the imagined world—those occupying the primary diegetic level—might say or do things that they do not know to be funny, though it is hilarious to onlookers watching from the safety of their sofas. In short, it does not matter if characters in a situation comedy get the jokes or find what happens in their world to be comical. What matters, what determines the success of the genre, is that the viewers do.

With these high stakes in mind, this essay outlines in broad strokes what, exactly, constitutes the situation in a situation comedy. The focus then shifts to the features of the typical sitcom situation that make it, when it works well, humorous; following this attempt to diagram humor—a dubious undertaking that, ironically, seldom ends in laughter—the analysis returns to the attendant importance of coherence mentioned above, noting why it is essential for a show's success. In the process of tackling each of these related issues, the essay focuses on three contemporary shows: *Arrested Development*, *The Office*, and *30 Rock*. Each, with varying degrees of effectiveness, illustrates the supple quality of time in contemporary television; each, due to the dramatic, public nature of laughter—makes the otherwise inexplicable concepts connected with narrative time/space evident and appreciable.

THE *SITUATION* IN THE SITUATION COMEDY

Although the word "situation" suggests something fixed and stable, the situations in sitcoms are anything but. They involve interplay between and among the various elements (meaning, the characters, their world(s), the viewers, the world, etc.) and the space/times connected with those elements. A joke, for instance, can originate in the world of the characters, allude to something beyond their realm in the real world, and, in the end, elicit the viewer's laughter because of something said or done subsequently or even previously at an extra-diegetic level. Humor, in other words, is as spatial as it is temporal, as much about context as it is about timing.

Like other novelistic constructs, these spatial/temporal texts involve a new "orientation in the world and time" that brings the story world (as opposed to the storied, epic, always distant one) closer in alignment with the realm of the viewers (Bakhtin 25). According to Bakhtin, novelistic narratives feature characters, language, and references to the real beyond the realm of the imagined, including embedded allusions to individuals and events familiar to the audience occupying the space/time of the text's production. This makes them relevant and unseemly. It means that what is happening in society around the time of the story's creation and reception can, and likely will, be reflected in and parodied by the narrative. Accordingly, novelistic texts such as sitcoms remain both in touch with and yet somewhat separate from the world of which they are a part.

Yet despite this complex and often ambiguous orientation toward reality, sitcoms seldom lose or confuse viewers. Instead, viewers are well aware that realistic narratives are not representations of reality but instead something similar to and yet separate from it. They know, moreover, that the worlds they imagine into existence occupy an essentially different realm, while remaining tied in significant—though often humorous—ways to their own world. Hence, viewers likewise know that what appears in another fictional world—though it might also exist in their own—differs from it in elemental ways. Still, despite the common viewer's comfort when it comes to negotiating these texts, the extent of this interplay is not often fully appreciated, especially when considering the temporal element common to both the real and imagined.

The fact that the fabricated worlds specific to sitcoms are similar to—though separate from—the viewers' allows them, strangely enough, to be more, rather than less, flexible, especially when it comes to playing with the rules of time and space, rules otherwise governed by the laws of physics. The reason for this elasticity stems from the site of the narrative's actualization, which is in the imagination of the viewer, or, more accurately, in the relationship between the text and the viewer's imagination. Nothing makes this otherwise elusive, dialogic situation more evident than a study of the situational comedy specific to it.

Almost without exception, the situation in a sitcom includes the dynamic and dialogic place/time/event involving the characters, their world, the numerous real and fictional worlds to which they have belonged at some point in their respective pasts, the viewers, and, finally, the world of the real to which the viewers belong, a fact illuminated by humor that cuts across these overlapping, intersecting frames like a line drawn across a palimpsest of concentric circles (Nelles 339–41).

WHY COHERENCE MATTERS

Comedic situations unfold in and through time/space. Hence, a single joke can originate in one episode involving something related to a storyline tied to one actor's actions in the sitcom world under investigation; this same joke can relate to still another sitcom from a different era; it can also simultaneously be tied to something said by a second character in the sitcom world in question, perhaps a reference to what he or she has done not as an actor but as an actual individual in the public realm. So, to describe a comic event and the situation in which it unfolds is to map a constellation that links words, actions, and actors in different frames, with the viewer, who keeps track of each reference and, in the end, completes the joke(s). In short, sitcoms are multifaceted entities with many moving parts. They thus represent the next stage in the development of novelistic genres, a stage that seems to be giving away to still more multifarious, dialogic narratives that require readers/viewers to be fully engaged in the act of processing and producing these eventful, irreverent, and surprisingly coherent works. In this regard, these texts again draw our attention to Bakhtin and his contentions about narratives in general and time/space in particular.

Well ahead of the theorists and critics who wrung their hands over the approaching specter of postmodern playfulness, Bakhtin warned in "Epic and Novel" of potential problems tied to the always-evolving and opportunistic novel. He cautioned that one important "phenomenon in the history of the novel" that producers and consumers of narratives need to be aware of "is connected with [the] new temporal orientation [of the novel] and with this zone of contact: it is the novel's special relationship with extraliterary genres" (Bakhtin 33). As if talking specifically about contemporary sitcoms, Bakhtin further explained that "the genres of everyday life" will become the most multifarious and *timely* of all narratives, meaning relevant and time focused (33). Speaking of the novel specifically, he argued that its open-endedness stems from its "contact with the spontaneity of the inconclusive present [which keeps it] from congealing" (Bakhtin 27). Combine this generic tendency to be diffuse with the idea that the novel represents a "new temporal orientation" toward the present and with its "special relationship with extraliterary genres," and one wonders how any novelistic text such as a sitcom could hold together as a stable construct, even if only temporarily.

But, to be sure, the potential problems do not end there with considerations of genre conventions and particulars, at least not when one is talking about televised sitcoms. Because of the ways that technology allows for such tricks and techniques as split screens, voice-overs, montages, and numerous examples of analepses and prolepses, even individual scenes have become chaotic intersections of references involving images and allusions from other time/spaces, rather than relatively isolated, stable scenes. The narratives speak to numerous audiences simultaneously, including the "newly hip" viewers who recognize the off-hand allusions, as well as all of those watching at home with laptops at the ready, eager to connect the dots between what they are seeing and hearing while watching and what it links to on the increasingly atemporal World Wide Web (Bordwell 7). For these reasons related to the sitcom's profoundly novelistic qualities, sources of stability and coherence have become ever more critical for the viability of a scene, episode, or show.

Against this measure, *Arrested Development* and *30 Rock* exhibit the requisite features for succeeding *and* enduring, while *The Office*, much more aesthetically simple, on the other hand, does not. Below, then, I will outline the important features specific to each show and demonstrate why a long-running "popular success" such as *The Office* lacks the kind of complexity and concomitant coherence common to *Arrested Development* and *30 Rock*.

ARRESTED DEVELOPMENT

Arrested Development commences by outlining the relationships among the various components. At the outset of the first episode—and in the opening segment of every subsequent show—we hear the familiar voice of Ron Howard, who explains the *situation* in this way: "Now the story of a wealthy family who lost everything, and the one son who had no choice but to keep them all together. It's arrested development" ("Pilot"). Combined as it is with banjo music, still-shot pictures, and juxtaposed videos showing the actors and actresses in character, Howard's voice-over introduces the comedic situation. Imaginatively moving past a series of paratexts, the viewer proceeds further and further into the layers of nested frames. Once "inside" this dialogic narrative world, we are not lost in a fictional place but instead reside at a cross-section, an axis point or plane representing the intersections of multiple time/spaces.

Within scenes and sometimes over a series of episodes, persistent themes, extended metaphors, and even simple wordplay prevent the show from unraveling while at once allowing it to resist "congealing." For example, in a scene from season two, episode thirteen, an allusion to an infamous event near the end of the series *Happy Days* (ABC, 1974–1984) and a series of offhand allusions to events occurring in the lives of the actors involved in the scene unifies the action and the many oblique references that spin centrifugally out from it. At the same time, a reference to product placement help create a humorous situation that holds the narrative together while allowing and requiring the viewer to move quickly in and around the numerous time/spaces specific to the many storylines. Concurrently, the narrative features temporal play at different levels in diverse ways.

This scene occurs when *Arrested Development*'s ratings were high but its revenues were low and there was concern among the producers that they might have but one season left. In addition to these variables pertaining to the show's popularity and production, the situation involves Michael Bluth (Jason Bateman), Buster Bluth (Tony Hale), Gob Bluth (Will Arnett), Barry Zuckerkorn (Henry Winkler), and, implicitly, Ron Howard, the narrator. It begins with a shot of Gob, who is holding a severed seal fin in his hand (the fin is from the seal that bit off the hand of Buster in a previous episode). Gob proclaims, "And I've got to staple this to a seal," which is followed by Zuckerkorn's response, "And I skipped breakfast, so I'm off to Burger King," a line delivered while he is jumping a dead shark lying at his feet on the dock ("Motherboy"). That is the whole of the dialogue and the action, but this scene has tentacles that reach in all directions into the space/time of this situation.

First of all, the reason Gob needs to staple the fin back on the seal relates to the fact that his wife in the show is a seal salesperson who is threatening to divorce him. Previously, he had released one of her seals into the wild out of spite, and that same seal later bit off Buster's hand. Meanwhile, after we find out about the possible lawsuit and before we arrive at this part of the episode, we encounter actor Carl Weathers (playing himself), who convinces character Tobias Funke (David Cross) to meet him at Burger King because, as he explains, "I'm trying to get them to underwrite a new TV project I'm working on. Get some money in exchange for setting a scene here at Burger King" ("Motherboy"). Tobias, residing firmly in the story level (or innermost, diegetic frame) and thus unaware of the humor tied to his proleptic statement, responds, "Well, as long as you don't draw attention to it," a statement that forecasts the irony that underlines the subsequent scene in question, one involving Henry Winkler, wherein Winkler's character announces that he is "off to Burger King."

Additional allusions to narrative worlds outside of and yet connected with this one involving Burger King include but are not limited to these: first,

Gob's wife (the woman whose name he can never remember, though he does at one time use "Amy" as an example of the kind of name he might use to refer to her if were to call her by a name) is played by Amy Poehler, Will Arnette's wife, a connection that typifies the kind of reach into reality common to contemporary sitcoms. Similarly, but still more convoluted, is Zuckerkorn's jumping of the shark, a fairly obvious reference to Henry Winkler's infamous jumping of the shark in the sitcom *Happy Days*, an allusion that functions on a number of levels. First, it links this scene and this world of *Arrested Development* to that of *Happy Days*; second, it implicitly ties Ron Howard—the voice and god-like, all-knowing narrator in *Arrested Development*—with the naïve, participant character Richie Cunningham in *Happy Days*; and, third, it links the series *Arrested Development*—which, as mentioned, was struggling with ratings when this episode first ran—with the phenomenon known in the television world as "jumping the shark," which is to say, a desperate attempt to do something out of the ordinary for higher ratings.

Still, though this scene exemplifies the intricate nature of the comedic situation specific to sitcoms, the question remains: what does any of this analysis have to do with narrative time and contemporary television? The answer pertains to the relative nature of time specific to the places in question. In other words, time in the realm of the viewer remains, as always, constant, while variations in such aspects of narrative temporality as "order," "duration," and "frequency" are nearly infinite (Genette 25–34). Hence, a thirty-minute show lasts thirty minutes and takes thirty minutes to watch (if one includes commercials and leaves out of the calculus the possibility of pausing and replaying individual scenes). In contrast, time specific to the comedic *situation*—that space/time involving the viewer, the episode, references to other episodes and sources of high and low culture, and the finite real world that envelopes these—is anything but fixed or linear. As a case in point, in the above example the viewer jumps in this space/time from the scene near the end of this episode in season two back to a point earlier in season one, then returns to a point earlier in this episode, then jumps yet again to a place outside the narrative to the actual marriage of Arnett and Poehler, then skips forward to the previous point in the episode involving Carl Weathers at Burger King, then makes a longer leap back several decades to *Happy Days*, then a considerably shorter one forward (though not to the present of the episode) to the time/space when "jumping the shark" became a common idiom in Hollywood; then, finally, the viewer returns to the present scene/episode, having made this extensive, desultorily journey through time/spaces without ever leaving her sofa. That, to be sure, is a considerable amount of imaginative travel through time/space; and proof that one has made this journey, or part of it, takes the form of laughter. To have gotten the jokes is to have visited in one's imagination all of these time/spaces in the course of eight seconds of real, ontological, linear time. To have made this imaginative journey possible is to have created and delivered a truly complex, brilliant piece of pop culture.

THE OFFICE

Like *Arrested Development*, *The Office* is a comedy that demands viewers be engaged enough to understand, appreciate, and, ultimately, complete jokes that begin in various time/spaces and conclude somewhere in the present specific to those watching/laughing along. Unlike *Arrested Development*, though, the NBC version of *The Office* has in recent seasons begun to become irrelevant and incoherent, a testament to the fact that the components required for consistency in a narrative that plays loosely with time have become insufficiently common and still less effective when present.

To understand how NBC's *The Office* works and, more important, why it is ceasing to do so with any consistency as of late, one need look no further than its precursor, the British version of *The Office* (BBC Two, 2001–2003), a highly successful show written and directed by Ricky Gervais and Stephen Merchant.

Most notably, *The Office* broke new ground by famously challenging viewers to make the situation specific to the characters in an otherwise mundane time and place cohere by employing the faux documentary camera, an invasive and yet somehow acceptable trope wherein the act of filming people at work became an integral part of the narrative. When it comes to understanding the way time/space functions in the show, the documentary style plays an important role by allowing the creative artist/mind conventionally behind the scenes to enter into the action/event. As such, Ricky Gervais—comedian, writer, director—plays the part of the clown and fool, one who, in Bakhtin's words, creates around himself his "own special little world, [his] own chronotope" (159). This "special little world" represents an amalgam of worlds, or time/spaces, including that of Gervais the comedian, that of his similar but essentially different character David Brent (the witless office manager who mistakenly thinks he is funny), that of an early 1990s English working-class town, that of the implied viewer (of the documentary), and, finally, that of the viewers required to follow the threads of humor that move in and through these time/spaces and arrive at their destinations within the realm of the real.

And, to be sure, the British *The Office* worked, so to speak: the highly postmodern, self-referential series managed to merge numerous worlds/realms while maintaining sufficient consistency. It was such an aesthetic success, in fact, that when brought to the United States, producers were able to change the setting, the actors, and everything but the specifics tied to sitcom's situation and still deliver a show that not only survived but also thrived.

The American *The Office* likewise worked as a sitcom built out of numerous time/spaces because of the above-mentioned characteristics borrowed from the British version; however, over (real) time, the show has migrated away from its roots and has thus become more insular and less connected with other worlds beyond that of the inner-most diegetic frame. In the 2009 season, writers and producers made few noteworthy references to recent or historical events or situations outside the world of Dunder Mifflin. Even veiled mention of happenings linked to the lives of the actors is relatively rare in these episodes. The results of these directorial decisions are isolated, congealing constructs that are threatening to become concretized and therefore unsuitable for accommodating multiple time/spaces.

More specifically, as of late, few jokes in *The Office* rely for their punch line on the viewer's understanding of other worlds (or time/spaces) to which he has access and the characters do not; consequently, viewers are beginning to sense on some level that scenes involving the characters stand alone, at a distant from the viewer and his or her world in isolation. In other words, the viewer while watching an episode soon begins to conclude that what happens between and among the characters and the operator of the faux documentary has little, if any, relevance to what is or has happened in other time/spaces to which the viewer has privileged admission. Viewing has become similar to watching a comedy in another country about an entirely separate culture: even when dubbed into English, the humor is lost on the viewer because all of the allusions—the origins of the jokes—begin in time/spaces foreign to the person watching, who is charged with completing the joke. Hence, in an office that is ever more unconnected from other realities, characters say and do things that they find funny but viewers likely do not.

30 ROCK

Though any number of episodes would illustrate the ways that *30 Rock* effectively plays with time, one in particular from season four is most especially impressive for its comical forays into the viewer's world. "Into the Crevasse" represents literally from start to finish why this sitcom and others with its generic characteristics constitute the cutting edge of novelistic narrative.

The show opens with familiar background music that viewers associate with the *world* of *30 Rock*; then, we see the central character in Liz Lemon (Tina

Fey) come strolling buoyantly down a busy street in New York City and into the frame. We watch from a close, familiar distance as she passes a display window of a Borders bookstore. A camera angle approximating a visual version of free indirect discourse makes synonymous Liz's view of the books on display with that of the viewer's, a vantage point that features a book about President Jimmy Carter titled *From Peanut to President*; another, *The Cigarette Diet*, by the alleged doctor in the series, Dr. Leo Spacemen (Chris Parnell); and a third, *Deal Breakers: A Girl's Guide to Shutting It Down*, by Tina Fey. We realize at some level from this intimate angle seemingly inside the story world that each book, in turn, introduces us to the broader universe of *30 Rock* into which we have entered, one clearly tied through humor to the actual, still wider world of the viewer, a world full of idiotic self-help books, presidential biographies, and oversized bookstores. Moreover, this opening scene reintroduces viewers not only to the central character—Lemon—but also to Fey's pervasive and oftentimes political brand of humor, which appears like fingerprints all over this and all other scenes in this show. (The book about Carter, we will eventually come to find out in a subsequent episode, is written by a liberal-leaning Democrat, who turns out to be the father of Jack Donaghy, the VP of GE in the world of *30 Rock*, and a staunchly conservative Republican, played by Alec Baldwin, an outspoken liberal Democrat in real life.)

In these twisted, roundabout ways, *30 Rock* in general and "Into the Crevasse" in particular reinforce the notion that the real and fictional are more than merely intersecting: they are enmeshed. This relationship produces an interpretative situation wherein the viewer must manage to maneuver back and forth and in and around the intersecting time/spaces specific to Lemon's world of *30 Rock* and Fey's world of 30 Rockefeller Plaza (as well as the many others, including her links to *Saturday Night Live* [NBC, 1975–Present], her political leanings, and her references to high and low culture, of which there is a seemingly endless reservoir).

"Into the Crevasse" begins with Lemon meeting with Donaghy in his palatial office. Donaghy is on the phone with Don Geiss, his mentor and boss—the archetypal Republican business tycoon Fey seems to enjoy lampooning. Jack, in an off-hand statement that quickly connects the time/space of these characters with others—Washington, D.C., the Smithsonian, and *Happy Days*, to name a few—says just before hanging up, "Uh, yes, Mr. Geiss, of course. Well I'll only be in D.C. for the day, but if I find time I will be sure to go see Fonzee's jacket" ("Into"). Chuckling, he adds, "You sit on it as well," a ludicrous attempt at humor among stuffy businessmen that plays out behind the superimposed words, "Executive Producer Tina Fey," that linger on the screen as the last of the opening credits dissolves. The conversation, the location, the characters, and the reference to Fey are all of a piece: brought together in this way, the sum of these parts underlines the fact that viewers are entering a coherent, consistent narrative event.

The exchange between Lemon and Donaghy begins with Lemon requesting of Jack that he keep an eye out for her retainer, which she lost when visiting during junior high. Donaghy cuts her off before she can finish her rambling story, asking, "What can I do for you, Lemon?" and she drops the request (one that will serve to close down and complete the episode twenty minutes later, when Jack hands Lemon the retainer and she pops it into her mouth) ("Into"). They are soon interrupted by Jack's assistant, who comes into the office to rush him on his way, explaining that his bus leaves in half an hour. Lemon laughs at the mention of Jack taking a bus, and he says in return that he is doing so because, as he states proudly, "I have to. Ever since these buffoons from Detroit took the private planes, the rest of us have to put on a show" ("Into"). Gratuitously, he proceeds with, "And now your president—who, by the way, is Kenyan and smokes cigarettes—has created an industry task force for microwaves and small appliances" ("Into"). And while Jack is saying these things with disgust in his voice, three cameras capture the scene and all the innuendo and related references: one camera focuses on Lemon/Fey's reaction to Jack's assertions (she rolls her eyes), one focuses on Jack and his haughty posturing, and a third on his assistant, who takes Jack's expensive watch before then affixing an American flag to his lapel. Moving back and forth from person to person, the camera work underlines the ways in which references reach from within to outside of this scene, each a kind of joke that those who know Fey's politics and humor can appreciate/complete. Driving this home, Lemon asks, "Why? Do you need to be bailed out with my tax dollars?" ("Into"). Breathy and overly serious as always—a perfectly cast character/caricature of the cold, corporate businessman—Jack avows, "Even if they wanted to I wouldn't take it. It's corporate welfare, Lemon," a statement that, minus the "Lemon," perfectly parodies statements conservatives at this time in this world have made about President Obama's policies ("Into"). But, and this is critical, the argument comes across as hollow and insincere in this scene because of the numerous ways the writing and direction have contextualized it.

The rest of the episode teases out the humor implicit in the relationship between the constructed, often inane events and individuals in *30 Rock* and those more serious, somber ones specific to the viewer's real world. These allusions gather force and substance en route through the various time/spaces and, ultimately, to the viewer. Hence the humor in this situation comedy made up of many diverse and tangential but related references/contexts/scenarios helps it all come together, if only for a scene, an episode, or a season. However, as soon as the show ceases to adhere to these conventions—as soon it elects to play it politically correct, to marginalize its unifying consciousness, or to focus on scenes in ways that do not privilege the viewer's the location at the extra-diegetic level—the situation will no longer cease to matter and the sitcom will cease to exist.

CONCLUSION
Why Comedy in a Sitcom Is Serious Business

Although it is tempting to assert that shows such as *Arrested Development* or *30 Rock* are classics—and in this way suggest they are somehow timeless—to do so would be to miss the point. It is the timely, truly contextual nature of these shows and the often irreverent ways in which they reach out from their constructed worlds into the real, ephemeral ones of which they are a part that matter. Moreover, it is the ways that these constructs involve the viewer's participation (often in the form of laughter) for their completion that makes them both humorous and, as importantly, dangerous. As noted above, despite that the situations in the shows draw heavily on both real and unreal, they need not abide by the same laws and sense of decorum that limit and control the viewers' thoughts and behavior. Hence, sitcoms are essentially ironical entities that, to quote Linda Hutcheon, "cannot be trusted" (13). In this regard, these shows—when they work well—cultivate the ability to think on multiple levels and to think through various scenarios and possibilities from different points of view simultaneously. The sitcoms thus encourage and even prepare viewers to be watchful and suspicious, to look askance at authority and to keep a safe psychological (sarcastic) distance from such ideals as patriotism and nationalism. In so doing, they remind us that we are fortunate to live in a *situation* where the most powerful people and most sacred ideas are subject to the same kind of scrutiny and ridicule as all other individuals and ideals.

SUGGESTED EPISODES FOR ADDITIONAL STUDY

30 Rock
1:1. "The Pilot." Writ. Tina Fey. Dir. Adam Bernstein. October 10, 2006.
1:15. "Hard Ball." Writ. Matt Hubbard. Dir. Don Scardino. February 22, 2007.
2:4. "Rosemary's Baby." Writ. Jack Burditt. Dir. Michael Engler. October 25, 2007.

3:22. "Kidney Now!" Writ. Jack Burditt and Robert Carlock. Dir. by Don Scardino. May 14, 2009.
5:5. "Reaganing." Writ. Matt Hubbard. Dir. Todd Holland. October 22, 2010.

Arrested Development
1:1. "Pilot." Writ. Mitchell Hurwitz. Dir. Anthony Russo and Joe Russo. November 2, 2003.
1:7. "My Mother, the Car." Writ. Chuck Martin. Dir. Jay Chandrasekhar. December 21, 2003.
2:15. "Sword of Destiny." Writ. Brad Copeland. Dir. Peter Lauer. March 27, 2005.
3:2. "For British Eyes Only." Writ. Richard Day and Mitchell Hurwitz. Dir. John Fortenberry. September 26, 2005.
3:9. "S.O.B.s." Writ. Richard Day and Jim Vallely. Dir. Robert Berlinger. January 2, 2006.

The Office
1:1. "Pilot." Writ. by Ricky Gervais, Stephen Merchant, and Greg Daniels. Dir. Ken Kwapis. March 24, 2005.
3:16. "Phyllis's Wedding." Writ. Caroline Williams. Dir. Ken Whittingham. February 8, 2007.
4:7. "Job Fair." Writ. Lee Eisenberg and Gene Stupnitsky. Dir. Tucker Gates. May 8, 2008.
5:13. "Stress Relief." Writ. Paul Lieberstein. Dir. Jeffrey Blitz and Paul Lieberstein. February 1, 2009.
6:5. "Mafia." Writ. Brent Forrester. Dir. Dave Rogers. October 15, 2009.

WORKS CITED

Bakhtin, Mikhail M. *The Dialogic Imagination: Four Essays*. Trans. Caryl Emerson and Michael Holquist. Ed. Michael Holquist. Austin: University of Texas Press, 1981. Print.
Bordwell, David. *The Way Hollywood Tells It: Story and Style in Modern Movies*. Berkeley and Los Angeles, California: University of California Press, 2006. Print.
Genette, Gerard. "Order, Duration, and Frequency." *Narrative Dynamics: Essays on Time, Plot, Closure, and Frames*. Ed. Brian Richardson. Columbus: Ohio State University Press, 2002. 25–34. Print.
Hutcheon, Linda. *Irony's Edge: The Theory and Politics of Irony*. New York: Routledge, 1994. Print.
"Into the Crevasse." *30 Rock*. NBC. October 22, 2009. Television.
"Motherboy XXX." *Arrested Development*. Fox. March 13, 2005. Television.

Nelles, William. "Stories with Stories: Narrative Levels and Embedded Narrative." *Narrative Dynamics: Essays on Time, Plot, Closure, and Frames*. Ed. Brian Richardson. Columbus: Ohio State University Press, 2002. 339–53. Print.

The Office. Prod. Greg Daniels, Ricky Gervais, and Stephen Merchant. NBC. 2005–Present. Television.

"Pilot." *Arrested Development*. Fox. November 2, 2003. Television.

16

CHANGE THE STRUCTURE, CHANGE THE STORY
How I Met Your Mother *and the Reformulation of the Television Romance*

MOLLY BROST

"Kids," an off-screen narrator announces to a teenage boy and girl. "I'm gonna tell you an incredible story: the story of how I met your mother" ("Pilot"). The story begins in 2005, when twenty-seven-year-old Ted Mosby's best friend, Marshall Eriksen, proposes to his longtime girlfriend, Lily Aldrin. Though Ted is happy for them, he quickly becomes concerned about the sorry state of his own love life, complaining to friend Barney Stinson that soon Marshall and Lily will have a family and he will just be "that weird middle-aged bachelor their kids call Uncle Ted" ("Pilot"). Then, fate steps in: "It was like something from an old movie," the narrator (Ted, speaking to his children in the year 2030) says. "Where the sailor sees the girl across the crowded dance floor, turns to his buddy, and says, 'See that girl? I'm gonna marry her someday'" ("Pilot"). The girl (a reporter named Robin Scherbatsky) agrees to go out with him, and the first date cements Ted's belief that she is perfect for him. Unfortunately, Ted comes on too strong, telling her that he thinks he is in love with her on that very first date, and it seems that he has scared her off. However, "that's the funny thing about destiny," the narrator says. "It happens whether you plan it or not. I mean, I never thought I'd see that girl again, but it turns out I was just too close to the puzzle to see the picture that was forming. Because that, kids, is the true story of how I met . . . your aunt Robin" ("Pilot"). The kids are aghast: "I thought this was how you met Mom," his daughter reproaches ("Pilot"). She is told to relax: "It's a long story" ("Pilot").

Thus, in one half-hour premiere episode, *How I Met Your Mother* (CBS, 2005–Present) laid the foundation for the series, introducing viewers to the premise (a middle-aged man tells his children the story of how he met their mother), and to the five main characters: Ted (Josh Radnor), an architect obsessed with meeting the love of his life; Marshall (Jason Segel), a law student who met *his* future wife, Lily (Alyson Hannigan), during his freshman year of college; Barney (Neil Patrick Harris), a womanizing bachelor; and Robin

(Cobie Smulders), the woman who rejects Ted's advances. "I don't know, Ted," she says. "We barely know each other, and you're looking at me with that look, and it's like—like—let's fall in love, and get married, and have kids and drive them to soccer practice" ("Purple Giraffe"). She says that it is a great look; unfortunately, he is looking at the wrong girl: "I don't want to get married right now, maybe ever, and—if we got together, I feel like I'd have to marry you or break your heart" ("Purple Giraffe"). Nevertheless, the two become friends and eventually date. However, viewers are reminded often (via narration from older Ted, voiced by Bob Saget) that Robin is not "the one," and that he will eventually marry someone else.

It is a unique premise. However, from the very beginning, critics expressed skepticism about whether telling the story in flashback from 2030 was necessary, or merely a gimmick. While *Variety*'s Brian Lowry lauded the framing device for helping to "skirt some of the 'Will they or won't they, and if they will, then when?' questions that have historically plagued episodic romantic comedies," the *Washington Post*'s Tom Shales called it "lame and intrusive," claiming that "you could jettison the narration and that gimmick and have essentially the same show" (59, C01). Further, the fact that built into the premise of the show is the promise that Ted will eventually meet and marry the mother of his children has many fans debating exactly when this will (and should) happen. As *Daily Variety*'s Alan Sepinwall notes, "some fans feel she shouldn't turn up until the final scene of the series, while others argue the show could run for several years after Ted finally meets and even marries his dream woman"; series co-creator Craig Thomas has quipped in response, "Our plan has always been to do it one of those two ways" (qtd. in Sepinwall). This chapter posits that, "gimmicky" or not, the series' unique narrative structure provides an opportunity for the romantic comedy to be reimagined. Within this reimagining, it then becomes possible—and even necessary—for traditional relationship expectations, as well as traditional gender roles, to be challenged and subverted.

TED AND ROBIN
Rethinking the "Ideal Romance"

Before examining how *How I Met Your Mother* reimagines the romance, it is first necessary to look at how romance typically works on the television sitcom. Janice Radway provides an apt description of this in *Reading the Romance: Women, Patriarchy, and Popular Literature*; though she observed the formula for what she calls the "ideal romance" after studying popular romance *novels*, rather than romantic *television series*, characteristics of the formula can be seen in stories told in multiple mediums, from novels to television series to film. As Radway describes, the "ideal romance" begins when "the heroine's social identity is destroyed"; she then "reacts antagonistically to an aristocratic male," who "responds ambiguously to the heroine" (134). Then, "the heroine interprets the hero's behavior as evidence of a purely sexual interest in her," which angers her (Radway 134). The heroine and hero are separated, either physically or emotionally; after this separation, "the hero treats the heroine tenderly" (Radway 134). Later, the hero "declare[s] his love" or "demonstrate[s] his unwavering commitment to the heroine"; the heroine "responds sexually and emotionally," and her "identity is restored" (Radway 134). This formula is often altered to some extent. In contemporary televisual texts, for example, the male is not always aristocratic. However, the story of a couple who initially despise each other, are separated following a misunderstanding, and reunite after a grand romantic gesture on the part of the male main character should not be unfamiliar to those who have read romance novels or viewed romantic comedies.

Scholars have pointed out the problems inherent in this formula. David Natharius notes that "Hollywood filmmakers . . . fulfill the perceived need for happy endings to romantic stories . . . even if the ending is, ultimately, severely limiting to the female characters involved. No matter how intelligent or self-sufficient or actualized a woman may be, her ultimate happiness is found in being loved and taken care of by a man" (179–80). Thus, the idea that a female character must be in a relationship to be happy is problematic. Further, scholars have pointed to problems with the idea that relationship problems are often solved with a "grand gesture"; as Laura Winn notes, "there is a pervasive *Carpe Diem* (Latin for 'seize the day') thematic within Hollywood romantic comedies, and this theme suggests a relational script in which dramatic gestures are upheld as the primary means of navigating important turning points in romantic relationships" (247). She warns that this suggests

> an unrealistic view of how the relational process may unfold . . . rather than working through a conflict, couples in these movies often jump in a moment to the state of "living happily ever after" . . . this happy ending script minimizes the extent to which real-life couples must work through conflict issues over time. (Winn 261)

Thus, the romantic formula so prevalent in popular culture paints a rather unrealistic picture of what real couples might expect from romantic relationships.

The notion that television and film are often unrealistic is certainly not new or surprising. However, many scholars warn that it *is* a cause for concern. As

L. Monique Ward and Kristen Harrison note, "frequent TV viewing is associated with holding more stereotypical associations about masculine and feminine activities, traits, and occupations" (5). It is further suggested that sitcoms might have a particularly strong influence on viewers. Richard Butsch states that "sitcoms' predominance on prime-time television throughout its history and their consequent share of the television audience . . . mean that they are preeminent examples of dominant culture, steadily presented to the largest population over the largest time. Pervasive and persistent images crystallize as cultural types" (113). Thus, because of the ubiquity of the sitcom, repeated formulas and images might begin to seem natural to viewers over time. Further, Aileen L. S. Busling and Anthony M. Ocana explain that "although sitcoms may seem relatively benign, research suggests that the use of humor in a message can influence people without their conscious understanding of that influence" (204). As a result of their pervasiveness and use of humor, then, sitcoms have great potential to influence viewers' perceptions of—and expectations for—romantic relationships.

Thus, it is important to examine how individual shows portray romantic relationships—and how they tweak existing, prevalent formulas. With regard to *How I Met Your Mother*, it is noteworthy that the formula is already altered somewhat by the fact that it is told from the point of view of a male character; romances are often told from the woman's point of view. Thus, the roles of the "heroine" and "hero" described in Radway's "ideal romance" formula are reversed. Though Ted and Robin's relationship does not follow the "ideal romance" to the letter (they do not start off hating each other, for example), they do have to overcome a series of conflicts, misunderstandings, and obstacles before they become a couple. The first is, of course, Ted coming on too strong; next, after the two decide to become friends, Robin begins dating someone else. By the time she realizes she has feelings for Ted, *he* has moved on. However, as on many sitcoms, they eventually get together (in fact, compared to many sitcoms, they get together rather quickly, uniting by the end of the first season). In this narrative, however, there is one important twist: the audience already knows that the relationship will not last.

This is important for multiple reasons. First of all, when Ted performs the "grand gestures" typical to the "ideal romance" formula, they come across as somewhat silly and desperate, rather than romantic. In the finale of the first season, for example, when Ted arranges for a quartet of musicians to be waiting in Robin's apartment when she gets home, she frustratedly asks him why he has to make everything so "big" ("Come On"). Both Robin and Marshall tell Ted that the relationship is not meant to be; he ignores them. Knowing that Robin will go camping that weekend with a would-be suitor unless it rains, he enlists an acquaintance to teach him a Native American rain dance. It does rain, and this is the grand gesture that gets Robin to finally give him a chance. However, the fact that the audience knows the outcome makes the moment less triumphant than it might be under other circumstances; while on many shows, audience members might be happy that the two have finally gotten together and feel upset if they break up, in this case viewers might feel impatient "waiting out" the relationship, wondering when Ted will meet the "real" love of his life. Thus, the "grand gesture" that is typically portrayed as romantic comes across as rather futile.

TED AND STELLA
"Trying to Skip Ahead to the End of the Book"

Though viewers know that Ted and Robin's relationship will end, the show devotes considerable time and attention—the entire second season, in fact—to its development and, eventually, its demise. When the older Ted's teenage daughter asks, in the premiere of the second season, if he can skip to the part of the story where he meets their mother, he assures her that this part is important, too. This in and of itself is unconventional; while on many sitcoms, the central romantic relationship might be the focal point of the narrative, the "be all/end all" in the story, we are reminded that other parts of life, as well as with relationships with people other than one's ultimate life partner, are also significant—something that the show's secondary characters repeatedly remind Ted of. For example, in season four, Ted enthuses that he cannot wait to get old—then he will not have to worry about where his career is going or who he is going to marry, because it will have already happened. Robin tells him that he cannot just jump to the end—the journey is the best part.

It is a lesson he should have already learned by that point. After Ted and Robin break up at the end of the show's second season when they realize that they want completely different things, Ted briefly goes wild, drunkenly getting a tattoo on his lower back; having a threesome; and accidentally making out with a married woman. However, by the end of the third season, he is in another serious relationship, this time with the doctor he enlists to remove the tattoo, Stella (Sarah Chalke). The two start their relationship slowly, largely because Stella has a young daughter and has little time to date; however, after Ted survives a car accident in the third season finale, he spontaneously proposes to her. She accepts; the early part of the show's fourth season focuses largely on their engagement; and, for a time, it seems possible that she might even be the mother of Ted's children, due both to things the narrator says in voice-over narration and clues placed in the narrative itself. In voice-over, the narrator refers to Stella by her first name only and does not (until it has become clear to both Ted and the audience that the relationship is not going to last) say anything to make it clear that she is not the mother, as he did very quickly with Robin. Further, certain clues within the narrative seem to have been placed with the specific intention of leading the audience to believe that Stella is the mother. For example, in an episode that takes place before Ted meets Stella, the narrator tells his children that while he would eventually learn that their mother was at a St. Patrick's Day party that he attended, he did not meet her that night; soon after Ted meets Stella, she makes a comment about going out on St. Patrick's Day, leading the audience to believe that she could have been at that party. Thus, the framing device works to create suspense in the narrative.

However, though both Ted and the audience might be hopeful that he has finally met "the one," Ted will soon learn that he hardly knows Stella at all. In the premiere of the show's fourth season, he will panic when his ignorance of her peanut allergy sends her to the emergency room. Further, he will soon realize that she wants him to make sacrifices he is not sure he is prepared to make—she expects him to move to New Jersey after the wedding. None of this is enough to make him call off the wedding, however; in fact, when Stella's sister cancels her own wedding at the last minute, he agrees to move his and Stella's wedding forward to her date and location so that she will not lose her deposit. Though his friends have reservations about this, it is Robin who tells him (in "Shelter Island") not to go through with it:

> Don't get married. Look, you're rushing into this. It's—it's like you're trying to skip ahead to the end of the book. Ted, you're the most romantic guy I know . . . but after all that, this is how your great romantic quest comes to an end? You're just disappearing into someone else's wedding, someone else's house, someone else's life, without a second thought! That's not the amazing ending that you deserve. That's not Ted Mosby.

Through this speech, we are reminded that marriage, in and of itself, is not a happy ending. While it can be wonderful with the right person, it does not guarantee happiness. Ted will not hear it; though Stella calls off the wedding when she realizes that she is still in love with her daughter's father, Ted is prepared to go through with it. He has to learn the hard way that he cannot "skip to the end" of the ideal romance.

BARNEY AND ROBIN, MARSHALL AND LILY
"Different Ways to Be in Love"

As Ted searches for the love of his life, the show's secondary characters provide alternate perspectives on love: through Barney and Robin, we are given the perspectives of two people who are happily single, and through Marshall and Lily, we get the perspective of two characters who have already found their "happy ending." It is through these characters that the "ideal romance" is, once again, challenged. Further, because the audience has been told from the beginning that Robin and Ted do not end up together, the relationships of these secondary characters create more narrative tension than the central romantic relationship does.

This tension is particularly alive in the characters of Robin and Barney. Flashforward scenes from the characters' futures interspersed throughout the series suggest that Marshall and Lily have a long, happy marriage (for example, at the end of an episode in which Marshall and Lily contemplate writing letters that they will read in the event of each other's deaths, fifty-something Marshall is shown opening his letter from Lily, only for fifty-something Lily to come in and chastise him for opening her letter early). However, older Ted tells his children (and the audience) very little about Barney's and Robin's respective romantic lives, meaning that the two could wind up with virtually anyone, or choose to remain single. This opens up numerous possibilities for the two. Very early in the series, it is suggested that Robin and Barney might actually be better suited for each other than Robin and Ted; as Barney himself points out, they both think that marriage and commitment are "a drag"; they both want something casual and fun; and they get along really well. Robin is inclined to agree—but what about Ted?

Following Ted and Robin's breakup, it would seem that nothing is standing in Robin and Barney's way, and the two sleep together. When Ted finds out, however, he is angry, and (temporarily) ends his friendship with Barney. Nevertheless, it soon becomes clear that Barney has real feelings for Robin—feelings that he is ill-equipped to deal with, given that he has avoided serious relationships for most of his adult life. Regardless, the two eventually date, and it seems, at first, that the two of them might have been wrong to think that they did not belong in serious relationships—they simply had not met the right people yet. Just as it seems that the show's producers are sending the message that everyone eventually can—and perhaps should—couple off, however, they turn that expectation on its head. A mere six episodes into Barney and Robin's relationship, after more than a season of build-up to the two getting together, it is revealed that the only reason that Barney and Robin seem so happy together is that they never talk about their problems. In the very next episode, it becomes clear that Barney and Robin are sucking the life out of each other—he is putting on weight, while she has stopped caring about her appearance. Thus, the show seems to imply that some people are better off alone.

While on the surface this might seem to be a positive message, it is problematized by the fact that Barney and Robin are presented as somewhat dysfunctional characters. Barney, for example, never knew his father; lost his virginity at age twenty-three to a friend of his mother's; and celebrates after crossing the milestone of sleeping with two hundred women. While his outrageous behavior is sometimes humorous, the other characters on the show often act as if he is disgusting. For example, when, in season three, Ted's careless, loutish behavior (ditching a date when he hears there will be "hotter and drunker" women at the bar he is waiting to get into and putting his own drinks on a stranger's bar tab) causes Marshall to accuse him of "turning into Barney," it is implied that this is a negative development ("No Tomorrow"). While the audience is presented with a character who eschews traditional romantic relationships, then, it can be argued that he serves as a cautionary tale—what Ted might turn into if he does not settle down.

Similarly, while Robin is presented as an attractive, intelligent career woman, she has baggage as well. The audience learns in season four that her father wanted a son so badly that he named her Robin Charles Scherbatsky Jr. and raised her as he would a boy. Indeed, Robin is, throughout the series, often shone to have stereotypically masculine interests (she has an affinity for scotch and cigars and is a self-proclaimed "gun enthusiast"). This is often played for laughs; for example, when Barney suggests that Robin deals with break-ups by eating Haagen Dazs and watching *Love Actually*, the scene immediately cuts to show her at the shooting range. While Robin's enthusiasm for male activities has led to humorous moments in the show, her lack of interest in marriage and children, things that women are "supposed" to want, often causes other characters to accuse her of being, at best, a little strange, and, at worst, heartless: "When you're done shaking off at the urinal, maybe you could ask the wizard to give you a heart," Ted tells her sarcastically in season four's "Not a Father's Day" (albeit in response to her teasing offer to grab him a tampon due to his more traditionally feminine enthusiasm over having children). Similarly, a few episodes later, when Robin fails to understand Marshall and Lily's rituals, Marshall lashes out at her: "You don't understand love, okay? You're like some robot who sees a person crying and says, 'Why is that human leaking?'" ("Three Days"). Again, such moments are played for laughs; however, they imply that while the other characters on the show like Robin, they also find her attitudes toward relationships to be odd and, perhaps, an indication that something is wrong with her. The characters with less conventional attitudes toward relationships, then, often inspire the anger, derision, and sometimes pity of the characters with more "normal" attitudes.

Fortunately, in the narrative of *How I Met Your Mother*, such characters do not often simply sit back and take such comments from their friends. For example, Robin responds to Marshall's claim that she does not understand love by asserting that he is wrong to think that "the only way to be in love is to have pet names and leave each other stupid little notes . . . There's lots of ways to be in a relationship, and you would know that if you ever left your little love snob country club" ("Three Days"). Robin seems determined to figure out what those ways are. While the character has rarely wavered in her views on marriage and children, she seems willing to try to figure out what kind of relationship works for her; following her relationship with Barney, she embarks on a serious relationship with a coworker, even briefly living with him before a new job sends him to Chicago. Similarly, while Barney enjoys the freedom to see as many women as he wants, he does occasionally develop more serious feelings, which he struggles to handle in his own way. Through these secondary characters, then, we are shown two people trying to negotiate love outside of the rules and boundaries of traditional relationships; while these characters are not always portrayed positively, their prominence on *How I Met Your Mother* provides an alternative to the "happily ever after" ending. Additionally, the show's narrative structure leaves virtually any romantic future open to the two of them, leaving their characters with more narrative possibilities than other characters have.

Further, even Marshall and Lily, the characters who have already achieved the "happily ever after" ending, are not shown as having perfect lives. Though the couple marry in the show's second season, this does not happen before Lily expresses worries about the experiences she might have missed by entering a serious relationship at a young age; the couple even breaks up briefly before getting married. Additionally, their marriage has not made them immune to the types of problems many contemporary young people face: credit card debt; first-time home-owner issues; career frustrations; and, as they attempt to conceive their first child in the show's sixth season, fertility concerns. Thus, through the example of Marshall and Lily, the audience is not simply shown an "ideal romance"; it is shown a couple experiencing realistic problems as they move into their first years of marriage. Though the brief moments we see of the characters' futures show us that the two stay together, achieve financial success, and, yes, become parents, the two are not shown as having all of the answers or the ideal life. The framing device, then, allows the creators to explore the problems that Lily and Marshall might reasonably face without worrying the audience that permanent damage will be done to their relationship. Thus, in the cases of the secondary characters' relationships, the framing device allows the show's creators to experiment with different possibilities for what it means to find and experience love.

TAKING "THE LEAP"
Life Outside of the "Ideal Romance"

As Robin, Barney, Marshall, and Lily make their way through their own problems and successes, they encourage Ted to let go of his preconceived notions of how life should be: "You can't design your life like a building," Lily tells Ted in season four after he experiences a series of career setbacks ("The Leap"). Though Ted has trouble accepting that, his future self has some perspective: "That was the year I got left at the altar," older Ted tells his children. ". . . The year I got fired . . . And damn if it wasn't the best year of my life. Because if any one of those things hadn't happened, I never would have ended up in what turned out to be the best job I ever had. But more importantly—I wouldn't have met your mother" ("The Leap"). The framing device in this instance serves to tell the audience things that Ted could not know in the present, as well as to lend an optimistic note to what is, in many ways, a rough time in the characters' lives. Far from being a gimmick, it proves instrumental. At the same time that it works to remind us that this is a love story with a conventional happy ending, it also reminds us that it is the things that happen on the way to that ending that determine the course of one's life. By employing such a framing device, the creators of *How I Met Your Mother* are allowed to critique and reimagine the traditional love story that has been told so many times.

SUGGESTED EPISODES FOR ADDITIONAL STUDY

How I Met Your Mother
1:13. "Drumroll, Please." Writ. Gloria Calderon Kellett. Dir. Pamela Fryman. January 23, 2006.
1:14. "Zip, Zip, Zip." Writ. Brenda Hsueh. Dir. Pamela Fryman. February 6, 2006.
1:15. "Game Night." Writ. Chris Harris II. Dir. Pamela Fryman. February 27, 2006.

1:16. "Cupcake." Writ. Maria Ferrari and Suzy Mamann-Greenberg. Dir. Pamela Fryman. March 6, 2006.

1:18. "Nothing Good Happens After 2 A.M." Writ. Craig Thomas and Carter Bays. Dir. Pamela Fryman. April 10, 2006.

2:1. "Where Were We?" Writ. Craig Thomas and Carter Bays. Dir. Pamela Fryman. September 18, 2006.

2:3. "Brunch." Writ. Stephen Lloyd. Dir. Pamela Fryman. October 2, 2006.

2:4. "Ted Mosby: Architect." Writ. Kristin Newman. Dir. Pamela Fryman. October 9, 2006.

2:8. "Atlantic City." Writ. Maria Ferrari. Dir. Pamela Fryman. November 13, 2006.

2:21. "Something Borrowed." Writ. Greg Malins. Dir. Pamela Fryman. May 7, 2007.

2:22. "Something Blue." Writ. Carter Bays and Craig Thomas. Dir. Pamela Fryman. May 14, 2007.

3:7. "Dowistrepla." Writ. Brenda Hsueh. Dir. Pamela Fryman. November 5, 2007.

3:11. "The Platinum Rule." Writ. Craig Thomas and Carter Bays. Dir. Pamela Fryman. December 10, 2007.

3:13. "Ten Sessions." Writ. Carter Bays, Craig Thomas, and Chris Harris II. Dir. Pamela Fryman. March 24, 2008.

3:16. "Sandcastles in the Sand." Writ. Courtney Kang. Dir. Pamela Fryman. April 21, 2008.

3:17. "The Goat." Writ. Stephen Lloyd. Dir. Pamela Fryman. April 28, 2008.

3:20. "Miracles." Writ. Craig Thomas and Carter Bays. Dir. Pamela Fryman. May 19, 2008.

4:1. "Do I Know You?" Writ. Carter Bays and Craig Thomas. Dir. Pamela Fryman. September 22, 2008.

4:3. "I Heart NJ." Writ. Greg Malins. Dir. Pamela Fryman. October 6, 2008.

4:12. "Benefits." Writ. Kourtney Kang. Dir. Pamela Fryman. January 12, 2009.

4:22. "Right Place Right Time." Writ. Stephen Lloyd. Dir. Pamela Fryman. May 4, 2009.

4:23. "As Fast As She Can." Writ. Craig Thomas and Carter Bays. Dir. Pamela Fryman. May 11, 2009.

5:1. "Definitions." Writ. Carter Bays and Craig Thomas. Dir. Pamela Fryman. September 21, 2009.

5:3. "Robin 101." Writ. Carter Bays and Craig Thomas. Dir. Pamela Fryman. October 5, 2009.

5:6. "Bagpipes." Writ. Robia Rashid. Dir. Pamela Fryman. November 2, 2009.

5:7. "The Rough Patch." Writ. Chris Harris II. Dir. Pamela Fryman. November 9, 2009.
5:17. "Of Course." Writ. Matt Kuhn. Dir. Pamela Fryman. March 8, 2010.
5:21. "Twin Beds." Writ. Theresa Mulligan Rosenthal. Dir. Pamela Fryman. May 3, 2010.
5:23. "The Wedding Bride." Writ. Carter Bays and Craig Thomas. Dir. Pamela Fryman. May 17, 2010.
5:24. "Doppelgangers." Writ. Craig Thomas and Carter Bays. Dir. Pamela Fryman. May 24, 2010.
6:16. "Desperation Day." Writ. Tami Sagher. Dir. Pamela Fryman. February 14, 2011.
6:17. "Garbage Island." Writ. Tom Ruprecht. Dir. Michael Shea II. February 21, 2011.
6:18. "A Change of Heart." Writ. Matt Kuhn. Dir. Pamela Fryman. February 28, 2011.
6:20. "The Exploding Meatball Sub." Writ. Steven Lloyd. Dir. Pamela Fryman. April 11, 2011.
6:23. "Landmarks." Writ. Carter Bays and Craig Thomas. Dir. Pamela Fryman. May 9, 2011.
6:24. "Challenge Accepted." Writ. Carter Bays and Craig Thomas. Dir. Pamela Fryman. May 16, 2011.

WORKS CITED

Busling, Aileen L. S., and Anthony M. Ocana. "Myths of Romantic Conflict in the Television Situation Comedy." *Critical Thinking About Sex, Love, and Romance in the Mass Media: Media Literacy Applications*. Ed. Mary-Lou Galician and Debra L. Merskin. Mahwah, NJ: Lawrence Erlbaum Associates, Publishers, 2007. 203–14. Print.

Butsch, Richard. "Five Decades and Three Hundred Sitcoms about Class and Gender." *Thinking Outside the Box: A Contemporary Television Genre Reader*. Ed. Gary R. Edgerton and Brian G. Rose. Lexington: University Press of Kentucky, 2008. 111–35. Print.

"Come On." *How I Met Your Mother: Season One*. Writ. Craig Thomas and Carter Bays. Dir. Pamela Fryman. 20th Century Fox, 2006. DVD.

"The Leap." *How I Met Your Mother: Season Four*. Writ. Craig Thomas and Carter Bays. Dir. Pamela Fryman. 20th Century Fox, 2009. DVD.

Lowry, Brian. "Clever CBS Sitcom Hits 'Mother' Lode." *Variety*. September 19, 2005: 59. *LexisNexis*. Web. August 3, 2010.

Natharius, David. "Gender Equity Stereotypes or Prescriptions? Subtexts of the Stairway Scenes in the Romantic Films of Helen Hunt." *Critical Thinking About Sex, Love, and Romance in the Mass Media: Media Literacy Applications*. Ed. Mary-Lou Galician and Debra L. Merskin. Mahwah, NJ: Lawrence Erlbaum Associates, Publishers, 2007. 177–88. Print.

"No Tomorrow." *How I Met Your Mother: Season Three*. Writ. Craig Thomas and Carter Bays. Dir. Pamela Fryman. 20th Century Fox, 2008. DVD.

"Not a Father's Day." *How I Met Your Mother: Season Four*. Writ. Robia Rashid. Dir. Pamela Fryman. 20th Century Fox, 2009. DVD.

"Pilot." *How I Met Your Mother: Season One*. Writ. Craig Thomas and Carter Bays. Dir. Pamela Fryman. 20th Century Fox, 2006. DVD.

"Purple Giraffe." *How I Met Your Mother: Season One*. Writ. Craig Thomas and Carter Bays. Dir. Pamela Fryman. 20th Century Fox, 2006. DVD.

Radway, Janice A. *Reading the Romance: Women, Patriarchy, and Popular Literature*. Chapel Hill: University of North Carolina Press, 1984. Print.

Sepinwall, Alan. "Producers Won't Reveal When They'll Let Title Character Shine." *Daily Variety*. January 7, 2010. *LexisNexis*. Web. August 3, 2010.

Shales, Tom. "'How I Met Your Mother': A Sweet Introduction." *Washington Post*. September 19, 2005: C01. *LexisNexis*. Web. August 3, 2010.

"Shelter Island." *How I Met Your Mother: Season Four*. Writ. Chris Harris. Dir. Pamela Fryman. 20th Century Fox, 2009. DVD.

"Three Days of Snow." *How I Met Your Mother: Season Four*. Writ. Matt Kuhn. Dir. Pamela Fryman. 20th Century Fox, 2009. DVD.

Ward, L. Monique, and Kristen Harrison. "The Impact of Media Use of Girls' Beliefs About Gender Roles, Their Bodies, and Sexual Relationships: A Research Synthesis." *Featuring Females: Feminist Analyses of Media*. Ed. Ellen Cole and Jessica Henderson Daniel. Washington, D.C.: American Psychological Association, 2005. 3–24. Print.

Winn, Laura L. "*Carpe Diem*: Relational Scripts and 'Seizing the Day' in the Hollywood Romantic Comedy." *Critical Thinking About Sex, Love, and Romance in the Mass Media: Media Literacy Applications*. Ed. Mary-Lou Galician and Debra L. Merskin. Mahwah, NJ: Lawrence Erlbaum Associates, Publishers, 2007. 247–64. Print.

17

LIKE SANDS THROUGH THE HALF-HOURGLASS
Nurse Jackie *and Temporal Disruption*

JANANI SUBRAMANIAN

Showtime has emerged in the last few years as a serious contender in the premium television league with its super-hits like *Dexter* (2006–Present), *The Tudors* (2007–2010), and *Weeds* (2005–Present) challenging HBO's reign over the "quality" (Emmy-winning, adult-oriented, original) television category. Four of its series—*Nurse Jackie* (2009–Present), *Weeds, United States of Tara* (2009–Present), *Secret Diary of a Call Girl* (2007–Present), and, most recently, *The Big C* (2010–Present)—are half-hour shows that center their narratives around a strong female protagonist who eschews conventional morality for personal or professional gain. Jason Mittell notes that "HBO has built its reputation and subscriber base upon narratively complex shows" (29), and, in a slightly different vein, Showtime has incorporated the female-centric, single camera, half-hour "dramedy" genre into its quality brand identity. Building on its success with the groundbreaking and controversial *The L Word* (2004–2009), the network has diverged from HBO in its efforts to push the boundaries of gender and sexuality within premium cable. In addition to the high production quality of the above shows, *Nurse Jackie, Weeds, United States of Tara,* and *The Big C* all feature accomplished actresses who have acted in both feature films and theater. HBO's half-hour series include *Bored to Death* (2009–Present), *Curb Your Enthusiasm* (2000–Present), *Hung* (2009–Present), *Entourage* (2004–Present), *Flight of the Conchords* (2007–2009), and *Eastbound & Down* (2009–Present), along with the retired *Sex and the City* (1998–2004). With the exception of *Sex and the City*, the shows mentioned are primarily motivated by male protagonists, forming a striking counterpart to Showtime's line-up. All of the aforementioned series are dark comedies, like Showtime's female-centric programs, yet the exploits of HBO's detectives, writers, prostitutes, actors, musicians, and baseball players (respectively) focus more on action-oriented narratives, heterosexual coupling, and personality quirks than on deeper character complexity.

In this chapter, I will argue, using *Nurse Jackie* (*NJ*) as my primary example, that the segmentation of these thirty-minute shows presents a reformulation of television time in a quality television context; along with continuing to develop Showtime's brand identity, the combination of situation comedy and melodrama in this thirty-minute time frame also turns conventional rituals of heterosexual coupling and domesticity on their head, creating a space in the television landscape for female characters' renegotiation of the traditional work/home binary.

TEMPORALITY, TELEVISION, AND WOMEN

The main characters of *NJ*, *United States of Tara*, *Weeds*, *Secret Diary of a Call Girl*, and *The Big C* are all, in some form or fashion, "working mothers." Like most television programs featuring female protagonists, the shows explore the conflicts arising from the division between home and professional life. What sets these dramedies apart from those of network television are the unique ways that these leading ladies cope with the tensions between work and home; Nancy Botwin creates a marijuana empire to support her upper-middle-class lifestyle, and Tara Gregson, while not having a traditional "career," tries to balance her role as mother with the six other personalities that are a product of her dissociative identity disorder. As the twentieth century, industrialization, and two world wars drastically changed gender dynamics in America, women's work moved from inside to outside the home, creating new ideological valences around domestic space, work space, and family dynamics. Time, within second-wave feminist discourses and their popular representations, seemed to be either an adversary that needed conquering, or a potential avenue for restless housewives to explore other facets of their feminine identity.

The demands of time, both in and outside of the home, have a distinct relationship to television style and programming. Along with the organization of television programming, the style and generic qualities of specific shows, such as situation comedies, also responded to a home-bound female audience.[1] The format of the situation comedy was generally half an hour, with commercial breaks, and it is the shorter time frame, as well as the general lack of serial narratives that extended past one episode, that led to a different negotiation of femininity and domesticity within the sitcom as a genre; women in situation comedies must constantly negotiate between containment and independence.[2]

I would argue that HBO has maintained a brand identity for its programming based on the complexities of the American family, often creating surrogate structures that attempt to re-create the nuclear family in other milieus.

Showtime, in a slightly different vein, still locates the majority of its programming within the nuclear family, and its female-oriented half-hour series presents serious challenges that continually threaten the inherent stability and comfort of this structure, suggesting a radically altered view of women and the domestic. Situating *NJ* in the context of women's television programming and the demands of both work and home perhaps sheds light on the show's use of the half-hour melodramatic format to explore these same issues within the institutional parameters of Showtime's "quality" original television productions. I use *NJ* as my primary example since the main character is one of the only two heroines of Showtime's half-hour programming who works outside the home, as opposed to *Weeds'* Nancy Botwin, *The United States of Tara's* Tara Gregson, and *The Big C's* Cathy Jamison, whose statuses as "housewives" are radically challenged by extenuating circumstances such as death, multiple-personality disorder, and cancer, respectively. The other working heroine is Belle/Hannah from *Secret Diary of a Call Girl*, and while thematically the show plays on similar themes as the previous shows, its younger protagonist and British production company and setting call for slightly different contextualization and analysis.

NURSE JACKIE'S DISCOURSE OF DISCONTENT

Nurse Jackie debuted on Showtime on June 8, 2009, to mixed reviews, including high praise for Edie Falco's performance as well as criticisms about the uneven writing and supporting cast. Critics praised the show's ability to mix drama and comedy in half an hour, which in premium cable is a solid twenty-seven to twenty-eight minutes, with no commercial breaks, as opposed to the roughly twenty-two minutes of narrative content and eight minutes of commercial breaks in network situation comedies. There are several precedents which set the stage for *NJ*'s thirty-minute format. One influence is the growing number of what Brett Mills calls "comedy vérité," programs like *The Office* (NBC, 2005–Present), *Arrested Development* (Fox, 2003–2006), *Parks and Recreation* (NBC, 2009–Present), *Modern Family* (ABC, 2009–Present), *Flight of the Conchords*, and so on, which—while still located within enclosed sets such as offices, apartments, and living rooms—removed the multiple-camera, proscenium arch, and canned laughter of the traditional situation comedy, and replaced them with single-camera, documentary-like cinematography. Another influence on *NJ*'s thirty-minute format is its network precursor *Weeds*, as well as the HBO mega-hits *Sex and the City* and *Curb Your Enthusiasm*. One of the characteristics of the network situation comedy is a narrative segmentation that allows for commercial breaks, where each segment is often designed with its own mini narrative structure and climax; "the function of this pre-commercial climax is not to resolve narrative dilemmas, but instead to heighten them, to raise our interest in the narrative as we flow into the commercials" (Butler 38). While the premium half-hour shows do not have commercial breaks, I would argue that they are equally, if differently, segmented into smaller narrative arcs, creating a rhythm that is often unique to each show. It is the arrangement and the pacing of these "nuggets" of narrative that not only allow an effective sitcom/melodrama, serial/series hybridity, but also create a specific brand of comedy-drama for Showtime as a network.

Looking at *NJ* specifically within these parameters, the show's pacing and segmentation not only form a compelling relationship with its female protagonist's experience of time, but also place the show within the ongoing televisual conversation about women, work, and domesticity. Jackie Peyton is a middle-aged, working-class nurse in New York City with two daughters and a husband who runs a bar; she is also having an affair with the hospital pharmacist and is addicted to painkillers. Like her fellow Showtime heroines, she has developed her own moral code to adapt to the pressures of work and home. One of the show's promotional posters features Jackie holding a syringe and the tagline "Life is full of little pricks"; Jackie metes out her own punishments to patients and colleagues to balance out life's unfairness. The promotional poster suggests a kinship to Showtime's other vigilante—Dexter—but while *Dexter*'s pace is often languorous and contemplative (aided by his voiceover), *NJ*'s hospital setting creates an undercurrent of urgency around Jackie's choices and decisions. The hospital is a Catholic faith-based institution, and another promotional poster for the series features Jackie with a halo of drugs around her head, holding up two fingers in the iconic style of Byzantine religious art. The show's deployment of religious iconography and spaces casts Jackie in the role of harried saint or martyr, and like all martyrs, Jackie suffers for a cause; if she only had more *time*, she could probably deal more effectively with her affair, her family, and the assorted "pricks" that come into her hospital.

One of the primary facets of female temporality that *NJ* addresses is age, specifically creating a representation of a woman's subjectivity when she is in a particular stage in her life. Jackie joins a growing group of older female protagonists across both network and cable programming. Julia Lesage's "Watching for Botox" deftly highlights the contemporary prevalence of plastic surgery for public figures but also perhaps touches on another point—that older female protagonists are becoming more ubiquitous in fictional media narratives. *Damages* starring Glenn Close (FX, 2007–Present), *The Good Wife* starring Julianna Margulies (CBS, 2009–Present), and *The Closer* starring Kyra Sedgwick

(TNT, 2005–Present)—are a few examples of series focused on middle-aged women who try to negotiate professional success with complex personal lives. While these series highlight the women's powerful professional profiles in the midst of male-dominated environments, they also tap into what Diane Negra defines as a kind of temporal anxiety that often structures women's lives. In "Time, Crisis and the New Postfeminist Heterosexual Economy," Negra argues that the convention of "cheating time" in contemporary media texts is often related to a sense of urgency that dominates the female characters' lives—in particular, an urgency to complete the requisite "stages" of the conventional heterosexual feminine life, including relationships, marriage, and children. Along these lines, Close's Patty Hewes, Margulies's Alicia Florrick, and Sedgwick's Brenda Leigh Johnson are represented as short on time, not only in terms of managing family and work on daily basis, but also within the larger arcs of their life choices. They sacrificed or continue to sacrifice stages of their personal lives for professional achievements and, from week to week, the narrative push behind these dramas is the continuing dissatisfaction of these women with their personal/professional choices, suggesting that they somehow "missed" something in the pursuit of careers. Each moment with husband or children for these female protagonists butts against the case or trial she is working on, and the brief segments she gets for family life within the hour-long drama leave her ultimately unsatisfied (and, of course, leave room for another episode).

Within the series just mentioned, different facets of temporality intersect—the age of the protagonist, the larger implications in a woman's timeline of choosing both a career and motherhood, the day-to-day challenges of balancing the two worlds, and the limitations imposed by the generic and commercial conventions of network television. *NJ* sits apart from these dramas in that Jackie is middle-aged and does balance a career and family, but the half-hour format, the mix of melodrama and comedy, and Falco's performance as Jackie establish different parameters for evaluating Jackie's choices. For example, in the pilot episode, viewers are introduced to Jackie, her quirky colleagues, her addiction, and her affair with Eddie, the hospital pharmacist. The only insight viewers get into Jackie's life are her thoughts, via voice-over, about her addiction, until the twenty-sixth minute of the twenty-seven-minute-long episode, where Jackie uses voice-over to tell the audience her opinions on sainthood. She says, "If I were a saint, which maybe I wanna be, which maybe I don't, I would be like Augustine. He knew there was good in him and he knew there was some not so good. And he wasn't going to give up his earthly pleasures before he was good and ready. 'Make me good, God, but not yet.' Right?" The camera follows her as she walks home from work, walks into a small house, and just as she stops talking, it pans over to the couch to reveal two little girls, whom Jackie refers to as "my loves." The theme song to the film *Valley of the Dolls* (1967), sung by kd lang, plays as Jackie continues through the house, puts a ring back on her finger, and, smiling, greets a man who is presumably her husband. Her last line in the episode is, "It bears repeating. Make me good, God. But not yet," and she steps out of our view into the shadows ("Pilot").

The sudden reveal of Jackie's family in the last minute of the episode functions, on one level, to create surprise, yet on another level perhaps indicates Jackie's own identification of priorities in her life. Her thoughts on sainthood indicate a hesitation to embrace what she considers "good," which presumably means no addiction and no lying to her family, but she does not want to be good "yet." The inclusion of the theme song from the cult film *Valley of the Dolls*, where viewers hear the lyric "When will I know why" adds a level of camp to the scene, for although the song itself is mournful, the "dolls" the movie refers to are the barbiturates the film's heroines are addicted to, a knowing wink to the savvy viewer. The tragedy of drug addiction and its effects on the family, a subject well suited for the generic conventions of melodrama, becomes something different in this last scene; as Jackie half-smiles/smirks when she greets her family, viewers get the sense that she (and the show) are holding them at a distance, and what could be maudlin ends up being tongue-in-cheek and wry. This literal last-minute revelation of a family, after it is assumed that Jackie is merely a drug-addicted, middle-aged, cranky but good-hearted nurse, pulls the rug out from under the show, suggesting through a literal allocation of episode time that the heroine likes her family, but likes her drugs, her affair, and the demands of her job just as much.

The half-hour format also forces the show to move at a fast pace, alternating scenes, spaces, and characters in a way that creates humor and reflects the chaos of the hospital setting. As Michael Z. Newman explains in his analysis of the PTS (prime-time serial), most television programs are organized around short, two-minute beats, which are strung together to form an episode (17). While the industrial context of television demands short segments to hold viewer attention, Newman argues that "by demanding that scenes be short, the networks create the conditions for a sophisticated mode of ensemble storytelling" (18). In *NJ*, the organization of melodramatic and humorous beats in unexpected ways not only stylistically marks the program as a Showtime product, but also frames the protagonist as alternately ill tempered, morally questionable, and tender in a manner that renders her startlingly complex. For example, the pilot episode begins with a dreamlike image of Jackie in a traditional nurse's uniform, lying on the floor, quoting T. S. Eliot from her tenth-grade English class (taught by a "smart fucking nun"). Jackie then begins to wax poetically about her drugs, with a close-up of the red medicine balls in her last pill, framed beautifully against a stark white background in slow motion, until Jackie lines them up and snorts them. The camera then zooms in on Jackie's eye and cuts to a scene with a patient who has just been in a bike accident. While Jackie tries to convince the arrogant Dr. Cooper (Peter Facinelli) that the patient is in more danger, he brushes her off, which leads to the patient's death. As the camera looks over the dead patient, eyes wide, Jackie stares at him and says baldly through voice-over "acute subdural hematoma. The brain puffs up so fast it rips the blood vessels and you bleed to death inside your skull" ("Pilot"). The scene then cuts to Jackie forging the patient's signature on the donor line of his driver's license, with a close-up of her carefully blowing the ink to make it dry faster, and then to the scene where she tells his family of his death. The scene presents the family in a medium-level tableaux shot, with two large brothers in uniform and their small mother in the middle, and as Jackie breaks the news to them that the patient was a donor, the brothers start fighting with each other in a comic manner.

Looking at the alternation of scenes in this opening sequence, first is the incongruous juxtaposition of Jackie and the pills bathed in soft white lighting and a flat, heavily accented New York voice, alternately quoting poetry and cursing. The dreamlike effect of the opening is disrupted by Jackie lining up and snorting the pills, an act that is startlingly out of character for a middle-aged woman in medical scrubs. Melodramatic music plays over the scene with the dead patient, but again the contemplative tone is undercut by Jackie's stark description of what killed him, her forging of the patient's donor signature, and the almost slapstick nature of the patient's family's reaction to his death and donor status. Medical shows like *Grey's Anatomy* (ABC, 2005–Present) usually heavily dramatize the moment when the doctor must tell families about a member's death, but in this case, the patient's brothers are represented as morons and his mother as pathetic. Assuming that this point of view is Jackie's, viewers have been presented up to this point with a character who is alternately poetic, crass, ethical, dishonest, sympathetic, and cynical, a vast array of qualities for the first five minutes of an episode. As Newman argues, the screenwriters have deftly combined beats to create an entertaining and intriguing series of shots, but, on another level, they have created a space for their female protagonist to express her complexity within a short period of time. By mixing moments of melodrama and humor, viewers are rarely left with the sense of longing for things lost or sacrificed that characterizes most television melodrama, but as the program moves from moment to incongruous moment, they get the sense that Jackie, while tender, mean, and constantly high on drugs, is also just impatient with the events unfolding around her.

The sense of incongruity from scene to scene in *NJ* is not typical of prime-time serials, which provide both resolution and "thematic parallelism" within their four acts or segments, leaving the ideal balance between "episodic closure and serial deferment" (Newman 21, 20). Newman says, "A closed form is one in which the elements all hang together in an integrated pattern" (22), but I would argue that not only the generic combinations of melodrama and comedy disrupt the "closed form" of each *NJ* episode, but also that Falco's performance as Jackie resists easy resolution within each episode and across the series as a whole. The casting of Falco is a mark of Showtime's procurement of "quality" film actresses to star in its series (Mary Louise Parker, Toni Collette, Laura Linney) but is also unusual within television programming because of Falco's age. As Negra discusses, a burgeoning cult of the "MILF" or the "desperate housewife" is evidence of the ongoing "time panic" of postfeminist culture, as there is growing pressure to get married, have children, *and* still be seen as a sexy and sexual female subject (179–81). Falco as Jackie resists the representational demands of the "sexually seasoned midlife woman" (180); Jackie wears scrubs most of the time, a short, no frills haircut, no makeup, and little jewelry—a stark contrast from her previous "quality television" portrayal of Carmela Soprano in HBO's *The Sopranos* (1999–2007). Sex is perfunctory and necessary for Jackie, but not sexy—the series' sex scenes are often represented as either humorous or awkward. Falco's performance as Jackie emphasizes her inscrutability; while viewers are occasionally granted access to Jackie's thoughts via voice-over, they do not reveal character motivation as much as create darkly humorous asides to Jackie's actions. Her motivations throughout the series are less obvious than those of her more ambitious television peers; she has to work, she dutifully takes care of her family, but she does not seem to like either one very much. Violating performative and narrative codes of melodrama, Jackie denies the viewer both the pleasure and the satisfaction of understanding her motivations and reactions to those around her, and in doing so, also rejects the transparency of other female protagonists' struggles to balance the priorities of work and the home.

The combination of Jackie's impatience with and ambivalence toward the world around her create what I call a "discourse of discontent,"[3] and it is through this discourse that I read the show's groundbreaking representation of a working-class, non-consumer-oriented femininity that adds shades of complexity not only to the work-life conflicts that mark other female-centric series, but also to the idea that a woman must move linearly down a particular timeline in order to achieve satisfaction. Each beat that focuses on Jackie's lined, tired, skeptical face, within the relatively short period of the show's half-hour context, rejects the idea that we must dissect a woman's motivations along the conventional melodramatic lines of exaggerated facial expressions and elaborately staged interpersonal interactions. She appears to care equally about her ex-pharmacist lover Eddie (Paul Schulze) as she does about her husband (Dominic Furmusa), yet there is no time in the show (or her life) for self-reflection on the moral ramifications of her affair. Her often unethical nursing practices and ongoing drug addiction are similarly left unquestioned, which has garnered criticism from reviewers that the show skims the surface of its characters. I would argue, though, that Jackie's ambivalence poses a challenge to viewers to critically consider her motivations in career and personal life and undoes assumptions that her desire must remain confined to either one or the other. In the second-season finale, both her husband and her best friend Dr. O'Hara (Eve Best) try to stage an intervention with Jackie about their discovery of her drug use. Jackie reacts badly as her house of cards comes crumbling down and storms into the bathroom. While this moment is fairly important in the show's narrative arcs—where the audience's knowledge and that of the other characters finally come together—Jackie's angry stomp into the bathroom is overlaid by a Melissa Etheridge song, "Nervous." The rock nature song lends a gritty edge to the scene as Jackie stares into the bathroom mirror, her expression unreadable, as she imagines herself on a beach and saying the words "Hi my name is Jackie and I'm a drug addict." The camera focuses on a close-up of Jackie for about ten seconds, as a smile creeps on to her face, she throws her head back in laughter, and tells the camera "Blow me" ("Years"). The discovery of her secret—a moment that usually leads to the resolution of tension within melodrama—is diffused into a moment that is neither completely dramatic nor comic, but styled through music and editing as beyond the understanding of either the viewer or Jackie's husband and friend. The moment is a cliffhanger in terms of the series plot and character arcs, but leaves no suspense or surprises in terms of Jackie's characterization. Viewers know that she does not accept the label "addict" or crumble in the face of her loved ones' concerns, but they do not know much more than that, and as the series as a whole suggests with its format, pace, and performances, perhaps they should not always automatically assume complete access to a female protagonist's subjectivity.

CONCLUSION

The reception contexts of "women's television" mentioned at the beginning of this essay must be reformulated in light of contemporary television contexts such as niche programming and premium cable, a changing woman's workforce, and viewing conditions among different classes and races. The relationship between women's programming and consumerism takes on a different valence within premium cable shows that do not have commercial interruptions; for example, *Sex and the City* marries a rampant consumerism with quality television aesthetics, narrative complexity, and postfeminist ideology, and shows like *The Sopranos* have created a thriving market of ancillary products like cookbooks, city tours, clothing, and more. *Nurse Jackie*, starring a working-class heroine and set mainly outside the home, does not fit perfectly into the consumerist fantasy mold of television in general, although supporting characters like the wealthy and fashionable Dr. O'Hara act as both foils for Jackie's Spartan aesthetic and symbols of an upper-class lifestyle that the viewers (and Jackie) can aspire to. The show's relationship to consumerism is perhaps most evident in its place within Showtime's line-up of half-hour female centered dramadies, which reinforce Showtime's brand appeal to particular segments (white, educated, upper middle class) of the female television demographic.

Jackie is in good company amid Showtime's line-up of quirky heroines in half-hour shows and is an integral part of Showtime's brand identity. One of Showtime's flagship shows, *The L Word*, was considered groundbreaking in terms of its frank portrayal of the lives and loves of LBGT denizens of Los Angeles and was also criticized for its representation of very attractive lesbians seemingly cast for the heterosexual male gaze (Sedgwick). While none of the shows that I have referred to—*Weeds, Nurse Jackie, The United States of Tara, The Big C*—explore alternatives to heterosexual relationships (with the exception of some of Tara's alternate personalities), they all explore alternatives to the conventional work/home divide that characterizes most female-oriented television drama. Dorothy Snarker says on the pop culture Web site *AfterEllen.com*, "But Showtime programming head Robert Greenblatt insists the network didn't set out to make shows about complicated women: 'It's not like we had some great strategy: "Let's do a series of shows about flawed women." *Weeds* was a great idea and it started a trend.'" But as Snarker points out, with several premium and network programs focused on "flawed men," Showtime's creation of a new niche fits well into the television landscape, and, most importantly, creates a differentiated brand identity for a network that is always competing with HBO (and now AMC) in the "original programming" category. I have argued that *Nurse Jackie*, with its half-hour format, combination of melodrama and comedy, and the inscrutable performance of its female star, challenges conventions of women's time in television and in life, creating a form that highlights the complexity of a middle-aged, working-class female subjectivity that must negotiate between the competing demands of a professional and domestic life. In a postfeminist climate that often embodies what Negra calls a "time crisis," *Nurse Jackie* rejects the idea that a woman must "have it all" both formally, through the limitations of the half-hour format, and thematically, through its female protagonists' cynical impatience and disappointment with the world around her. There is definitely more work to be done about the relationship of Jackie to her "network sisters" Nancy Botwin, Tara Gregson, and Cathy Jamison and these programs' relationship to Showtime's brand-name definition of a new kind of "desperate" housewife.[4]

SUGGESTED EPISODES FOR ADDITIONAL STUDY

Nurse Jackie
1:3. "Chicken Soup." Writ. Mark Hudis. Dir. Craig Zisk. June 22, 2009.
1:6. "Tiny Bubbles." Writ. Rick Cleveland. Dir. Craig Zisk. July 13, 2009.
1:10. "Ring Finger." Writ. Liz Brixius. Dir. Paul Feig. August 10, 2009.
2:1. "Comfort Food." Writ. Liz Brixius. Dir. Paul Feig. March 22, 2010.
2:4. "Apple Bong." Writ. Christine Zander. Dir. Alan Taylor. April 12, 2010.
2:8. "Monkey Bits." Writ. Liz Flahive. Dir. Paul Feig. May 10, 2010.
2:9. "P.O. Box." Writ. Mark Hudis. Dir. Paul Feig. May 17, 2010.
3:1. "Game On." Writ. Liz Brixius and Linda Wallem. Dir. Steve Buscemi. March 28, 2011.
3:4. "Mitten." Writ. Liz Flahive. Dir. Michael Lehmann. April 18, 2011.
3:7. "Orchids & Salami." Writ. Ellen Fairey. Dir. Bob Balaban. May 9, 2011.
3:11. "Batting Practice." Writ. Liz Flahive. Dir. Linda Wallem. June 13, 2011.
3:12. ". . . Deaf Blind Tumor Pee-Test . . ." Writ. Liz Brixius. Dir. Linda Wallem. June 20, 2011.

NOTES

1. See Tania Modleski (1983), Patricia Mellencamp (1986), Lynn Spigel (1992 and 2000), Lauren Rabinowitz (1989), and Mary Beth Haralovich (1992).
2. See Mellencamp (1986).
3. See Subramanian (2010).
4. I would like to thank Veena Hariharan for her insightful comments on this essay.

WORKS CITED

Butler, Jeremy G. *Television: Critical Methods and Applications*. 3rd ed. London: Lawrence Erlbaum Associates, 2007. Print.

Haralovich, Mary Beth. "Sitcoms and Suburbs: Positioning the 1950s Homemaker." *Private Screenings: Television and the Female Consumer.* Ed. Lynn Spigel and Denise Mann. Minneapolis: University of Minnesota Press, 1992. 111–42. Print.

Lesage, Julia. "Watching for Botox." FlowTV 11.11. April 8, 2010. Web. May 15, 2010.

Mellencamp, Patricia. "Situation Comedy, Feminism, and Freud: Discourses of Gracie and Lucy." *Studies in Entertainment: Critical Approaches to Mass Culture.* Ed. Tania Modleski. Bloomington: Indiana University Press, 1986. 80–95. Print.

Mills, Brett. "Comedy Verite: Contemporary Sitcom Form." *Screen* 45.1 (2004): 63–78. Print.

Mittell, Jason. "Narrative Complexity in Contemporary American Television." *The Velvet Light Trap* 58 (2006): 29–40. *Film and Literature International Index with Full Text.* Web. March 4, 2010.

Modleski, Tania. "The Rhythms of Reception: Daytime Television and Women's Work." *Regarding Television: Critical Approaches.* Ed. E. Ann Kaplan. Frederick, MD: University Publications of America, 1983. 66–74. Print.

Negra, Diane. "Time Crisis and the New Postfeminist Heterosexual Economy." *Hetero: Queering Representations of Straightness.* Ed. Sean Griffin. Albany: SUNY, 2009. 173–90. Print.

Newman, Michael Z. "From Beats to Arcs: Towards a Poetics of Television Narrative." *The Velvet Light Trap* 58 (2006): 16–28. Web. March 4, 2010.

"Pilot." *Nurse Jackie.* HBO. June 8, 2009. Television.

Rabinowitz, Lauren. "Sitcoms and Single Moms: Representations of Feminism on American TV." *Cinema Journal* 29.1 (1989): 3–19. *JSTOR.* Web. December 5, 2010.

Sedgwick, Eve Kosofsky. "'The L Word': Novelty in Normalcy." *The Chronicle of Higher Education.* January 16, 2004. Web. December 5, 2010.

Snarker, Dorothy. "Cable Brings us Complex Women, while Networks Think We're Uninteresting." *AfterEllen.com.* N.p., March 26, 2010. Web. October 10, 2010.

Spigel, Lynn. *Make Room for TV: Television and the Family Ideal in Postwar America.* Chicago: University of Chicago Press, 1992. Print.

———. "Women's Work." *Television: The Critical View.* 6th ed. Ed. Horace Newcombe. New York: Oxford University Press, 2000. 73–99. Print.

Subramanian, Janani. "A Bitter Pill: *Nurse Jackie* and a Discourse of Discontent." *FlowTV* 12.01. June 3, 2010. Web.

"Years of Service." *Nurse Jackie.* HBO. June 7, 2010. Television.

18

THE TELEVISION MUSICAL
Glee's *New Directions*

JACK HARRISON

> "If I were you, I'd recognize who your true friends are, and I'd practice a little more because you obviously have a lot you need to express," geeky glee club star, Rachel Berry (Lea Michele), says accusatorily to her social antagonist, cheerleading captain Quinn Fabray (Diana Agron). The two lock eyes, "Oh you have no idea." Drums begin in the background and then, just before turning to march off, Quinn breaks into song—"You Keep Me Hangin' On" by The Supremes.
> *GLEE* ("THROWDOWN")

Debuting in 2009, Fox's *Glee*, created by Ryan Murphy, Brad Falchuck, and Ian Brennan, has become the first successful musical television program to grace American screens. Television has, of course, always included music. Talent contests like *The Gong Show* (NBC, 1976–1978), televised music videos on channels like MTV, and, perhaps most notably, variety shows like *The Ed Sullivan Show* (CBS, 1948–1971) have played major roles in television history. However, up until this point, narrative fiction punctuated by break-out song and dance numbers has primarily been restricted to film and stage.

When Quinn sings "You Keep Me Hangin' On," she begins her performance walking down a set of stairs in her high school hallway, but the view of the camera soon cuts to cheerleading practice on the football field. It shifts again to feature the cheerleaders dressed in football costumes on the auditorium stage, and then rotates through these spaces for the remainder of the song.

Though the show's musical numbers differ, this scene signals *Glee*'s importation of the film genre's defining characteristic. In her seminal work on musical convention, *The Hollywood Musical*, Jane Feuer describes how these song and dance numbers transform an otherwise standard narrative by opening out into the fantastic. She writes:

> Musicals are built upon a foundation of dual registers with the contrast between narrative and number defining musical comedy as a form. The dichotomous manner in which the story is told—now spoken, now sung—is

a very different mode of presentation from the single thread of the usual Hollywood movie. (Feuer 68)

However, even as it confirms the linkages with musical film, this rendition of "You Keep Me Hangin' On" also illustrates what is distinct about *Glee* as a twenty-first-century U.S. televisual text.

The musical number on television is a decisive example of what Amit Rai has dubbed the media interval. In his book, *Untimely Bollywood*, Rai describes this concept within a Deleuzian framework as "the qualitative durations constituting the continuous multiplicity of a media assemblage, their mode of self-organization" (19). For Rai, the interval is a lens for reading multiple temporalities into media. Even as previous television scholarship has emphasized runtimes, scheduling, and commercials, Rai's analysis makes legible the importance of attending to manifold intervals, particularly as the definition of TV continues to blur into new media. These may include the ontological durations of reception as well as shorter intervals within episodes such as individual shots or, here, song-and-dance scenes.

To these points, this chapter is animated by three questions about *Glee*. First, how does televisual seriality shift the musical's generic formula? Second, how do *Glee*'s musical numbers operate temporally to disrupt the tradition of televisual realism? And finally, why *Glee* and why now?

Accordingly, the remainder of this essay is organized into three sections, each addressing *Glee*'s temporal dimensions. The first explores how musical conventions are changed by seriality, arguing that Feuer's notion of narrative synthesis in the musical film is still relevant to this show, but that the indefinite temporal expansion of televisual seriality creates opportunities for multiple and experimental romantic ruptures and unions. Thus, even as the promise of narrative synthesis remains ever-present, it is ultimately always postponed for another episode, another season. In the second section, closer attention is paid to the cause of the ruptures that necessitate this drive to synthesis—the musical numbers themselves—reading the lyric time of these scenes against the history of televisual realism to highlight the break from tradition they represent. This is followed by an examination of the tactics undertaken to re-ground an audience in danger of being alienated by the text. Finally, in order to begin to address the question of why *Glee* was the show to bring the musical format to television where other series have failed, the third section will read the show's musical numbers through the lens of Rai's interval, showing how their circulation, independent of the greater text, has tapped into novel flows of sensation and revenue, particularly through digital downloads.

This essay aims the scholarly spotlight on a television program that has enjoyed critical acclaim and mass popularity in order to make legible how it has taken both television and the musical in New Directions. Appearing at the conclusion of the twenty-first century's first decade, the shifts that *Glee* represents may be emblematic of new pleasures and expanding narrative possibilities in this cultural moment. But equally important is the way these formal changes correlate with new temporal, aesthetic, and technological tactics to encourage consumption, obliging media scholars anew to map the dynamics between the culture industry, the text, and its viewers.

SERIALITY AND SYNTHESIS

Glee does not constitute a seamless importation of the musical film genre from big to small screen. This shift in medium has brought the discursive arrangement of the televisual into conversation with musical conventions resulting in new formations for each. For the musical, these novelties include the introduction of commercial breaks and a flexible and ever-expanding list of creative collaborators writing and directing the text, but the most significant shift away from the show's filmic antecedents is its temporal reformatting to fit the model of televisual seriality.

The term seriality here is not meant to cite the decreasingly meaningful distinction between the TV series, designating distinct narratives linked by characters or settings, and the television serial, a single narrative split into installments (Mazdon 9). Rather, it gestures toward both—the tightened narrative schemes emerging from what television scholars term the *quality* shows of the eighties, as well as the longer history of intertextual programming in U.S. television (Feuer, Kerr, and Vahimagi 16; Hammond 75–82).

The serial musical has rarely been attempted and has almost never been successful. There have been a few examples of failed musical TV shows, most notably 1990's *Hull High* (NBC) and *Cop Rock* (ABC), neither of which aired more than eleven episodes. And even in film and on stage, musical sequels have almost always flopped.

The reason for this can be connected to what Feuer describes as "the musical's drive toward synthesis" (81). She writes of the genre, "In the Hollywood musical, heterogeneous levels are created so that they may be homogenized in the end through the union of the romantic couple" (Feuer 68). In other words, the departure from realism in the spatial and temporal ruptures of the musical numbers raises the stakes for a climactic heterosexual union to re-ground the spectator's viewing, which, in turn, necessitates a narrative finality that has no opening for a sequel or other continuation.

But the televisual convention of seriality does not allow this pat finality. Instead, its narratives are constructed to play out repeatedly every season. However, it is not this essay's contention that seriality makes Feuer's drive to narrative synthesis irrelevant for *Glee*. Rather, it hangs like a specter, always seemingly just beyond the text, and the promise of its ever-postponed fulfillment is made to encourage a committed audience rather than alienate it. This is executed through tantalizing, smaller moments of coupling at key junctures within this indefinite temporal expansion that create the opportunities for multiple and experimental romantic ruptures and unions.

It is no mistake that the setting for this type of musical is a high school. The fast-paced movement between couplings that this model encourages is perfectly suited to adolescent experimentation. When she sings, "You Keep Me Hangin' On," for example, Quinn's repurposing of the Supremes centers both on the emotional challenges of her pregnancy as well as how these challenges are inextricably bound up with the complex web of romantic relationships she finds herself in.

It is revealed over the course of the show's first season that although she is dating Finn (Cory Monteith), the football quarterback whom she feels is an appropriate and reliable boyfriend, Quinn's true romantic inclinations are toward his best friend, Puck (Mark Salling), the show's bad boy figure. Puck is also revealed to be the actual father of Quinn's baby. The moment that starts the Supremes number highlights another complication: though Quinn has eschewed her socially inappropriate lover to stay with Finn, the feelings between Finn and Rachel have grown, causing her to feel even more unmoored.

All four possible heterosexual combinations of these characters serve at various times to tease viewers with the promise of a coupling that also sates "the musical's drive toward synthesis between fantasy and reality" (Feuer 81). However, in each instance, the synthesis is undermined even as it is achieved. For example, in episode four, Finn and Quinn are shown coming together for an intimate embrace after Finn leads the football team to victory even in the wake of the startling news of Quinn's pregnancy. This shot is immediately followed by one in which Puck is shown watching their interaction, foreshadowing the inevitable revelation of the baby's parentage that will mark the dissolution of their union ("Preggers"). Quinn and Puck also come together in several scenes, such as in episode eleven when they babysit together, successfully cooperating to wrangle three children. However, by the end of the episode, the veneer of the union is shattered when Quinn discovers that Puck was also engaging in text message sex with another woman the entire time ("Hairography").

The first season's focus on these four protagonists already constitutes a change from what Rick Altman describes as the musical's "dual focus" (19). Altman maps the classic Hollywood musical as being dyadic in form, organizing its every element "around parallel stars of opposite sex and radically divergent values" (19). It is notable then that these four are still not the only characters used to arouse viewers' desire for union. Beyond the Quinn-Finn-Rachel-Puck web, the show's rich supporting cast is also involved in an ever-shifting mosaic of relationships that both gesture toward the narrative synthesis of the musical film while also highlighting how *Glee* more broadly distributes its character focus. For example, Brittany (Heather Morris), a supporting cheerleader turned glee club singer, dates both Artie (Kevin McHale), following his summer breakup with Tina (Jenna Ushkowitz), and Kurt (Chris Colfer), a gay character trying to be straight in order to bond with his father. Additionally, she is shown coming together in sexual union with her romantic best friend and peer cheerleader, Santana. That there is time to build moments of synthesis even around figures billed as "recurring characters" speaks to the differences of filmic and serial temporality.

Even more disruptive to what Feuer lays out as formulaic in the classic Hollywood musical is the way *Glee* experiments with partial synthesis through moments of union between combinations of characters whose relationships are not romantic and among the group as a whole. Among the first season's most memorable moments are those between Kurt Hummel and his father, Burt, in which a kind of synthesis is achieved between parent and child as they negotiate his coming out as gay. In episode four, following his success on the football team, Kurt reveals his sexuality to his father (Mike O'Malley). He responds, "I guess I'm not totally in love with the idea, but if that's who you are, there's nothing I can do about it, and I love you just as much," before their bodies come literally into the physical union of embrace ("Preggers"). Additionally, a majority of the episodes conclude with musical numbers intended to highlight the solidarity among the glee club members overall. Interestingly, this kind of synthesis need not be undermined immediately because it is not romantic, as it still provides a level of climactic satisfaction.

Romantic hijinks have often been part of the musical, but their function has not historically been to arouse the climactic pleasures of union. However, as mentioned, this adaptation is key to the successful importation of the genre onto the small screen. Rather than denying closure altogether and leaving audiences particularly disoriented because of the rapturous bi-modal narrative style, *Glee* leans on a structure of ever-delayed resolution, teasing its audience with the vast open field of possibilities.

LYRICISM AND REALISM

In *Television Studies: The Key Concepts* Bernadette Casey and colleagues describe realism as "a system of conventions, which represents the world to us through a series of devices. For example, television presents the viewer with narrative structures that are tightly patterned ways of organising reality" (Casey et al. 194). Concerning the prevalence of this system for the small screen, the authors argue that "Television narratives tend to be recognisable, reassuring and comforting" (Casey et al. 194). This can be connected to the profit structures of broadcast television, which have traditionally relied on attracting a mass audience. Any divergence from a standard, realistic narrative even within fiction threatens to alienate some viewers, which in turn may alienate advertisers and threaten profits.

Having discussed what television changed about musical temporality, attention now turns to the other side of this dialogue to examine how televisual norms are subverted by the musical's defining characteristic: the song-and-dance number. Unlike other prime-time network programs that focus on a single narrative mode, an episode of *Glee* allocates its time between standard story and five to seven scenes of lyric musical expression. This challenges the norm of televisual realism but navigates that challenge through two ameliorating factors—the use of familiar music and the excuse of live performance—in order not to alienate its audience.

Formally, the surrealism of the musical number has been discussed in terms of spatial metaphors. Feuer describes them as creating "a secondary, more stylized fictional world," opening up "the secondary, the unreal, the dream world" (68). In the case of *Glee* and "You Keep Me Hangin' On," this is most easily understood in terms of the third performance space—the stage. While the school hallway and football field both appear as they do in other scenes, the auditorium stage is transformed by a lighted backdrop, blinking in time with the rhythm; the cheerleaders' whimsical football costumes; and the sports props they use in their choreography, all of which suggest Feuer's dream space.

In terms of time, these numbers operate two ways. On the one hand, temporal fantasy play opens up along with that of the spatial. This is evident, for example, in the way Quinn's performance seems to take place *simultaneously* in three locations. On the other hand, however, the music itself actually anchors the scene into a comprehensible temporality. This effect is an example of what Michel Chion ascribes more broadly to sound in moving-image media when he suggests that "sound endows shots with temporal linearization" (13). He writes:

> When a sequence of images does not necessarily show temporal succession in the actions it depicts—that is, we can read them equally as simultaneously or successive—the addition of realistic, diegetic sound imposes on a sequence a sense of real time, like normal everyday experiences and, above all, a sense of time that is linear and sequential. (Chion 17–18)

This is linked to Chion's conceptualization of synch points, the "audiovisually salient synchronous meeting of sound event and sight event" (223). In this case, the sound in question is Quinn's singing and the synch point is her moving lips so that even as viewers may be disoriented by the scene's whimsy, the linear narrative of the song emanating from her realistically moving mouth keeps them temporally grounded in the scene.

In terms of the narrative, these numbers diverge from realist storytelling in their mode of expression and use of time. The musical numbers are lyric in their substantive focus on emotional content and the delimitation of particular moments for deeper expression of those feelings. For the almost two minutes that Quinn sings "You Keep Me Hangin' On," the audience is absorbed into an exploration of her angst. As Chion writes, "Music makes space and time pliable, subject to contraction or distention," highlighting its utility in marking off separate space and time for content that is substantially divergent from the norms of television (82).

Amid this emergent form, *Glee*'s creators have taken steps to stabilize their viewers. First, where *Cop Rock* and *Hull High* attempted to produce original music, the *Glee* team opted to repurpose existing songs, adding familiar content to Chion's observation about the song's linearizing and thus grounding effects. Of course not all the music is familiar to everyone. For example, it is likely that a large portion of *Glee*'s audience did not know the Supremes' song when Quinn sang it, but taken as a whole, the show's selections bear a comforting referential quality. This extends beyond the sonic as well in that the numbers often take visual cues from the songs' sources. These references range from the facial cosmetics of Kiss to Lady Gaga's costumes and choreography, and even full-scale recreations of Britney Spears's music videos.

The second militating factor is the excuse of live performance. Feuer points out the importance of the internal audience for constructing a rationale for the musical's song-and-dance scenes (23–48). By staging them as actual performances, the television audience is better able to understand why the characters are singing and dancing even if other surrealistic elements such as spatial and temporal drift are incorporated. For *Glee*, this manifests in the glee club's rehearsal numbers, school performances, and competitions.

In addition to these intentional tactics for maintaining *Glee*'s viewership, contemporary consumers may also feel more comfortable with such diegetic play because of increased familiarity with new media. Exemplary here is the Internet short-form video such as that found on youtube.com, which may integrate diverse temporalities and narrative devices within a single piece. Nevertheless, *Glee*'s musical numbers represent a significant risk in their divergence from the tradition of televisual realism, which is imbricated in the economic structures of network TV reliant on attracting as many viewers as possible. Their lyric temporal and substantive operations risk alienating viewers because of this shift away from a basic realism assumed to be universally appealing. However, as shown, *Glee*'s creators guard against this possibility through the use of familiar music and the excuse of live performance. Additionally, the following section explores specific advantages of this storytelling mode as it builds connections with affective and monetary flows formerly unheard of for TV.

HISTORY, TECHNOLOGY, AND AFFECT

This essay is haunted by the question of why *Glee* and why now? Even in discussing the dialogue the show creates between musical convention and televisual norms, it has already touched on ways *Glee* has mobilized the tension between the two to encourage rather than alienate its viewership. But the question remains, why after so much ambivalence and failure was *Glee* ultimately successful at the end of the first decade of the twenty-first century?

A complete examination of this question is beyond the scope of this chapter, but this section will offer two ways *Glee*'s creators have used the interval of the musical number in ways that are specific to the present cultural moment and tap into flows of sensation and revenue to cement its success.

This analysis takes Rai's concept of the media interval as its point of departure. In laying out this model, Rai suggests a three-part method for identifying significant intervals in media. He suggests they are "stochastic *and* patterned," that they "render assemblages in perpetual nonequilibrium," and that they are "temporally bound structures through which definite sets and forms of information circulate" (Rai 19). *Glee*'s musical numbers, then, qualify on all three counts. To the first point, they are dispersed throughout episodes at moments that are unpredictable to the audience but that are determined by the creators to have an optimal impact. To the second, they are divergent from the main diegesis of the text and potentially disorienting as discussed in section two. And to the third, they occur in durations of three to seven minutes, and, most important here, tap into specific affective flows meant to encourage certain forms of engagement. In what follows, two such habituated forms of engagement are explored: viewer loyalty encouraged by structures of feeling in music and audience desire to extend that feeling through purchase of mp3s and soundtrack albums.

In her essay, "The Writer/Producer in American Television," Roberta Pearson describes the shift in the way shows were valued in the era of the post-network oligarchy:

> By the twenty-first century, shows succeeded, that is, warranted profitable advertising rates, with ever lower audience numbers . . . The increasing fragmentation of the audience among the networks and their competition meant that a programme's demographic profile counted for more than sheer numbers. (15)

During the period of network domination, then, it is clear that the model for building programming was based on a unified text with a singular, specific affective charge meant to have universal appeal. However, following the shift Pearson describes, the industry's focus has changed, fragmenting audiences and evaluating and emphasizing their differences. It is only within this latter milieu that *Glee*'s complex strategy for building a heterogeneous audience could have emerged. This is particularly emblemized by *Glee*'s use of music from a diverse range of generic and temporal-historic moments of origin and the variety of sensations it encourages.

The earliest songs adapted and rerecorded for *Glee* were from the 1920s, Louis Armstrong's "When You're Smiling" and "Happy Days Are Here Again" by Milton Ager and Jack Yellen. These are followed by "Get Happy" from *The Nine-Fifteen Revue* and four other songs from the 1930s, and, of course subsequent decades are well represented including "You Keep Me Hangin' On" from 1966 and the show's iconic Journey covers from the 1970s and 1980s.

In the second section of this essay I explored how this use of existing music mobilized sensations of familiarity to guard against viewer alienation by the show's experimental format. However, familiarity is not the only effect being tapped by the show's diverse musical selections. By using this range of music, *Glee*'s creative team has knit together an audience of viewers whose relationships to individual songs vary significantly from nostalgic and reminiscent to sentimental or excitable. This appeals to various groups who were familiar with songs from across the historic and generic map. For those who did not know a given song, like the potentially large group of youth who might not immediately recognize "You Keep Me Hangin' On," the show performs a similar operation to what John Mundy describes as occurring with early television broadcasts of rock 'n' roll. He writes, "What most characterizes television's relationship with the new youth music and culture is its insistence on rendering it safe and comprehensible to . . . mixed audiences" (Mundy 8). However, in this case, the operation potentially moves both ways, making older music relevant to youth as well as making contemporary music accessible to older audience members.

In addition to the multiple affective flows tapped by *Glee*'s stochastic musical intervals, so too have these break-out scenes allowed for new flows of revenue. Similar to Lalitha Gopalan's description of the circulation of Bollywood songs independent of their filmic origins (Rai 8), recordings of *Glee*'s songs have been sold on CDs and as digital downloads on iTunes. Because of this, thirteen million copies of digital singles have been downloaded, and as of 2009, the show had already had twenty-five singles chart on the *Billboard* Hot 100, the second highest number in history next to the Beatles (Trust; "Glee").

This process of commodity re-creation and circulation hearkens back to a line in *The Hollywood Musical*, in which Feuer describes a common theme for the genre: "In its more literal form, the process of bringing music to a world lacking in music is common to a dozen musicals" (72). Although she may not have had this commercial operation in mind particularly because of its reliance on the contemporary technologies of iTunes, Feuer's pronouncement literalizes the way that *Glee*'s creators have made their franchise profitable through the enduring power and texture of song.

CONCLUSION

This essay relies to a degree on generic and medium-based generalizations for academic convenience. Of course *Glee* is not the first musical to disrupt the drive to narrative synthesis; the film genre has come a long way in the half century since the period Feuer discusses most. American musicals like *Hedwig and the Angry Inch* (2001) have remained concerned with synthesis as a narrative device but challenged its normatively gendered heterosexuality, while U.S. audiences have also been increasingly exposed to musicals from abroad drawing on divergent traditions like the Danish production *Dancer in the Dark* (2000), which ends in death. Likewise, *Glee* is not the first television production to employ surrealistic temporalities as the other chapters in this book well illustrate. However, building these arguments on the conventions of both has allowed me to make legible how the intersection of the musical genre and the medium of television creates novel tensions resulting in transformation for both.

Of course, my assertions do not constitute the limit of the analytic possibilities the concepts of rupture and union may offer in revealing *Glee*. Particularly vital opportunities for analysis lie in the show's politics of minority and diversity and how, even amid so-called *positive representations* and *inclusion*, the unity and solidarity of the characters may be read as being built at the expense of disability and race. Further, *Glee* must be interrogated against the histories of stolen black music. Even as appropriation culture becomes the norm in both grassroots and commercial media, these vectors of sampling remain crucial for understanding revenue flows, those who benefit, and those who do not. Additionally, although the analysis here has been limited to the United States context, *Glee*'s global circulation offers another area for productive future analysis. As of 2010, ABS-CBN's *1DOL* had just been canceled after a successful thirty-five episode run in the Philippines. Citing *Glee* as a primary inspiration, *1DOL* could provide a point of departure in further making visible the contingencies of the texts, genres, and media associated with both franchises.

Glee has brought the generic conventions of the film musical in dialogue with the practices of television as a medium. Televisual seriality transformed the musical by disallowing the traditional closure of narrative synthesis through climactic heterosexual coupling meant to homogenize the narrative otherwise rife with rupture from the musical numbers. Lyric musical time has also transformed television in its departure from realism, even as *Glee*'s creators have sought to mitigate the potential negative effects by building in the excuse of live performance and using familiar music. Further, this familiar music was adapted from all over the American historical music map, knitting together a mass audience by attracting various styles and periods of existing fans while making the music relevant to all. This music was then sold on iTunes instantly, connecting households to the songs in order to generate money for the franchise in a whole new way.

The stakes of this chapter are tripartite. Reflecting much of the rhetoric about the broader project of television studies, *Glee*'s popularity, alone, begs the question of how and what kinds of meanings are being made in and through the text. But for this show, its appearance in a new century when increasing experimentation is rapidly dislodging assumptions as well as marking out major lines of continuity with the past makes it even more crucial that these processes come under critical scrutiny. The painful pleasure of the ever-postponed closure offered in the televised musical is recognizable even as it compels loyal viewing. Likewise, the joy of instant access to mp3 audio files of the show's music immediately following each episode is inextricably bound up with the text as commodity. Media scholars, however, must accept these contradictions, allowing for growth and transformation of genre theory, television studies, and media studies as they move in New Directions.

SUGGESTED EPISODES FOR ADDITIONAL STUDY

Glee
1:1. "Pilot." Writ. Ryan Murphy, Brad Falchuck, and Ian Brennan. Dir. Ryan Murphy. May 19, 2009.
1:6. "Vitamin D." Writ. Ryan Murphy. Dir. Elodie Keene. September 9, 2009.
1:13. "Sectionals." Writ. and dir. Brad Falchuck. December 2, 2009.
1:22. "Journey to Regionals." Writ. and dir. Brad Falchuck. June 8, 2010.
2:1. "Auditions." Writ. Ian Brennan. Dir. Brad Falchuck. September 21, 2010.
2:4. "Duets." Writ. Ian Brennan. Dir. Eric Stoltz. October 5, 2010.
1:7. "The Substitute." Writ. Ian Brennan. Dir. Ryan Murphy. November 16, 2010.
2:19. "Rumours." Writ. Ryan Murphy. Dir. Tim Hunter. May 3, 2011.
2:22. "New York." Writ. and dir. Brad Falchuck. May 24, 2011.

WORKS CITED

Altman, Rick. *The American Film Musical.* Bloomington: Indiana University Press, 1987. Print.
Casey, Bernadette, Neil Casey, Ben Calvert, Liam French, and Justin Lewis. *Television Studies: The Key Concepts.* New York: Routledge, 2002. Print.
Chion, Michel. *Audio-Vision: Sound on Screen.* New York: Columbia University Press, 1994. Print.
Feuer, Jane. *The Hollywood Musical.* 2nd ed. Bloomington: Indiana University Press, 1993. Print.
Feuer, Jane, Paul Kerr, and Tise Vahimagi, eds. *MTM "Quality Television."* London: BFI, 1984. Print.
"Glee: The Music, The Rocky Horror Glee Show in Stores October 19." PRNewswire.com. September 28, 2010. Web. October 5, 2010.
"Hairography." *Glee.* Fox. November 25, 2009. Television.
Hammond, Michael. "The Series/Serial Form." *The Contemporary Television Series.* Ed. Michael Hammond and Lucy Mazon. Edinburgh: Edinburgh University Press, 2005. 75–82. Print.

Mazdon, Lucy. "Introduction: Histories." *The Contemporary Television Series*. Ed. Michael Hammond and Lucy Mazon. Edinburgh: Edinburgh University Press, 2005. 3–9. Print.

Mundy, John. *Popular Music on Screen: From Hollywood Musical to Music Video*. New York: Manchester University Press, 1999. Print.

Pearson, Roberta. "The Writer/Producer in American Television." Ed. Michael Hammond and Lucy Mazon. Edinburgh: Edinburgh University Press, 2005. 11–26. Print.

"Preggers." *Glee*. Fox. September 23, 2009. Television.

Rai, Amit. *Untimely Bollywood: Globalization and India's New Media Assemblage*. Durham, NC: Duke University Press, 2009. Print.

"Throwdown." *Glee*. Fox. October 14, 2009. Television.

Trust, Gary. "Best Of 2009: By-The-Numbers." Billboard.com. December 29, 2009. Web. October 25, 2010.

PART V

PLAYING OUTSIDE OF THE BOX
The Role Time Plays in Fan Fiction, Online Communities, and Audience Studies

19

"NOTHING HAPPENS UNLESS FIRST A DREAM"
TV Fandom, Narrative Structure, and the Alternate Universes of Bones

MELANIE CATTRELL

> We should certainly avoid celebrating a process that commodifies fan cultural production and sells it back to us with a considerable markup.
> —HENRY JENKINS ("AFTERWORD" 362)

In the tradition of *Remington Steele* (NBC, 1982–1987) and *Moonlighting* (ABC, 1985–1989), the current Fox series *Bones* (Fox 2005–Present) aims to be more than just a crime procedural, striving for a mix between drama and romantic comedy. At the center of *Bones* is the relationship between forensic anthropologist Temperance "Bones" Brennan (Emily Deschanel) and her partner, FBI agent Seeley Booth (David Boreanaz). In this chapter, I will discuss the way *Bones* creator Hart Hanson manipulates conventional storytelling methods to explore a romantic relationship between the two lead characters without disrupting the larger narrative of the program. I argue that Hanson borrows narrative techniques that fan fiction writers have been using for decades—techniques that allow fans to create their own stories without disturbing the narrative flow of the primary text.

This play with narrative time first becomes evident in the fourth-season finale, "The End in the Beginning," or "EitB." This episode portrays an alternate reality where Brennan and Booth, who are not romantically paired on the show, are shown as a happily married couple. Furthermore, "EitB" places both full and recurring characters in an alternative universe, creating a dreamlike reality for them to operate within. Hanson followed up the romantic tension created in "EitB" in the fifth-season episode, "The Parts in the Sum of the Whole," in which the audience was presented a different type of alternate universe: an episode which, through flashbacks, told of Brennan and Booth's first meeting. In both scenarios, Hanson did what he cannot do within the narrative structure of the show: place the two lead characters in a romantic relationship.

Hanson's attempts to play with narrative structure and time are remarkably similar to writers of fan fiction, who often place romantic pairings in situations that do not occur within the actual series. Through his narrative play, Hanson has found a way to give fans what (he believes) they want, while continuing to present a weekly show that builds on his characters' unresolved sexual tension. Furthermore, Hanson complicates the already tense relationship between producer and fan, as he appears to be using the tools of both.

INTERNET COMMUNITIES AND TV FANDOM

One of the most popular cultural productions of fan communities is fan fiction. Loosely defined by fan scholar Sheenagh Pugh as "fiction based on a situation and characters created by someone else" (9), fan fiction serves as a way for fans to work through their own expectations and desires for their favorite fictional characters. Although early fan fiction was distributed through mailing lists and fanzines, the Internet has allowed for endless fan communities to develop, communicate with one another with ease, and to share their work. Fan scholars often reference Janice Radway's *Reading the Romance: Women, Patriarchy, and Popular Literature* as a starting point for this research. In this foundational text, Radway examines the reactions that various women have to romance novels and attempts to learn why women continue to become involved in works that can be seen as misogynistic. More important, she argues that the romance novels can be read as texts with multiple meanings:

> whatever the theoretical possibility of an infinite number of readings, in fact, there are patterns or regularities to what viewers and readers bring to texts in large part because they acquire specific cultural competencies as a consequence of their particular social location. Similar readings are produced . . . because similarly located readers learn a similar set of reading strategies and interpretive codes that they bring to bear upon the texts they encounter. (8)

Therefore, the meaning of the text does not come from the original author, but by the group interpreting it. This principle is also found in Camille Bacon-Smith's *Enterprising Women: Television Fandom and the Creation of Popular Myth*, as she takes an ethnographic approach to women who have formed *Star Trek* fan clubs to discuss their multiple interpretations of the series. Unlike the women profiled in Bacon-Smith's writing, the Internet now allows fans to trade fan fiction, fan videos, and so forth more quickly, not having to wait until a convention or a mailed newsletter. Furthermore, open Internet communities allow viewers to dabble in fan culture without needing to take the time or expense of traveling to a fan convention or meeting.

In *Textual Poachers: Television Fans and Participatory Culture*, fan scholar Henry Jenkins combines many of the ethnographic approaches used within the work of Radway and Bacon-Smith and applies them to a fan community of which he is a member. Jenkins—who is, among other things, a *Star Trek* fan—traces the history of fan culture from an insider perspective. His work echoes that of Radway as he discusses the impact that groups have upon the reading of texts: "Fan reception cannot and does not exist in isolation, but is always shaped through input from other fans and motivated, at least partially, by a desire for further interaction with a larger cultural community" (Jenkins, *Textual* 76). This statement is important not only because it emphasizes the notion that groups of fans form collective readings of texts, but also because it emphasizes the social aspect of fandom. As Jenkins explains in the first chapter of his text, fans are often encouraged to "get a life" and to dismiss their fannish pursuits (*Textual* 9–49). Jenkins's work dismisses that notion by explaining that fan culture is neither lonely nor isolating, but rather, it is a social atmosphere where relationships and connections are formed.

Furthermore, the inclusion of Internet fan communities into the study of popular culture is not always an easy one, as Nancy K. Baym discuses in *Tune In, Log On: Soaps, Fandom, and Online Community*. In her text, she discusses her personal experiences as a soap opera fan and graduate student posting in a soap opera online discussion group primarily dedicated to the discussion of *All My Children*. While she claims that her work is ethnographic and follows in the tradition of Radway, she also states that ethnographic definitions of community are not always applicable when discussing groups of Internet users, as ethnographers have often placed too many limitations on their definitions of community (Baym 18–19). Perhaps by studying the interaction of posters on various online communities, a new methodology will eventually appear, one that understands that folk groups and communities are not always bound by language or location.

Baym's notion that Internet communities challenge concepts of temporality is also an interesting one. Certainly, TV fans, for example, can chat with one another during or immediately following the broadcast of an episode, creating both a sense of immediacy and intimacy among the community members. Internet discussion boards, however, may also be viewed by newcomers to the fandom months, even years, after their original postings. Thus, many discussion boards serve as a place for timely discussion and as an archive of fans' thoughts and reactions to a particular episode or storyline. Baym believes that Internet communities have changed the way in which audiences are viewed, and that perhaps this will lead to a difference in the way these communities are studied: "In short, even if one wanted to find a nicely bounded, self-defined audience community of interrelated members, it has not been easy. The Internet has changed that, in part by making audience communities more visible and in part by enabling their proliferation" (19).

Although much scholarship exists in the realm of television fan communities and fan production, little has been produced discussing fan relationships to crime dramas. This lack of scholarship is surprising, given their popularity and longevity. In *Prime Time Law Enforcement*, author James Carlson explains that crime shows have risen in popularity over the last twenty-five years. Carlson argues that viewers expect their shows to follow a specific formula: "Each program must include a crime, someone who commits it, someone who is victimized by it, and someone to bring the criminal to justice" (32). This predictably is certainly one of the reasons why the procedural crime drama is so popular; the viewer receives satisfaction when justice is brought to the criminal. This predictability extends to the way such narratives unfold. Crime dramas rarely play with narrative time; they—in the tradition of the crime novel, to which many current TV crime dramas, including *Bones*, owe a great debt—follow a strict formula that allows for little deviation. This tight format allows each episode to stand alone, thereby making crime dramas popular in syndication, as they do not have to be watched sequentially or with prior knowledge of the program. This lack of serialization, however, works against the development of the main characters. Fans of these shows, therefore, often take it on themselves to fill in the gaps, creating "personal" lives for their favorite characters through fan fiction. Fan communities for such programs are difficult to analyze, however. Episodic, rather than serial, dramas tend to lead to a broad audience, from viewers who watch only on a periodic basis to those who immerse themselves within the fan culture surrounding a specific show. Whereas a cult program, for example, may have a targeted audience—and, consequently, an easily identifiable and centralized fan community—the audience of the episodic crime drama is far more difficult to determine.

ALTERNATE UNIVERSE I
"The End in the Beginning"

In March 2009, Emily Deschanel and David Boreanaz appeared on the cover of *TV Guide* with the headline "He's Just that Into Her." In the article, which operates under the premise that Bones and Booth will "seal the deal in May," the actors are questioned about how "Booth and Brennan are moving from the lab to the bedroom" (Keeps 29). Interestingly, Deschanel mentions her favorite TV couples are Liz Lemon and Jack Donaghy from the sitcom *30 Rock* and Olivia Benson and Elliot Stabler from the crime procedural *Law & Order: SVU*. Although both pairings maintain significant fan followings, neither are romantically paired within the text of their respective shows. Along with this article, the actors appeared on a variety of different talk shows and media outlets during the season, always proclaiming the same "party line"—that the season would end with the characters in bed together.

As previously mentioned, *Bones* focuses on the partnership of FBI special agent Seeley Booth and forensic anthropologist Temperance Brennan. Partially based on the life of author Kathy Reichs—a forensic anthropologist and creator of the *Temperance Brennan* crime novels—*Bones* takes on many characteristics prevalent in crime dramas. Each episode stands alone, and character development is often secondary to crime solving. As with most crime dramas, the lead characters are supported by a larger cast of characters: Dr. Camille Saroyan (Tamara Taylor), forensic pathologist and head of the Forensic Division of the Jeffersonian; Angela Montenegro (Michaela Conlin), Brennan's closest friend and an artist who uses her talent to reconstruct the faces of crime victims; Dr. Jack Hodgins (T. J. Thyne), an entomologist who specializes in "bugs and slime"; Zack Addy (Eric Millegan), Brennan's doctoral student and assistant, who, in later seasons, is replaced by a revolving door of various interns; and Dr. Lance Sweets (John Francis Daley), a psychologist added to the cast in later seasons, both to serve as a criminal profiler and to study the relationship between Brennan and Booth for his own research on workplace dynamics. Although the characters are more developed than some on procedural crime dramas, such as those within the *CSI* and *Law & Order* franchises, in most episodes, the personal lives of the characters are secondary to the "crime of the week." At times, however, *Bones* does delve into the personal lives of its characters. In the episodes leading up to "EitB," Booth experienced several hallucinations. In the episode directly preceding "EitB," Booth entered the hospital to have brain surgery, as it was revealed that he had been suffering from a brain tumor. It was with this anticipation that "EitB" was greeted by fans.

From the first scene, "EitB" is clearly not a typical episode of *Bones*. It begins (and ends) with voice-over narration by Hodgins. His introductory voice-over, heard as Brennan is shown climbing into Booth's bed, alerts the viewer that this episode will be unique:

> People say you only live once, but people are as wrong about that as they are about everything. In the darkest moments before dawn, a woman

returns to her bed. What life is she leading? Is it the same life the woman was living half an hour ago? A day ago? A year ago? Who is this man? Do they lead separate lives, or is a single life shared?

Hodgins's commentary questions the boundaries of time, hinting to the possibility of alternate universes. Furthermore, his words give the viewer permission (not that permission is needed, of course) to view this episode outside of the narrative space and time of the series.

Indeed, the universe presented in "EitB," is unique. The characters exist in an alternate reality where, instead of working in the forensic laboratory at the fictitious Jeffersonian Institute, they work at a nightclub called "The Lab." The fourth-season interns, along with the main characters and some frequent guest characters, play a unique role in this universe. The characters within "EitB" are all intriguing; for the most part, they are either similar to the real characters or (in another referential sense) direct opposites of them. Uptight intern Clark, for example, is a flamboyant rap artist; globe-trotting artist Angela struggles with visual aids and geography. Zack, as in "real life," is revealed to be "the kind of guy who would go away for a crime he didn't commit" (a fact unknown to anyone outside of Sweets, and, of course, the audience), and Sweets is a bartender, which he concludes is "practically a psychologist." Hodgins, our narrator, is a "best-selling pulp crap crime novelist." Booth and Brennan's relationship stays the same; although they are not "crime-solvers," they still attempt to solve a murder committed in their nightclub. While doing so, they operate in the same fashion familiar to viewers; Booth operates from a place of emotion, while Brennan operates from a place of logic. The only change to this partnership—which is always a refreshing reversal of gender stereotypes—is their marriage. "EitB" allows the viewers see how Booth and Brennan would exist simply as a couple.

At the end, the episode is revealed to be a combination of Booth's comatose dream and Brennan's most recent novel, which she is writing and reading aloud to Booth while sitting at his hospital bedside. In the last moment of "EitB," Booth awakens only to ask Brennan quizzically, "Who are you?" This ending, like the rest of the episode, led to a great deal of discussion and outrage among fans. Furthermore, it spawned a great deal of fan fiction from authors who were unsure what Booth's final comment really meant. When season six began, would he have amnesia? If so, how would this affect the show?

In order to understand the way in which "EitB" borrows from cult fandom, one must first understand the impetus behind creation of fan fiction. In "So, What's the Story? Story-Oriented Fans and Series-Oriented Fans: A

Complex of Behaviors," the Internet and TV fan scholar Mary Kirby-Diaz addresses fan fiction:

> Fans write fan fiction to "correct" what they perceive as poor script writing and incorrect characterization, to deepen a relationship they'd like to see—or see subtextually, on the shows they are engaged in, and to amuse/entertain themselves and other fans . . . Consequently, fans who would like to see particular relationships occur—or who want to read more about a particular relationship, will search for, read, and sometimes write fan fiction. Fan fiction—which is available on the Internet, for free—thus reinforces "ship loyalty." (69)

Fan fiction serves as a way for fans to create romantic narratives for their favorite TV couples—regardless of whether the characters are actually a couple within the text of the television show. It also serves as a way to play with time, and to reimagine new or different realities for one's favorite fictional characters. Pugh concurs, describing alternate universe (AU) fiction, as one of the various types of fan fiction—along with "sequels, prequels, crossovers, and missing scenes" (47) that play with narrative time and structure. While some of these genres simply add to an existing canon, the AU fiction complicates time in a different way:

> AU's, in some fandoms, are known as "what ifs." They are deliberate departures from canon; what if this, and not that, had happened. [. . .] The name "AU" comes from the idea, familiar in futuristic fiction, that there might be any number of parallel universes in which the same people live out different destinies. (Pugh 61)

Pugh further acknowledges that "the idea that one man might have different potential fates . . . is a lot older than science fiction," but is a common literary trope (61). These descriptions of alternate universe fiction mirror Hodgins's voice-over at the beginning of "EitB," as he reminds the viewers that characters can lead multiple lives and have multiple realities. Like authors of alternate reality fan fiction (or fan videos), in "EitB," Hanson takes his own characters and places them in another created universe, while continually referring back to the original text. By doing so, he both stretches the boundaries of the procedural crime drama and achieves his goal of placing the two lead characters in a romantic relationship. Furthermore, he acknowledges to fans that he is aware of their writing techniques. *Bones* fan fiction abounds on the Internet, and Hanson is acutely aware of *Bones*'s fan base, engaging with them at conventions and on Twitter. In fact, Hanson is so known for his engagement with fans through his Twitter account that he was profiled in a *Los Angeles Times* article about celebrities who Twitter, described as "an active Twitterer known for his gently ironic on-set updates and affectionate exchanges with the show's hard-core fans" (Collins par. 2).

After the airing of "EitB," Hanson spoke to *TV Guide* again, claiming that he did not technically lie when stating Bones and Booth would consummate their relationship: "It wasn't an out-an-out lie . . . It [the alternate reality] was a strange combination of two people's experiences—a book Brennan wrote and then deleted and a dream in Booth's head" (Keck 21). Despite this explanation, both Hanson and *TV Guide* writer William Keck admitted to receiving many "nasty emails" (Keck 21) about the episode after its airing. However, Hanson believed "EitB" served a purpose within the larger context of the series and remained undeterred by negative fan response. He maintained that "EitB" marked a significant development in Booth and Brennan's relationship, as "they can no longer pretend that there is not something in them that is screaming out for that alternate reality" (21). However, he claimed that although fans claim to want Booth and Brennan together, this might not be the case: "Fans desperately want it, but if they get what they want, they could be very, very disappointed" (21). Hanson's comments were not well received by fans, who still insisted that Hanson did not deliver on his promise to place Booth and Brennan together in the season finale.

Hanson's dismissive, paternalistic attitude toward fans continued at the Bones panel during the 2009 Comic Con. Clearly nervous and prepared to, once again, defend "EitB," Hanson proclaimed:

> I always saw the season finale . . . as a love letter to our loyal fans . . . The season finale was full of inside jokes and layers and echoes from our four seasons and with the extra added blitz to see what it might look like if Booth and Brennan were a married couple. Also, I think with a lot of the other characters, we kind of showed what they're like inside . . . In retrospect, I hope the season finale will become more and more likable to our loyal fans, although I think our loyal fans got it. The people who tune in every once in a while didn't like it as much, and boy did I hear from them.

Hanson's distinction between "loyal fans" and casual viewers is troubling. Certainly, casual viewers would not, as he states, send him messages through Twitter. The notion that "EitB" was, in fact, not as well received by fans seems to be one that he cannot accept. Although the proliferation of discussion boards within the *Bones* fandom make it nearly impossible to gauge fan response, an examination of 206 Bones, a popular Live Journal fan community, shows that many fans were not pleased. Immediately following the episode, one poster expressed her frustration to community members by directly addressing Hanson:

> Dear Hart Hanson, That was, without a doubt, one of the worst season finales. That was the big cliffhanger? "Who are you?" I know you don't care, because, really, why should you? But honestly, the fans have spoken. THAT WAS HORRIBLE. NO LOVE. Me.

The post was quickly followed up with a brief rebuttal by another poster, who simply stated, "Well, I'm a fan and I liked it, just so you know . . ." This exchange, like many within the community, is useful. Both posters identify themselves as fans of the show, the first taking it upon herself to speak for "the fans." (When the first fan's opinion was challenged, however, she immediately followed up by stating that she was "ranting.") This brief exchange is useful in that it shows an awareness of production and also resists it. The poster directly challenges Hanson, operating on a level that shows she is aware of his role within the series.

While Hanson's assumption is that "loyal fans" would enjoy the episode, this seems to be untrue. Instead, they felt misled by his earlier statements that the season finale would end with the characters together. Certainly, fans of the show would appreciate an episode filled with clever inside references and a unique perspective. However, the downfall of this episode is not in its disruption of the traditional crime narrative format, but the misleading publicity surrounding the outcome of the episode.

ALTERNATE UNIVERSE II
"The Parts in the Sum of the Whole"

In "The Parts of the Sum of the Whole," the one-hundredth episode of the series, Hanson clearly tries to repair some of the damage done to the fan base through "EitB." "Parts" serves as a follow-up episode to "EitB"—even more so than the similarly titled "The Beginning in the End"—as it is filled with references to "EitB." Like "EitB," "Parts" plays with narrative time and structure, borrows from fan writing, and serves as a vehicle to place the two lead characters in a romantic relationship. Instead of the alternate universe of The Lab, however, "Parts" takes place as a recreated flashback—the story of Booth and Brennan's first meeting. Because the characters already knew one another in the pilot episode, "Parts" serves as a way to construct their backstory, as well as to offer more information on the other members of the Jeffersonian team. Sweets, as a late addition to the cast, functions as a representative of the audience, as Brennan and Booth recount their meeting and first case to him. Sweets has finished a book about Brennan and Booth, and (like the fan writers and viewers themselves) formed his assumptions about their relationship without knowing the dynamics of their first case. He begins the episode by explaining his conclusion to Booth and Brennan: "the two of you are in love, and the sublimating energies of that connection are responsible for the energy, rigor, and vigor that you bring to your homicide investigations" ("Parts"). Within their flashback, Booth and Brennan openly address their attraction to each other, discuss the possibility of starting a romantic relationship, and share a kiss. By doing so, their characters bring to light the discussions that typically do not exist within the parameters of a crime drama, but, instead, exist as a subtext developed by fans. Through this play with narrative time, fans are given a window into Booth and Brennan's past relationship that they did not have before; a glimpse that supports the theory that they have always been attracted to one another.

Although, like "EitB," "Parts" includes a murder mystery, it is secondary to the development of the characters. This is rare, as character development typically is secondary within crime dramas. As noted earlier, this lack of development opens a space for fans to create their own backstories for their characters, but these stories can often be contradicted within the canon of the series. This chance for contradiction is high after an episode like "Parts"—one that attempts to fill in narrative gaps of the series. Numerous fans had already written fan fiction that recounted the characters' pre-series interaction; such stories could now be negated by the canonization of "Parts." After all, not only does "Parts" provide more development of the Booth/Brennan, relationship, it also expands on Angela's introduction to the Jeffersonian, Angela and Brennan's early friendship, and the formation of the crime-solving unit itself.

"Parts" differs from "EitB" in one important way, however. Instead of the unsatisfactory ending of "EitB," the break in narrative time in "Parts" is actually used to move the larger narrative forward. At the end of the show, Sweets (again, operating as a surrogate viewer/fan) urges Booth and Brennan to act upon their feelings for each other. Poised in front of a structure displaying the Carl Sandberg quotation, "Nothing Happens Unless First a Dream," Booth urges Brennan to reconsider their relationship. (This quotation, a direct reference to "EitB," serves as yet another inside reference for fans.) Although Brennan rejects Booth's proposal of a romantic relationship, the characters share a kiss. More important, they have acknowledged what was previously only subtext: a romantic connection.

Because it was marketed to viewers differently than "EitB," "Parts" was met with positive fan reception. However, I would argue that it poses interesting questions for fans and fan writers. While the history of the characters once belonged to fans, it is now, like the present, in the hands of production. While it could be argued that Hanson *borrowed heavily* from fan techniques for "EitB," it did not disrupt fan writing in the way that "Parts" must have. By proposing a new history for the characters, "Parts" negates fan fiction that attempts to create a history for the characters before the pilot episode of the series, thus rendering it to the realm of "alternate reality." How should fans react to the rewriting of the history of a television program? What happens when fan writing contradicts the narrative text?

Perhaps these questions belong to a larger framework of discussions about textual ownership and technology. In "TV.com: Participatory Viewing on the Web," June Deery concludes that "there is little doubt that a closer link between television and the computer is coming. What also seems certain is that the convergence of our era's two most significant media will require a more complex understanding of what is meant by 'the viewer' and 'the televisual text'" (179). Certainly, "The End in the Beginning" and "The Parts of the Sum of the Whole" both play with concepts of time and narrative. This play raises questions about the limits of fan fiction and audience participation. Furthermore, it disrupts traditional ideas of authorship, text, and narrative. Most important, this narrative play allows *Bones* to move beyond the framework of the traditional procedural crime drama and into the realm of cult television status.

SUGGESTED EPISODES FOR ADDITIONAL STUDY

Bones
1:1. "Pilot." Writ. Hart Hanson. Dir. Greg Yaitanes. September 15, 2005.
1:9. "The Man in the Fallout Shelter." Writ. Hart Hanson. Dir. Greg Yaitanes. December 13, 2005.
2:9. "Aliens in a Spaceship." Writ. Janet Tamaro. Dir. Craig Ross Jr. November 15, 2006.
5:22. "The Beginning in the End." Writ. Hart Hanson and Stephen Nathan. Dir. Ian Toynton. May 20, 2010.
6:22. "The Hole in the Heart." Writ. Carla Kettner and Karyn Usher. Dir. Alex Chapple. May 12, 2011.

WORKS CITED

Bacon-Smith, Camille. *Enterprising Women: Television Fandom and the Creation of Popular Myth*. Philadelphia: University of Pennsylvania Press, 1992. Print.

Baym, Nancy K. *Tune In, Log On: Soaps, Fandom, and Online Community*. Thousand Oaks, CA: Sage, 2000. Print.

Bury, Rhiannon. *Cyberspaces of Their Own: Female Fandoms Online*. New York: Peter Lang, 2005. Print.

Carlson, James. *Prime Time Law Enforcement: Crime Show Viewing and Attitudes Toward the Criminal Justice System*. New York: Prager, 1985. Print.

Collins, Scott. "TV Industry Looks for a Game Plan on Using Twitter." *Los Angeles Times*. October 16, 2009. November 1, 2010.

Deery, June. "TV.com: Participatory Viewing on the Web." *Journal of Popular Culture* 37.2 (2003): 161–83. Print.

"The End in the Beginning." *Bones*. Writ. Hart Hanson. Dir. Ian Toynton. Fox. May 14, 2009. Television.

Hanson, Hart. *Bones* Panel. *Comic Con*. You Tube. July 26, 2009. Web. January 15, 2011.

Keck, William. "*Bones* Doesn't Put Out." *TV Guide*. June 1, 2009: 21. Print.

Keeps, David A. "Yes, They Will!" *TV Guide*. March 9, 2009: 28–30. Print.

Kirby-Diaz, Mary. "So, What's the Story? Story-Oriented and Series-Oriented Fans: A Complex of Behaviors." *Buffy and Angel Conquer the Internet: Essays on Online Fandom*. Ed. Mary Kirby-Diaz. Jefferson: McFarland, 2009. 62–86. Print.

Jenkins, Henry. *Textual Poachers: Television Fans and Participatory Culture*. New York: Routledge, 1992. Print.

———. "Afterword: The Future of Fandom." *Fandom: Identities and Communities in a Mediated World*. Ed. Jonathan Gray, Cornel Sandvoss, and C. Lee Harrington. New York: New York University Press. 357–64. Print.

"The Parts of the Sum of the Whole." *Bones*. Screenplay by Hart Hanson. Dir. David Boreanaz. Fox. April 8, 2010. Television.

Pugh, Sheenagh. *The Democratic Genre: Fan Fiction in a Literary Context*. Bridgend, Wales: Seren, 2005. Print.

Radway, Janice. *Reading the Romance: Women, Patriarchy, and Popular Literature*. Chapel Hill: University of North Carolina Press, 1991. Print.

20

TWO DAYS BEFORE THE DAY AFTER TOMORROW
Time, Temporality, and Fandom in South Park

JASON W. BUEL

South Park (Comedy Central, 1997–Present) is infamous for its crude sense of humor, frequent use of profane language, and depictions of sex and violence that often involve children. It also happens to be one of the most popular programs on television and has become a cultural institution unto itself. It is somewhat ironic to analyze the show because it often directly criticizes those who attempt to take it (or anything else) too seriously. It is difficult to seriously discuss the show on a more practical level because it is hard to establish a reasonable, stable context through which to frame it, particularly because *South Park* defies any simple genre classification (Gournelos 67). While the show may seem to fit into the category of the family sitcom fairly well at some points, there are other times when it could not resemble a family sitcom any less. To say *South Park* is a genre and style unto itself is also inaccurate, as the storytelling conventions and animation styles are constantly changing—much more so and more self-consciously so than most other programs. While any given episode may fit squarely into a given stylistic category, the series as a whole is no one thing, nor are there distinct periods of the show that fit neatly into any sort of classification. Even the storytelling conventions and patterns that have developed with the show are constantly and often intentionally shifting. If for no other reason, *South Park* is interesting in terms of temporality because the storytelling conventions of the show are themselves constantly in flux, just like the subjects of the stories they tell. As Doyle Greene points out, *South Park*'s construction paper cutout animation style makes it look as though it could be made by the same elementary school characters that the show is about (212). The show's changing conventions similarly seem to mimic a child's sense of time—though curiously, as much as the show has evolved, the main characters have only moved from third to fourth grade and, despite having progressed forward in time, they show no signs of aging or developing over the course of the series.

As complex and unusual as *South Park*'s temporality may be in and of itself, this chapter is particularly interested in analyzing the show's use of narrative time in relation to the ways fans have responded to it. I will focus on two storytelling devices that are relatively common in the show: the cliffhanger and the flashback. I argue that while some early uses of nontraditional temporality in *South Park* confused and angered fans, the program's playfulness with time has come to be one of its defining characteristics and has played a key role in differentiating between fans and casual viewers.

DUE TO ITS CONTENT IT SHOULD NOT BE VIEWED BY ANYONE
Background and Literature Review

South Park tells the stories of four boys—Stan, Kyle, Cartman, and Kenny—and their adventures in the town of South Park, Colorado. Even such a simple description of the show will often prove wholly inaccurate: there are many episodes where none of the boys plays a significant role, several where none of them appear at all, and many times when none of the action takes place anywhere near South Park. Though the boys are often the protagonists of their narratives, there are many instances when this is not the case. Often one boy serves as another's antagonist (as is often the case with Cartman). Sometimes it is up to the viewer to decide who is the protagonist.

While there is some existing scholarship on *South Park*, it pales in comparison to the abundance of writing available on a show like *The Simpsons* (FOX, 1989–Present), which it is frequently compared to in terms of its importance and its representations of American culture. Most of the available writing on *South Park* seems primarily interested in the politics of the show or, more specifically, in its ability to generate controversy in the media for its representations of politicians, religious figures, and celebrities. Though there is some work that deals with *South Park*'s online fan communities, most of it is focused on the emergence of *South Park*'s Web presence, which is interesting but does not reflect the modern fan experience.

Helen Nixon observes that the character Kenny is killed off in nearly every episode only to resurrect offscreen and die again. Nixon argues that this regular pattern with slight variations provides the audience with pleasure in a way similar to repetition in nursery rhymes (14). She also suggests that such thematic rhyming becomes a "shared code" between fans of the show (15). The ability to recognize such repetition within the story world provides a key distinction between true fans and casual viewers and accordingly allows the same text to take on another level of meaning (and humor) for viewers who are more familiar with the show.

Kenny's recurring deaths bring up an important point about the continuity of narrative time in *South Park*. Comedy Central initially objected to the ritualistic killing off and reviving of Kenny on the grounds that it "destroyed the logic of the show" (Weinstock 9). Though Kenny often dies and is reborn between episodes without comment, other narrative events do have long-standing repercussions. Sometimes even Kenny's death has long-standing repercussions, such as in the episode "Kenny Dies" (2001), after which he stays dead for eighteen episodes. In season fourteen, the episode "Coon vs. Coon & Friends" (2010) gives narrative logic to Kenny's deaths and reincarnations—as it turns out, Kenny was cursed after his parents attended a cult meeting at an undisclosed time in the past. The revelation of this information reframes nearly every preceding episode of the series.

Ted Gournelos observes that *South Park* indiscriminately switches between serial and episodic narrative structures. He suggests that the show does not operate according to the rules of "a traditional episode framework, nor does it return to normalcy within the same show," which is contrary to the sitcom model (Gournelos 44). Gournelos continues: "It often does return to normalcy by the next episode, but changes occasionally occur and often episodes reference each other as a lived past with consequences" (44). So, as if from a child's perspective, sometimes events have obvious, long-lasting consequences while other times things inexplicably return to normal with the passage of time.

There is one key point about *South Park*'s relationship to time that has been widely discussed: the show's quick production schedule allows it to reference specific, recent events, a characteristic that is unprecedented in animated television. As Jeffrey Weinstock points out, "The program's accelerated production schedule, that is, episodes can be put together in a week's time, allows it to achieve a level of currency generally only reserved for news programs" (14). Typically, each episode is produced in less than a week and not finished until the day it is set to air (Driver 1). This quick pace of production allows the show to address specific, recent issues, as opposed to a show like *The Simpsons*, which relies on satirizing broader issues and trends (Gournelos 16). The relationship between the production of *South Park* and time has led to a unique relationship between the story world of *South Park* and the outside world. It also sets up the expectation among fans that each new show generally will, in some way, reference some recent event ("A Conversation"). Accordingly, *South Park* is not just set in the present, but in a sort of hyper-present: one that is as self-consciously instantaneous and up-to-date as a twenty-four-hour news network.

TEETERING ON THE EDGE WITH CLIFFHANGERS

The first season of *South Park* came to a close with the episode "Cartman's Mom is a Dirty Slut." In the episode, Cartman observes that all of his friends have fathers. He asks his mother, who we know to be a single parent, why he does not have a dad. Then, Cartman sets off on a quest to find his father based on his mother's best estimation of who it might be. Over the course of the episode, Cartman manages to round up everyone who had slept with his mother around the time he was conceived (which is no small feat, as she seems to have slept with nearly every male character in town). At the end of the episode, just as the results of a paternity test are about to be revealed, a voice-over tells viewers to tune in to an "all new *South Park* in just four weeks" to find out the true identity of Cartman's father.

Four weeks later happened to be April Fools' Day. Accordingly, Trey Parker and Matt Stone decided that, as a joke, they would not resolve the cliffhanger—instead, they showed an entire episode featuring Terrence and Phillip (the boys' favorite cartoon characters, whose television show is analogous to *South Park*) in a story that has nothing to do with the unresolved plotlines from the first season and does not involve any of the characters from the town of South Park at all. The episode, "Not Without My Anus," became one of the most infamous episodes among *South Park* fans. Many fans were outraged and took to the Web in droves, voicing their grievances to anyone who would listen—mostly other fans of the show. Parker and Stone were quickly and fully aware of fans' disapproval. They had expected that their audience was only interested in *South Park* for its humor and would not particularly care about the resolution of the previous plot (Parker and Stone). Fans clearly did not find it funny; Comedy Central received nearly three thousand complaints via e-mail by noon the following day, which prompted the network to air the episode that resolved the cliffhanger a month earlier than they had originally scheduled it in an attempt to placate the angry fan base (Huff). Though the episode lacks the level of potentially offensive content that the series is known for, the fact that it did not reveal the promised cliffhanger resolution was enough to earn it a spot on several lists of the most controversial episodes of the series (Lake; Vary).

"Cartman's Mom is Still a Dirty Slut" aired three weeks later. The episode begins with a voice-over: "Who is Eric Cartman's father? At the end of tonight's episode, you will know the answer." The voice-over is a blatant attempt to placate fans and prevent any worries that this episode will again delay the cliffhanger payoff. It also sets up the voice-over convention for the episode—many of the most mundane, uneventful moments of the episode are punctuated by the voice-over narration asking questions and listing possible answers, progressing from the logical ("Who shot Mephisto?") to the insignificant ("Who will the director cast first?" and "Who is screwing with the lights?") to the nonsensical ("Who framed Roger Rabbit?" and "Who built the pyramids?")

"Cartman's Mom is Still a Dirty Slut" delays the cliffhanger payoff until the very end. The narrative action in the episode begins with Dr. Mephisto beginning to announce who Cartman's father is. Before he can make it that far, however, he gets shot. He is taken to the Hell's Pass Hospital, where he is in critical condition. At this point, a television crew from *America's Most Wanted* comes to South Park to produce a dramatic reenactment of the mysterious shooting. This embedded narrative not only serves to delay the payoff, but also recreates the main narrative, which is still developing. A third storyline is introduced as Cartman's mom, feeling she has been an inadequate mother, petitions the government to allow her to abort him—we later find out that she has confused the terms "abortion" and "adoption," but in the meantime she has convinced President Clinton to legalize fortieth trimester abortions (which is, in and of itself, an unusual take on how we typically think about time and aging). With the secondary and tertiary plots resolved, the episode writes off the mystery surrounding the inciting event—Mephisto, after recovering in the hospital, reveals that his brother tries to shoot him every month and dismisses the significance of the shooting outright. Finally, Mephisto reveals that Cartman's mother is a hermaphrodite and is actually his father. Using a technique that would later come to be a defining narrative characteristic of *Lost* (ABC, 2004–2010), the episode resolves the plot with an answer that only raises another more baffling mystery. The voice-over then asks the obvious question, "Who is Eric Cartman's mother?" Cartman responds directly to the voice-over as he shouts, "Forget it!" This resolution did not prompt outrage from fans as the previous episode had. For whatever reason, the episode that resolved the cliffhanger in an illogical way while raising an equally important, nearly identical mystery proved relatively satisfying compared to "Not Without My Anus," which ignored the previous plots of the show altogether ("Episode"; "Spoilers/New").

Time heals all wounds, or so the case would seem to be in this context. Fan discussions of "Not Without My Anus" after the initial fallout tend to view it much more favorably. The following sentiments expressed by pricey123 seem to be indicative of most fans' attitudes toward the episode in retrospect: "i didn't like it the first time i saw it but after about 5 years, i watched it again yesterday and think its one of the best from series 2 [*sic*]" ("Episode"). The above positive reaction to the episode after a more recent viewing confirms that the episode's offensiveness to fans was not based as much on its content as its temporal context. That is, fans expected the episode to reveal a specific bit of narrative information based on its placement as the episode immediately following a cliffhanger. The lack of that information and further delay in the revelation of that information was more troubling than the episode's decision to eschew the story world and characters audiences had come to expect from the series. The negative experience of having the cliffhanger payoff postponed seems to have served a larger, unintended purpose as well: "Not Without My Anus" and its placement in the middle of an unresolved story arc served as a bonding function for those who were around to witness it when the episodes were first broadcast (an experience that viewers who have since seen the episodes on the Web, on DVD, or via some other time-shifting device would have missed out on).

Though Parker and Stone have not since blatantly violated the expected temporal conventions of the cliffhanger by airing another non sequitur episode (admittedly because they were afraid to in light of fan responses to "Not Without My Anus"), they have referenced the episode several times since (Parker and Stone; "A Conversation"). In "Professor Chaos," a voice-over narration introduces three questions and strongly implies that the episode will be a cliffhanger. Instead, the narrator lists a single-word answer to each question and the episode abruptly ends. "Cartoon Wars Part II" begins with a "previously on *South Park*" segment that recaps the events of the previous episode. Then, a voice-over announcer tells the audience "the thrilling conclusion of 'Cartoon Wars' will not be seen tonight so that we can bring you the Terrance and Phillip television special." The title sequence for Terrance and Phillip in "Mystery at the Lazy J Ranch" plays. The show begins and an image of Muhammad is censored. The embedded narrative ends and we see the "real" Terrance and Phillip confronting network executives about the censorship of their show. Then, the show cuts to an entirely different time and space, where Cartman continues the storyline from the previous episode. Such moments in *South Park* are clearly inside jokes to fans and play off of longtime fans' shared negative experiences with the postponed cliffhanger at the beginning of season two.

South Park later calls upon fans' memories of the cliffhanger debacle to encourage fans to empathize and identify with the boys featured in the show when, several seasons later, the boys experience a similar situation. In "Eat, Pray, Queef," the boys tune in to watch the conclusion to a cliffhanger on their favorite television series *Terrance & Phillip*. The same voice-over that had been so ubiquitous in "Cartman's Mom is Still a Dirty Slut" and "Not Without My Anus" comes on to announce that the cliffhanger will not be resolved so they can bring viewers a special presentation, which mirrors what had happened to *South Park* fans at the beginning of the second season. As diehard fans of *Terrance & Phillip*, the boys are outraged. Besides simply mirroring the structure of past *South Park* episodes within the story world of the show itself, this situation also calls attention to the vital importance that fandom plays within the boys' lives.

The mystery of Cartman's father would be raised again and finally resolved in the episodes "200" and "201," twelve seasons after the question was initially raised. The episodes garnered attention from mainstream news media for their attempted portrayal of an image of Muhammad (Martinez). While many fans expressed anger over Comedy Central's decision to censor images of Muhammed, an equally common reference in fan forums was to the revelation of the true identity of Cartman's father. One might think that bringing the plotline back up after twelve years would be so radically unconventional in terms of temporality that it would be on par with the original delay of the cliffhanger payoff and potentially offend fans in the same way, but this was not the case. On the contrary, most fans loved the episode. Several even hoped that, after the mystery had been raised again in "200," it would not be immediately resolved. Some fans eagerly awaited another *Terrance & Phillip* episode the following week. A few hoped the payoff would be postponed until the three or four hundredth episode of *South Park* ("Episode"; "Spoilers/New"). Instead, the plot was finally resolved in the following episode, "201." The idea that fans would wind up caring as much or more about Cartman's storyline than the ensuing Muhammad controversy is even predicted during "201" as Cartman (correctly) guarantees the other boys that people care more about who his father is than the fact that the town of South Park is about to be destroyed (again) or than the fact that Muhammad is unable to show his face in public in the episode.

WAS THAT HOW IT HAPPENED?
Flashbacks and Misremembering

Much of the temporal play in *South Park* occurs between episodes. While the show rarely requires narrative recaps, it assumes viewers have a certain level of knowledge of the show's history and encourages fans of the show to view every episode in order to appreciate the frequent inside jokes and self-reflexive references. Details from past episodes not only recur for the sake of humor, but often they will become major plot points in later episodes. For example, in "Cancelled" the boys reenact the first few scenes from the pilot episode before observing that everything seems oddly familiar. After recognizing that they are being pulled through the narrative of the first episode, they are able to confirm their suspicions by successfully predicting the next few events, at which point they realize that they are stuck in a repeat. Their awareness of the past episode's narrative structure (and this sort of meta-temporality) allows them to split from the past narrative sequence and set out to discover what is happening (all of Earth is actually just a reality show and it is about to be canceled). This is a prime example of the show's nontraditional temporality and tendency toward revisionism.

South Park often self-consciously lapses into narrative conventions of the sitcom in order to parody them and mark its own place in television history. It places itself in the context of the sitcom (often with explicit references to syndication as a means of distribution), yet makes itself distinct through its satire and its meta-awareness of form and convention. "City on the Edge of Forever" a.k.a. "Flashbacks" might look like a conventional sitcom flashback episode to a casual viewer because of its structure, but it functions in an entirely different way for viewers who are aware of the previous episodes that are referenced. Instead of simply replaying clips from past episodes, "Flashbacks" changes key narrative elements. While the boys remember aloud the events of "Cartman Gets an Anal Probe," viewers see a flashback to a scene where Cartman is standing in a field as a large satellite dish telescopes out of his backside, only this time instead of a satellite dish it is an ice cream truck. When Cartman remembers back to the revelation of his father's identity, a flashback ensues that reveals that his father is actually John Elway (there is another reference to the cliffhanger debacle in "Flashbacks" as the boys are stranded inside a school bus that is literally hanging over the edge of a cliff for most of the episode). There is even a flashback to an earlier moment within the episode that, in its flashback form, is misremembered.

The idea of misremembering is not unique to the use of flashbacks in the show (and likewise, there are many flashbacks that reveal new information rather than misremembering information that had already been presented). David Larsen identifies the boys' teacher, Mr. Garrison, as a major source of misinformation who encourages a misremembering of American history (69). In one emblematic lesson, Mr. Garrison tells the children, "Christopher Columbus discovered America and was the Indians' best friend. He helped the Indians win their war against Fredrick Douglas and freed the Hebrews from Napoleon and discovered France" ("Cartman Gets"). Larsen suggests that Garrison's convolution of history and temporality is "a Jamesonian nightmare" and his teaching methods represent an "implosion of linearity in the black hole of the mass media" (69).

A TEMPORALITY OF SELF-REFLEXIVITY AND INTERTEXTUALITY

Brian Ott cites intertextuality as one of the key pleasures of watching *South Park*. He argues that the show's frequent use of allusion "fosters a sense of in-group superiority among those viewers who poses the special pop cultural literacy to recognize or 'get' the allusion" ("Pleasures" 45). In turn, the pleasure principle behind such intertextual references helps to create fan communities since "intertextual media encourage viewers to identify with others in a manner that less consciously intertextual media do not" (Ott and Walter 441). Particularly with a show like *South Park* that commonly uses devices like flashbacks and time travel within the story world, it is important to note that self-reflexivity plays an equally significant if not larger role in developing fan communities for some of the same reasons intertextuality does. Ott also notes that *South Park*'s audience experiences a temporality of viewing that is distinct from that of most television: "The structure of the TV series *South Park* is, in many ways, the televisual equivalent of hypertextuality" as watching the show becomes an active event of surfing from one popular allusion to the next rather than passively receiving a story ("Oh My" 227). Ott suggests this notion of hypertextual allusion surfing as a way that fans derive pleasure from moving outside the text, but anyone with the cultural awareness to recognize an intertextual reference would presumably take the same sort of enjoyment from watching the show as the most thoroughly initiated fan. Recognizing self-reflexive references, however, would operate on the same pleasure principle, but would only apply to fans and would provide more opportunities for enjoyment among fans who are the most familiar with past episodes of the show.

South Park's story world is complex and encompasses a wide range of time—from prehistory (in an episode when the character Timmy travels back in time) to several different points in the distant future (in episodes when characters travel forward in time or when characters from the future travel back into the present time). Audiences have also seen into the main characters' pasts and futures via flashbacks and flashforwards. The ability to take pleasure in recognizing references within the mythology of *South Park* does not depend on general cultural literacy. Rather, it depends on fans' specialized knowledge of past episodes (and a keen attention to detail or desire to interact with other fans who have such an eye for details) and more general understanding of history of the show (the evolving aesthetics of its animation, the patterns and variations of its narrative structures, the backstories of secondary characters). As most episodes are self-contained narratives and knowledge of past narrative information is not necessary to follow and understand them, such fan knowledge as I have described above serves to add another layer of humor to the show and seems to function solely for the purposes of fan enjoyment and community building. A casual viewer may be able to follow the narrative of an episode (which would be more difficult for a casual viewer of a show like *Lost*), but a great deal of the humor would be obscured, as would the ability to be drawn into a community with fellow fans and, through the shared experience of fandom, with the characters in the show.

South Park is a deceptively complex program, whether or not it means to be. Its temporality, like its style of animation, is playful and experimental at heart and helps keep even its most controversial images and ideas lighthearted and funny, at least to fans. As Toni Johnson-Woods writes: "*South Park* delights in deliberately subverting conventions. It disregards the structures of institutions such as the family, politics, religion, and school" (76). As I have argued, it also delights in subverting the conventions of time and fan expectations. Fans that started watching *South Park* for its subversion of social institutions have learned to delight in the subversion of their own expectations as well.

SUGGESTED EPISODES FOR ADDITIONAL STUDY

South Park
3:14. "The Red Badge of Gayness." Writ. Trey Parker and Matt Stone. Dir. Trey Parker. November 24, 1999.
5:4. "Scott Tenorman Must Die." Writ. Trey Parker. Dir. Eric Stough and Matt Stone. July 11, 2001.
7:9. "Christian Rock Hard." Writ. and dir. Trey Parker. October 29, 2003.
7:11. "Casa Bonita." Writ. Trey Parker and Matt Stone. Dir. Trey Parker. November 12, 2003.
7:12. "All About Mormons." Writ. and dir. Trey Parker. November 19, 2003.
8:14. "Woodland Critter Christmas." Writ. and dir. Trey Parker. December 15, 2004.
9:11. "Ginger Kids." Writ. and dir. Trey Parker. November 9, 2005.
10:8. "Make Love, Not Warcraft." Writ. Trey Parker and Matt Stone. Dir. Trey Parker. October 4, 2006.
14:2. "The Tale of Scrotie McBoogerballs." Writ. and dir. Trey Parker. March 24, 2010.
15:7. "You're Getting Old." Writ. and dir. Trey Parker. June 8, 2011.

WORKS CITED

"200." *South Park*. Dir. Trey Parker. Comedy Central. April 14, 2010. Television.
"201." *South Park*. Dir. Trey Parker. Comedy Central. April 21, 2010. Television.
"Cancelled." *The Complete Seventh Season*. Dir. Trey Parker. Warner Brothers, 2006. DVD.
"Cartman Gets an Anal Probe." *South Park: The Complete First Season*. Dir. Trey Parker. Warner Brothers, 2002. DVD.
"Cartman's Mom is a Dirty Slut." *The Complete First Season*. Dir. Trey Parker. Warner Brothers, 2002. DVD.
"Cartman's Mom is Still a Dirty Slut." *The Complete Second Season*. Dir. Trey Parker. Warner Brothers, 2003. DVD.
"Cartoon Wars pt. II." *The Complete Tenth Season*. Dir. Trey Parker. Warner Brothers, 2007. DVD.
"City on the Edge of Forever." *The Complete Second Season*. Dir. Trey Parker. Warner Brothers, 2003. DVD.
"A Conversation with Trey Parker and Matt Stone, Co-Creators of *South Park*." *The Charlie Rose Show*. PBS. UNC-TV, Research Triangle Park, NC. September 26, 2005. Television.
"Coon vs. Coon & Friends." *South Park*. Dir. Trey Parker. Comedy Central. November 10, 2010. Television.
Driver, Dustin. "South Park Studios: No Walk in the Park." *Profiles*. Apple Inc., 2010. Web. September 22, 2010.
"Eat, Pray, Queef." *The Complete Thirteenth Season*. Dir. Trey Parker. Warner Brothers, 2010. DVD.
"Episode Discussion." *Awesom-o.com*. Awesom-o.com, 2010. Web. August 20, 2010.
Gournelos, Ted. *Popular Culture and the Future of Politics: Cultural Studies and the Tao of South Park*. New York: Lexington Books, 2009. Print.
Greene, Doyle. *Politics and the American Television Comedy*. Jefferson, NC: McFarland, 2008. Print.
Huff, Richard. "Not an Eternity to Cartman Paternity." *New York Daily News*. April 9, 1998. Web. July 3, 2010.
Johnson-Woods, Toni. *Blame Canada: South Park and Contemporary Culture*. New York: Continuum, 2007. Print.
"Kenny Dies." *The Complete Fifth Season*. Dir. Trey Parker. Warner Brothers, 2005. DVD.
Lake, Dave. "The 10 Most Controversial *South Park* Episodes." *tv.msn.com*. Microsoft, 2010. Web. August 31, 2010.
Larsen, David. "*South Park*'s Solar Anus, or, Rabelais Returns: Cultures of Consumptions and the Contemporary Aesthetic of Obscenity." *Theory, Culture & Society* 18.4 (2001): 65–82. Print.
Martinez, Edecio. "*South Park* 201 Censored: Radical Islamic Death Warning Follows Muhammad Episode." *CBSnews.com*. CBS, 2010. Web. September 20, 2010.
Nixon, Helen. "Adults Watching Children Watch *South Park*." *Journal of Adolescent & Adult Literacy* 43.1 (1999): 12–16. Print.
"Not Without My Anus." *The Complete Second Season*. Dir. Trey Parker. Warner Brothers, 2003. DVD.

Ott, Brian L. "Oh My God, They Digitized Kenny!" *Prime Time Animation: Television Animation and American Culture*. Ed. Carol A. Stabile and Mark Harrison. New York: Routledge, 2003. 220–42. Print.

———. "The Pleasures of *South Park* (An Experiment in Media Erotics)." *Taking South Park Seriously*. Ed. Jeffrey A. Weinstock. Albany: State University of New York Press, 2008. 39–57. Print.

———, and Cameron Walter. "Intertextuality: Interpretive Practice and Textual Strategy." *Critical Studies in Media Communicaton* 17.4 (2000): 429–46. Print.

Parker, Trey, and Matt Stone. "Matt and Trey Answer the Twenty Questions." *SPscriptorium.com*. The *South Park* Scriptorium, n.d. Web. July 2, 2010.

"Professor Chaos." *The Complete Sixth Season*. Dir. Trey Parker and Matt Stone. Warner Brothers, 2005. DVD.

"Red Sleigh Down." *The Complete Sixth Season*. Dir. Trey Parker. Warner Brothers, 2005. DVD.

"Spoilers/New Episode Discussion." *SouthParkStudios.com*. South Park Studios, 2010. Web. July 22, 2010.

Vary, Adam B., and Kate Ward. "*South Park*: 20 'They Did WHAT?!' Episodes." *EW.com*. Entertainment Weekly, 2010. Web. October 10, 2010.

Weinstock, Jeffrey A. Introduction. *Taking South Park Seriously*. Ed. Jeffrey A. Weinstock. Albany: State University of New York Press, 2008. 1–20. Print.

21

LOST IN TIME?
Lost *Fan Engagement with Temporal Play*

LUCY BENNETT

In May 2007, the finale of the third season of *Lost* (ABC, 2004–2010) was aired. A double episode entitled "Through the Looking Glass," the finale employed a significant time puzzle. In its final few moments, the program offered viewers an abrupt revelation: what was presumed to be a flashback was actually a flashforward. The surprising scene, set in the present day, showed Jack Shephard (Matthew Fox) and Kate Austen (Evangeline Lilly), two of the *Lost* castaways, off the island and discussing the funeral of a fellow character, with Jack declaring "we have to go back, Kate . . . we have to go back" ("Through"). These declarations of needing to return to the island immediately informed viewers of the eventual rescue or escape of the characters and thereby answered a primary question of the show that compelled many viewers and fans for the first three seasons: would the islanders ever return home?

The program, detailing the survivors of Oceanic Flight 815 and their lives on a mysterious island, concluded in May 2010, after six seasons. The show used experiments with time as an important part of its structure, employing flashforwards, flashbacks, flashsideways, time travel, and multiple plot threads to create a novel narrative development.[1] In fact, time has even been regarded as a major character in the show (Larsen), being used to lead the audience "through a labyrinth of potential storylines, character connections, enigmas and puzzles" where "the path to narrative resolution is marked by twists, turns, dead ends and misleading clues" (Abbott 10). In this sense, the program was specifically constructed as "the central text in a cross-platform experience, encouraging shared research and textual analysis" (Brooker, "Man").

This chapter, by focusing on a specific example of the flashforward employed in season three, seeks to examine how online fans of the show engage with, and respond to, the use of these devices surrounding narrative time[2] and the rationale that underlies this participation in the program as a puzzle to be solved. To achieve this, I will consider how these fans "read" and try to make sense of the show's use of temporal play in terms of their placement as viewers following characters in past, present, and alternate timelines, often simultaneously.

To examine the "debate, and circulation of meanings" between fans that these time experiments initiate, discussions by members of the largest online community for *Lost* fans, www.lost-forum.com, will be drawn upon (Jenkins 137). The data for this study was collected through an examination of all posts within the season-three subforum in this community and also an additional archive search, with any identifying usernames removed to protect anonymity. I seek to not only determine the methods used by fans to understand these disruptions of narrative progression, but also to illuminate how the loyalty and knowledge of these fans may be tested in these instances by the program's use of temporal play as part of its puzzle, and also within discussions among members of the fan community itself.

"THROUGH THE LOOKING GLASS"
Time Manipulations in Lost

During the first three seasons the program frequently incorporated flashbacks[3] into its narrative structure, using them to develop the backstory of a character and subsequently contrast it with island life. Indeed, "*Lost*'s formal complexities offer intricately crafted puzzles which partially reveal themselves each week while adding new wrinkles and mysteries to the richly drawn characters and the snapshots of their pre-crash lives" (Mittell, "Film" 167). It is this very narrative composition that Steven Johnson views as challenging, and consequently, smartening television viewers today (*Everything* 62–63, 11–114). As he writes about *Lost*: "The genius of [the show] is that its mysteries are fractal," with the program delivering "a consistent payload of confusion" (Johnson, "What's"). He expands: "Narratives by definition work by withholding information about future events; you tune in to find out what will happen next. But with *Lost*, the mystery lies in the present tense: half the time, you have no idea what's happening right now" (Johnson, "What's").

The flashbacks were an integral piece of this puzzle, working as "revelatory insights, explaining why a character responds or acts in a certain way," and also "providing information as to why they were on the plane and, more subtly, hinting at the reason for their presence on the island" (Drangsholt 213). Hence, viewers slowly became accustomed to this temporal device that became an integral part of the show, with the process of narrative comprehension offering pleasures based on the cognitive energy it demanded (Mittell,

"Lost" 167). However, it was this particular learnt familiarity with the show's narrative strategies that was manipulated by the writers with the inclusion of the flashforward in "Through the Looking Glass." Presented as a flashback, this narrative deception played on viewers' learned patterns of comprehension when watching the show, and subverted them, prematurely answering a central enigma of the show, while simultaneously, and vitally, revealing new mysteries. This specific example is representative of how fans of *Lost* cope with the time puzzles, and, as this chapter will now show, illuminates the key themes in their responses to this narrative strategy.

UNDERSTANDING THE TEMPORAL PLAY

The three main coping tactics through which fans responded to and understood the flashforward in "Through the Looking Glass" were (1) engagement in forensic fandom, (2) trust in the *Lost* writers, and (3) evaluating and questioning the narrative structure. These will be outlined in turn, followed by a focus on the reactions from viewers who rejected the program as a result of the time puzzle contravening their expectations of the show.

LOST AND FORENSIC FANDOM

The narrative universe of *Lost* is formed on interlocking mythology, time travel, and unexplained phenomena, creating a complex and curious web of intrigue for viewers. Jason Mittell and Will Brooker, both drawing on Henry Jenkins's study of *Twin Peaks* fans, have convincingly argued that this mode of storytelling promotes a "forensic fandom" from viewers of the show that involves "research, collaboration, analysis and interpretation" (Mittell, "Sites"). The launch of a *Lost* wiki in 2005, Lostpedia, illustrates the point. Boasting over 25,000 registered users and more than 5,000 pages, it soon became one of the most popular wikis of all time, receiving over 150 million page views by 2009 (Mittell, "Sites"). *Lost* online communities also appeared soon after the show began airing; with www.Lost-forum.com reaching over 88,000 members by 2009, who had amassed roughly 1,138,000 posts on all aspects of the *Lost* universe (Livelsberger 9). This forensic inspection of the show is therefore encouraged by the narrative structure and form of the program, which is often littered with clues left by the writers to puzzle and engage these detective-like fans. It is no surprise therefore that the composite of the show has been seen to share similarities with video gaming:

> The writers seem to have based the formal structure and narrative possibilities of the show itself on video game conventions . . . in order to better create the kind of networked community or fanbase usually associated with games—a potential audience ready not just to watch but also "play" *Lost*. (Jones 20)[4]

With this in mind, we need to determine how fans engage in this "play" surrounding time puzzles, with regard to their forensic fandom.

As outlined in this chapter, the flashforward at the end of "Through the Looking Glass" was a carefully constructed narrative device that toyed with fans' learnt familiarity of the show. However, as part of the learnt familiarity for many rested in engagement with the program as a puzzle or game, some fans used their forensic detection skills to work out the flashforward before the revelation in the final scene, solving clues left by the writers. For example, the make and model of the mobile phone used by Jack in the episode was immediately discovered by a number of fans as dating from 2006, therefore indicating that the episode was set in the future or present and not the past:[5]

> Jack was using a black Razr phone . . . They didnt come out in 2004 or pre 04, so it HAD to be a flashforward! (May 23, 2007)
>
> I realized it was a flash forward in the beginning because jack is using a KRZR phone that came out 5 months ago. I couldn't imagine the makers of lost would have goofed that up! They are too good! (May 23, 2007)

As we can ascertain from this exchange, the *Lost* writers encourage a sharpness and intellect from their fans,[6] so every detail is inspected and examined closely. In *Lost*, a mobile phone is not just a prop, but an important and revelatory clue. As Ian Askwith observes: "*Lost*'s narrative is similar to, if more complicated than, traditional detective stories. If the characters themselves fail to act like detectives . . . there is no question that *Lost*'s viewers are positioned as detectives" (171). Another major clue left by the writers in the episode for the detective-like forensic fans involved the name of the funeral parlor, which was a revealing anagram:

> The funeral home name was HOFFS/DRAWLAR. Anagram for: FLASHFORWARD. Of course we all know it was now, but there it was, plain as day, about halfway through the episode! (May 23, 2007)

Although the sign was only shown briefly, the writers were aware that it would be noticed by fans due to their forensic detection activities. M. J. Clarke explains that the sign is a "comment by the creators on the textual construction of the episode itself . . . [it] can be understood solely as an instance of the creators using the diegetic space as a palette to indirectly communicate with viewers over the head of fictional representation" (128–29). This communication therefore shows that "through such distractions and clues in both the fictional space of the show, cyberspace and real space, the audience itself becomes part of that mythological fabric, essentially participating in the story similar to the way the characters do" (Wood xiii).

As Jason Mittell observes, "While many fans do watch the show in a more self-contained fashion, *Lost*'s moments of information overflow . . . seem to demand a mode of forensic engagement to organize and uncover a wealth of narrative data" ("Lost" 129). This is further explained by Gray and Mittell in their examination of the spoiler habits of *Lost* fans:

> There is no doubt that the chief reason that *Lost* fans consume the show and its cross-media experiences is to crack its secrets. Discovering the answers to the island's mysteries was our respondents' most commonly shared reason for watching the show and most cited primary rationale . . . it is clear from their broader responses that there is a ludic sense of imaginative speculation and problem-solving that motivates most viewers' fandoms.

Therefore, it can be seen that the flashforward in "Through the Looking Glass," with its mystery, obscure clues, puzzling twist, and manipulation and tease of the narrative expectation of viewers, perfectly complemented this "imaginative speculation" and "problem solving" rationale that motivated forensic fandom.

TRUST IN THE *LOST* WRITERS

Another process used by fans in an effort to understand the time puzzle involved placing trust and control in the creators and writers of the show, even when they could not comprehend the narrative development. For fans that did not detect and interpret the clues placed in the episode, and who were confused and shocked by the flashforward, many still revelled in the latest twist, and saw the narrative turn as a new level in the *Lost* experience:

> This is lost. it ain't really going to play out that way. Especially with all the future/past stuff. I think the series ending now will be how they decide to go back to the island? or change their pasts to stay on the island. I don't

know. All I know is, after this episode, all bets are off as to where the brilliant writers are taking us. (May 23, 2007)

Simply unbelievable, you can sit and wonder what the writers could possibly do that would completely surprise us at this point, and they drop this on us. Didn't feel at all like a Desmond vision. I don't know how this is going to work in the future (no pun intended), but it seems that this may be how "everything is going to change". Best Show EVER!! (May 23, 2007)

What the writers have done, more or less, is reboot the series. Same characters, same setting, totally different direction. (May 24, 2007)

For these fans, although they expressed confusion, not knowing where the narrative would now lead became a pleasure—with the knowledge that the writers would take them to a surprising and different experience than before. In addition, this particular time puzzle brought along a new collection of mysteries that they could try to solve, such as: How did the characters get off the island? Who is left there? Why is Jack trying to get back to the island? Why is Kate not in jail for the crimes she committed before arriving on the island? And, which character's funeral was taking place in the episode? As one fan explained, to be engaged in the game of *Lost* is to understand how the show is written and works as a labyrinth of mysteries, with viewers actively involved in the detection process:

We need more questions. And to answer those questions, with questions. That is how a series works, at least, the best of them IMO. Give us little resolutions, make us find little rewards, but string us along, like little fishes on your treble hooks. Lost . . . is one of the best television shows of all time. Period point blank. (May 24, 2007)

This complements Matt Hills's argument that cult television is marked by "sustained enigmas, and by ongoing or unresolved mysteries about their characters, character relationships, or aspects of their invented worlds" (190). When the enigma of the flashforward arose, some fans then reminded themselves and urged others to put their faith in the writers, trusting that it would later become clear as to where they were being led as viewers engaged in the program:

I thought that this was the best lost episode ever, until the last scene that is . . . I was utterly blown away, and not in a good way. So LOST . . . I don't know where they can go with this . . . I am struggling . . . I need to remember that the writers have created this show (greatest show in the history of TV) and I need to trust that they won't let it slip . . . (May 23, 2007)

Trust the writers. Everyone gets all wound up when they are not certain about where things are headed, yet LOST is still the best thing on television . . . Whatever direction the show takes, I believe it will continue to be the best show on television until proved differently. I rather enjoy the idea that they may be taking me places I haven't imagined yet. (May 31, 2007)

I agree, we should trust the writers. After all, they have done an amazing job the first three seasons. There's no reason they won't continue to do so for the remaining seasons, especially considering the fact that they are ending the show when they want instead of continuing on for too long. (June 2, 2007)

For these fans, although they may be unclear on how the narrative will now progress after the flashforward, there is an air of positive expectation based on the "invented world" (Hills 190) of the program and their confidence in the creators that guide them through this. These responses suggest that fans view the show as an enjoyable game between themselves and the creators, whom they see as absolutely in control.

EVALUATING AND QUESTIONING THE TIME MANIPULATIONS

As outlined throughout this chapter, "to be a *Lost* fan is to embrace a detective mentality, seeking out clues, charting patterns and assembling evidence into narrative hypotheses and theories" (Mittell, "Lost" 128–29). In alignment with this, some viewers immediately contemplated whether the flashforward presented an accurate depiction of the future, or just a suggestion of what could happen:

I'm really frustrated by how everyone seems to be taking the flashfowards at face value as what is without a doubt going to happen. We have no reason to believe that these "visions of the future" are necessarily accurate. The thing about the past is that it cannot be changed, but things can always be done to change the future. I think the Island is Smurfing with Jack's mind to make him want to stay . . . (May 23, 2007)

However, this detective mode of viewing can also be directed against the writers themselves and the narrative structure, with some fans questioning whether the apparent flashforward and the clues found within was simply just an illusion, or trick intended to mislead them onto another narrative path:

> I still am not convinced it was a flash forward. The writers did a brilliant job at leaving it ambiguous. The writers know that lost fans pay meticulous attention to detail, and they shoved that razor phone right in our face. It was almost too obvious to be the proving sign that jack was in the future. I think it is just as plausible to assume the writers intentionally put the phone there knowing we would notice it in hopes to make us believe it took place in the future. It would be quite simple for them to create a scenario were jack could have gotten an advanced copy or something of the phone. I am simply saying, that there is still a plausible scenario that would allow jacks flash to have taken place in the past, and if it did take place in the past, my god does that change things. (May 23, 2007)

Therefore, being a forensic fan can involve not only using detective skills to decode the clues presented to them, but also, in some cases, to mistrust the clues and reconsider different solutions to the narrative mysteries. A poll conducted on www.lost-forum.com attempted to discover the most popular reading of the narrative time device, asking members: "What do you think the flashforward is?" Out of the 566 respondents, 49.82 percent agreed that it was "a faithful account of the future," 44.35 percent saw it as a "vision or just one possible future," and 5.83 percent believed it to be a "flashback in disguise." From this, we can view how members of the forum had different interpretations of the intended meaning and construction of the time puzzle, an occurrence that forms the heart of the show. "As an interactive experience, *Lost* allows and encourages its viewers to become agents and participants in the building of meaning—or at least allows them a glimpse of what sort of viewer they have the potential to become" (Shyminsky). This "building of meaning" then, was perfectly encapsulated by the flashforward, with the numerous theories and debates keeping many fans occupied until the beginning of the next season:

> We certainly don't know ANYTHING about the flash-forward. It was a great sleight of hand on the part of the writers, and it opens wonderful new doors for the series. And it was probably the only way they could guarantee we'd all be frothing at the mouth come February. They couldn't have presented a better mystery than the flash-forward to keep all us LOSTies theorizing and debating and screen-capping until 2008. (May 24, 2007)

However, it will now be important to examine the reactions and debates circulated by fans that saw the temporal play as not a harbinger of more mystery and introducer of fresh direction, but rather as an abrupt end to their participation as viewers engaged in the show. For these fans, the flashforward was understood and received as an end to the game and puzzle of *Lost*, rather than introducing a new level or beginning.

GAME OVER?
The Test of Temporal Play

As evident in this chapter, engaging with the mysteries and puzzles in *Lost* is an intrinsic part of the viewing pleasure for many fans. However, for others, the mysteries of the show seemingly proved too complex, frustrating, and failed to continue holding intrigue. As one ex-viewer and critic has argued, the writers of *Lost* made the "story even more convoluted and mysterious every episode . . . [being] too consumed with giving viewers something else to wonder about . . . they drop each mystery after a few minutes and then run to the next one, hoping viewers will follow" (Dehnart). What I now want to illuminate are the responses from fans who shared this perspective with regard to the flashforward, and failed to gain pleasure or intrigue from the forensic and temporal play employed by the writers.

The inclusion of the flashforward ensured that the narrative arc of the program was immediately disrupted. We learn that "the flashforwards show us that whilst the serial has a way in the sense that the survivors continue to relate themselves to the island in some manner, [the show] does not have a way in terms of a straightforward journey from a beginning to an end" (Drangsholt 221). However, this proved quite testing for some fans, who struggled with this alteration of the narrative progression and questioned their future relationship with the show based on the light that it would not be a "straightforward journey" in terms of progressing from plane crash to rescue in a linear manner:

> So what's the point of watching the show anymore now that we know they got off the island? I don't really care about the rest really. (May 23, 2007)

> I have to agree with what a fair few have said in here. As much as you want to see them get off the island. What's the point in viewing the show if we know they got off the island? Isn't that the whole point in Lost? The wonder of them getting off the island . . . (May 27, 2007)

For these viewers, the time puzzle resulted in frustration and an immediate voiced rejection of the principles of the *Lost* universe. Their expectations of the show being formed around a single mystery (the wonder of leaving the island) that they desired to solve, were then disrupted. This premature conclusion of the central enigma ("will they get off the island?") being replaced by another ("how did they get off the island?") then resulted in their disappointment. They wanted the mystery resolution to remain delayed and saw the "game" as now being "over," with the writers changing the rules and solving the primary detective mystery too early.

As the program had used temporal play in the form of flashbacks up until and throughout season three, the learnt familiarity held by the audience meant that they followed the linear path of the narrative through two strands—the past and the present—and were placed in these two timelines simultaneously. However, the narrative comprehension of viewers was intercepted by the startling flashforward time manipulation, and the strand previously approached as the present (life on the island), then became the past. Consequently, the post-island life of some of the castaways was now regarded as the present, with the past eventually catching up to this. This disruption of learned conventions, linearity, and their placement in the timelines therefore unsettled some fans, who voiced serious doubt concerning their involvement in viewing the program:

> I feel like I have little reason to continue caring about the series now that we know that they leave the island only to end up miserable. (May 23, 2007)

> That's about how I felt while watching . . . part of the mystery of the island is not knowing if they ever get off the thing. I'm not sure I'm going to care too much about Jack or Kate from now on. Anything that happens to them from now, I'll just think "Oh well. They'll get off the island eventually so no biggie." (May 27, 2007)

As we can see, these reactions are contextualized in terms of how they would stop emotionally investing in, or "caring" about, the program and characters in the light of the abrupt narrative twist. Throughout these responses there is also evident a sense that for these individuals the main intrigue of the show had now been answered. For these viewers then, the motivation for continued engagement in *Lost* and the seemingly most intriguing piece of the puzzle centered on whether the castaways would ever be rescued or escape from the island. They expected this single mystery to continue throughout the show, and did not foresee a change of rules and focus halfway through. Now that this central enigma appeared to be answered, "the point" in viewing the show had to be reconsidered, a prospect quite different to some forensic fans that, as shown in this chapter, had a different conception of narrative. Rather than engage in the more traditional approach to enigma-resolution and narrative drive, whereby the mystery is resolved at the climax of the show, these fans gained pleasure from asking more questions in response to the time puzzle, rather than view it as an end to the involvement in the game of *Lost*.

We can conclude therefore that *Lost*'s use of the flashforward constitutes quite a vivid example of how fans can react when temporal play is employed within narrative structure. Although the narrative format of the show encouraged complexity and a detective engagement boarding on the microscopic, the use of a time manipulation that explicitly depicted elements of the future central to the narrative arc resulted in the confusion and consequent displacement of some viewers. In this sense, these audience members quite literally became *Lost* in time.[7]

SUGGESTED EPISODES FOR ADDITIONAL STUDY

Lost
1:1. "Pilot." Writ. Damon Lindeloff. Dir. J. J. Abrams. September 22, 2004.
1:4. "Walkabout." Writ. David Fury. Dir. Jack Bender. October 13, 2004.
2:1. "Man of Science, Man of Faith." Writ. Damon Lindeloff. Dir. Jack Bender. September 21, 2005.
3:5. "In Translation." Writ. Damon Lindeloff. Dir. Tucker Gates. February 23, 2005.
3:8. "Flashes Before Your Eyes." Writ. Damon Lindeloff and Drew Goddard. Dir. Jack Bender. February 14, 2007.
3:20. "The Man Behind the Curtain." Writ. Elizabeth Sarnoff and Drew Goddard. Dir. Bobby Roth. May 9, 2007.
4:5. "The Constant." Writ. Carlton Cruse and Damon Lindeloff. Dir. Jack Bender. February 28, 2008.
5:7. "The Life and Death of Jeremy Bentham." Writ. Carlton Cruse and Damon Lindeloff. Dir. Jack Bender. February 25, 2009.
6:11. "Happily Ever After." Writ. Damon Lindeloff and Carlton Cruse. Dir. Jack Bender. April 6, 2010.
6:17. "The End." Writ. Damon Lindeloff and Carlton Cruse. Dir. Jack Bender. May 23, 2010.

NOTES

1. As Vellar states, the show was "intentionally designed with a complex plot and narrative hooks, with the aim of involving internet users in an intellectual challenge" (5).
2. David Lavery has described *Lost* fans as an "ingenious fan base" and "a deeply inquisitive viewership, determined to puzzle out its mysteries."
3. For an examination of the show's "mastermind narration" within *Lost* flashbacks, see Clarke and also Anderson (88).
4. See also Millmann and Abbott.
5. The "past" of the show was therefore pre-2004, with the off-island footage taking place between 2005 and 2007.
6. As show creator J. J. Abrams declared while being interviewed on *The Jimmy Kimmel Show*, "People who post online—they're infinitely smarter than anyone working on the show" (Lavery).
7. The author would like to thank Will Brooker for his valuable comments and insights on this article.

WORKS CITED

Abbott, Stacey. "How *Lost* Found Its Audience: The Making of a Cult Blockbuster." *Reading* Lost: *Perspectives on a Hit Television Show*. Ed. Roberta Pearson. London: I. B. Tauris, 2009. Print.

Anderson, Tonya. "'24,' 'Lost,' and 'Six Feet Under': Post-traumatic Television in the Post 9/11 Era." M.A. thesis. University of North Texas, 2008. Print.

Askwith, Ivan. "'Do you even know where this is going?': *Lost*'s Viewers and Narrative Premeditation." *Reading* Lost: *Perspectives on a Hit Television Show*. Ed. Roberta Pearson. London: I. B. Tauris, 2009. Print.

Brooker, Will. "Man Out of Time: Lost Season 3 Finale." *Media Commons*. N.p., February 12, 2008. Web. October 25, 2010.

———. "Television Out of Time: Watching Shows on Download." *Reading* Lost: *Perspectives on a Hit Television Show*. Ed. Roberta Pearson. London: I. B. Tauris, 2009. Print.

Clarke, M. J. "Lost and Mastermind Narration." *Television & New Media* 11.2 (2010): 123–42. Print.

Dehnart, Andy. "Why 'Lost' Has Lost Me As a Viewer." *Today Television*. MSN, October 8, 2006. Web. October 25, 2010.

Drangsholt, Janne S. "World Without End or Beginning: Structures of Dis-placement in *Lost*." *New Review of Film and Television Studies* 7.2 (2009): 209–24. Print.

Gray, Jonathan, and Jason Mittell. "Speculation on Spoilers: Lost Fandom, Narrative Consumption and Rethinking Textuality." *Particip@tions* 4.1 (2007). Web. October 25, 2010.

Hills, Matt. "Cult TV, Quality and the Role of the Episode/Programme Guide." *The Contemporary Television Series*. Ed. Michael Hammond and Lucy Mazdon. Edinburgh: Edinburgh University Press, 2005. 190–206. Print.

Jenkins, Henry. *Fans, Bloggers, and Gamers: Exploring Participatory Culture*. New York: New York University Press, 2006. Print.

Johnson, Steven. *Everything Bad Is Good for You: How Today's Popular Culture Is Actually Making Us Smarter.* New York: Riverhead Books, 2005. Print.

———. "What's Going On? Don't Ask Me, I'm Lost . . ." *The Times*, September 2, 2005. Web. October 25, 2010.

Jones, Steven E. *The Meaning of Video Games: Gaming and Textual Strategies.* New York: Routledge, 2008. Print.

Larsen, Kristine. "The Art of World Making: Lost and Time Travel." *Lost Studies Online* 2.1 (2008): n. pag. Web. October 25, 2010.

Lavery, David. "Get Lost in a Good Story." *Flow* 3.2 (2005): n. pag. Web. October 25, 2010.

Livelsberger, Tara. "'Lost' in Conversation: Complex Social Behavior in Online Environments." M.A. thesis. Ohio University, 2009. Print.

Millman, Joyce. "Game Theory." *Getting Lost: Survival, Baggage and Starting Over in J. J. Abrams' Lost.* Ed. Orson Scott Card. Dallas, TX: Benbella Book, 2006. Print.

Mittell, Jason. "Film and Television Narrative." *The Cambridge Companion to Narrative.* Ed. David Herman. Cambridge: Cambridge University Press, 2007. Print.

———. "*Lost* in a Great Story: Evaluation in Narrative Television (and Television Studies)." *Reading* Lost: *Perspectives on a Hit Television Show.* Ed. Roberta Pearson. London: I. B. Tauris, 2009. Print.

———. "Sites of Participation: Wiki Fandom and the Case of Lostpedia." *Transformative Works and Cultures* 3 (2009): n. pag. Web. October 25, 2010.

Shyminsky, Neil. "Finding Lost, Getting Lost." *Lost Studies Online* 2.1. 2008: n. pag. Web. October 25, 2010.

"Through the Looking Glass" *Lost.* ABC. May 23, 2007. Television.

Vellar, Agnese. "'Lost' (and Found) in Transculturation. The Italian Networked Collectivism of U.S. TV Series and Fansubbing Performances." *Broadband Society and Generational Changes.* Ed. F. Colombo and L. Fortunati. Oxford: Peter Lang, 2011. Print.

Wood, J. *Living* Lost: *Why We're All Stuck on the Island.* New Orleans, LA: Garrett County Press, 2007. Print.

CONTRIBUTORS

MELISSA AMES is an assistant professor at Eastern Illinois University specializing in media studies, television scholarship, popular culture, and feminist theory. Her work has been published in a variety of anthologies, journals, and encyclopedias, ranging in topic from television study, new media, and fandom to American literature and feminist art. Her most recent publications include her books, *Feminism, Postmodernism, and Affect: An Unlikely Love Triangle in Women's Media* and *Women & Language: Essays on Gendered Communication Across Media*, and chapters in *Grace Under Pressure: Grey's Anatomy Uncovered, Writing the Digital Generation, Bitten by Twilight: Youth Culture, Media, and the Twilight Saga*, and *Manufacturing Fear*.

FRIDA BECKMAN is a research fellow at Uppsala University as well as a visiting lecturer at Stockholm University, Sweden. She is the author of various articles on Gilles Deleuze, focusing on topics such as idiocy, masochism, sexuality, history, and temporality. She is the coeditor of two special issues of *Angelaki: Journal of the Theoretical Humanities* as well as the editor of *Deleuze and Sex*.

LUCY BENNETT obtained her Ph.D. from the Cardiff School of Journalism, Media, and Cultural Studies in 2009, conducting her thesis on normative behavior of online fans of the band R.E.M. Her main research interests are audiences and fandom; communication, identity, and participation online; social media; online research methods; and popular music and culture. From 2007 to 2010 she was a research assistant at Cardiff University, working on a media analysis project funded by civil service, as well as two other projects funded by the BBC Trust, examining accuracy and impartiality in the news coverage of the four nations. She is currently editorial assistant for the journal *Social Semiotics*.

MOLLY BROST received her Ph.D. in American Culture Studies from Bowling Green State University in 2008. She also holds an M.A. in English from Colorado State University and a B.S. in Journalism and English from the University of Nebraska at Kearney. She is currently an assistant professor of English at the University of Southern Indiana, where she teaches composition and introductory literature courses. Her scholarly work has appeared in *Americana: The Journal of American Popular Culture* and *Scope: An Online Journal of Film and TV Studies*. Her research interests include the biographical film, class issues on film and television, and narrative and genre.

JASON W. BUEL is a graduate student in film at North Carolina State University. He holds bachelor's degrees in English and psychology from Appalachian State University. His current projects include a history of the western genre in videogames and an analysis of piracy and paratexts in the *Star Wars* universe. His research interests include American pop culture, paratexts, fan cultures, and transmedia narratology.

SARAH HIMSEL BURCON teaches composition and literature courses at Lawrence Technological University in Southfield, Michigan. She completed her doctoral work at Wayne State University in 20th Century American Literature, with a specialization in feminist theory. Her other research interests are popular culture and linguistics. Among her recent publications are her coedited collection, *Women & Language: Essays on Gendered Communication Across Media*, as well as a chapter in *Revisiting the Past through Rhetorics of Memory and Amnesia*. Additionally, she has written articles for *Women and Popular Culture Encyclopedia*.

KASEY BUTCHER earned her undergraduate degree from Ball State University and is currently pursuing her Ph.D. at Miami University where she studies English literature and teaches first-year composition courses. Her research interests include Victorian literature, popular culture, and girlhood studies, focusing especially on gender performance, education, and the media. Her past writing projects have analyzed Gothic convention and childhood in *Harry Potter*, masculinity and monstrosity on *Dexter*, and the portrayal of overachieving girls on *Glee*.

MELANIE CATTRELL completed a Ph.D. in American Studies at the University of New Mexico. Her dissertation, "Gendered Crimes, Gendered Fans: Intersections of Gender, Sexuality, and Fandom in the Contemporary American Television Crime Drama," analyzes the intersection of fandom with changing representations of gender and sexuality in the television crime drama. Her research interests include gender studies, queer theory, fan studies, new media, television studies, and aging studies. She is currently a visiting assistant professor in the Department of English and Rhetoric at Georgia College and State University.

MICHAEL FUCHS is currently a research and teaching associate in the Department of American Studies, University of Graz, Austria. He recently coedited a collection entitled *Landscapes of Postmodernity: Concepts and Paradigms of Critical Theory*. Currently, he is coediting two books, *ConFiguring America: Iconic Figures, Visuality, and the American Identity* and *Placing America: Space and American Culture*, and finishing his Ph.D. dissertation on self-reference in horror cinema. Michael has published essays on horror and adult cinema, video games, and American television.

NORMAN M. GENDELMAN is a Ph.D. student in the Department of Film and Media at the University of California, Berkeley. In 2002 he received an M.A. in Media Studies from the Media Department of the New School for Social Research, completing a master's thesis entitled "The Implosion of Everyday Life: *Fight Club* and the Narrative of the Commodity Cyborg." His current research interests center on theories of the American actor, media theory, and the historical interconnections between avant-garde practice and popular culture. His dissertation, "The Media West: the Nuclear Family as New Frontier," concerns the relationship between the westerns of the 1950s and early 1960s and their intermedia expression.

JACK HARRISON is an M.A. candidate in the Communication, Culture, and Technology program at Georgetown University in Washington, DC. He received his B.S. from Georgetown in Asian Studies in 2008. His academic interests include remix culture, sound studies, new media, sexuality, race, and queer theory.

COLIN IRVINE is an associate professor of English at Augsburg College. His most recent publications include his book *Teaching the Novel Across the Curriculum: A Handbook for Educators*; chapters in *Papa, PhD: Essays on Fatherhood by Men in the Academy* and *Does the Writing Workshop Still Work*; and articles in the *Journal of Philosophy Literary Studies*, *The International Journal of the Humanities*, the *Midwest Modern Language Association Journal*, the *Journal of the West*, and *Academic Exchange Quarterly*. His current research projects focus on narrative theory and, specifically, the use of frames and embedding in film and fiction.

J. P. KELLY is a Ph.D. student in the Institute of Film and Television Studies at the University of Nottingham. His current dissertation, "Prime *Times*: Technology, Temporality and Narrative Form in Contemporary US Drama," examines the relationship between industry, technology, and narrative time in series such as *24* and *Lost*. He has published on this topic in *Ephemeral Media: Transitory Screen Culture from Television to YouTube*. He has also contributed reviews and other original research to *Popular Communication: The International Journal of Media and Culture*, *Scope: An Online Journal of Film & TV Studies*, and *In Media Res*.

JORDAN LAVENDER-SMITH is working toward his Ph.D. in English with a Certificate in Film Studies at CUNY Graduate Center. His academic interests include reflexivity in literature and film, seriality and addiction, early and postmodern dramaturgy, and, more generally, the cultural causes and consequences of narrative forms. He teaches in the English department at CUNY Queens College.

CASEY J. MCCORMICK is a Ph.D. student in English at McGill University, concentrating in cultural studies and critical theory. She received both her B.A. and M.A. degrees in Literary Studies from Georgia State University. Her research interests include television and new media, posthuman theory, and digital culture.

KRISTI MCDUFFIE is currently earning her Ph.D. in English Studies at Illinois State University with a concentration in rhetoric and composition. Her research interests include public and cultural rhetorics, new media studies, composition studies, and language ideologies. Her publications include "Helping Students Negotiate Dialects in the Writing Center" in *The Writing Lab Newsletter* and "*Kairotic* Moments in the Writing Center," a joint publication in *Praxis: A Writing Center Journal*.

ARIS MOUSOUTZANIS is a visiting lecturer at the Department of Media and Cultural Studies at Kingston University, United Kingdom. He has researched and published in areas such as critical and cultural theory (especially psychoanalysis and trauma theory), technoculture and cyberculture, media and globalization, popular culture, science fiction, and the Gothic. He is currently coediting a collection on *New Media and the Politics of Online Communities* and *The Continuum Handbook of Science Fiction*.

TONI PAPE is a Ph.D. candidate and research assistant at the Department of Comparative Literature at Université de Montréal. His areas of research include the studies of narrative, television, and intermediality as well as the philosophy of time. In his dissertation project, Toni analyzes representations of time in contemporary North American television series. He has contributed to a translation of P. B. Shelley's early works into German (*Zastrozzi. Eine Romanze und andere Frühschriften*. Passau: Stutz, 2007). Furthermore, his publications include a comparative reading of *Heart of Darkness* and *Apocalypse Now*, in *Post-Scriptum*, and a note on performance and performativity in *Intermédialités* (dossier électronique).

GRY C. RUSTAD is a Ph.D. fellow at the Department of Media and Communication at the University of Oslo. Her dissertation addresses questions of television drama and spectatorship. She has forthcoming publications on television aesthetics and the "new" American sitcom.

TODD M. SODANO is an assistant professor at St. John Fisher College in Rochester, New York, where he teaches classes in television studies and video production. He earned his Ph.D. from Syracuse University, where he wrote his award-winning dissertation on the HBO series *The Wire*. At Syracuse, Sodano taught one of the first college classes on *The Wire* in the spring of 2008, when the show was still on the air. He also once appeared as an extra in *The Sopranos*.

JANANI SUBRAMANIAN is a visiting assistant professor in the Critical Studies Department at the University of Southern California, School of Cinematic Arts. As a postdoctoral fellow at USC, she edited the "Post-Identity" issue of *Spectator*, The University of Southern California Journal of Film and Television Criticism. Her research interests include race and representation in science fiction, fantasy, and horror; critical race theory; popular culture; and histories of technology and science. She is currently working on a book manuscript about race and fantasy across a variety of visual media.

TIMOTHEUS VERMEULEN is a lecturer in Cultural Studies and Theory at the Radboud University Nijmegen. He has written and spoken extensively on contemporary aesthetics, inter- and transmediality, cinema, television, the aesthetics and poetics of space, and the work of Jacques Rancière.

INDEX

Abbot, H. Porter, 164n1
Abbott, Stacey, 308n4
Abrams, J. J., 100, 112, 308n6
accelerated temporality, 43–44
active viewing, 15, 19, 188, 304
active/passive binary, 188
Adam and Eve, 129–30, 133–34
adolescence, 261
advertisements, 28–29, 162
aesthetics, 6, 32, 65, 71, 82, 259
agency, 197
Akass, Kim, 3
Al Jazeera, 4
albums, 43
Alias, 45–46, 97, 155
All My Children, 275
Allan, Stuart, 20n5
allegory, 7, 19
Allen, Robert C., 29
allusion, 27, 220, 222–24, 293
alternate reality, 15, 18–19, 89, 195, 197, 273, 279–82
Altman, Rick, 261
American Idol, 142, 148
America's Most Wanted, 289
anachronism, 208
analepses, 22. *See also* flashbacks
Anderson, Bonnie, 20n9
Anderson, Steve, 20n21
Anderson, Tonya, 308n3
Andrejevic, Mark, 20n8
animation, 285, 294
anxiety, 13–14, 74, 111, 139–40, 144–45, 167, 175
apocalypse, 111
appropriation, 267
Aristotle, 5, 20n12, 180

Arrested Development, 6, 14, 92n3, 142, 154–55, 161–64, 218–19, 222–25, 229
art, 156–57
Askwith, Ian, 64, 57, 300
audience, 4, 11, 16–18, 27–28, 49, 51, 56, 58, 60, 62, 83, 86, 142, 179, 190, 195–97, 205, 235, 237–39, 246, 258, 262–63, 265–67, 276, 283
Augustine, 5, 20n12, 249
automation systems, 72, 79
avant-garde art, 71
avatars, 180, 183, 186

Back to the Future, 7, 103
backshadowing, 59
backstories, 57
Bacon-Smith, Camille, 20n2, 274
Bakhtin, Mikhail, 16, 20n15, 90, 218, 220, 221
Bal, Mieke, 16, 209–10
Barnett, Jo Ellen, 20n14
Barthes, Roland, 181
Battlestar Galactica, 11, 56–68, 211
Baudrillard, Jean, 104
Baym, Nancy K., 20n2, 275
behind-the-scene footage, 48
Benjamin, Walter, 6, 82
Bergson, Henri, 5, 85, 170–71, 182
Big C, The, 245–47, 254
Bignell, Jonathan, 193–94
billboard hits, 266
binge viewing, 28, 31–33
Birds, The, 143
Bodroghkozy, Aniko, 20n3
Bollywood, 258
Bones, 18, 273–84
Booker, M. Keith, 20n1

Bordwell, David, 63
Bored to Death, 245
Braga, Brannan, 113
Brennan, Ian, 257
British television, 20n22
broadcast era, 3, 66n1, 70
Broe, Dennis, 20n5
Brooker, William, 299
Brooks, Peter, 20n15
Buffy, the Vampire Slayer, 62
Bush, George W., 131
Busling, Aileen L. S., 235
Butsch, Richard, 235
Butterfly Effect (scientific concept), 119
Butterfly Effect, The (film), 7
Byzantine, 70, 248

cable, 17, 27, 205, 245
cable era, 3, 17, 27
Cain and Abel, 88, 132–34, 137n4
calendar time, 45
callbacks, 58, 63
Cantor, Muriel, 28
capitalism, 71
Cardwell, Sarah, 154
Carlson, James, 276
Carnivàle, 15, 178–89
Carpek, Karel, 207
Carr, David, 30
Carter, Bill, 31
Carter, Chris, 56, 99
Carter, Jimmy, 227
cartoon, 8. *See also* animation
Casey, Bernadette, 262
Castells, Manuel, 54n1, 54n2
catastrophe, 105
causality, 15, 64, 180, 185, 188
CD, 43
celebrity culture, 286
censorship, 290
chaos theory, 119
characterization, 8, 78, 276
Chatman, Seymour, 159, 180–81
Chion, Michel, 263
Christmas Carol, A, 7
chromos, 14

chronological order, 7, 9, 12, 90, 125, 166, 194
chronontype, 16, 90, 218
cinema. *See* film
Clarke, Bruce, 16, 206, 209, 211, 215
Clarke, M. J., 300–302, 308n2
Clayton, David, 20n20
cliffhanger, 18, 29, 46–47, 50, 73, 286, 288–90
climax, 17, 29, 89, 248, 307
Clinton, Bill: family, 147; president, 289
clock-time, 45, 74
Closer, The, 248
closure, 262, 268
cognitive theory, 206
coherence, 221–22
cold war, 102
collective experience, 98
comedy, 257
Comic Con, 280
comic strips, 51
comics, 113
commercials, 10, 28–29, 32, 35–37, 103, 179, 248, 258
commodity culture, 267
Community, 29
complexity, narrative, 4, 14, 30, 70, 126, 179, 297
computer code, 71
consciousness, 15, 85, 90
constructivism, 71
consumption, 9–10, 28, 30, 34, 43, 69
continuity, 11, 15, 49
convenience technologies, 28, 30–31, 38, 69
Cop Rock, 259, 263
corporeality, 188
Couric, Katie, 20n10
court television, 98
credit sequence, 72
crime dramas, 14, 15, 98, 103, 113, 140, 167, 190–91, 197, 205, 207, 273, 276, 281, 283
Crime Traveller, 8
critics, 38, 64
Cronkite, Walter, 5
CSI, 191–92, 194, 199, 277
cult television, 56, 60, 98, 125, 142, 148, 211, 276, 283

cultural studies, 9
Curb Your Enthusiasm, 245, 247
Currie, Mark, 166, 168–69, 176n2, 176n3, 176n6
Cuse, Carlton, 59, 61, 63
cyclical structure, 13

da Silveira, Luciana Hiromi Yamada, 211–12
Daily Show, The, 5
Damages, 14–15, 165–77, 248
Dancer in the Dark, 266
David, Anna, 20n8
Davies, Paul, 19
Dayan, Daniel, 106
Deadwood, 40n3
death, 83–85, 89, 167, 181, 191, 194
Deery, June, 283
Deja Vu, 7
Deleuze, Gilles, 78, 154, 159–60, 170–71, 182, 184, 188, 258
Desperate Desmond, 51
Desperate Housewives, 158–59
destiny, 59, 87–89, 111, 125–26, 129, 135
detective novels, 303
Dexter, 29, 245, 248
Dickens, Charles, 33
Dickens, David, 20n16
diegesis, 16, 17, 51, 59, 65, 74, 83–84, 178, 181, 207, 216n3, 219–20, 265
digital downloads, 17, 61, 258
digital era, 3, 66n1
dimensionality, 71, 75, 77
disability, 267
disaster, 105. *See also* catastrophe
discontinuity, 98, 167
discourse, 15, 29, 165, 190, 194, 252
discussion boards, 19, 275, 281
distribution, 10–11, 27, 46–50, 53, 61–62, 258
Doane, Mary Ann, 20n17, 105, 123n2
Doctor Who, 8
documentary, 225, 247
Dolan, Marc, 57
Dollhouse, 16, 205–17
domesticity, 17, 246, 248
do-over, 7, 110, 113, 126, 132, 143

Douglas, Susan, 20n5, 20n7
drama, television, 8
dramatic irony, 59, 62
dramedy, 17, 245
dreams, 85, 184–85, 193–94, 198
Dupuy, Jean-Pierre, 167
duration, 69–70, 224
Durkeim, Emile, 19
DVD: collectible box sets, 31, 48, 53, 59; commentary, 180, 290; extras, 31, 35; unaired episodes, 210; watching on, 10, 27–28, 31–32, 35, 37, 60–63, 70, 126, 162, 187
DVR, 10, 28, 30–31, 34, 53, 61, 70, 104
Dynasty, 49–50, 53

Eastbound and Down, 245
Eco, Umberto, 193
economic recession, 14, 139
economy, 14, 43, 49, 103 264
Ed Sullivan Show, The, 257
editing, 5, 53, 78, 86–87
Einstein, Albert, 5, 170
Eliot, T. S., 250
ellipsis, 210
Elsaesser, Thomas, 62
End of Eternity, The, 7
ensemble casts, 8
Entourage, 245
episodic series, 11, 15, 44, 47, 61, 70, 190–92, 194, 207, 287
epistemology, 16, 69, 169
Epstein, Michael, 3, 66n1, 102, 106
Eriksen, Thomas Hylland, 49, 54n2, 54n4
Ermarth, E. D., 20n16
escapism, 123n1
eternal return, 182
eternity, 186
ethnography, 274–75
Event, The, 13, 101–2, 105
Ewing, Dale, Jr., 140

fabula, 212
Facebook, 32
faith, 13, 59, 63–64, 129–30, 135
Falchuck, Brad, 257
Family Man, The, 7

fan fiction, 18, 273–74, 279, 283
fandom, 3, 8–9, 18–19, 32, 58, 205, 273–74, 276, 279–83, 285–86, 288, 291, 293, 297–309
fantasy, 257
fanzines, 274
Farrell, Kirby, 98
fate, 13, 59, 87, 125–26
Faulkner, William, 93n7
femininity, 235
feminism, 98, 247
Feuer, Jane, 20n3, 257, 263, 266
Fight Club, 62
film, 6–7, 28, 50, 63, 70, 86, 98–99, 103, 156–57, 174, 234, 258
film noir, 140–43
Fire Walk with Me, 99
Fiske, John, 141
flashbacks, 9, 13, 15–16, 69, 77–78, 84, 100–101, 125, 127, 129, 132, 143, 145, 194, 197–98, 213, 233, 273, 286, 292, 293, 297–99, 304, 306
FlashForward (television show), 13, 46, 50, 97, 101, 111, 113–16, 120–21, 167, 198
flashforwards (narrative device), 13, 18, 69, 77, 100–101, 125, 127, 132, 194, 198, 238, 293, 297, 302–5
flashing arrow, 145
flashsideways, 13, 18, 69, 77–78, 125, 127, 132, 297
flexi-narratives, 14, 155
Flight of the Conchords, 245, 247
Flitterman-Lewis, Sandy, 103
flow, 10, 27–29, 33
Flow TV, 205
Fludernik, Monkia, 215n2
fluidity, 90, 191
Fontana, Andrea, 20n16
forensic fandom, 37, 60, 66n2, 299, 304
foreshadowing, 57, 59–60, 62–64
formula, 190, 192–93, 235, 258, 261, 276
Forster, E. M., 20n15
4400, The, 101
fragmentation, 12, 29, 43–44
frame theory, 16
framing device, 89, 237, 241
free will, 13, 19, 88–89, 125–26, 129–30

frequency, 224
Freud, Sigmund, 84, 100, 104
Friday Night Lights, 57
Friedberg, Anne, 85
Friedman, Susan Stanford, 164n1
Fringe, 13, 97, 105, 111–17, 120–21, 191, 205, 207
futurity, 167

Gallo, Phil, 188n2
gaps, in viewing, 28, 33–35, 37, 45–48, 59
gender roles, 17, 233, 245–46
Generation Kill, 32
generations, 15, 19, 180, 183, 186
Genette, Gerard, 16, 176n1, 176n2, 208, 211
genre, 4, 6, 8, 14, 16, 56, 62, 65, 70, 98, 103, 154, 179, 190, 192, 199, 205, 215, 218, 222, 246, 249, 259, 261, 268, 285
Gessler, Nicholas, 63
Ghost Whisperer, 191, 199
Ghosts of Girlfriends Past, 7
Gibson, Charles, 20n10
Gilligan's Island, 77
Glee, 17, 34, 46, 257–69
globalization, 102, 108n3
Gong Show, The, 257
Good Wife, The, 192, 248
Goodnight Sweetheart, 8
Gopalan, Lalitha, 266
Gournelos, Ted, 287
Goya, David, 113
Gray, Jonathan, 35, 301
Greenblatt, Robert, 254
Greene, Doyle, 285
Grey's Anatomy, 251
grief, 13
Grillet, Robbe, 78
Grosz, Elizabeth, 110, 169
grotesque, 178
Grusin, Richard, 21n26
Guattari, Felix, 154, 159–60

Hagedorn, Roger, 61
hallucination, 13, 97, 100, 129
Halyes, N. Katherine, 63
Hanson, Hart, 273, 280–81
Happy Days, 223–24

Harrison, Kristen, 235
Hassan, Robert, 43, 54n2
Hawk, Julie, 210
Hawking, Stephen, 5, 21n13
Hayward, Jennifer, 57, 60
Hedgwig and the Angry Inch, 266
Hegel, Georg Wilhelm Friedrich, 171
Heidegger, Martin, 5, 20n12
Heise, Ursula, 6, 20n25
Hendrix, Grady, 32
Heroes, 13, 111–13, 115, 117–19, 121, 205
Hess, Stephen, 20n5
heteronormativity, 246
heterosexuality, 17, 245, 259–61, 266
Hill, Matt, 302
Hill Street Blues, 192
Hills, Ken, 140
historization, 10
history, 6–7, 9, 12, 82, 90, 98, 102, 141
Hollinger, Veronica, 20n20
Hollywood, 181, 234, 261
Holmes, Su, 20n8
holocaust, 98
homosexuality, 261
Honeymooners, The, 103
horror movies, 98
How I Met Your Mother, 16, 232–44
Hull High, 259, 263
Hulu, 34, 142
humor, 16, 219–21, 225, 227, 235, 250–51, 285
Hung, 245
Husserl, Edmund, 5, 20n12
Hutcheon, Linda, 229
Huyssen, Andreas, 90, 104
hyper-present, 287
hypertextuality, 293

identity, 15, 179, 186, 246
ideology, 14, 71, 114, 141, 246
IDOL, 267
immediacy, 46, 72, 75, 275
industry, 49, 71, 259
infotainment, 4–5
inheritance, 186
interface, 69, 72–73, 79

Internet, 11, 49, 103, 126, 222, 274–76, 279, 290
intertextuality, 14, 27, 62, 87, 89, 141, 191, 293
iPod, 34, 70
It's a Wonderful Life, 7
iTunes, 34, 43, 267

Jameson, Fredric, 10–12, 20n24, 70–71, 79, 82
Jenkins, Henry, 20n2, 147, 273, 275, 299
Jermyn, Deborah, 20n8
Jimmy Kimmel Show, The, 308n6
jingoism, 4
Johnson, Steven, 8, 20n1, 30, 58, 126, 145, 179, 298
Johnson-Woods, Toni, 294
justice, 172

Kafalenos, Emma, 212
kainos, 14
Kalb, Marvin, 20n5
Kaplan, E. Ann, 97
Katz, Elihu, 105
Kennedy Family, 141
Kermode, Frank, 6
Kindred, 7
Kirby-Diaz, Mary, 279
Klevan, Andrew, 156
Knauf, Daniel, 178, 179, 188n1
knowledge, 14–15, 165–66, 169
Kompare, Derek, 31, 40n1
Kozloff, Sarah, 15, 29, 190, 193
Kring, Tim, 111
Kripe, Eric, 93n8
Kurtzman, Alex, 112

L Word, The, 245
Lacan, Jacques, 99
Lambert, Josh, 50
Landes, David, 20n14
Larsen, David, 292
Lashley, Marilyn, 146
Last Year at Marienbad, 63, 79
Late Spring, 156
late-capitalism, 9, 11
Lavery, David, 20n6, 308n2

Law & Order, 27, 162, 166, 172, 277
legal drama, 15
Lesage, Julia, 248
Liebes, Tamar, 105
Life on Mars, 167
Lightman, Alan, 90
Lim, Bliss Cua, 170
Lindelof, Damon, 59, 61, 63
linearity, 10, 12, 14, 27, 89–90, 101, 103, 110, 181, 306
literary studies, 9
literature, 6, 28, 33, 60, 179, 218
Live Journal, 281
live television, 4, 8
Lone Star, 29
Lost, 11, 13, 18, 27, 34–37, 45–47, 56–81, 97, 103, 105, 113, 125–38, 155, 190, 192, 197, 205, 289, 297–309
Lotz, Amanda, 3, 27, 30, 38, 142
Lowry, Brian, 233
Luckhurst, Roger, 97
Lukacher, Ned, 100–101
Lynch, David, 56, 178

Mad Men, 14, 38–39, 153–61, 163–64
mapping, 69–72, 76–79
marketing, 267, 281
Marlevich, Vladimir, 71
marriage, 237–38
Marriott, Stephanie, 20n18
masculinity, 235
materiality, 69–72
McCabe, Janet, 3
McCain, John, 146
McLuhan, Marshall, 125
mediation, 70, 104
Medium, 15, 190–201
Meek, Allen, 104
Mellencamp, Patricia, 255n2, 255n3
melodrama, 17, 247, 250–51
Memento, 7, 62, 64
Memories of the Twentieth Century, 7
memory, 7, 11, 15, 61, 78, 85–86, 88, 98, 101, 108n1, 178, 184, 186, 188, 215
Mentalist, The, 191
metacognition, 83, 97, 199
meta-textuality, 12

mid-season breaks, 46–47
Miége, Bernard, 31
MILF, 252
Millmann, Joyce, 308n4
Mills, Brett, 247
Milton, John, 13, 130, 135
mind/body dualism, 206
miniseries, 57
misremembering, 18, 292. *See also* memory
Mitell, Jason, 4, 14, 20n4, 29, 32–34, 40n2, 40n3, 57, 64, 66n2, 70, 79, 82, 103, 127, 155–56, 190, 207, 245, 299, 301
mobile technology, 103
mockumentary, 225
Modeleski, Tania, 20n19, 255n1
Modern Family, 32, 247
modernism, 6
montage, 222
Monty Python, 162
Moonlighting, 273
Moore, Ronald D., 56–57, 61, 63
morality, 114, 190, 196
mp3, 43, 265
Mr. Destiny, 7
MTV, 257
Mulholland Dr., 7, 63
Mundy, John, 266
Murphy, John, 131
Murphy, Ryan, 257
Murray, Susan, 20n8
musical, 8, 17, 34, 257–69
mystery, 57, 140, 306
mythology, 188n3

Nagl, Manfred, 20n20
narrative arc, 18, 44, 47–49, 50, 52, 248
narrative theory, 29, 180–81, 192
narratology, 9, 205–6, 209, 214
Natharius, David, 234
Negra, Diane, 249
Nelson, Robin, 14
Netflix, 34
network era, 3–4, 43, 45
network television, 28
network time, 11, 54n1
new media, 4–5, 7, 27, 62, 97–98, 102–4, 258, 264

Newman, Michael Z., 31, 250, 252
news coverage, 4, 287
Newton, Isaac, 5
niche programming, 252
Nielsen Ratings System, 31
Nietzsche, Fredrich, 5, 20n12, 120, 182
9/11, 4, 9–10, 13–14, 105, 110–14, 120, 126, 130–31, 141
Nintendo Wii, 34
Nixson, Helen, 286
nonlinearity, 6–7, 12–13, 16, 70, 89, 97, 101–2, 104, 206
nostalgia, 141
novelistic television genres, 11, 33, 57, 62, 220
Numb3rs, 191
Nurse Jackie, 17, 245–56

Obama, Barak, 139, 141–42, 146–47, 149, 228
Ocana, Anthony M., 235
Oedipus, 120
Office, The, 16, 218–19, 222, 225–26, 247
Olt, Brian, 293
on-demand video systems, 10, 48, 70, 126
online streaming, 27, 53, 103–4
onotology, 16, 69, 182
open texts, 63–64
optimism, 14, 139–40, 143–44, 146
Orc, Roberto, 112
O'Sullivan, Sean, 33–34, 40n3
Oullette, Laurie, 20n8

pacing, 248
Paradise Lost, 13, 130
parallelism, 139
paranormal, 12, 190–91, 195
paratexts, 10, 32, 35, 37–38, 83
Parks and Recreation, 247
parody, 35, 198, 292
Pearson, Roberta, 265
perception, 90
performance, 262–64
personal computers, 103
pessimism, 14, 139–40, 143–44
philosophy, 5, 13, 19, 125, 127, 136, 171, 182
physics, 170, 220

podcasts, 60
Poe, Edgar Allan, 125
poetics, 154
point of view, 80, 188, 235
police procedural. *See* crime drama
politics, 13–14, 267, 286, 294
pornography, 98
Porter, Lynnette, 20n6
post-apocalyptic, 88
postfeminism, 252, 255
posthistory, 6, 9
posthuman, 16, 206, 210, 214
postmodernism, 6, 9, 62–63, 82, 90, 104, 156, 205–6, 221
post-network era, 3–4, 9, 27, 30–31, 38, 69, 71, 79
post-9/11. *See* 9/11
posttraumatic stress disorder (PTSD), 98
power, 15, 166
Pozner, Jennifer, 20n8
pre-credit sequences, 50
prediction, 183–84, 188
premediation, 13, 21n26, 111
premonitions, 190, 193
present tense, 16, 43, 54
previews, 10, 35
previouslies, 10, 35, 39, 57, 60
Prison Break, 11, 43–54
product placement, 223
production, 4, 9–10, 28, 30, 43, 45, 60, 71–72, 103, 105, 220, 287
prolepsis, 166, 168, 222–23. *See also* flashforwards
promos, 28–29, 32, 35
Proust, Marcel, 85
psychic, 190
psychoanalysis, 99
psychology, 13, 97, 136
psychopathology, 13
Pugh, Sheenagh, 274
Pulp Fiction, 7
Pushing Daisies, 14, 138–50
puzzle films, 62–63, 66n5, 127

quality television, 65, 154, 252, 255, 259
Quantum Leap, 8, 123n4, 197
quantum physics, 87

race, 83–84, 267
radio, 103
Radway, Janice, 233–34, 274
Rai, Amit, 17, 258, 264
Rancière, Jacques, 154, 157
ratings, 57, 224
real time, 9, 30, 43, 46, 49–50, 69, 73, 75, 80
realism, 258–59, 262, 264, 267
reality television, 4, 140, 292
recap episodes, 48
reception, 70
redemption, 132, 134, 214
Redfield, Marc, 20n5
Reeves, Jimmie L., 3, 66n1, 102, 106
religion, 13, 87–89, 90, 125, 127, 129–34, 286, 294
Remington Steele, 273
repetition, 13, 15, 70, 72–73, 97, 100, 103, 111, 141, 180, 184, 186, 193, 195
repression, 84, 100
resolution, 18, 262, 307
resurrection, 85, 181
revisionism, 292
rhizomatic, 14
Richardson, Brian, 20n16
Ricoeur, Paul, 6, 159
Rimmon-Kenan, Schlomit, 181
Robson, Hillary, 20n6
Rogers, Mark C., 3, 66n1, 102, 106
romance, 14, 17, 140, 232, 235, 241, 259–61, 273–74, 280, 282
romantic comedy, 16–17, 233
rupture, 17, 98, 102, 258

salvation, 111
sampling (music), 267
Sarah Connor Chronicles, The, 97, 101, 106
satire, 207, 287
scaffolding, 197
schedule (network), 27, 29–30, 32, 34, 45, 258
Scheuring, Paul, 45
Schivelbusch, Wolfgang, 106
science, 5, 9, 19, 112, 125, 166, 170–71
science fiction, 8, 13, 16, 97–109, 113–14, 191, 199, 205–6, 211, 214–15

Scrooged, 7
Secret Diary of a Call Girl, 245–47
Sedgwick, Eve Kosofsky, 254
segmentation, 53
Seinfeld, 9, 58, 62
selfhood, 15
self-reflexivity, 56, 72
semiotics, 12
Sepinwall, Alan, 233
sequels, 260
seriality, 11–12, 17, 27, 32, 40n3, 44, 69–72, 258–60, 287
serialization, 179, 276
serialized season, 44, 47
Seven Days, 8
17 Again, 7
Sex in the City, 245, 247, 285
sexuality, 245, 285
Shales, Tom, 233
Shutter Island, 62
signifier, 73–74, 76
Simon, David, 33
Simpsons, The, 27, 62, 286–87
simultaneity, 73
sitcom, 8, 16, 30, 103, 218–31, 232, 235, 246–47, 285, 287, 292
situational comedy. *See* sitcom
Sixth Sense, The, 62–64
Slaughterhouse-Five, 7
Smith, Mark, 161
Snarker, Dorothy, 254
soap operas, 8–9, 29, 65, 70, 103, 192, 205, 275
Sobchack, Vivian, 90
social media, 11, 38
Sopranos, The, 29, 34, 252
soundtracks, 265
South Park, 18, 285–96
space, 15, 16, 80, 82, 84, 89, 90, 98, 184, 188, 215, 218, 220, 222, 224–25, 227
space-time continuum, 84
special episodes, 48
Spigel, Lynn, 3–4, 20n6, 255n1
Spinoza, Baruch, 182
Spivak, Gayatri, 170–72
spoilers, 10, 35, 38–39, 301
sponsors, 30

St. Elsewhere, 61, 65
stacking, 49, 53
standardization of time, 5
Star Trek, 274
Stein, Gertrude, 83, 92n4
stereotype, 239
Stevens, Hampton, 30
Stewart, Jon, 5, 20n10
Stilwell, Cinnamon, 20n6
storytelling, 18, 29, 33, 50, 53, 264, 273, 285
Strang, Michael, 188n3
Strayer, Kristen, 213
streaming devices, 30
structure of feelings, 265
subjectivity, 12, 74
Super Bowl, 142
Supernatural, 12, 82–94, 191, 198
suprematism, 71
surrealism, 266
surveillance, 74–75
sweeps week, 54
symbolism, 119–20, 125
synchronicity, 34, 37, 46, 76
syndication, 61, 276, 292
systems theory, 215

tabula rasa, 207
talent competition, 257
talk shows, 31, 98, 277
teasers, 58
technoapocalyse, 207–8
technology, 10–11, 27, 43, 49, 61–62, 65–66, 70, 74, 82, 97, 100, 102–3, 105–6, 222, 259
technophobia, 106
television industry, 4, 10–12
telos, 166
temps mort, 159
Terminator, The, 101
terrorism, 4, 69
theology, 13
theory of relativity, 116, 170
30 Rock, 16, 29, 218–19, 222, 226–29, 277
Thomas, Craig, 233
Thompson, Kristin, 179, 181, 185, 187
Thompson, Robert J., 20n1, 61, 66n2
Thussu, Daya, 20n9

time compression, 9, 14, 44, 46
time loops, 84, 99, 291–92
Time Machine, The, 7
time shifting, 10, 27, 30, 103
time travel, 7, 18, 86–89, 101, 103, 112–14, 116–18, 120, 123n3, 137n6, 297
Time Traveler's Wife, The, 7
Time Trax, 8
Timeline, 7
Timely Persuasion, 7
Time's Last Gift, 7
Timeslip, 8
title sequence, 72, 76–77, 83
TiVo, 126
Todreas, Timothy M., 66n1
Toffler, Alvin, 20n23
transmedia, 14
transmediation, 147
trauma, 9, 97–109, 111
trauma theory, 13, 98, 100
Traveller in Time, A, 7
Treme, 32
True Blood, 57
Tryon, Charles, 7
Tutors, The, 245
TV Guide, 276, 280
TV I, 66n1, 102. *See also* network era
TV II, 66n1, 102. *See also* cable era
TV III, 56–57, 66n1, 66n2, 102. *See also* digital era
Twelve Monkeys, 7
24, 11, 27, 30, 43–51, 69–81, 97
Twin Peaks, 56–57, 65, 98–99, 178, 299
Twitter, 140, 280
Two and a Half Men, 162
2008 Presidential Election, 14, 139–40, 146–47
Tyree, J. M., 20n17

Ugly Betty, 50
Uhlin, Graig, 20n17
United States of Tara, The, 245–47, 254
univocity, 182
Usual Suspects, The, 62

V, 46
Valley of the Dolls, 250

variety shows, 257
VCR, 28, 31, 103
Veller, Agnese, 308n1
Veronica Mars, 140, 198
Vertigo, 143
VHS, 62–63, 103
videogames, 93n5, 299
Vietnam War, 98
violence: domestic violence, 102; sexual abuse, 102; on television, 98, 167, 285
Virilio, Paul, 72
virtual, 182
visions, psychic, 85, 193, 198
Voyagers!, 8
voice over, 83–84, 92n3, 145

Waldeni, Dana, 53
Walker, William, 130
Wall Street, 141
Wallace, David Foster, 66n4
war, 105, 131
Ward, L. Monique, 235
water-cooler discussion, 10, 37–39, 142
webisodes, 148
Weeds, 245–47, 254
Weiner, Matthew, 38
Weinstock, Jeffrey, 287
Wells, H.G., 87
Whedon, Joss, 205, 207
White, Hayden, 105
wikis, 299
Williams, Brian, 20n10
Williams, Raymond, 28
Winn, Laura, 234
Wire, The, 14, 29, 32–33, 154–55, 161–64
wish fulfillment, 113
Wood, J., 20n6
work/home binary, 17
world wide web. *See* Internet
wrestling, 65
Writers Guild of America, 2007–2008 strike, 14, 139, 148–49
Wurtzel, Alan, 31

X Files, The, 56–57, 65, 99–100, 106

YouTube, 140, 264

zaumism, 71
Zelizer, Barbie, 20n5
zero degree, 71–75
Žižek, Slavoj, 99, 167

www.ingramcontent.com/pod-product-compliance
Lightning Source LLC
Chambersburg PA
CBHW031900220426
43663CB00006B/702